D1485040

The Fertility Handbook

BAINTE DEN STOC

WITHDRAWN FROM DLR LIBRARIES STOCK

ERRATUM

With reference to *The Fertility Handbook*, please note that there are errata on pages 13 and 318.

On page 13, in the legend for the table at the bottom of the page, *for* Menstruation (period) *read* Fertile window; *for* Fertile window *read* Menstruation (period).

On page 318, in the captions under the graphs at the bottom of the page, in both instances *for* Livebirth Rate *read* Livebirth Rate per embryo transfer.

For corrected versions of these pages, please go to www.gillbooks.ie/the-fertility-handbook

These errata were made by the publisher and not the author, for which the publisher apologises.

BAINTE DEN STOC
WITHDRAWN FROM DLR LIBRARIES STOCK

The Fertility Handbook

EVERYTHING YOU NEED TO KNOW
TO MAXIMISE YOUR CHANCE OF PREGNANCY

Professor Mary Wingfield

Gill Books

Gill Books
Hume Avenue
Park West
Dublin 12
www.gillbooks.ie

Gill Books is an imprint of M.H. Gill and Co.

© Mary Wingfield 2017

978 07171 7274 0

Edited by Jane Rogers
Index by Cliff Murphy
Design and print origination by O'K Graphic Design, Dublin
Printed by GraphyCems, Spain

All illustrations by Derry Dillon except page 57 © Andriy Yankovskyy

For permission to reproduce photographs, the author and publisher gratefully
acknowledge the following:
© iStock: 6B, 82, 99; © Phanie/Alamy Stock Photo: 303.

The author and publisher have made every effort to trace all copyright holders,
but if any have been inadvertently overlooked we would be pleased to make the
necessary arrangement at the first opportunity.

This book is typeset in 11/15 pt Minion with titles in Advert Light.

*The paper used in this book comes from the wood pulp of managed forests. For
every tree felled, at least one tree is planted, thereby renewing natural resources.*

All rights reserved.
No part of this publication may be copied, reproduced or transmitted in any form
or by any means, without written permission of the publishers.

A CIP catalogue record for this book is available from the British Library.

5 4 3 2 1

To my parents, Marie and Joe Wingfield, who loved me so much.

Contents

List of Abbreviations

AFC	antral follicle count
AHR	assisted human reproduction
AMH	anti-Mullerian hormone
ART	assisted reproductive technology
ASAs	anti-sperm antibodies
ASRM	American Society for Reproductive Medicine
BFS	British Fertility Society
BMI	body mass index
CAHR	Commission on Assisted Human Reproduction
CASA	computer-assisted semen analysis
CBAVD	congenital bilateral absence of the vas deferens
CFRA	Children and Family Relationships Act 2015
CMV	cytomegalovirus
DAHR	donor assisted human reproduction
D&C	dilation and curettage
DNA	deoxyribonucleic acid
EACC	European Assisted Conception Consortium
ED	erectile dysfunction
eSET	elective single embryo transfer
ESHRE	European Society for Human Reproduction and Embryology
FET	frozen embryo transfer
FSH	follicle-stimulating hormone
GnRH	gonadotropin-releasing hormone
hCG	human chorionic gonadotropin
HFEA	Human Fertilisation and Embryology Authority
HPRA	Health Products Regulatory Authority
HRT	hormone replacement therapy
HSG	hysterosalpingogram
HyCoSy	hysterosalpingo contrast sonography
ICMART	International Committee Monitoring Assisted Reproductive Technologies
ICSI	intracytoplasmic sperm injection

IFCA	Irish Fertility Counsellors' Association
IFFS	International Federation of Fertility Societies
IFS	Irish Fertility Society
IMSI	intracytoplasmic morphologically selected sperm injection
IUD	intrauterine device
IUI	intrauterine insemination
IVF	in vitro fertilisation
IVM	in vitro maturation
LH	luteinising hormone
LLETZ	large loop excision of the transformation zone
LOD	laparoscopic ovarian diathermy
MRI	magnetic resonance imaging
NICE	National Institute for Clinical Excellence
NK cells	natural killer cells
NTD	neural tube defect
OHSS	ovarian hyperstimulation syndrome
OPK	ovulation predictor kit
PCO	polycystic ovary/ies
PCOS	polycystic ovarian syndrome
PGD	pre-implantation genetic diagnosis
PGS	pre-implantation genetic screening
PID	pelvic inflammatory disease
PN	pronucleus
POI	premature ovarian insufficiency
PUL	pregnancy of unknown location
RM	recurrent miscarriage
ROS	reactive oxygen species
SHBG	sex hormone binding globulin
SIDS	sudden infant death syndrome
SLE	systemic lupus erythematosus
SPRMs	selective progesterone-receptor modulators
SSR	surgical sperm retrieval
STI	sexually transmitted infection
TCM	Traditional Chinese Medicine
TESA	testicular sperm aspiration
TESE	testicular sperm extraction
TSH	thyroid-stimulating hormone
UI	unexplained infertility
WHO	World Health Organisation

Introduction

For some years now I have been thinking about writing a book. I meet people every day who have reproductive and fertility problems and it is a joy if I can have a meaningful discussion with them, give them information, suggest options and come up with a plan that may help them. As I am sharing information, I often think – wouldn't it be wonderful to be able to capture this in writing so that people could take it home, study it and truly empower themselves? It's so hard for people to remember everything that comes up during a consultation and taking notes interferes with our flow of ideas. So my first thought in writing this book was to get my knowledge down on paper – knowledge gained, not just from studying and reading, but from experience and from just having 'seen it before'.

Once I started putting my knowledge and views down on paper, I realised that I also needed to support those views with evidence. Information is useless (and even harmful) if it is not correct. Nowadays we live with a plethora of material on the internet and on social media and it can be extremely difficult to distinguish between good and bad information. So what I had originally thought would be easy soon became a mammoth task. But a rewarding one. I have trawled the medical and scientific literature, including writings on lifestyle, ethics and law. And I have learned a lot. I really hope that this book will act as a sound and reliable source of balanced and factually correct information. I have listed reliable websites and I have included references after each section, so I hope that the book will also be of value to students and to other doctors and health professionals (and maybe even also to policy makers).

I have been working in the area of fertility and obstetrics and gynaecology for almost 30 years and it is a truly exciting, challenging and rewarding field. However, it can also be heart-breaking. In my work I have met amazing colleagues in medical, nursing and other health professions and also wonderful scientists, ethicists, lawyers and, above all, patients.

Fertility patients come from all walks of life and have a fascinating variety of medical, social and relationship issues. As a doctor, I am very privileged to be able to gain a unique insight into people's innermost lives and for this I feel truly grateful. Last summer, I wrote to current and ex-patients and asked them to contribute any of their experiences that they felt might be of benefit to others with fertility issues. I was overwhelmed by the honesty, openness and generosity of the many men and women who replied. I have included some of their quotes throughout the book and I think these truly heartfelt insights are invaluable.

In this book I have tried to explain natural fertility, fertility problems, fertility investigations and fertility treatments in as clear and factual a way as possible. I have divided the book into five main sections. **Section 1** is about natural biology and covers issues such as ovulation, sperm, the male and female reproductive systems and sex. **Section 2** describes the hugely important influence of lifestyle. I hope Sections 1 and 2 will be helpful for all women and men who would like to have a child or children, irrespective of whether or not they have fertility problems. It may also help young people and students understand the miracle of 'making a baby' and the normal workings of a woman's menstrual cycle and sperm production in males. I also explore relationship issues, including reproduction for single people and those in 'non-traditional' relationships.

I am delighted to have excellent contributions by some of my colleagues, including Sinead Curran, Dietitian and Kay Duff, Fertility and Relationship Counsellor (Section 2). Meg Fitzgerald, Psychosexual Therapist, has also written a wonderful piece about sex, which of course is central to natural reproduction (Section 3). Lifestyle affects absolutely every part of our health and fertility is no exception. It is reassuring to see that stress does **not** cause infertility and that you are not unusual if infertility affects your sex life. But alcohol may be more of a problem than people realise, e-cigarettes are not ideal and fertility apps may not be all they are made out to be.

Section 3 deals with fertility problems, tests and investigations and advice on when and how to seek help if you have a problem. There are sections on endometriosis and polycystic ovaries and, of course, male fertility problems. I also discuss ovarian reserve, tubal disease, unexplained infertility and the heart-breaking issues around miscarriage and ectopic pregnancy.

Section 4 relates to treatment, including medical and surgical options for women and for men. It addresses assisted reproduction such as intrauterine insemination (IUI), in vitro fertilisation (IVF) and intracytoplasmic sperm injection (ICSI), donor pregnancies, surrogacy and exciting advances in this fascinating field. There is also a discussion of closure, dealing with 'when it doesn't happen' and coping with a life without children. I am grateful to my editor, Deirdre Nolan, for stressing the importance of addressing this and also to the patients whom I quote there.

The final section, **Section 5**, covers thorny ethical issues including the lack of public funding in Ireland and summarises the law with regard to fertility treatment in Ireland and internationally. Finally, there is discussion regarding closure, dealing with 'when it doesn't happen' and coping with a life without children. I am grateful to my editor for stressing the importance of this and also to the patients quoted there.

Having a fertility problem can be a really lonely and miserable place to be. Fertility treatment and the fertility journey are, without doubt, some of the most stressful experiences that any of us can go through. I sincerely hope that this book will help fill some of the gaps for everyone, but particularly for the 1 in 6 couples who are unlucky and experience difficulty conceiving. A book can't replace medical and professional help or cover every possible clinical scenario or individual variation, but accurate knowledge can empower people and sometimes even avoid the need for medical intervention. I also want to reassure people that, in the vast majority of cases, help is at hand and that most people will achieve their dream if they can manage to persist with treatment. For those who are not successful in forming a family, I hope that the sections on emotional wellbeing and counselling will be of some comfort and help in coming to the realisation that, even without children, life can be very rewarding and fulfilling.

Personally, I am blessed to have two wonderful children and they make me thankful every day for the joy and quality of life they bring me. This is something I want for all my patients and for everyone who reads this book. I sincerely hope my book will help.

I want to thank all my colleagues at Merrion Fertility Clinic who have been such a support and help and who tolerated me over the last year while I was undertaking this challenging work. I am so lucky to be part of such a wonderful team. I am particularly grateful to my PA, Liz Gallagher, who has helped with typing, and most importantly, has, with a smile, put up with my mood, which has swung from excitement to despair as I have tried to pull this work together. I want to thank my editor, Deirdre Nolan, who suggested the project and Sheila Armstrong – their enthusiasm kept me going. Most of all, I want to thank all my patients who have given me such an insight over the years and particularly those patients who have contributed some of their personal and extremely helpful experiences, which will, I feel, definitely benefit others. Finally I can't adequately thank my husband, Toss, a GP, who has been an endless support throughout my career and, most recently, while writing this book, and also my two wonderful children, Fionnuala and Fiachra, who have given me the joy of parenthood.

Biology of Natural Pregnancy

The way a human pregnancy and child can develop following a single act of sex between a man and a woman is indeed a miracle of nature and something that, even after all these years, still leaves me in awe. So many minute steps have to happen in a highly co-ordinated and precise pattern – all at a microscopic level. When we realise how intricate it all is, it is not surprising that things can go wrong. And so, before we look at treatments and tests we need to understand the basic biology.

In this chapter I hope to explain the biology of reproduction in a clear fashion and give points as to how to optimise your chances of natural conception. There is a detailed section on ovulation and whether women should try to monitor it, and how. I also speak about sex and give advice about 'how and when' is best for sex to maximise fertility.

Basics of conception

In order to conceive a baby a sperm must fertilise an egg. This fertilised egg then develops into an embryo, which implants in the woman's womb (uterus) and subsequently develops into a foetus and eventually a baby.

A woman produces one or two eggs in one or other of her ovaries every month and this is called ovulation (described in detail later). The egg is released from her ovary at the time of ovulation and, by some miracle, the woman's Fallopian tube, which lies close to the ovary and connects with the uterus, is able to pick up this egg. If the woman has sex around the time of ovulation, some of the sperm that is deposited in her vagina swim through her cervix and uterus up to her Fallopian tube. The hope is that one egg and one sperm will meet in the Fallopian tube. The sperm will penetrate the egg and hopefully fertilise it.

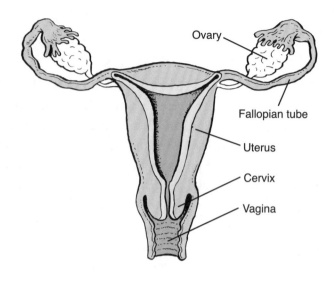

Female reproductive system

The process of fertilisation takes about 24 hours and then the fertilised egg, which is one cell, divides into two cells, which subsequently divide into four cells and then eight cells and so on. Once the fertilised egg has started dividing into numerous cells we have what is called an embryo. (See the section on IVF for more details about embryos.) After 2–3 days in the Fallopian tube, the embryo begins to move down towards the uterus or womb. If the lining of the womb is appropriate, which it should be at this time of the woman's menstrual cycle, the embryo will start to implant in the woman's uterus – this is approximately five days following ovulation and the embryo at this stage is called a blastocyst. As implantation progresses, the placenta part of the embryo starts producing a hormone called hCG (human chorionic gonadotropin), which supports the pregnancy. This hormone, which is excreted into the woman's blood and urine, forms the basis of a pregnancy test and will give a positive pregnancy test 10 to 16 days after ovulation.

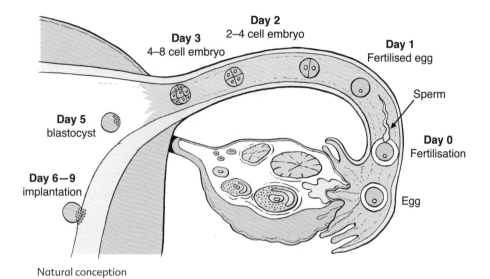

Natural conception

In order for all of the above to happen, it is really important that the couple have had sex in the days leading up to and around the time the woman is ovulating as that is the only time when there will be an egg available for the sperm to fertilise.

If a couple have an active sex life and are having sex every two or three days, they don't need to concern themselves with the 'fertile window' (see page 12) – they will be having sex often enough.

Sperm and semen

Sperm are the male 'reproductive cells'. They are produced in the testes (testicles) in a process called spermatogenesis. During development, the testes start off in the abdomen but by the time a male child is born, they have usually moved down to the scrotum. The germ cells that produce sperm lie dormant until puberty and then spermatogenesis starts. Other cells in the testis are Sertoli cells, which support the development of the sperm, and Leydig cells, which produce testosterone, a hormone that is essential for normal sperm development. Testosterone production and sperm development are controlled by the hormones FSH (follicle stimulating hormone) and LH (luteinising hormone), which are released from the pituitary gland in the brain.

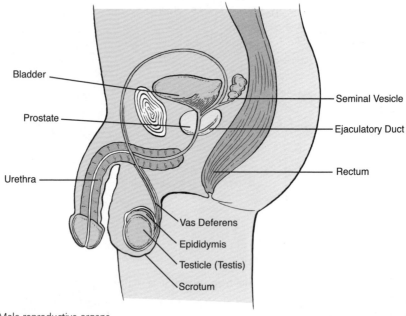

Bladder

Prostate

Urethra

Seminal Vesicle

Ejaculatory Duct

Rectum

Vas Deferens

Epididymis

Testicle (Testis)

Scrotum

Male reproductive organs

Healthy sperm

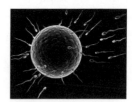

Sperm and egg

Sperm travel from the testis into the epididymis, a tubular structure at the back of the testis. This connects the testis with the vas deferens, another tube, which carries the sperm down along the penis from which they are ejaculated. Along the way the seminal vesicle and prostate gland produce other fluids and secretions that surround the sperm cells, supporting them and providing a medium through which they can swim. Semen therefore contains sperm (about 5% of it) and supporting secretions.

During the early stages of sperm production in the testis, immature sperm cells divide to produce immature sperm, each of which contains a half set of the man's chromosomes (23 chromosomes). These will later join the half from the female egg to produce one fertilised egg with a full complement of chromosomes (i.e. 46 – 23 from each parent). Once the chromosomes have divided, the sperm cell is then shaped to form a head and tail, but at this stage it is not motile. These non-motile sperm are transported to the epididymis, where they mature, becoming capable of swimming and fertilising an egg. They are then stored here until ejaculation.

THREE-MONTH EFFECT

The entire process of producing a capable sperm takes about three months. Therefore any intervention to improve sperm (e.g. stopping smoking) takes about three months to have an effect.

Semen is the fluid produced by a man at ejaculation. As described above, it contains sperm and supporting secretions. Semen is usually white or grey, or may have a yellowish tint. If it is pink or red it may contain blood and this should be discussed with your doctor. After ejaculation, semen coagulates or becomes sticky and jelly-like. This may help to keep the semen in the vagina. After about 15 minutes, it becomes more watery (liquefies) and this is thought to help sperm to swim up through the cervix and uterus to the Fallopian tubes. It is therefore normal for semen to flow out of the vagina after sex and this is nothing to worry about. Sufficient sperm will have got to the female reproductive tract after a few minutes.

Ejaculation

Ejaculation results in the release of sperm from the penis and is a complex event. Many processes are involved. Firstly, sexual arousal causes areas in the brain to send signals via the spinal cord to the sacral area. This leads to a release of chemicals from the nerves in the penis, leading to relaxation of the muscles and an increase in blood flow into the penis, which causes the firmness necessary for an erection and sexual activity. When the man has achieved a sufficient level of stimulation, orgasm and ejaculation begin. Muscles in the penis undergo rhythmic contractions, leading to ejaculation of the sperm. The length of time from initial stimulation to ejaculation, the force of propulsion achieved with ejaculation and the numbers of sperm in the ejaculate all vary from man to man. Testosterone is a necessary hormone for sexual function and ejaculation. Problems related to ejaculation are discussed in the section on male fertility problems.

Frequency of ejaculation: We know that the quality and number of sperm in the ejaculate is affected by the frequency of ejaculation. If ejaculation is very infrequent, men get a build-up of dead, old and poor-quality sperm. On the other hand, if they ejaculate very frequently, the numbers of sperm can be reduced. In terms of conceiving, frequent ejaculation is fine; it doesn't matter if the numbers are low if you are having sex often – the cumulative results will be fine. However, when we are organising a sperm test or getting a sperm sample to use for fertility treatment, we generally advise men to abstain from ejaculation for 2–5 days prior to producing his sample. This is because, for a test, we need to reach specific criteria and, for a treatment, we need as many healthy sperm as possible.

Eggs

Eggs are the female 'reproductive cells' and are also called ova or oocytes. They are stored in the ovaries, in small sacs called follicles. These follicles can be seen on an ultrasound scan. Women are born with all their eggs in their ovaries. At birth, the ovaries contain one to two million eggs and these are arrested at an early stage of development. After puberty, several eggs begin to mature each month but only one or two are ovulated and the final stage of development of the egg does not happen until the egg is fertilised by a sperm.

The egg is one of the largest cells in the human body, and can even be just about visible to the naked eye. Like sperm, eggs contain half the normal number of chromosomes (23) in their nuclei and these combine with the 23 male chromosomes at fertilisation to produce one fertilised egg with a full complement of chromosomes (46). The egg also contains other structures, such as mitochondria, which are essential for normal development of the early embryo (mitochondria produce energy for the cell). Indeed the first three days or so of an embryo's life is controlled and determined by the egg, rather than by the sperm.

The effect of age on a woman's eggs is described in Section 2. AMH and ovarian reserve are discussed in Section 3, as is the hormonal control of ovulation.

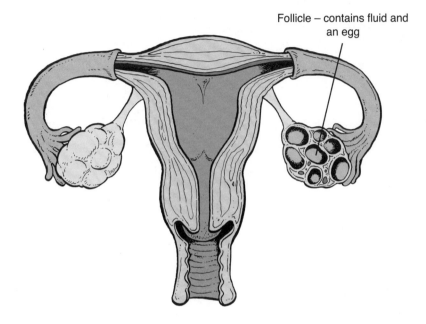

Follicle – contains fluid and an egg

Ovaries with follicle

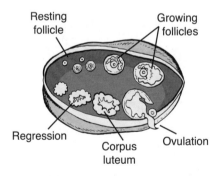

Resting follicle

Growing follicles

Regression

Corpus luteum

Ovulation

Egg in follicle

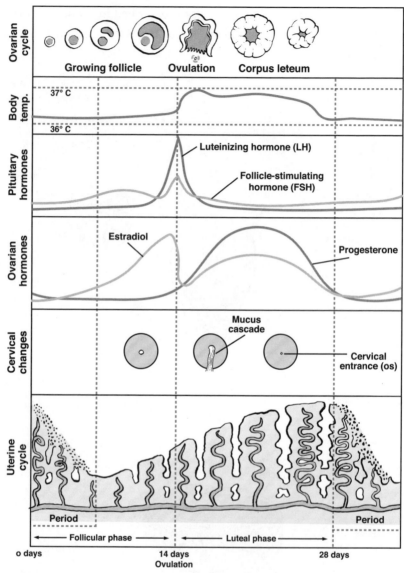

Menstrual cycle

Ovulation and the menstrual cycle

The menstrual cycle is the series of changes a woman's body goes through every month as she ovulates (releases an egg) and her uterus prepares for a possible pregnancy. It is a fascinating series of events controlled by the ovary and the hormones which regulate it.

The cycle is described as starting on the first day of the woman's period or menstruation – Day 1 – and ends on the day before the next period – typically Day 28 (but normal can be anywhere from Day 24 to Day 35). The diagram opposite shows the changes that occur in the woman's ovary, temperature, hormones, cervix and uterus during this time. Each cycle can be divided into three phases based on events in the ovary or in the uterus. In the ovary the three phases are called the follicular phase, the ovulatory phase and the luteal phase. The phases in the uterus are called the menstrual, proliferative and secretory phases. During the cycle, there is a lot going on at many levels – the various events are summarised in the diagram.

In the follicular phase in the ovary, under the influence of follicle-stimulating hormone (FSH) and, to a lesser extent, luteinising hormone (LH), several follicles begin to develop, but after a few days all but one (or sometimes two) stop growing and what is called the 'dominant' follicle continues to grow. The growing follicles produce oestrogen hormone. Once this reaches a certain level, the pituitary gland in the brain is triggered to release LH in a surge. This LH surge starts around Day 12 of the average 28-day cycle and lasts 24–36 hours. It triggers the dominant follicle to release its egg in an event called ovulation. This typically occurs on Day 14 of a 28-day cycle. Meanwhile, in the uterus, rising oestrogen levels stimulate the lining to get progressively thicker in preparation for pregnancy. The oestrogen also stimulates the cervix to produce fertile cervical mucus.

After ovulation, the dominant follicle in the ovary becomes what is called a corpus luteum. This produces the hormones oestrogen and progesterone, which continue to develop the lining of the uterus. This is called the secretory or luteal phase and lasts for two weeks. During this phase the uterine lining is soft and thick and suitable to allow the embryo to implant. The corpus luteum continues to produce progesterone. If the woman conceives, the implanting embryo begins to secrete the pregnancy hormone hCG (human chorionic gonadotropan). If the woman does not conceive, the corpus luteum in the ovary fails after about two weeks, causing a sharp drop in the levels of both progesterone and oestrogen. The fall in progesterone hormone causes the uterus to shed its lining and the woman's next menstrual bleed (period) begins.

Which of the two ovaries ovulates each month appears to be random. Occasionally, both ovaries will release an egg. For an individual woman, the follicular phase (before ovulation) often varies in length from cycle to cycle; by contrast, the length of her luteal phase (after ovulation) will be fairly consistent at 14 days from cycle to cycle.

The fertile window

Over the last 20 years much research has been done on ovulation and what is called the 'fertile window'. This is a period of about six days starting five days prior to ovulation and ending on the day of ovulation and is the time when pregnancy is most likely to happen. While an egg only stays capable of being fertilised for about 12 hours after ovulation, we know that healthy sperm can remain actively motile and capable of fertilising an egg for at least 72 hours (three days) after intercourse. So if a couple have sex a few days before ovulation that is still sufficient for them to conceive because the sperm will be healthy and 'sitting there' waiting for the egg to arrive. Sex a few days after ovulation is, however, too late because the egg will have deteriorated too much. It has been shown that over 80% of pregnancies happen when the couple have sex on the day of ovulation or in the five days leading up to ovulation. There is therefore generally a **six-day fertile window.**

MY ADVICE ON THE FERTILE WINDOW

If a couple are having sex often, e.g. every 2–3 days, they will be having sex during the fertile window and they don't need to worry about timing ovulation. However, for various reasons, couples may be having sex less often, and, if so, it is important to have some idea of when a woman is most fertile.

An average woman's menstrual cycle is typically 28 days, counting from the first day of her period (Day 1) to the first day of her next period – for example if a woman with a 28-day cycle has a period starting on 1 January, her next period is expected on 29 January and the one after that on 26 February. In such a cycle ovulation occurs approximately 14 days before the anticipated next period, so on a 28-day cycle that is approximately Day 14. For the woman above that would be 14 January, 11 February, 10 March. This woman's six-day fertile window would therefore occur from 9 to 14 January, from 6 to 11 February and from 5 to 10 March.

Cycle lengths, ovulation and fertile window

January	1	2	3	4	5	6	7
	8	9	10	11	12	13	14 ovulation
	15	16	17	18	19	20	21
	22	23	24	25	26	27	28
	29	30	31				

28-day cycle

February				1	2	3	4
	5	6	7	8	9	10	11 ovulation
	12	13	14	15	16	17	18
	19	20	21	22	23	24	25
	26	27	28				

March				1	2	3	4
	5	6	7	8	9	10 ovulation	11
	12	13	14	15	16	17	18
	19	20	21	22	23	24	25
	26	27	28	29	30	31	

■ Menstruation (period)   ■ Fertile window

Cycle lengths, ovulation and fertile window

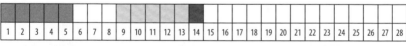

28-day cycle

26-day cycle

35-day cycle

■ = Menstruation (period)   ■ = fertile window   ■ = day of ovulation

But women are not machines, so the length of their menstrual cycles can vary a lot. If a woman has a 35-day cycle, ovulation occurs 14 days before the end of her cycle, which would be around Day 21. For this woman the fertile window would be the six days ending on that day, i.e. Days 16–21. If a woman has a 26-day cycle, ovulation would occur around Day 12 and her fertile window would start on Day 7.

What actually happens is that most women tend to have slightly varying cycles, so it would be perfectly normal for a woman to have a 26-day cycle one month and a 32-day cycle another month. We generally assume that any variation up to about seven days is completely normal. For a woman with varying cycles it can be difficult to predict the time of ovulation, so it is recommended that she observes her cycle for three or four months, noting the time of her periods. She can then work out approximately when her fertile time is likely to be. But in order to cover long and short cycles she might need to have a ten-day window when it is important to be having sex if she is trying to conceive.

Generally, if a woman's cycle is between 26 and 35 days, if she has sex between Days 8 and 21 of her cycle she will catch the fertile window. The recommended frequency of sex during this time is discussed later in this section.

Monitoring ovulation

For women who have very regular cycles it is easy to predict the day of ovulation based on a calendar or an app that records the cycle (see page 17). Some women get symptoms or signs of ovulation. It is also possible to measure the woman's level of the hormone LH, which surges in her bloodstream about 24–36 hours before ovulation and is present in her urine 12 to 24 hours before ovulation.

Apart from knowing the days of your cycle, there are several signs and devices available to help you know your fertile time.

Signs of ovulation

Some women will have signs of ovulation and these include changes in the cervical mucus, a rise in body temperature, ovulation pain, alterations in libido or sex drive, and mood swings.

Cervical mucus: Most women will have some degree of vaginal discharge and part of this is made up of cervical mucus. This typically undergoes dramatic changes around the time of ovulation, but not all women will see this. For those who do see changes, it can be a very useful way of predicting ovulation. Early on in a woman's cycle the mucus is usually cloudy or white and if you try to stretch it between your fingers it will break apart. As you get closer to ovulation the amount of mucus increases and it becomes thinner, clearer and has a slippery consistency, similar to raw egg white. If you try to stretch it between your fingers you will be able to stretch it out into a string. This is what we call fertile mucus and it has been shown that pregnancy rates are highest when intercourse occurs on the day of maximum mucus. This is usually two to three days prior to ovulation, so I would always suggest to a woman that if she sees this clear mucus she should really try to have sex during the following 24 hours.

The amount of mucus varies according to the size and nature of the woman's cervix. It can be higher in women who have been previously pregnant and lower in women taking certain fertility drugs or who have had surgery to their cervix (e.g. a LLETZ (large loop excision of the transformation zone) procedure for abnormal smears). Some women will notice ovulation mucus on their panties: others may find it if they place a finger inside their vagina; other women will never see it. It is a help if you see it, but don't worry if you don't.

Basal body temperature: When a woman ovulates, her progesterone hormone level increases. This in turn causes the woman's temperature to rise and can be a way of demonstrating ovulation. It is possible to buy specific fertility thermometers called basal thermometers (an ordinary thermometer is not sensitive enough) and if a woman measures her temperature every morning (before she gets up, starts any activity and before she eats or drinks) she should find that her temperature will rise one-fifth to one-half a degree a day or two after ovulation. This is a useful way of confirming that you *have* ovulated but, because the temperature only rises after ovulation, it is not a useful way of *predicting* ovulation. Certainly if you wait until the temperature has risen it is too late – you will have already gone past the fertile window which, as we described above, happens for the five days prior to ovulation and the day of ovulation.

Monitoring your temperature for a few cycles can be useful just to confirm that you are ovulating – but not to time it. I don't recommend doing it on a regular basis because it's just another job and another stress.

Ovulation pain: Around the time of ovulation some women get a pain in one or other ovary. This is triggered by the release of the egg from the ovary and is called 'mittelschmertz', which means in German 'middle pain'. The pain can occasionally be severe enough to cause the woman to be admitted to hospital. It is a useful way of detecting ovulation and, if the woman has not had sex coming up to this time, it would be important for her to do so as this is marking the end of the fertile window. Ovulation pain is very normal and can vary from cycle to cycle but women with endometriosis (see Section 2) can be more likely to experience it consistently. Again, if you don't feel it, don't worry. It doesn't mean that you are not ovulating.

Mood and libido changes and ovulation: There is a general consensus that women's libido, or sex drive, increases coming up to ovulation and this is seen as something that has evolved in humans to maximise fertility. Much fascinating research has been conducted on this topic, but the results are conflicting. Some studies show an increase in libido only in women who have a steady partner likely to be a suitable provider/parent; others show that libido is more related to the 'sexual desirability' of the male. If there is an increase in sexual activity around this time it seems more likely to be instigated by the woman. All the studies acknowledge that there may be flaws in interpreting the time of ovulation. But I suppose if libido increases prior to ovulation in women trying to conceive, it can only be a good thing!

In contrast, progesterone hormone levels rise after ovulation and this can cause generally unpleasant 'premenstrual' symptoms such as bloating, breast tenderness and low mood or PMS (premenstrual syndrome). While not pleasant, these at least are signs that the woman has ovulated.

Ovulation predictor kits (OPKs)

There are lots of home ovulation test kits available in pharmacies or online. These all act by measuring LH hormone, which is produced by the woman's pituitary gland and which triggers the egg to be released from her ovary. LH surges in the bloodstream about 24–36 hours before ovulation and is present in the urine 12 to 24 hours before ovulation – it takes longer to get to the urine because it has to go from the blood through the kidneys and into the urine. Some kits also measure oestrogen, which also rises before ovulation – but the oestrogen rise is slower and not as specific. The vast majority of these kits measure the hormone levels in the woman's urine, but there are some that use saliva. Once the LH level begins to rise it is very important to have intercourse around this time. However, some studies have shown that the kits may underestimate the fertile window and there is always a risk that if a woman is waiting for an LH surge, she may miss the critical five days coming up to ovulation.

There is some controversy over the use of OPKs. International guidelines, such as NICE (National Institute for Clinical Excellence) in the UK, advise against using them as they feel they increase stress levels (1.1). However, a large UK-based study showed that this was not the case and that the use of kits 'empowered women' and 'might' increase fertility (1.2). A cautionary note, however: this study was sponsored by a company that made the kits!

MY ADVICE ON OPKS

My advice is usually that it can be helpful for women to use an ovulation kit for a few cycles to help her become aware of when she is ovulating and to become familiar with and more confident in the workings of her own body. But I don't recommend them routinely because they are 'medicalising' sex and making it a big project! Having said that, some women feel much more in control when using the kits and are slow to stop. Cost may also be a factor – they can be expensive, especially if the woman's cycle is irregular, because she will need a lot of tests. Some studies have shown that observing changes in cervical mucus are probably better than, or certainly at least as good as, using LH kits – and certainly cheaper. Like most things in medicine, different approaches help different people and it is important to go with what works for you.

Apps and websites to detect ovulation

Recently, a number of websites and mobile phone apps have been developed that offer predictions of ovulation dates and a 'fertile window' during which couples are most likely to conceive. These programs generate the information by prompting the user to enter the date of the last menstrual period and the usual cycle length. Researchers in New York recently performed a study of 20 such websites and 33 apps to determine their accuracy in predicting the fertile window (1.3). Only one website and three apps predicted the precise fertile window. The researchers found that the programs were accurate 75% of the time but that the majority over-estimated the length of the fertile window. The researchers only used an example of a woman with a regular menstrual cycle and noted that the results would be even poorer for a woman with an irregular cycle.

My advice would be to use these apps, if you want, to keep a record and as a rough guide to when you may be fertile, but don't rely on them. Watch your body and put all the clues together. As a doctor, it's always useful when a woman comes to the clinic with all her recent period dates written down or noted in an app. It helps planning blood tests, treatments, etc.

Here are some examples from patients about how easy it is to get caught up in 'monitoring', which can take over your life and, in the long run, is not helpful.

'I temp every morning to see if I ovulate, how long my luteal phase is and even see if I'm pregnant if my temperature stays above a base line. I use home ovulation predictor sticks, take vitamins and even drink pomegranate juice to help our chances of conceiving. You can see how fertility becomes the main focus of my life every minute of every day. Time stands still when you can't conceive despite everyone around you falling pregnant. Treatments can't happen quick enough and the months of testing and repeat testing are gruelling and frustrating.'

'The advice is to relax as much as possible and while I think this is obviously good advice, as a woman there is no getting away from it. You can't get away from your own body, even if trying to take a relaxed approach you cannot not notice CM (cervical mucus) or blood or you cannot not feel cramps. Even without actively trying to notice you have a general idea where you are and what is going on in your body.'

> **WHEN TO SUSPECT PROBLEMS WITH OVULATION**
>
> Generally, when a woman's cycle is too short or too long it is unlikely that she is ovulating well and it is recommended that she see a doctor to discuss this. Cycles that are less than 25 days or more than 36 or 37 days in length are likely to be associated with ovulation problems and such women may need medical help to ensure that they are ovulating. See Section 3 on ovulation problems.

Ultrasound Scans

The use of ultrasound to track ovulation is discussed in the section on ultrasound scanning in Section 3.

Sex

If a couple have a very active sex life and are having sex a few times a week, they don't need to think about timing ovulation or worry about missing the fertile window. In keeping with this, many international guidelines recommend that couples don't think about timing and just have regular sex. This is good advice and aims to reduce the stress that couples are under and to keep sex as 'normal', spontaneous and enjoyable as possible. But I'm afraid it's not always that simple!

Sex and timing

A lot has been written about the benefits of trying to time intercourse. Indeed lots of companies promote and make money out of urinary testing kits and, more recently, apps to predict ovulation.

I come across many couples who lead very busy lives. They rush out the door in the morning and come home from work exhausted. Sex is often the last thing on their minds. Others work away from home or travel a lot and are not together every day/night. Others share their accommodation with parents or have disruptive small kids at home. Finally, if they have been trying to conceive for a long time, they may just be fed up with having sex and it can become a chore rather than a joy. These couples are not having rampant sex a few times a week! For these couples, it is important that they make that extra effort to ensure that they have sex during the fertile window. (See more on sexual problems in Section 3.)

Studies have shown that having intercourse daily during the fertile time makes pregnancy slightly more likely than having sex on alternate days, but the difference is not great. A study of 221 couples trying to conceive showed that the pregnancy rate was highest in the group who had sex every day during the fertile window (37% conceived), but was almost as high in those having sex every second day (33%). However, if couples were only having sex once a week the pregnancy rate was much lower (15%) (1.4). Another study has shown that for women with generally regular 28- to 33-day cycles, the possibility of pregnancy increased from 3% on cycle day 8 to 9% by cycle day 12 and decreased to less than 2% on cycle day 21 (1.4).

It is really important not to put too much emphasis on exact days or times. This is often counter-productive. Many studies have shown that the stress associated with trying to conceive can reduce sexual satisfaction, and even have a negative effect on pregnancy rates. I have had women come to my clinic with complicated Excel files, detailing almost to the minute every time they have had sex and their symptoms at the time. I have had men who can relate in minute detail the intricacies of their partner's menstrual cycle. I have had women who try to hide any sign that it is their fertile time so that they appear 'just in the mood for sex' and I have even had women who set an alarm clock or their phone alarm for when they think the time of ovulation will be. I can imagine few things that could be a greater disincentive to enjoyable sex.

While it is so easy to see why couples can get caught up in this detail, it is not helpful.

MY ADVICE ON TIMING

Trying to get the balance right between being too careful and too careless can be really difficult. My advice is generally that if couples are having vaginal sex three or four times a week, they certainly don't need to think about timing. If, however, sex is less frequent, they need to have a rough idea of when the woman's fertile time is. It can be useful to look at ovulation for a few cycles so that the woman has some idea as to when her fertile time is, and then to try to have sex two or three times, or roughly every second day, during that time. But a day or two here or there isn't going to make any difference. If the woman notices clear ovulation mucus just before ovulation, that is absolutely the best time to try, if possible.

Couples sometimes worry that they might be having sex too often if they do so every day. The answer is no – it is absolutely fine. Some of this confusion comes from the fact that, when we are arranging sperm tests or asking men to provide sperm for treatments such as IUI or IVF, we ask them to abstain for 2–5 days beforehand. This is because for those tests and procedures, we need a certain concentration of sperm and we know that the concentration diminishes with frequent ejaculation. But for natural sex and conception, there will be enough sperm and the sperm can remain healthy in the woman's body for up to three days, so if the couple are having sex frequently, plenty will accumulate. On the other hand, we know that if a man ejaculates very infrequently, large numbers of dead and poor sperm will accumulate, so ejaculating at least every 2–5 days is best.

Sexual practices

Position: I'm often asked by couples what is the best position for sex in order to conceive. The answer, I am pleased to say, is that no one position is preferable to any other and the most important thing is that sex is as comfortable and as enjoyable as possible. There are some crazy reports on the internet suggesting that elevating the woman's pelvis or even standing on her head may help. There is absolutely no truth to this.

Studies have shown that sperm can reach the Fallopian tubes within two minutes of intercourse and certainly there would be an abundance of sperm in the Fallopian tubes 10–15 minutes following intercourse. It is normal for some semen to trickle out of the vagina when a woman sits up or stands up; this happens with every couple and is normal. I generally suggest that the woman relaxes for five to ten minutes following sex and then gets up and about if she wishes, but there is no proof that resting makes any difference.

There have been some small studies which have suggested that female orgasm can improve the transport of sperm up into the Fallopian tube, but this has not been shown to actually affect fertility.

Lubricants: The vagina naturally produces lubrication during sexual arousal. However, many couples find that using a lubricant improves comfort and pleasure, for both sexes. One US study of over 2,000 women showed that 62% had used a lubricant at some time (1.5). Lubricants can be helpful, particularly for women who find sex painful (e.g. women with endometriosis) or who feel vaginal dryness, or in couples who are finding sex a 'chore'. It is therefore important to know whether or not they affect fertility.

Unfortunately the science is not as clear as we would like. Many laboratory-based studies have been done and the majority show that most lubricants reduce sperm motility in a test tube within 15–60 minutes (1.5). These include natural agents like water, saliva and olive oil, petroleum-based oils (e.g. Vaseline), water-based gels (e.g. KY jelly, Replens, Astroglide and Surgilube). However, canola oil had no effect. In addition, newer lubricants have been developed that are promoted as being sperm-friendly (Pre-Seed, Conceive Plus) and several laboratory studies confirm that they have minimal effects on sperm. In contrast to the lab-based studies, studies of fertility and pregnancy in couples using lubricants do not give a clear answer as to their effect on pregnancy. There is some evidence that the effect when a couple uses them may be considerably less than the effects in the lab because of the vagina's in-built protective mechanisms and also the fact that sperm get to the Fallopian tubes so quickly after ejaculation in the vagina.

In summary, couples need to be able to have sex comfortably, so I would recommend using canola oil or one of the newer 'sperm-safe' lubricants mentioned above. This was also the conclusion of an American Society for Reproductive Medicine (ASRM) committee opinion in 2013. However, if you don't need a lubricant, I'm not convinced that there is any reliable evidence that they actually improve fertility.

When to seek help

Sex is not always enjoyable or comfortable and it is important that you don't feel embarrassed or silly because of this. It is really important to discuss any issues with your medical professional (see our later discussion of this in Section 3). And it is better to do this sooner rather than later because sexual problems tend to get worse if ignored. As mentioned earlier, trying to have sex at particular times to 'get pregnant' can sometimes take all the fun out of it and can in itself cause problems. This is discussed in detail by psychotherapist Meg Fitzgerald in her excellent piece in Section 3.

Section 1 References

1.1   NICE (2013) *Fertility Problems: Assessment and Treatment.* Royal College of Obstetricians and Gynaecologists, London.

1.2   Tiplady, S., Jones, G., Campbell, M., Johnson, S. and Ledger, W. (2013) 'Home ovulation tests and stress in women trying to conceive: a randomized controlled trial'. *Human Reproduction* 28(1): 138–51.

1.3   Setton, R., Tierney, C. and Tsai, T. (2016) 'The accuracy of web sites and cellular phone applications in predicting the fertile window'. *Obstetrics and Gynecology* 128(1): 58–63.

1.4   ASRM Practice Committee in collaboration with the Society for Reproductive Endocrinology and Infertility (2013) 'Optimizing natural fertility: a committee opinion'. *Fertility and Sterility* 100(3): 631–7.

1.5   Mesen, T. B. and Steiner, A. Z. (2014) 'Effect of vaginal lubricants on natural fertility'. *Current Opinion in Obstetrics and Gynecology* 26(3): 186–92.

Lifestyle

I n all aspects of health, it is becoming clear that lifestyle has a major impact on wellbeing. This is also true for fertility. While improving lifestyle doesn't resolve all fertility issues, it certainly helps with each and every problem I see and every treatment we recommend. One of the most distressing aspects of infertility or difficulty conceiving is that it can cause a sense of helplessness and lack of control. But with lifestyle, the patient or client is in control. And if lifestyle changes can get you the child you so desire, without needing to have expensive and draining fertility treatment, that is fantastic. Also remember that your end goal is a baby – so any lifestyle improvements you make are going to help your pregnancy and baby too. And all of this applies to men as well as to women.

Changing one's lifestyle is, however, not a quick fix, so the sooner you start, the better. In this section I try to cover all the ways in which people can optimise their health naturally without medical intervention. Even for those who need fertility treatment, the advice in this section will help improve your chances of success. Probably even more important, it will help you remain fit and healthy, both physically and emotionally. I am delighted to include here some excellent contributions from some of my colleagues and from ex-patients.

Unfortunately, even though hundreds of studies have tried to analyse the effects of lifestyle on fertility in men and women, the results are often conflicting and inconclusive. I have researched each topic and I am happy that the advice I give is based on sound evidence where available and on common sense where the evidence is conflicting. My overall belief is that moderation is the key. I also believe that small changes may be just enough to tip the scales favourably or unfavourably towards fertility: every little helps. So I hope this section will help you to optimise your fertility. But, remember, you also have to live – and live happily – so remember moderation and don't overdo things.

Age

Now for the bit that no one wants to hear! The effect of age on fertility, and specifically the effect of the woman's age. Few things related to fertility upset, irritate and annoy women more. Journalists, in particular, don't like to hear doctors telling women to try to have their babies in their twenties. Fertility specialists are often called scaremongers, dramatists, busybodies – How dare they tell women what to do with their lives?

But if you asked me how I would improve women's fertility, I would, like any fertility specialist I know, say simply, 'Change our society to make childbearing at a young age the norm.'

If someone asks me to see a couple with a fertility issue, the first question I ask is 'How old is the female partner?' because – even if one of the couple has a major problem e.g., severe sperm issues or severe endometriosis – the key to success is the woman's age. If she is 30, we have a real chance of success one way or another, but if she is 43, my heart sinks.

Unfortunately, many women (and their partners) don't realise that a woman's biological clock is ticking rapidly – from her late 20s and early 30s. Our bodies are designed to have children when we are young. Technology and medicine can help, but they can't replace natural fertility, if it has been lost. Fertility in men also declines with age, but not as early and not with as big an effect.

Several age-related factors are important for fertility and they include:

- the number of eggs
- the quality of the eggs
- the general gynaecological health of the woman
- the general health of the woman
- the quality of the sperm
- the general health of the man.

Sadly, all these factors deteriorate as we get older.

The number of eggs

Women are born with all their eggs already in their ovaries and the number left in each ovary declines with time. At birth the ovaries contain one to two million eggs and these are arrested at an early stage of development. When a woman reaches puberty and starts to menstruate the number of eggs in her ovaries will have reduced to about 400,000. After puberty, each month several of these eggs develop but only one or two reach full maturity and actually ovulate. Therefore over a lifetime a woman will ovulate about 400 eggs. Between puberty and menopause the number of follicles containing eggs diminishes and by menopause there are actually no eggs remaining in the woman's ovary. Menopause means that the woman's periods (*men*struation) have stopped.

Women lose their eggs at different rates. Some women are lucky and even at the age of 43 or 44 will have lots of eggs left in their ovaries. Others are not so lucky and by the age of 30 have very few eggs left. Two to three per cent of women undergo what we term 'premature ovarian insufficiency' or early menopause – menopause before the age of 40.

But as regards fertility, it is not really menopause we are concerned about – once that occurs it is definitely too late (periods have stopped completely). It is the years prior to menopause that are critical for women. We know that fertility diminishes rapidly up to ten years before the woman's periods stop, i.e. ten years before menopause. Most women go through menopause at around 51 and this means that their fertility has virtually gone by the age of 41. In contrast, some women go through menopause at 48 and they will find that their fertility is almost gone by the age of 38.

Unfortunately it is not possible to predict which women are going to go through an early menopause. However, if you have a family history of a sister or a mother who has had an early menopause you need to watch out for this.

As women and their ovaries get older, most women will notice a gradual shortening of their menstrual cycle (it may go from 28 days to 25 or 26 days). If the cycles are getting as short as 21 or 22 days, this may mean that the woman's ovaries are failing rapidly.

We can make some attempt at determining a woman's ovarian reserve (how many eggs she is likely to have left) by measuring a hormone, AMH (Anti-Mullerian hormone), in her blood or by doing an ultrasound scan and counting her follicles (which contain eggs) – this is called an antral follicle count (see Section 3).

Quality of the eggs

In addition to the age-related decline in the number of follicles or eggs in the woman's ovaries, we also know that the quality of the eggs diminishes. This means that the eggs are less able to be fertilised by a sperm and lead to pregnancy and they are also more prone to developing chromosomal (genetic) abnormalities. This is discussed in more detail later.

Unfortunately, there is currently no simple test (other than age) to determine the quality of a woman's eggs. Even in IVF, where we can look closely at the eggs, it is very difficult to grade them. This is because eggs are just one cell and, unlike sperm, they don't move or have particular shapes. Lots of research is being carried out to try to find biomarkers of egg quality, but that will be in the future.

The information we currently have about egg quality comes from studies looking at how eggs behave in natural and IVF pregnancies – how they fertilise, form embryos and lead to healthy pregnancies. Sadly, all the studies show that as the woman, and therefore her eggs, age, her fertility reduces and her chance of miscarriage and foetal abnormalities increases.

Fertility and female age

A study carried out in the USA as long ago as 1986 (2.1) showed that, of women who married between the ages of 20 and 24, only 6% remained childless over their lives, compared to 64% of women who married at the age of 40–44. This study looked at different populations all around the world and showed very clearly that fertility rates began to drop significantly once the woman was aged 30.

Another study has shown that if women start trying to conceive at the age of 30, 75% will conceive within one year. This falls to 66% if the woman starts at 35 and 44% if she waits until 40 to start trying to conceive (2.2).

According to the Central Statistics Office, the average age of mothers giving birth in Ireland in 2014 was 32.4 years, which is the highest average age of mothers at maternity, since the age of mother at birth was first recorded in 1955 (2.3).

There is a tendency in modern times to assume that if a woman waits to try to conceive and then has problems she can at least go for IVF and this will sort the problem. However, sadly, this is not so. A French study in 2004 (2.4) showed that, for women who postpone a first attempt at conceiving from the age of 30 to 35, IVF will only make up for half of the births lost by waiting those five years. If women postpone from age 35 to 40 IVF will only make up for a third of the lost pregnancies.

Another study of women having donor insemination in 1991 showed that a woman of 35 is only half as likely to have a healthy baby as a woman of 25 (2.5).

If you look at any fertility clinic that publishes its success rates by age, you will see that the success rates of IVF fall dramatically for women over 40 years of age. In our own fertility clinic, Merrion Fertility Clinic, women who are under 35 have a 50% chance of having a healthy baby following one cycle of IVF, and women up to the age of 39 have an almost 40% chance. But the chance of a healthy pregnancy and live birth in women 42 years and above is down at 5–7%. This is despite every effort made by clinics to improve the success rates for older women.

CSO Ireland figures on maternal age when giving birth

Miscarriage, other pregnancy problems and female age

Sadly, the incidence of miscarriage also increases with age and is nearly 50% once a woman is into her forties. We know that this is predominantly related to an increase in chromosomal abnormalities in the embryos formed by older eggs.

A Danish study published in 2000 (2.6) looked at over 1.2 million pregnancies in 634,000 women between 1978–1992. The risk of miscarriage according to age was as follows:

20–24 years:	11.1%
25–29 years:	11.9%
30–34 years:	15%
35–39 years:	24.6%
40–44 years:	51%
45 or more:	93.4%

You will see that there is a dramatic increase in miscarriage after the age of 40. This increase happened both in women who had never been previously pregnant and also in women who had been previously pregnant.

Ectopic pregnancy is less common than miscarriage, but this also increases with age and in the Danish study was shown to be 1.4% at the age of 21 compared to 69% at the age of 44. The incidence of stillbirth follows a similar pattern. The researchers concluded that at 42 years of age, more than half of all pregnancies resulted in a miscarriage, ectopic pregnancy or stillbirth.

Because of the increased age of her eggs and the consequent increase in genetic abnormalities in the embryos, it has been known for a long time that foetal abnormalities increase as the mother gets older. Pregnancy problems such as pre-eclampsia, high blood pressure, haemorrhage, premature birth, placenta praevia and diabetes are also all more common in older women.

Chromosomal abnormalities

By far the most important cause of miscarriage and foetal loss is chromosomal abnormalities. Chromosomes are what carry our genes and all humans have 46 chromosomes in every cell. Embryos can be referred to as euploid or aneuploid. Euploid means that the chromosome content of the embryo is normal, i.e. there are 46 normal chromosomes – 23 from the mother and 23 from the father. An aneuploid embryo is one where there is either an extra chromosome or there is one chromosome missing. Chromosomes that are commonly affected by aneuploidy are chromosomes 21, 18 and 13. Trisomy 21, where the embryos have an extra number of chromosome 21, leads to Down syndrome. Trisomy 18, which leads to an extra chromosome 18, causes Edwards' syndrome. Trisomy 13 causes Patau syndrome. We know that the children actually born with these syndromes represent less than 10% of the embryos that originally started out with these abnormalities as the pregnancies for most of these embryos will end in miscarriage.

A genetic study published in the USA in 2014 looked at genetic screening results for over 15,000 embryos from 2,700 patients having IVF (2.7). Of these embryos, 9,000 were found to be normal and 6,000 were abnormal or aneuploid. The authors correlated the incidence of abnormal chromosomes with the age of the woman and the results are startling. The incidence of abnormal or aneuploid embryos was lowest for women between 26 and 30 (<25%). In women aged 35, 35% of embryos were abnormal. This rose to 60% of embryos at the age of 40 and 83% of embryos at the age of 43. One-third of patients at age 42 had no normal embryos and over half of the women aged 44 were in this situation.

Gynaecological and general health

In addition to the problems with female eggs as they age, women are also more likely to develop other gynaecological and general health problems as they get older. Any of the conditions mentioned in the section on female causes of infertility are likely to be more common in older women. These include endometriosis, adenomyosis, fibroids, ovarian cysts and even pelvic infection. Becoming pregnant later in life also overlaps with the onset of chronic and general diseases such as arthritis, depression, cancer, heart disease and diabetes. Also, BMI (body mass index) increases with age and this is problematic, especially for women with polycystic ovarian syndrome (PCOS).

Fertility and male age

Studies on fertility in men also show a decline with age, though the results are not as clear as they are in women because it can be hard to tease out the contribution of the effect of the female partner's age (2.8). However, it appears that natural fertility rates in men over 40 years of age may be half those of younger men. It is not known whether this is due to a reduction in sperm quality or a reduction in sexual activity as men age. One study has shown that success rates with IVF can be almost halved in men over 40. The older the man's partner, the more significant this difference (2.9). Another study showed that men who are over 45 had between a four and 12 times higher chance of infertility than men who are under 25 years of age (2.10).

Laboratory studies show changes in the testes and in sperm production with age and also hormone changes, with a reduction in testosterone levels in men over 50 (2.8). Although some changes have been noted in men over the age of 35, we know that sperm is affected by various factors such as the last time of ejaculation and lifestyle issues such as diet and smoking. While some of the studies try to take these into account, it is difficult to do so. Studies of DNA damage in sperm also suggest that the level of damage increases as men get older (2.8), but the precise age at which this happens has yet to be determined. Again, it is likely to be significant after the age of 45.

Much more study and research is required to accurately determine at what age men's fertility may decline, but it is likely that sperm quality begins to deteriorate progressively from the age of 35 and significantly after the age of 45.

Male age has also been associated with an increased risk of miscarriage and health problems in their offspring, though this tends to be not as well known as the effects of female age. There is some evidence that Down syndrome may be associated with male age and that conditions such as bipolar disorder and autism may also be higher in the children of older men (2.8). Again the risks seem to be in men aged over 45. For these reasons international bodies such as the American Society for

Reproductive Medicine and the British Andrology Society set the upper age limit for sperm donors at 40 years of age.

So what can we do?

This really is a difficult and touchy subject. The last thing I want to do is to be negative and depressing. Most of the people I see who are trying to conceive in their forties are only too well aware of the issues of age but it never ceases to amaze me how many people just don't know these facts. And this applies to doctors as well as to patients!

I have had a 44-year-old patient who didn't want to do IVF because she wanted to try everything else first. How do you tell someone like that that it's too late, even for IVF? I have had a doctor refer a 43-year-old woman whom he described as a 'young' 43-year-old. I'm sorry, but there is no such thing as a 'young' 43-year-old when it comes to fertility!

The media don't help – every day we see reports of celebrities conceiving well into their forties and fifties. Most of these reports don't tell us that these women have conceived using donor eggs – i.e. eggs from a younger woman. Partly this is due to people's understandable need for privacy around the circumstances of their pregnancy, but it can also be a lack of knowledge and education. As recently as 2016, Ireland's main evening television news reported a pregnancy in a 72-year-old Indian woman as being 'thought to be with her own eggs'. This is simply fantasy and shows a deep level of misunderstanding about the effects of age on female fertility. While natural pregnancies have been reported around the world in women in their fifties, this is exceedingly rare (*Guinness Book of Records*-type stuff) unless they have had IVF with eggs donated by a younger woman or had their own eggs frozen many years earlier.

Fertility clinics must also take some of the blame for misinformation. Sadly, fertility treatment is commercialised around the world and this makes for intense competition between clinics. This can put pressure on clinics to over-inflate their pregnancy success rates, particularly for older women, in whom the results are poor. No clinic wants to tell a couple that their chances of a live birth are less than 5%. But honesty is what people want and what people need. So what can one do?

The most important advice I can give people, particularly women, is to think about pregnancy sooner rather than later. This is not possible for many women. Recent research shows that the commonest reason for women to delay pregnancy is because they haven't yet met 'Mr Right'. I see this so often – many couples don't find a meaningful long-term relationship until the woman is in her forties. And there is little we can do about that.

But if you do find someone, don't delay. If you are over 38 and are not pregnant within six months or if you have a known fertility-related health problem, see your doctor straightaway. And if your doctor doesn't take you seriously, contact a fertility clinic.

Don't postpone pregnancy for things that can wait. Most things can wait. I regularly see people who are waiting because they are building a house, or they are studying for a degree, or they have a career, or they want to travel, or they want to get married first (and planning a wedding can take 18 months!). These are all valid things to put into life plans but I, and all fertility experts, would say – hold it there. Focus on your family first and the rest will fall into place. Having a baby is expensive, but it's not necessary to have everything in place before the baby.

YOUR BIOLOGICAL CLOCK

I say to women that, as regards career, there is never a good time to have a baby. But no matter how inflexible and demanding you think your career is, it is not as inflexible as your biological clock. If you miss out on a career opportunity now, there will be another one some time, some place. But if you miss out on that fertility window, there is no second chance.

All too often, I see very successful, competent women with really good careers who have 'left it too late'. And I know that, if they had taken a chance and taken a career break to have kids, they would still have been successful in their career – but maybe a few years later. A career will wait. Your ovaries won't.

Thankfully, modern medicine and technology offer hope for age-related fertility decline. Assisted reproduction, in particular ICSI, has been a major breakthrough for male subfertility (see Section 3). Egg freezing is showing promise for women who aren't in a position to conceive (e.g. they haven't met a person they want to have kids with), but frozen eggs require ICSI (IVF) and are not anywhere near as successful as fresh eggs (see Section 3). They should also be frozen in that 25–34 age group. Ovarian reserve testing with AMH and antral follicle counts is helping women predict whether they might be in trouble at an earlier age than average. And slowly the medical world is beginning to make an impact on education – but there is still a long way to go.

Here are some patients' comments on age:

> 'Basically I spent all my years studying a degree, doing a PhD, looking for a stable job ... by the time we were ready for a child I am 37 years old. Maybe too late for it. My results show a low egg count. My husband's results are all very good. I am trying to conceive for two years with a miscarriage along the way. The option offered is IVF.'

> 'Even though I knew my age was an issue, the fact that I have been pregnant before, that my AMH levels are high, and that my mother became pregnant at 47 (and had a healthy baby, who is 21 years my junior!), all led me to believe that my fertility wasn't really an issue.'

> 'As a teenager you are educated by your parents and perhaps school about contraception and not getting pregnant! However, while I understand it's not relevant to that exact time, it would also be nice to be educated on the subject of possible infertility issues later on in life.'

> 'Whatever the reasons are for your infertility, I think it's important to try to share them and to educate people about not leaving it so late in life to start a family, the fact that it's far more common than people think, that it's nothing to be ashamed of and that, as my sister-in-law (who also had IVF) said to me recently, "at the end of the day, it doesn't matter how the baby arrives!"'

Nutrition, diet and body weight

Adequate nutrition is essential for our general health and wellbeing. As a doctor, and also as a human being who is getting older, I am realising more and more how a healthy diet and good nutrition can make us feel better and contribute to all aspects of our health and longevity. And fertility is no exception. In addition, medical problems related to obesity are now probably the biggest challenge we face in medicine.

Sinead Curran has written an excellent section on diet and nutrients and how to ensure that your diet is giving you what you and your (hopefully) future baby need to optimise health. This is essential reading for anyone hoping to embark on pregnancy, irrespective of your weight and diet.

In the following pages I will discuss the difficult issue of weight and how this affects fertility in both sexes, including treatment success, subsequent pregnancy and even the health of our children. In both men and women, hormone production is influenced by nutrition, and being either underweight or overweight is not good. This is discussed in further detail in the sections on PCOS, ovulation problems and male infertility. Even conditions such as endometriosis will often respond to dietary changes and there is growing evidence that obesity significantly affects our immune systems because it causes the body to be in a chronic inflammatory state.

The evidence regarding supplementing with vitamins for fertility is confusing and I have tried to summarise this as well as possible, given the poor quality of studies available.

A healthy BMI

BMI stands for body mass index and it is an internationally agreed calculation based on your weight and height. Sinead shows how to calculate your BMI in her essay, but there are many apps and websites that will also do this.

- If your BMI is less than 18.5, it falls within the underweight range.
- If your BMI is 18.5 to <25, it falls within the normal range.
- If your BMI is 25 to <30, it falls within the overweight range.
- If your BMI is 30 or higher, it falls within the obese range.
- If your BMI is 40 or higher, it is categorised as extreme or severe obesity.

BMI does not measure body fat directly, but it correlates with more specific measures of body fat such as measurement of skinfold thickness and with various adverse health outcomes.

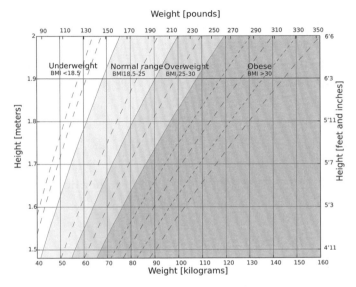

BMI chart for adults

Another way to estimate your potential disease risk related to weight is to measure your **waist circumference**. Excessive fat in the abdominal area may be serious because it places you at greater risk of developing obesity-related conditions, such as type 2 diabetes, high blood pressure, and coronary artery disease. A waist circumference in excess of 102 centimetres (40 inches) for men and 88 centimetres (35 inches) for (non-pregnant) women places you in the at-risk category, but ideally it should be less than 94 cms (37 inches) in men and less than 80 cms (32 inches) in women.

In populations such as those of Asian descent, BMI will be lower and waist circumference is a better indicator of disease risk than BMI.

Underweight women

We know that a certain amount of body fat (approximately 22%) is necessary for women to maintain normal hormone levels. I describe later how low body weight, particularly in combination with high levels of exercise, can lead to reduced or absent ovulation (hypogonadotropic hypogonadism, or hypo hypo). Studies have shown that if women lose 15% of their ideal body weight, their periods will become irregular and if they lose 30% their periods will stop altogether. Women with a history of eating disorders such as anorexia nervosa and bulimia are particularly at risk and some of these young women may never have a period. The good news is that gaining weight helps – though it may take over a year for the increase to affect periods and ovulation. Being underweight also has very significant effects on the health of your baby – see later.

In my experience, it is often harder to help women who are underweight to gain weight than to help overweight women to lose weight. Often those with a BMI below 19 are eating only healthy food and they may also be exercising and doing 'healthy things'. It is hard for them to accept that things are not optimal and, unlike obese women, they don't get strong messages from friends, social media, etc.

Underweight men

I can find very little written regarding fertility problems in men who are underweight but the principles outlined later by Sinead Curran on the benefits of a healthy diet apply to us all. As discussed in the section on exercise, we regularly see men whose sperm parameters decline when they put their bodies under excessive stress e.g. doing marathons, triathlons, etc.

Overweight women

There is no doubt that being overweight (BMI over 25) or obese (BMI over 30) increases the chances of infertility and miscarriage. Many obese women have no problem conceiving, but if we look at any study, they are proportionately a much smaller proportion of women of that weight than the proportion of women of normal weight who conceive. It's a bit like smoking; we know that smokers die younger, but there will always be exceptions who smoke and live into their nineties.

Infertility has been shown to be almost three times higher in obese women, and obese adolescents have a greater chance of remaining childless than normal-weight women (2.11). While overweight women with polycystic ovarian syndrome (PCOS) will have irregular menstrual cycles, the adverse effect of weight on fertility is also seen in women with regular cycles (2.11). Some of these effects relate to increased oestrogen production in fat tissue, but there are also studies suggesting that egg quality is affected too.

Studies in women undergoing assisted reproduction treatments (ART) such as IVF and ICSI also show a negative effect of increased weight (2.12). Obese women have been reported to have a 68% lower chance of having a live birth following their first ART cycle compared with non-obese women; this seems to be related to poor ovarian response and lower rates of fertilisation, embryo transfer, implantation and pregnancy. Blastocysts (embryos) developed from eggs of high-BMI women have been shown to be smaller, contain less cells, and have higher fat content, lower glucose consumption, and altered amino acid (protein) metabolism compared with embryos from normal-weight women (2.13). There is also evidence of an effect on the endometrium or womb lining. In addition, obesity is related to the requirement for increased doses of fertility drugs in treatment, more frequent cancellation of cycles and more difficult egg collection and embryo transfer procedures.

Miscarriage risk also increases with increasing BMI and has been shown to be one and a half to two times higher in obese and very obese women, both following natural pregnancy and following IVF/ICSI pregnancies (2.11). Even in women who have a successful pregnancy, pregnancy in overweight and obese women is associated with an increased risk of complications – for both the mother and the foetus – including diabetes, high blood pressure, pre-eclampsia, pre-term delivery, stillbirth, Caesarean or instrumental delivery, shoulder dystocia, foetal distress, early neonatal death and foetal abnormalities. They also risk having either abnormally small or large babies – see below.

Overweight men

Overweight and obese men also have increased fertility issues. These include reduced semen quality (reduced sperm count, concentration and motility), impaired erectile function, and other physical problems, including sleep apnoea and increased scrotal temperatures (2.14). There may also be effects on sperm DNA, embryo development, pregnancy rates and miscarriage. Obese men have been shown to have decreased levels of testosterone and other hormones, possibly related to increased oestrogen production in fat tissue. One recent study reports that in patients seeking treatment for male infertility, there has been a three-fold increase in the prevalence of obesity.

The benefits of weight loss

The good news is that weight loss in overweight and obese women (2.12) (and less obviously so in men) has been shown to increase both natural conception rates and IVF success rates and also to improve the course of pregnancy.

This is particularly so for women who are overweight and have irregular ovulation (PCOS and non-PCOS): a reduction of 10% in weight leads to pregnancy in over 50% of couples. The classic study on this was published in Adelaide, Australia, in 1998 (2.15). Of 67 obese infertile women who were not ovulating and who lost an average of 10 kg each during a six-month weight-loss programme, 60 (90%) started ovulating and 52 (78%) conceived, with a miscarriage rate of 18%.

I have seen this numerous times. As the woman loses weight, her periods first come back or start getting more regular and then she conceives. This is beautifully illustrated in the following wonderful account by one of my patients.

> *'I was first diagnosed with PCOS in 2011. I have always had irregular cycles. I did not know what PCOS was at the time and the information that you usually get on the internet can be even more confusing. We tried for nearly five years before seeking help. It might not be a long time to some of you reading this but when you want to be a mum so much it can feel like a lifetime.*
>
> *I was referred by my GP on 21 December 2012 to MFC's Dr Wingfield and she provided us with the right information on how to tackle my PCOS from the get go. First of all I needed to control my **weight**.*
>
> *I went home feeling defeated because I was always on the heavy side despite being active. I did not think any amount of dieting would work as it had not in the past but I really wanted a baby. I was armed with a prescription for Glucophage and advice/encouragement from my doctor.*

*I started by devising a meal plan for the whole day and with that I kept a diary registering my calorie intake every day (I would aim for 1,500 calories per day). Getting active 6/7, which consisted of a one-hour walk every evening (I kept at it whether it rained, snowed, I felt tired or on my own). I stopped smoking to improve my chances as recommended by Dr Wingfield and thought since I was at it and needed to lose weight, plus my workout would have been pointless, I **stopped drinking** (not even one glass of wine after a hectic day at work).*

I cut out my take-out nights completely and dined out only if it was a special occasion and even then would stick to light meals, e.g. soup or salads. I am also a dessert person so I would make sugar-free jelly to help whenever I was tempted.

*It all paid off four months after. I looked great, dropped two dress sizes ... and **success** in April 2013 I was pregnant! For a girl who was not regular for years and could not get pregnant despite trying for a long time I was over the moon. I also realised that the doctor was right – I could do this by just changing my lifestyle and a little something to control my sugar level.*

All the best to you all. Please don't give up on your dream of becoming a parent. The change is painful and some days you will feel like what's the point? But it's so worth it. I am the proud mum of a beautiful baby boy and it's a whole new adventure ...'

Here is another woman who was successful:

'I was carrying a lot of weight and doctors advised me to try and lose some of that weight as being overweight can also affect fertility. My husband and I really wanted another child so I was determined to get down to a healthy weight, so I did. I lost four and a half stone and got down to a healthy BMI .'

And here is another woman with PCOS and diabetes embarking on the weight-loss journey:

'With my history I want to give the baby the best chance for his/her future and me being at my healthiest is really important. I visualise the

PCOS and diabetes as a circle; one has a knock-on effect on the other. I needed to eat foods that won't cause an insulin spike to ensure my insulin levels don't get out of control, as the more insulin I had in my body the more my hormone levels got imbalanced. Getting the diabetes under control was paramount and I have reached a HbA1c level of 47 and counting it down further with food control and moderate exercise such as walking. The Meformin has helped me have regular periods, though they are still painful. I just live in hope that my husband and I will hold our bundle of joy soon. I'm just motivated to do everything I can to make that happen. I've lost 20 pounds so far. I wish anyone else out there going through a similar story every hope and success.'

As regards couples undergoing fertility treatments like IVF, the news is also good. A group in Sydney reviewed the literature and published a systematic review in 2014, looking at the effect of weight loss in overweight and/or obese women undergoing ART on their subsequent pregnancy outcome (2.12). Weight loss was significantly associated with increased pregnancy rates and/or live birth in eight of the 11 studies reviewed. In addition, regularisation of the menstrual pattern, a decrease in cancellation rates, an increase in the number of embryos available for transfer, a reduction in the number of ART cycles required to achieve pregnancy and a decrease in miscarriage rates were reported. There were also a number of natural conceptions.

When they looked at methods to achieve this weight loss (e.g. diet and lifestyle changes, very-low-energy diets, medical interventions and bariatric surgery), all were effective but they cautioned that more research is required into the effects of very-low-energy diets and bariatric surgery on foetal health. These are associated with a reduction in nutrients, so it is recommended that women wait at least a year to increase their nutritional status after these treatments before trying to conceive. Lifestyle programmes that included support and a multi-disciplinary approach were preferable to either diet or exercise alone and also led to significant improvements in psychological measures, such as self-esteem, and decreased anxiety and depression.

The health of future generations

Nutrition and optimising weight are not just about your own health. In the late 1980s, researchers in the UK started reporting high levels of coronary heart disease in people who had been born with low birth weight. This led to the 'developmental origins of adult disease' hypothesis, often called the Barker hypothesis. This states that adverse influences early in development, and particularly during intrauterine life, can result in permanent changes in physiology and metabolism, which result in increased disease risk in adulthood. This theory has been researched worldwide and there is now ample evidence from all around the world that poor nutrition of mothers leads to poor nutrition and growth in their offspring and significant subsequent increases in cardiovascular disease (strokes and heart disease), high blood pressure, insulin resistance and type 2 diabetes as these offspring age. The undernourished foetus is 'programmed' in the womb to develop these conditions in later life.

We know that if the mother is underweight due to poor nutrition (even if she thinks she has a good diet but is exercising too much and not getting enough essential carbohydrates and nutrients) that the health of her baby is compromised. However, what is less well known is that many mothers who are obese are equally putting their babies at risk. They are often overweight because they are eating high-calorie, low-nutrient foods and are thus 'undernourished' from the point of view of having enough essential nutrients. Other research has shown that the odds of adult obesity are two-fold greater in babies weighing more than 4 kg at birth. These effects can be mimicked in mice if they are fed 'cafeteria diets' (which resemble a human diet rich in fats and simple sugars), proving the concept of 'pre-programming'.

Obesity in men may also affect the health of their offspring. Studies have shown that obese fathers have a higher likelihood of fathering obese children (irrespective of maternal obesity) and studies in animals are showing that poor sperm development in obese animals are transmitted to the embryo and may lead to health issues in their offspring (2.14).

Vitamins

Sinead Curran describes micronutrients, which include vitamins, in her contribution and also how we can get them from foods and what they do. Getting what we need from our food and drink is ideal, but it can be difficult with a busy lifestyle, eating on the go, etc. Many of the couples I see are taking vitamin supplements and, apart from recommending folic acid and vitamin D for women, it is really hard to offer good advice. This contrasts with the vitamin or supplement 'industry', which bombards us with 'evidence' about the merits of its products. But when one looks for properly designed, good-quality studies regarding vitamin supplements and fertility, they are hard enough to find. In addition, vitamin and supplement manufacturers are not required to go through the same rigorous standards and controls as pharmaceutical companies, which produce medical products. Most of the studies on vitamins and fertility involve very small numbers of subjects and are therefore not very meaningful. Also, most of them study preparations that include many vitamins, so the effect of any one vitamin is difficult to determine.

Vitamins and men

The effects of vitamins on men and on sperm are difficult to assess because a sperm sample contains millions of sperm, and sperm development takes about 12 weeks, so we need to know the vitamin intake over those 12 weeks. Then there are all the other environmental factors that can affect sperm. And when it comes to pregnancy rates, there are also all the female factors. Having said that, we do have some worthwhile evidence on vitamins and sperm quality.

A lot of work has been done on chemicals called antioxidants. When cells are affected by infection, cancer, trauma or chemicals they release substances called oxygen free radicals or reactive oxygen species (ROS) and these can cause damage, called oxidative stress, in tissues and cells. These oxygen free radicals have been found in semen where they have been shown to have detrimental effects on sperm function. Our bodies naturally produce 'antioxidants' to counteract the effects of these oxygen free radicals and various antioxidants have been trialled in male infertility. These include vitamins A, C and E, carnitine, carotenoids, glutathione, lutein, lycopene, selenium, coenzyme Q and polyunsaturated fatty acids such as omega 3, 6 and 9.

A review of antioxidant therapies was conducted by the Cochrane Library in 2014 (2.16). This included 48 studies in 4,179 subfertile men. Most of the men enrolled in these trials had low total sperm motility and sperm concentration. Some men were undergoing IVF or ICSI. The evidence was graded as 'very low' to 'low' . The review showed that antioxidants 'may have increased live birth rates'. However, this result was based on only 44 live births from a total of 277 couples in four small studies. There was insufficient evidence to show a difference in miscarriage rates between the antioxidant and placebo or no-treatment groups. The authors concluded that 'there is low quality evidence from only four small trials suggesting that antioxidant supplementation in subfertile males may improve live birth rates for couples attending fertility clinics.'

Dietary antioxidants can be obtained through the intake of food products (see Sinead's section below) or by taking supplements but be careful if choosing supplements that you don't take ones with very high doses of vitamins because animal studies show that very high levels may have some toxic effects. And be aware that there is no consensus in medical circles on the optimal type, dose or duration of antioxidant intake.

Vitamins in women

There is less evidence of a beneficial role of vitamins and antioxidants in female fertility. A Cochrane review in females in 2014 looked at 28 trials involving 3,548 women and concluded that 'there was no evidence that taking an antioxidant may provide benefit for subfertile women; however, there did not appear to be any evidence of obvious adverse effects. At this time, there is no evidence to recommend supplemental oral antioxidants for subfertile women.'(2.17)

So I would feel that a balanced diet, as described below, and supplemental folic acid and vitamin D are best. However, for those who are concerned that their diet may not be optimal, supplementary vitamins seem to be safe. But if you do choose to take supplements, be careful that you don't take ones with very high doses of vitamins.

Getting help

Diet and weight are huge problems in modern western society and Ireland is no exception. Couples with fertility problems are no different from the rest of the population and will have a wide range of diets, exercise patterns and weights. It is important not to make people already struggling with infertility feel worse or guilty, and that is absolutely the last thing I would want to do. On the other hand, people have a right to correct information and this is not always available. And if lifestyle can improve your chances, that is better (though in many ways harder) than medical intervention.

In dealing with weight problems, whether you are overweight or underweight, it's really hard to do it on your own. Having a buddy or friend to work with and who will encourage you is a great help – and even better if your partner needs to make lifestyle changes too. Failing that, I have seen many people make fantastic progress (and get pregnant) with the help of weight loss and exercise programmes. Consulting a suitably qualified dietitian is also a good idea – particularly if you are underweight or have PCOS.

Nutrition, Fertility and a Pre-conception Plan
BY SINEAD CURRAN, FERTILITY DIETITIAN

As a young undergraduate dietitian, I couldn't wait to advise 'real' people. With four years of study under my belt, I knew all about metabolic processes, physiology, biochemistry, nutrition science and the composition of foods from avocado to zucchini. I honestly presumed that most people already knew that a healthy diet is important and that they also knew what a healthy diet looks like. People know fizzy drinks are 'empty calories', don't they? They know that you can't eat junk food all the time and live a healthy life, don't they? Everyone knows that you need lots of vegetables to get the vitamins you need to best use other nutrients, and that without them you're like a car engine with petrol, but no oil or water, don't they? Of course they do!

Guess what. I was wrong. It took about one week of hectic outpatient clinics and a morning in the ICU with some very generous, experienced dietitians for a few things to dawn on me. First, most people are confused about food and diet; second, knowing that something is good for you and doing it are not the same thing; third, making calculations about nutrients is the easy part – helping people to make meaningful changes to their diet is much more difficult.

Fast forward more than 20 years, and those three things still hold true. Even with the best of intentions, many people still make unhealthy or less than optimal choices when it comes to food and nutrition, for all sorts of reasons.

When you started taking an interest in your fertility, if you considered making some lifestyle changes, you may have noticed that there are lots of different opinions out there. We live in a culture where there are countless mixed messages about food, health and body image. Lots of us eat out and watch cookery shows, and we travel more than ever, giving us exposure to different cuisines and food styles; but because of our busy lives, we cook less often. The rates of both obesity and eating disorders are headline news, and every magazine has an article on who's eating what and how much weight they've lost or gained. Whether it's your colleague at work, who's convinced that her latest weight loss plan is the one for you (even though it's the third different one she's been on this year), or your friend's suggestion to cut out gluten, part of the problem is that not everyone understands nutrition well enough to spot a fad. But is gluten really a problem? Should you eat carbs or not? Is paleo worth a try? What about organic? Add trying to conceive or planning for fertility treatment into the mix, throw in a few internet searches, and who wouldn't be confused?

So, what should you do? Usually the best thing is to get back to basics. In our work at Merrion Fertility Clinic, a healthy, balanced diet for *both* partners is recommended as part of your pre-conception plan, with or without fertility treatment. In the following pages, I hope you'll get enough information to focus your attention on key aspects of your diet to improve your nutrition and your health overall.

Nutrition and fertility

When you are trying to conceive, you can feel vulnerable, frustrated and defeated. I see many couples who are under a lot of stress because they are doing 'everything right', but not getting the result they want. Good nutrition is one of several factors that can optimise your wellbeing and add to the chance of a successful pregnancy. For some couples, it might be just part of a more complex picture, but eating well is never a bad thing – it will benefit your health in so many ways beyond your fertility, and that's a result worth getting. For others, making changes to your lifestyle can be all that's needed to help you conceive – and how great is that?

For starters, though, let's clarify some of the language we use. The word 'diet' can be loaded with negative associations for people. When I use the word 'diet', I'm talking about a way of eating. I don't use it to mean a temporary fix or a weight-loss plan. 'Dieting' is even more problematic as a concept. It seems to mean denying or punishing in many people's minds, and usually takes a short-term view – you'll do it for a while and then it's back to business as usual. Labelling foods or nutrients as 'good' or 'clean' is not especially helpful either; it's far too simplistic and implies that we are bad or dirty if we stray at all. No wonder we might be afraid of being judged on what we eat. Also, while some people do have food allergies, the words 'intolerance' and 'allergy' are used far too often without a proper diagnosis.

I'd love it if we could take the approach of choosing 'nutritious' and 'nourishing' foods as part of your plan for fertility and pre-conception. No single food will treat or cure infertility, and no single food causes infertility, but looking at your diet overall there will almost certainly be ways to make it more nutritious.

Your pre-conception plan

I've included a section below that takes you through the basics of nutrition. I'd recommend that you read it for your own information, but the fact is, we eat food, not nutrients, so to put nutrition science to work, you need a pre-conception plan. See Table 2.1 for a summary of what you need, why you need it and how to build it into your lifestyle. Having evaluated the scientific information available to date, and after many years of experience, I'm confident that your plan can focus on four key principles:

1. Get your weight right
2. Balance your macronutrients
3. Optimise your micronutrients
4. Build in exercise

Whether or not you will undergo fertility treatment, these principles hold true, and they apply to both men and women.

Make any necessary changes well in advance of when you start trying to conceive to ensure that your nutrition is optimal at the time of conception. There is very good evidence that both partners' diets and nutritional wellbeing at the time of conception affects the gene code. You need to have a folic acid tablet on board well in advance, too – at least three months before you get pregnant. If you have been trying to conceive for a while, remember that you still need to take your supplement with 400 mcg of folic acid every day (or 5 mg per day if your BMI is over 30 – this requires a prescription).

When you want to get pregnant, the thought of delaying at all can seem unbearable, but your plan is not just about getting pregnant; it is also about staying pregnant, having as healthy a pregnancy and as healthy a baby as possible. Investing a few months in your lifestyle now can make a healthy outcome much more likely.

When I see couples at our clinic for the first time, we spend most of the appointment talking about what they are eating now and what is typical for them. It can feel a bit confessional, and sometimes I know that people don't want to tell me the full truth about how they eat, either because they are embarrassed or they already feel 'judged' as being responsible for their fertility difficulties. And quite often, most of us just haven't been paying that much attention to what we eat day to day, so it is genuinely difficult to remember.

But even the best map in the world isn't going to help you reach your destination unless you know where you're starting from, so before you make changes, you need to look at your current behaviour. There's good research showing that gaining this insight into your current habits makes you more likely to succeed in building a healthy lifestyle.

Keep a food and activity diary for a week or so – you don't need anything special to do this – just write down in a notebook everything you eat and drink and any activity you get as you go through the day. If you prefer, you can use one of the many tracker apps available; some smartphones come with one included.

At the end of the week, take a clear-eyed look at what you do now. Then assess what specific changes you need to make based on the four key principles, and make a plan.

Give your plan some thought. Do you need to get more information or support before you start? Think honestly about what 'barriers' might be in your way. Do you have a long commute and feel too tired to cook in the evenings? Are you prone to snack attacks when you're watching TV? Then think about work-arounds. It might be as simple as making a shopping list, cooking dishes for the freezer and checking that your walking shoes fit; or you might decide to join a weight management group, or that you would benefit from seeing a registered dietitian for more individualised advice and support. Write down your plan, decide on a realistic timeframe, enlist the support you need, and once you're ready, get started.

Get your weight right

Dr Wingfield has talked about body weight already, and checking your weight is probably one of the most useful things you can do to help your fertility or to improve your chance of success with fertility treatment. Taking account of your height makes weight more meaningful. Picture this: two people both weigh 68 kg, but the person who is 1.75 m tall is slimmer than the one who is only 1.6 m tall. Your body mass index (BMI) is a measure of the relationship between your weight and your height. It is simple to calculate, and if your BMI is outside the healthy range, you most likely have too much (high BMI) or too little (low BMI) body fat to be healthy. At a clinic, a dietitian will often use waist circumference as another measure alongside BMI. Changes in your waist measurement usually mean that you are losing fat mass from the tummy area, even if your weight isn't changing.

You can calculate your BMI using this formula, or use one of the reference tables or calculator apps available online.

BMI = weight in kg ÷ (height in m x height in m)
Healthy range = $18.5 kg/m^2 - 24.9 kg/m^2$

In women, the fat cells in your body make and store hormones. Your body fat also affects levels of other hormones in your gut and brain that influence your fertility. The mechanisms behind it are complex, but if you have too much body fat, it affects your ability to get pregnant and to stay pregnant.

Equally, too little body fat means that there are lower levels of the hormones needed to stimulate ovulation and this causes fertility problems. You can be lean with a low body fat mass and be healthy, but if you are thin because you exercise a lot and restrict what you eat, it can limit your ability to get pregnant. If your BMI is too low, check that you're not over-exercising or eating restrictively, increase your portion sizes at meal times and include some additional snacks.

Either way, balancing your diet through steps 2 and 3 above will help you to achieve a healthy weight.

It's important to remember that very restrictive plans which rely on leaving out an entire food group aren't ideal; you won't be able to get enough of the key nutrients you need from food to optimise your nutritional status. For many people, cutting out junk, adjusting portion sizes and increasing exercise will get your weight to a healthy level.

A difficulty with very unbalanced or restrictive dieting is that you make complex metabolic and hormonal adaptations to low-calorie diets, ultimately helping you to use calories more efficiently. Your appetite will increase on a restrictive regime, because of adaptations involving hormones you may never have heard of, such as leptin and ghrelin, making you feel more hungry than usual. Often, dieters end up even more focused on 'forbidden' foods. For some people, banning so-called 'bad' foods will make them focus on what they can't have. It's a bit like this: if I told you *not* to think of an elephant, I'll bet you'd immediately have a mental image of a large mammal with a trunk. Another consideration is that losing weight never means losing just unwanted fat; you will also lose muscle mass and bone density, and this is more marked on an extreme diet. Exercise alongside dietary change is important for your fertility, not only to use calories, but to protect against muscle and bone loss.

Being a healthy weight when you conceive reduces the chance of developing pregnancy complications like pre-eclampsia, gestational diabetes (overweight mothers have a higher risk), and of your baby being born pre-term (underweight and poorly nourished mothers have a higher risk) and has a lasting effect on your baby's genes.

If you struggle with your weight, or have any issues with food or eating that negatively affect other aspects of your life, now is the time to get some specific advice and support from a health professional.

Give this some serious thought. Eating disorders of all types can affect fertility, but with effective treatment and support, recovery is possible, and many women who recover go on to have healthy pregnancies. I see far too many women who have been contending for years with what is clearly an eating disorder presenting for fertility treatment without their condition ever having been addressed. No more than for a medical condition like diabetes, managing an eating disorder is important, not just to get pregnant, but to improve the likelihood of healthy pregnancy outcomes for both women and babies and for your long-term wellbeing.

Balance your macronutrients

Carbohydrate, fat, protein and water are the macronutrients in your food. The best pre-conception plan contains a balance of all the macronutrients, with a wide range of food types included. This is an important step in optimising your nutrition. Having a balanced intake of carbohydrate, protein, fats and oils and enough water is the best way to ensure that you have the right amount of calories for energy, building blocks for growth and repair, and fluids for hydration.

In Ireland, we use a food pyramid as a guide to which foods have a similar nutrient content. The shelves of the pyramid are divided by food group, and the size of the shelves represent the proportion of your diet overall that should come from each group. The Irish food pyramid was updated in 2016, and now places even more emphasis on the need for a high intake of vegetables and fruit as part of a healthy diet.

The use of the food pyramid seems to have generated a lot of airtime recently, with discussion about its validity, and some individuals have even gone so far as to claim that it 'causes' obesity. In my experience of well over 20 years in dietetics, I have yet to meet a single person who was overweight because they were correctly following the guidelines promoted by the Irish food pyramid. The real problem is when people are not following it.

By all means, chop the 'top shelf' off the food pyramid if you want to. Humans love the magic combination of sugar, fat and salt in the junk foods represented there – and they're fine occasionally. But we can't eat them every day and expect to be healthy.

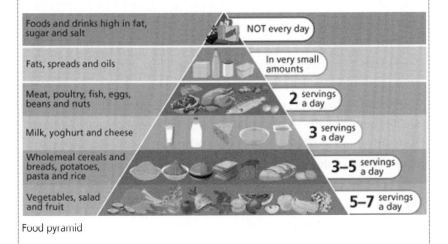

Food pyramid

As I've said before, it's a false economy to cut out entire food groups. For example, if you exclude carbohydrates from your diet, you will see rapid weight loss initially as your body uses up stores of glucose and loses water that was stored with it. But you will also miss out – not just on the easy-to-use energy that carbohydrate foods provide, but the associated fibre that helps your gut to eliminate waste, and to regulate levels of the hormone precursors of oestrogen and testosterone. Vital B vitamins, which help your brain to function and to use energy well, and polyphenols with antioxidant properties are also associated with wholegrains. All these nutrients are important for fertility.

The advice sums up the approach we take at our clinic: a nutritious, balanced diet with a low glycaemic index, wholegrain starches, lots of vegetables, a moderate amount of protein from a variety of sources, some fruit, milk, cheese or yogurt, and some healthy fats and oils.

Carbohydrates: Choose wholegrain or 'unrefined' starchy foods – baby potatoes with skins on, sweet potatoes, granary or stoneground breads (even better if they have added seeds) in moderate amounts. Have slightly less than half a plate, or two open handfuls, of complex starchy foods at each meal. Don't be afraid of carbohydrates, but choose the right type and watch your portion size. 'Rough' high-fibre or 'unrefined' and wholegrain versions are converted into glucose energy more slowly than white or refined types, which helps to balance blood glucose and insulin levels – this is why they are called 'low glycaemic index' carbs. Wholegrains are also rich in micronutrients.

Protein: Choose two palm-sized servings of good-quality protein-rich foods daily to provide the amino acid building blocks your body needs. We know from large-scale surveys, such as the National Adult Nutrition Survey (NANS 2011) that most people in Ireland eat more protein than they need. Quality beats quantity when it comes to protein, and you are much better to have a small amount of beef, lamb or chicken which contain useful nutrients, than a larger serving of processed meats like bacon or sausages, which are lower in vitamins and minerals but higher in fat, salt and nitrates. Because animal sources of protein and vegetable sources have a different nutrient profile, it's also a good idea to have at least one meat-free day a week, using beans, lentils or chickpeas as your protein source. These will be your main source of protein if you follow a vegetarian or vegan diet. Remember, you will also get protein from calcium-rich dairy foods like milk, cheese and yogurt and from nuts and seeds.

Fats and oils: I consider good choices here to be part of your pre-conception plan's secret weapon. Don't be too concerned about whether you choose full fat or low fat versions of wholesome foods like milk, yogurt or hummus, but do cut down on your intake of fats from spreads and especially oils that have been heat treated, which changes their chemical structure. Look out for hydrogenated fats or oils on food labels. In practice this means cutting out deep-fried foods as much as possible, avoiding margarines, biscuits, crisps and snacks, sauces in jars and many 'convenience foods', including highly processed meat products and takeaways. A useful side-effect of avoiding these types of fats is that you will also reduce your salt, sugar and nitrate intake as all three are usually present in high amounts in the same foods.

Cooking from scratch is usually a good strategy, but it needn't be complicated and there are lots of simple recipes online that don't require gourmet skills. Using fresh, quality oils as a dressing for salads and vegetables or as a dip for bread is a good strategy, as it helps you to feel full, adds unsaturated fatty acids and also helps the absorption of some polyphenols.

Increasing your intake of foods like nuts, seeds, olives and avocado is also a good idea. In addition to the omega 3 fatty acids found in oily fish and flaxseed, the oils in these foods are a very useful component of your pre-conception plan as some of them are sources of polyphenols and have anti-inflammatory properties. This can be especially helpful for women with endometriosis.

A word about meal timing: The hormones in your gut are influenced by the timing of your meals and food intake. It seems like the oldest advice in the book, but eating regularly is very important for you, because it helps to regulate some of the wide array of hormones that influence fertility. Ideally, your food intake will be spread out evenly across the day. This serves a few other purposes, in that it gives you several opportunities to 'fuel up' without overdoing it, and makes it more likely that you will eat fewer calories while having a greater variety of foods, giving you a more nutritious diet overall. You might like to have three meals in the day or slightly smaller portions at mealtimes, with small healthy snacks in between (my preferred recommendation), depending on what suits your lifestyle. I usually advise that you eat something within an hour of getting up in the morning and that your evening meal is at least three hours before bedtime. See Table 2.2 for an example of a daily meal plan.

In practice, I find that to get a healthy balance at mealtimes, the 'plate model' is especially useful. Every cuisine and culture will have a preferred option for the three sections on the plate, but once you have the balance between vegetables, starchy carbohydrate and protein foods, you're all set.

Wholegrain, unrefined starchy foods: breads, rice, pasta, couscous, noodles, potatoes.

Vegetables of all kinds: Lots of colour and variety. Salad, cooked veg, side dishes, soups, stews.

Protein food: meat, fish, eggs, beans, lentils, chickpeas, tofu.

Balanced plate

Optimise your micronutrition

Micronutrients are the vitamins, minerals and polyphenols in your food. There is some evidence that certain vitamins and minerals play an especially important role in aspects of human fertility. However, most of the evidence for specific nutrients is in the 'promising' category. The best of the science currently available tells us that, in general, it is preferable to get your vitamins and minerals from food sources, with a couple of exceptions. To optimise your micronutrient intake, follow the basic principles of healthy eating, with extra emphasis on these key points:

Eat lots of vegetables every day. All types are useful, but the more colour in your diet from vegetables (and fruit), the wider the variety of water-soluble vitamins – vitamin C, folate, other B vitamins – and phytonutrients such as the polyphenols, carotenoids and flavonoids. Because these nutrients can't be stored in your body, you need a good intake of vegetables every day. Look at the plate model as a guide. Each meal should have as much vegetables as starchy food. You can eat your veg raw or cooked, as you like, and choose fresh or frozen, but include some raw at every meal – perhaps a small side salad or fresh herbs added at the end of cooking. This helps to maximise your absorption of key nutrients such as folate. There's no need to go all-out raw, though; cooking makes some nutrients easier to absorb. The more colour and variety in your veg the better, and eating vegetables in season means they will be fresher and taste delicious.

Include good-quality red meat about three times a week, oily fish once a week and poultry or eggs on other days. Use beans, lentils, chickpeas as often as possible. This is important for your iron intake. About one-third of women in Ireland don't have enough iron in their diets, and iron is an essential part of haemoglobin, which transports oxygen. Iron is especially important if you have risk factors for anaemia, heavy periods or any pregnancy losses. These iron-rich foods are also a source of valuable B vitamins (B2, B3, B6, B12) and protein.

Have slightly less than half a plate of complex starchy foods at each meal for energy, important B vitamins, polyphenols and fibre. These foods are the backbone of your energy intake. 'Rough' or 'unrefined' and wholegrain versions are converted into glucose energy more slowly, which helps to balance blood glucose and insulin levels, and wholegrains and fortified breads and cereals contain the B vitamins needed for energy balance. These foods are an important source of vitamins B6 (potatoes, oats), and of added folic acid in fortified breads or cereals.

Include a piece of fruit as part of your lunch and dinner. Focus especially on fruit that is high in vitamin C, which is a powerful antioxidant. Including vitamin C in your meal will help your absorption of iron. Kiwi fruit, mandarins and berries of all kinds are a great choice, as are orchard fruit like apples, pears and peaches because they contain polyphenols. Fruit will also increase your fibre intake.

Choose a calcium-rich snack three times a day. You most likely know that calcium is essential for healthy bones, but it's also essential for muscle function and healthy blood pressure. Around a quarter of women in Ireland don't get enough calcium from their diets. Try a yogurt, a milky drink or some cheese on oat or rye crackers between your meals or in the evening. These foods are also the main source of iodine in Irish diets. For those who don't like dairy, try tinned fish such as sardines, hummus or some nut butter on your crackers instead and use a fortified version of a non-dairy milk that has calcium and vitamin D added. Green leafy vegetables and beans also contain some calcium.

Take a multivitamin that contains 400 mcg folic acid and at least 10 mcg vitamin D3. These are the two key exceptions to the 'food first' rule. Every woman needs folic acid (the more stable form of folate) in a tablet for at least three months before getting pregnant and for the first three months of pregnancy. (If your BMI is over 30 or you have diabetes you should take 5 mg, available by prescription from your doctor.) This is the best way to ensure that your body will have enough folate available to help a baby's brain and spinal cord (also known as the neural tube) form properly. Errors in formation result in neural tube defects, or NTDs, such as spina bifida. Adequate levels of folate are most important 21–28 days after conceiving, and because natural folates in food are temperamental nutrients, prone to destruction during cooking, processing and digesting, a supplement is the best policy. If you have a medical condition or a family history of NTDs, talk to your doctor about getting a 5 mg prescription dose of folic acid.

Humans get 90% of their vitamin D through the action of sunlight on our skin. As you can imagine, lack of sunlight makes living in Ireland an indication for taking a vitamin D supplement. In fact, in addition to eating foods rich in vitamin D, such as salmon and fortified milk, a vitamin D supplement is recommended for every man, woman and child, especially during the winter months. In Ireland, at the time of print, the recommended amount is for everyone to get 5 mcg vitamin D3 from supplements in addition to at least 5 mcg from vitamin D-rich foods. The European Food Safety Authority recently increased the amount they recommend to 15 mcg daily. The British Fertility society recommends 10 mcg a day for women trying to conceive. You don't need larger doses of vitamin D than that unless you have a known deficiency, because as a fat-soluble vitamin, it can be stored in your body and build up over time.

While you can take a folic acid tablet and a separate vitamin D supplement if you prefer, the simplest thing is probably to take a multivitamin with the right amount of both in it. Remember, though, that a multivitamin will not replace a healthy diet – it's a supplement to the nutrition you need to get from foods. See Table 2.3 for a breakdown of functions of nutrients.

Build in exercise

There's no way around it. Everyone needs to be active. If your BMI is in a healthy range, you need to be sure that you are getting at least half an hour of physical activity every day and up to an hour on at least two days a week. Walking is ideal – it's free and you don't need any special equipment, though a friend to walk with is a great motivator. When you're trying to conceive, going for a walk together can be a great way to reconnect. Talking while walking is optional.

If you are trying to lose weight, you need to get at least an hour of aerobic activity on four or more days every week. Anything you enjoy is fine: brisk walking that gets your heart pumping; or you might consider a Zumba class; or perhaps a swim is more your style.

I also recommend that you include some resistance exercise, Pilates or yoga in your week to strengthen your muscles and improve your core stability. Exercise of all kinds has the added benefit of helping to relieve stress, and choosing to do something positive that you incorporate into your lifestyle now will pay dividends as an investment in your physical and mental wellbeing long into the future.

A word of caution, though – excessive exercise, especially if you are very lean or have a low BMI can be highly problematic. Those complex mechanisms of metabolic and hormonal control that are affected by your body composition and food intake are also affected by intensive or excessive exercise.

Other nutritional considerations

Cooking methods

How you cook your food can make a difference to how nutritious your diet will be. Many water-soluble vitamins, like folate, are destroyed by heat.

Cooking fresh food for a short time preserves more of the vitamin content. When you boil vegetables, nutrients leach into the cooking water and are thrown out. I recommend that you choose either quick, flash cooking like steaming, stir-frying or grilling or one-pot cooking like casseroling or stewing to cook your food where possible. These cooking methods also have the advantage of keeping calories lower than frying in oil.

Drinks

Respond to your thirst. You don't necessarily need to drink more than two litres of any kind of fluid in the day to stay well hydrated and keep your bowel working well, because you get water from vegetables and fruit too, but your drink of choice should be water. It seems that fizzy drinks are not especially good for bone health, so cutting down on daily use is wise, but occasional fizzy drinks are not a real problem.

There is some evidence that excessive intakes of caffeine are not good for fertility, and it's advisable to stick to the level recommended for pregnancy: a maximum of 3–4 cups of tea, weak coffee or cola drinks a day.

Alcohol

While the only amount of alcohol that is definitely safe in pregnancy is zero, the evidence of its effect on fertility isn't straightforward. We know that more than a moderate amount of alcohol affects oestrogen levels, for example. While you don't need to cut out alcohol completely when you're trying to conceive, it is best for both men and women to limit it, and Prof. Wingfield discusses this later in this section. For reference, a 750 ml bottle of wine contains eight standard drinks. Alcohol is a significant source of calories, with few associated micronutrients, so if you're trying to lose a few pounds, cutting down on alcohol is a good idea.

Organic options

There is some concern that high levels of pesticide residue in foods can affect human fertility. In the European Union, strict regulation and monitoring makes contamination with pesticides and other chemical residue less of an issue than in other parts of the world. A recent European Food Safety

Authority (EFSA) report, for example, showed that 97% of the 83,000 food samples tested from across Europe were well below the limits for residues, and 53.6% of samples were completely residue-free. Organic versions of foods don't necessarily contain any more nutrients than their non-organic cousins, but they have been produced without the use of pesticides and other chemicals. The EFSA report found that 98.8% of organic foods tested were residue-free.

Some vegetables and fruits are not prone to pesticide contamination (see the 'Other' list below), so there is no need to buy organic versions of these to avoid pesticides. If you want to, you can spend your money instead on the organic fruit and veg listed here, especially if they are grown outside the EU.

Organic: strawberries, apples, peaches, nectarines, celery, grapes, cherries, spinach, grapes, peppers.

Other: avocados, asparagus, aubergine, onions, mushrooms, kiwi fruit, grapefruit, melons, papaya, peas, pineapple, mangoes, sweetcorn, cabbage, sweet potato.

Herbs & spices, marinades & dressings

In any healthy eating plan, it's wise to cut down on salt and convenience foods. Using herbs and spices in your cooking is a great way to add flavour. Fresh herbs can add quite a few micronutrients such as folate and iron, and many spices also add phytonutrients and polyphenols. Using marinades and dressings will also make food taste more delicious and often reduces cooking time, which helps preserve nutrition. Use lemon or lime juice, yogurt, soy sauce, teriyaki, curry paste or pesto to add flavour to chicken, pork, fish or tofu before you cook it and add herbs at the end of cooking for best effect. Dress salad leaves and vegetables with fresh cold-pressed oils and a splash of cider or balsamic vinegar or a squeeze of citrus juice and a twist of black pepper just before you serve them.

Specific fertility-related conditions

Aside from weight management, two conditions in particular will benefit from dietary interventions: PCOS and endometriosis. I have incorporated the key things that are beneficial for both these conditions into the pre-conception plan outlined here, but I recommend that you seek individualised advice from a registered dietitian, ideally with expertise in fertility nutrition.

Polycystic ovarian syndrome (PCOS)

Women with PCOS have a lower than average calorie requirement, which means that they will typically gain weight very easily, especially around the middle. This is an immense source of frustration for many of the women I see, who gain weight despite eating what would seem like a reasonable diet for another woman. Insulin resistance and high cholesterol are also common features, and even women who are not overweight benefit from dietary change and exercise if they have PCOS. The plan most widely recommended is based on choosing wholegrain 'rough', low-glycaemic index starchy foods in small portions, regular meals with lots of vegetables, moderate amounts of protein foods and getting lots of exercise.

Any recommended regimen will focus on:

- a low-calorie, low-glycaemic index diet
- weight loss of at least 5–10% if overweight
- exercise and overall increase in activity.

Endometriosis

Endometriosis is a complex condition. Symptoms can vary between women, and the extent of the endometriosis doesn't always predict the severity of the symptoms. A woman with a lot of endometriosis might feel fine while a woman with less extensive endometriosis might suffer a lot of pain. Many women with endometriosis can have bowel involvement, with symptoms presenting as 'irritable bowel' or 'food intolerance'. While there isn't any proven dietary treatment for endometriosis, a healthy diet can help a lot with symptoms and will optimise your wellbeing alongside surgical and medical management. Changing the types of fat in your diet can help, and increasing your fibre intake, especially from vegetables and legumes, is also beneficial.

The recommended regimen will focus on:

- a healthy eating, high-fibre diet
- a high intake of vegetables and legumes
- foods rich in polyunsaturated fatty acids.

Medical conditions

There are several medical conditions in which your diet is a key part of your treatment or management plan for life. I can't overstate this: *It is crucial before you attempt to get pregnant that you have a consultation with your own doctor and your dietitian to be sure that everything is under control, and that you've made all necessary changes to your diet well in advance, before you ever try to conceive.* For example, if you have diabetes, your blood glucose control will have a major effect on your ability to get pregnant and you need to take a high dose of folic acid, which your doctor will prescribe. High blood glucose is harmful to foetal development and low blood glucose can be highly problematic in the first trimester. If you have inflammatory bowel disease, high blood pressure, a heart condition, cystic fibrosis or a thyroid condition, for example, you will also need specific advice. Getting your diet right is a key investment in your health now, and it will also make a big difference to your risk of complications during a pregnancy.

So what are you waiting for? Start now. Get your plan in place. Anything that you do to make your lifestyle healthier is worthwhile, not just for your fertility, but for any future pregnancy and for the rest of your life.

Issues with research

Research into human nutrition and the effects of diet on health is difficult to do well, for many reasons. There are so many different factors to consider that can influence outcomes. This is called the number of 'variables'. For instance, food is made up of lots of different nutrients, many of which are changed by cooking; various factors in a food itself, or in other foods that it's eaten with, can affect how nutrients are absorbed; different biological factors also affect how much of any given nutrient is absorbed. So, with all these variables to consider, it is a stretch to prove that because a food is high in a given nutrient it will have a biological effect.

It seems easier to do research using individual vitamins or minerals in a tablet and to measure levels in blood or serum. But because nutrients interact with each other, and the levels that you have in your body already will affect the amount you will absorb, and because the effects of different levels are not always well defined, it's not always true to say that taking more of one nutrient will be of any specific benefit. Also, while some studies might find an effect of a particular nutrient or food on some aspect of health, unless there were a large number of people included in the research, the results can't be applied to other people. The number of people included is referred to as the 'power' of the study, and because of the high number of variables in human nutrition, studies need to be highly powered with large numbers of people taking part to have meaning.

Complex science doesn't make for good headlines and even with the best of intentions, it's difficult to communicate the information well.

Having said all that, it is an interesting time for nutrition, and from the good-quality research that is available, there are some things that are clearly important and some that look promising for fertility.

Table 2.1 Planning Tool for Pre-conception

What?	Why?	How?
Regular meals	Regulate gut hormones Regulate appetite Variety of nutrients	Plan ahead Use recipes Use a shopping list Prepare meals in advance Use your freezer
Regular exercise	Regulate hormones Weight management Stress relief Protect muscle & bones	Walk with a friend Cycle to work Join a class Take the stairs every time
Large portions of vegetables every day. Choose a wide variety: leafy greens, red/ yellow/ orange veg	Fibre Vitamins – folate Polyphenols/antioxidants Water	Fresh in salads, sandwiches, and as snacks Cooked from fresh or frozen with meals or added to soups, stews, casseroles
Some fresh fruit every day	Vitamins – vitamin C, folate Polyphenols/antioxidants Fibre Water Energy	Add to breakfast As dessert and snacks
Moderate protein from meat, poultry, fish, eggs daily	Amino acids Iron, zinc B vitamins Essential fatty acids	Medium portions daily Oily fish at least 1 meal weekly Red meat 3 meals weekly
Wholegrain or low-glycaemic index, starchy carbohydrates at each meal	Energy Fibre B vitamins Vitamin E Magnesium Polyphenols	Jumbo oats as porridge or oat crackers Wholegrain rye or multiseed bread or wraps as toast or for sandwiches Baby potatoes or sweet potatoes (skins on) with lunch or dinner Use a variety of grains – brown rice, wild rice, bulgur, buckwheat, quinoa, barley, millet
Oily fish (e.g. salmon, trout, sardines, herring) every week	Vitamin D Amino acids Essential fatty acids Iodine	Grilled fish at dinner Tinned fish in sandwiches, fish cakes or on crackers

What?	Why?	How?
Eat some nuts, seeds, avocado or olives every day	Essential fatty acids Polyphenols Fibre Amino acids Magnesium	As snacks Added to oats, yogurt, salads and stir-fries In dips and spreads like nut butter, pesto, tapenade, guacamole
Cut down on 'junk': sweets, cakes, biscuits, crisps, takeaways	Reduce trans fatty acids, sugar, salt and nitrates	Cook from scratch Plan healthy snacks Use a shopping list or shop online
Eat legumes: lentils, beans, chickpeas, soybeans	Fibre Amino acids B vitamins	In soups, stews, casseroles and curries As hummus and falafel In mixed dishes like chilli In salads and side dishes
Include 3 portions of fortified milk, cheese or yogurt daily (or calcium- and vitamin D-enriched substitutes)	Calcium Vitamin D Iodine Amino acids	Breakfast – yogurt and fruit, milk in cereal As snacks – cheese with oatcakes In drinks, e.g. latte, hot chocolate

Table 2.2 Example of a Pre-conception Meal Plan*

	Quick and easy – low calorie	A little fancier ...
Breakfast	Jumbo oats with fortified milk, linseeds and mixed berries	Poached egg with grilled tomatoes and mushrooms on sourdough toast
Morning snack	Natural yogurt	Cheese with pear and walnuts
Lunch	Mixed bean and vegetable soup with wholegrain bread Apple	Seeded wrap with chicken/mozzarella[†], avocado, beetroot, tomato, carrot Fruit salad
Afternoon snack	Almonds	Oatcakes with nut butter
Dinner	Chicken/tofu[†] & cashew stir-fry with broccoli, peppers & noodles Kiwi fruit	Grilled salmon/halloumi[†] with couscous & griddled vegetables Rocket salad Strawberries & crème fraiche
Evening	Low GI hot chocolate (fortified milk, cocoa powder, stevia)	Flatbread/pitta and veggie sticks with pesto, hummus, guacamole dips

* *some people will need more calories, and portions are not detailed – this is a general guide*

†*vegetarian option*

Table 2.3 Functions of Nutrients

Nutrient	Role in fertility	Food sources
B group vitamins: B1 B2 B3 Biotin B6 Folate (folic acid supplement needed too) B12	Cell function Energy metabolism Cell division Nerve function DNA synthesis Red blood cell manufacture	Wholegrains Vegetables Legumes Nuts & seeds Meat Green vegetables Yeast extract Mushrooms Fruit
Vitamin C	Semen quality Antioxidant	Fruit – especially berries and citrus Vegetables
Polyphenols	Antioxidants – protect cell structures Semen quality	Vegetables – all kinds; different polyphenols/ antioxidants associated with different colours Fruit – all kinds Wholegrains Olive oil
Fibre	Hormone regulation Satiety (feeling full) Gut function Blood glucose regulation	Wholegrain versions of starchy foods: breads, cereals & grains Vegetables – all kinds Fruit – all kinds Legumes Nuts and seeds
Calcium	Muscle function Blood pressure	Milk, cheese, yogurt, tinned fish, tofu, green leafy vegetables, tahini, baked beans, almonds, sesame seeds
Iron	Red blood cells – oxygen transport	Meat, fish, eggs, beans, lentils

Nutrient	Role in fertility	Food sources
Essential fatty acids	Anti-inflammatory properties Cell structure	Nuts, seeds, olives, avocado; & oils made from them Oily fish, e.g. salmon, trout, sardines, herring
Zinc	Sperm production Hormone function Immune function	Oysters, other seafood, meat, eggs, dairy, legumes
Magnesium	Energy balance – glucose regulation Protein synthesis Bone health Muscle & nerve function – pain	Legumes, nuts, seeds, fish and whole grains
Selenium	Antioxidant Immune function Thyroid function – hormones & metabolism	Brazil nuts, mixed nuts, oysters, seafood, meat, eggs, seeds, wholegrains

Exercise

The association between exercise and fertility is a typical situation where moderation is 'what this is all about'. A healthy level of exercise is essential for general wellbeing and also improves fertility, particularly in women who have difficulty keeping their weight within the normal range. However, excessive exercise is not good. It is often difficult to determine what a good level of exercise is and what is excessive. The ideal level of exercise may be different for every woman. There is no ideal amount that is best for everyone.

Medical benefits for women

Exercise releases endorphins (chemicals in the brain) which make people feel better, and this can only be good from a fertility point of view. Exercise has also been shown to increase self-esteem among women and this again can only be good.

The effects of exercise and weight loss on fertility are closely linked and we saw earlier that overweight women who lose approximately 10% of their body weight, whether that be with diet or exercise, will experience a 50% increase in their fertility (2.12, 2.15). This is particularly true for women with polycystic ovarian syndrome (PCOS). A combination of diet and exercise is the most healthy way to achieve this weight loss and studies have shown that a combination of exercise and diet works better than either diet or exercise alone.

There are other benefits of exercise apart from weight loss and improved emotional wellbeing. These include healthier bones and a healthier heart, with a reduction in the risk of diabetes. Physical activity improves glucose metabolism and reduces intramuscular fat. It also helps with pre-menstrual syndrome and even reduces the risk of endometriosis. Finally, it lowers the risk of breast cancer (2.18).

Medical benefits for men

The relationship of exercise and fertility in men hasn't been studied as much as in women. However the beneficial effects of exercise on general health, bones and mental health are the same as for women.

Lots of studies show that excessive exercise can affect sperm counts but it has not been proven whether or not this actually affects fertility. Certainly, I have seen men whose sperm counts deteriorate if they do very extensive exercise, such as running a marathon. If a man has a very good sperm count and quality to start off with, this probably doesn't make a huge difference, but if his sperm quality is borderline, something like running a marathon may just tip him over. Again as with women, I recommend moderation, so a regular amount of moderate exercise is ideal; but try to avoid putting your body under excessive stress.

On the other end of the spectrum, obesity in men (which usually goes along with not doing enough exercise) is also bad for sperm and fertility. Excessive heat is not good for sperm so it's best to avoid hot yoga, saunas or jacuzzis.

See also the section on recreational drugs, specifically food supplements and performance enhancers and their effects.

Risks with excessive exercise

As with obesity, the effects of exercise are very much tied up with body mass and body fat composition, and sometimes women who exercise excessively will not have enough calories in their diet to compensate. Excessive physical exercise, combined with low body weight, is interpreted by the body as a state of stress and defence mechanisms kick in to help the body save energy and avoid the extra strain that pregnancy would place on it.

The hypothalamic gland in the brain reduces its production of the hormone GnRH (gonadotropin-releasing hormone), which in turn reduces the amount of hormones FSH (follicle-stimulating hormone) and LH (luteinising hormone) released by the pituitary gland – see the description of normal control of ovulation in Section 3. This has a knock-on effect on the ovaries, which reduce the production of oestrogen. Oestrogen is also produced in fat tissue, so if there is very little fat, the levels of oestrogen drop further.

These reductions in the hormones oestrogen, FSH and LH have a very detrimental effect on menstruation and ovulation (2.19). At first the woman's ovulation and periods become irregular and as the situation worsens ovulation and periods become infrequent (occurring every few months). Eventually ovulation and periods stop altogether. Not surprisingly, the woman is then infertile. Another serious consequence of these low hormone levels (especially of oestrogen) is that bone formation and strength is reduced and there is a risk of osteoporosis.

A condition called 'the female athlete triad' has been described by the American Congress of Sports Medicine. It refers to women who have amenorrhea, osteoporosis and disordered eating (i.e. no periods, reduced bone density and inadequate calorie intake). Osteoporosis and osteopenia (low bone density) lead to an increased risk of scoliosis and bone fractures. It has been shown in studies that up to 50% of female athletes have some negative effect on their bones (2.18). In athletes with reduced bone density and no periods, up to 17% can develop stress fractures. Other groups that suffer these problems are ballerinas, gymnasts and ice skaters and those with eating disorders such as anorexia and bulimia.

Because exercise releases endorphins which make us feel good, it can be extremely difficult for people to reduce their exercise levels – indeed, it is well recognised that they may be 'addicted to exercise'. Don't be afraid to seek help with this.

Excessive exercise and the resultant reduction in oestrogen and bone density is particularly harmful for adolescents and young teenagers who exercise excessively as these are the years that are critical for ensuring adequate bone density for life.

In contrast, athletes who maintain a normal body weight and who continue to have regular periods and continue to ovulate tend to have normal or increased bone density.

Types of exercise

Exercise is great in so many ways and can be an ideal 'stress buster' for couples with fertility problems and all the stresses that can cause. The amount of exercise that is ideal varies from person to person, but most doctors would agree that three episodes of aerobic exercise for half an hour three times a week is optimal. It is also useful to consider being active rather than passive throughout the day, e.g. taking the stairs rather than the lift at work or walking or cycling to work if at all possible. These activities sometimes do not take up much time and can be built into your day, which is undoubtedly going to be busy. It is fine to do more exercise than this as long as your weight is in the normal range (BMI 18.5 to 25) and you take extra calories to fuel the extra exercise. But if your periods start becoming irregular or you feel you have stopped ovulating every month, you should seek professional advice – from your GP or a sports medicine expert/clinic. You may be seriously damaging not just your fertility but also your general health and that of your future baby. Try to reduce aerobic exercise and replace it with more strength and mindfulness exercises.

There is no great evidence that any one form of exercise is best. Some studies have looked at aerobic exercise versus resistance exercise and there is some evidence that a combination may be best. For those with low bone density, weight-bearing exercise such as walking or running is best, while some women with pelvic pain (such as endometriosis) or joint problems may find swimming good. Yoga, Pilates, tai chi, etc. can be very helpful for women, particularly if they find it difficult to switch off from their fertility problems and to relax.

I am sometimes asked whether 'hot yoga' is okay when trying to conceive. While various non-medical websites say it is safe, I can find no medical or scientific evidence showing this and we know that a significant increase in body temperature is not good in pregnancy. I would therefore advise against this.

When choosing your exercise, the most important thing is to choose something that you enjoy, that makes you feel good and that you are likely to be able to keep up. Doing it with others or a friend helps to keep you committed, and planning and scheduling exercise as part of your week is also important: try putting it in your diary as an event, rather than hoping you will just do it when you feel like it – there will often be lazier, easier things you will feel like doing. Remember how wonderful you will feel after doing the exercise and let that help motivate you.

Sometimes it is really hard to change the habits of a lifetime and professional help may be a good idea. For those trying to lose weight, professional weight loss and exercise programs, group activities or personal trainers can really help. As mentioned above, those with the opposite problem of too much exercise and low body weight may benefit from seeing someone trained in sports medicine.

Here is some advice from one of my patients.

'You will also need your exercise support team. You will want to stay in shape as you go through IVF. In the beginning you may have more energy but as you go through the process trying to balance work and appointments, taking the medication at the prescribed times, what your body is going through, it's going to be hard. Rope in friends and family where possible to meet you at lunchtimes, or just after work for a walk. Make sure that you have a support system to have a giggle, distract you, and exercise with you.'

Smoking

There is no doubt that smoking reduces fertility in both men and women. In addition, it has a significant adverse effect on pregnancy and the growth and health of the baby during pregnancy. There is even growing evidence that smoking in pregnancy affects the future fertility of male and female infants born.

Effects in women

Fertility: Many studies show that natural fertility in women who smoke is approximately half of that of women who don't smoke (2.20). Women who smoke take on average a year longer to conceive. The more the woman smokes, the lower her fertility and certainly smoking 20 or more cigarettes per day is associated with much lower fertility.

Studies in women undergoing fertility treatment such as IVF also show that cigarette smoking reduces pregnancy rates. A large study was published in 2009 by a group in Sheffield (2.21). They summarised the results of 21 previous studies looking at the effect of smoking on the success rate of 1,300 smokers and 4,000 non-smokers undergoing IVF. The results are quite striking. The success rates in terms of live birth and clinical pregnancy rates in women who smoked were half those of women who did not smoke.

There are many reasons why smoking affects female fertility. The authors of the study quoted above (2.21) state that 'a strong body of evidence indicates that the negative effect of cigarette smoking on fertility is evident in every system involved in the reproductive process'. There is strong evidence that smoking reduces the woman's ovarian reserve, so cigarette smokers have lower AMH levels, lower oestrogen levels, fewer eggs in their ovaries and they get fewer eggs during IVF and ICSI. It has been shown that menopause occurs between one and four years earlier in women who smoke than in non-smokers. Other authors state that smokers add ten years to their reproductive age – a 25-year-old smoker has the same reproductive potential as a 35-year-old non-smoker. The degree of damage to the ovaries is dependent upon the amount and length of time a woman smokes.

It is also clear that cigarette smoking affects the development of the egg prior to ovulation. Toxic factors found in tobacco smoke, such as cadmium, cotinine and nicotine, have all been found in the fluid surrounding the egg. These toxins can damage the genetic DNA content of the egg and some studies have even shown that the outer covering or shell of the egg is thicker in women who smoke. Smoking has also been shown to reduce implantation of the embryo in the womb, while studies in animals have shown that tobacco can affect the Fallopian tubes and this may be the reason for the increased risk of ectopic pregnancy in smokers.

Pregnancy and children: In the IVF studies mentioned above (2.21), smokers also had 15 times the rate of ectopic pregnancy and a 2½ times greater chance of miscarriage. The link with miscarriage is strong. A study published in 2014, which summarised 98 previous studies, showed a definite link between smoking and miscarriage and, again, the more the woman smoked, the higher the risk (2.22).

In fact, smoking has been shown in numerous studies worldwide to increase virtually every single complication of pregnancy – such as high blood pressure, bleeding and haemorrhage and Caesarean section. Effects on the baby include reduced growth of the baby, greater chance of being born premature (early), stillbirth and death in the first few weeks of life. There is also a higher risk of foetal abnormalities such as heart defects and genetic abnormalities. Children born with lower than expected birth weights are at higher risk for medical problems later in life (such as diabetes, obesity and cardiovascular disease) and children whose parents smoke are at increased risk of sudden infant death syndrome (SIDS or cot death) and of asthma. Nicotine use during pregnancy has also been associated with poor academic performance and behavioural disruptions such as ADHD in children.

Effects in men

Smoking in men is also detrimental to their fertility and to the health of their offspring. There is ample evidence that smoking significantly affects sperm quality. A recent study summarising 20 previous studies of 5,865 men showed that cigarette smoking was associated with reduced sperm counts, reduced sperm motility and reduced numbers of normally shaped sperm (sperm morphology) (2.23). The effects of smoking were more dramatic in men with fertility problems than in the general population and were more profound in moderate and heavy smokers compared to mild smokers. Smoking by men also reduces the success rates of IVF by at least 40% (2.21). There is also evidence that smoking affects the DNA content of the sperm and DNA fragmentation has been found to be higher in smokers (2.21). Tobacco consumption has also been shown to affect sexual function (increases erectile problems). While the link is not as strong as in women, smoking by men has been shown to increase genetic damage in sperm, causing an increase in the risk of miscarriage. Finally, it appears that passive smoking has a negative effect on female fertility, so this is another way in which male smoking can affect fertility (2.21).

The effect of mothers smoking in pregnancy on the fertility of their sons is also interesting. An Australian study of over 400 men showed that men whose mothers smoked in pregnancy had a lower sperm count and this seemed to be related to higher levels of oestrogen in the placenta during pregnancy (2.24). Men born to smokers have also been shown to have smaller testicles and a greater chance of needing testicular surgery in childhood.

Stopping smoking

Thankfully, for both men and women, it seems possible to reverse some of the detrimental effects of smoking on fertility. It is not clear how long a woman needs to be off cigarettes to improve her chances, but there is evidence that egg quality and pregnancy rates improve within 3 to 6 months of stopping (2.25). Her number of eggs will never be as good as if she had never smoked, but fertility definitely improves.

In men, stopping smoking for three months allows sperm quality to improve. One study showed that on average, sperm counts increased from 29 to 72 million per sample and motility increased from 33% to 79%.

It's never too late to stop and stopping can only help in every way. I am not going to write a book about stopping smoking, but here are just a few points. Different people like to do it in different ways and preparing for pregnancy and children is a fantastic incentive. It gives me so much pleasure when people stop smoking as preparation – there is such a feel-good factor all round. And it is so gratifying to see how many people actually make that enormous effort and stop. Tobacco is extremely addictive (more so, apparently, than heroin), so I really say 'hats off' to anyone who has been addicted and who fights it.

There is help available and evidence that seeking help improves success. The HSE runs a free information and advice service to take smokers through the first important weeks and months. Smoking Cessation services are provided by the HSE in locations nationwide, in hospitals and in primary care, and these offer personal or group support courses for quitters – visit www.quit.ie.

GPs and pharmacists and other healthcare professionals also play a key role in helping smokers to quit. Books such as that by Alan Carr work for some people, as do acupuncture or hypnosis.

E-cigarettes: E-cigarettes work by heating a solution that contains nicotine and causing a nicotine-containing aerosol that is then inhaled rather than burning tobacco leaves. To date there are no studies looking at the effect of e-cigarettes on pregnancy and they are not recommended by the WHO. Evidence is emerging that they are *not* as safe as people might think. There is evidence that lung problems such as childhood wheezing and asthma are more common in the children of smokers and this seems to apply to women who smoke e-cigarettes as much as to women who smoke conventional cigarettes. This is because these effects on lung development seem to be related to the inhaled nicotine and other compounds in e-cigarettes rather than the actual smoke. Based on the current evidence I can't recommend e-cigarettes to men or women hoping to conceive.

Nicotine replacement: Nicotine replacement works by substituting nicotine in patches, sprays or lozenges for nicotine which would have been inhaled by tobacco smoke. It is estimated that there are roughly 4,000 toxins in tobacco smoke which are avoided by using a nicotine replacement. It is therefore felt that nicotine replacement is likely to be safer than non-tobacco smoked nicotine.

The Cochrane Library recently reviewed the evidence regarding nicotine replacement and concluded that 'There is no evidence that nicotine replacement therapy had either a positive or negative effect on pregnancy and infant outcomes' (2.26).

My advice would be that for men and women who smoke heavily and have tried and failed with other methods of giving up smoking, nicotine replacement therapy in the form of patches, sprays or lozenges is safer than continuing to smoke. They should, however, be used in as low a dose as possible.

Drugs to stop smoking: Several drugs have been developed to help people give up smoking. These include Zyban (bupropion) and Champix (varenicline). Zyban is an anti-depressant which interferes with the action of nicotine, but its precise mechanism of action is not known. Champix reduces the pleasurable effects of smoking and helps with cravings and withdrawal symptoms. The effects of these drugs on pregnancy have not been studied adequately and current advice is that they should not be used by pregnant women.

Alcohol

International research regarding the effect of alcohol on fertility is conflicting and confusing and certainly not as clear as that on smoking and recreational drugs. We know that excessive alcohol consumption is very harmful to the developing foetus and there is a syndrome known as foetal alcohol syndrome which occurs in women who are taking large amounts of alcohol (it causes facial abnormalities, behavioural problems and mental retardation). But in my experience, couples who have a fertility problem will not be drinking that heavily – though most of us in our society are probably drinking a bit more than we should be.

Alcohol in pregnancy

We know that alcohol affects foetal health in pregnancy. A Canadian study in 2003 (2.27) showed that alcohol consumption of more than one drink a day during pregnancy was associated with low birth weight, pre-term birth, and foetal alcohol spectrum disorders, and the effect increased in line with increasing levels of alcohol intake. International guidelines regarding alcohol intake in couples trying to conceive range from the CDC Guidelines in the United States, which say that no amount of alcohol is safe before and during pregnancy, to the Department of Health in the UK, which advises that women 'who are pregnant or trying to become pregnant should drink no more than one or two units of alcohol once or twice per week and should avoid episodes of intoxication' (1.1). Intoxication or binge drinking is generally defined as four or more drinks at one time.

Units of alcohol: a half pint of beer (284ml), a 100ml glass of wine or a pub measure (35.5ml) of spirits

Effects in women

In women, studies on natural fertility and alcohol are surprisingly difficult to find and one study even found that moderate consumption of wine (more than two glasses per day) might reduce the time taken to conceive. A large Danish study has just been published (August 2016 in the *British Medical Journal* (2.28)). Over 6,000 women who did not have infertility but who were trying to conceive were followed for one year or until they got pregnant. The study found that alcohol intake by women of up to 14 servings per week did not seem to affect fertility, but those who drank 14 or more servings had an 18% decrease in fertility. However, the age of these women was relatively low (median age 28 years), they did not have infertility (69% conceived in the year) and the amount of alcohol consumed was low (median two drinks per week, and only 8% drank more than seven servings per week). The 'servings' in this study were slightly larger than our standard units. The authors concluded that, 'Nonetheless, because the foetus may be particularly vulnerable to alcohol during the first few weeks after conception, it would seem prudent for women who are actively trying to become pregnant to abstain from alcohol during their fertile window until a pregnancy has been ruled out.'

Effects in men

There are several studies showing that alcohol has a reversible detrimental effect on sperm. A study of over 1,200 young Danish men (2.29) showed that sperm numbers and shape were definitely reduced by alcohol intake of more than five units* per week, and very much affected in men who drank more than twenty five units per week. However, other studies have not confirmed this.

The UK NICE guidelines (1.1) state that 'The current recommended guidelines on safe drinking limits for men allow three to four units per day'. But this is disputed by others. Alcohol can also exacerbate difficulties in men with erectile dysfunction or impotence. The effects on men having IVF are discussed below.

IVF

There have been two studies specifically focusing on the effects of alcohol on IVF success rates (2.27, 2.30). Both studies showed a link between alcohol intake in both men and women and lower success rates and higher miscarriage rates, and the effect was greater when greater amounts of alcohol were consumed. The most important time seemed to be during the IVF cycle and the month before it. The authors suggested that maternal and paternal alcohol consumption in excess of one unit daily up to one year before assisted reproduction was associated with a significant decrease in the success rates of IVF. They advised couples undergoing IVF to avoid drinking any alcohol.

Suggested intake

I must admit that my advice about alcohol has changed in recent times. People who are having difficulty conceiving are under considerable stress and need to be able to relax, socialise and enjoy life while also trying to conceive. I would have advised no more than seven units of alcohol per week for women and ten for men, and no more than three drinks on any one occasion. This seems to be okay for those who are young and unlikely to have a major fertility problem (see the Danish study described above). However, in couples with infertility who have been trying to conceive for over a year, I would advise that it is wise to try to cut alcohol down as much as possible. So I would suggest no more than three to four units per week for women and seven to eight for men, and I would advise both partners to consider cutting it out completely during an IVF cycle and for the month prior. Having said that, if there is a special occasion coming up, one or two drinks isn't going to make a difference, but avoid binge drinking. The time during and coming up to an IVF cycle is relatively short so it's easier to 'be good' for this period. For couples trying naturally, they may be looking at a year or more of trying, so a low level of alcohol is probably more workable than 'zero tolerance'. It's also best for women to avoid alcohol between ovulation and a pregnancy test and during the first three months of pregnancy.

Other lifestyle

Caffeine

Again, the evidence regarding caffeine intake and fertility and pregnancy is not very clear. Caffeine is present in coffee, tea, colas and chocolate, so an individual's precise intake of caffeine can be difficult to estimate. There are lots of online sites that calculate the caffeine content of different drinks.

Some recent studies have suggested that drinking more than three cups of coffee per day may be associated with infertility and early miscarriage. A recent American study looked at 344 couples who conceived and documented their caffeine intake prior to and in the first seven weeks of pregnancy (2.31). More than two drinks per day of caffeinated beverages was associated with an increase in the rate of early miscarriage – interestingly, this applied to both men's and women's caffeine consumption. There is also evidence from one study that caffeine reduces the live birth rate with IVF – possibly two- or three-fold (2.32). Unfortunately, it is not possible from this research to deduce what, if any, is a safe level of caffeine intake.

I would therefore advise women not to have more than two cups of coffee per day (total of 300 mg) and to consider cutting it down to one or none prior to and during IVF. There is no significant evidence showing a relationship between caffeine intake and male fertility but more than two or three cups of coffee per day is probably not good for anyone. Again, it is important not to get too hung up about this, and if you are reducing your intake, do it slowly to allow your body to adjust. Unfortunately, no one has studied whether or not decaffeinated beverages have an effect.

Recreational drug use

There is a lot of evidence that the use of recreational drugs such as marijuana and cocaine can adversely affect health. This negative impact also applies to fertility. The effects are often associated with weight loss and poor diet. These drugs also have a very significant effect on the health of the pregnancy and baby.

Cannabis/marijuana: This has been shown to have very adverse effects on fertility in both men and women. Cannabis is eliminated very slowly compared with tobacco, and the harmful effects are more significant.

In women, cannabis interferes with ovulation and also with the development of eggs and with embryo implantation. Women who smoke cannabis are therefore more likely not to ovulate and, even if they do, fertility is reduced at the level of implantation.

In men, cannabis lowers testosterone levels and has been associated with ejaculation problems, a loss of libido (sexual desire), impotence, gynecomastia (breast enlargement) and reduced sperm counts and motility. One study showed that more than a third of chronic marijuana smokers had very low sperm counts associated with low levels of hormones.

Use of cannabis in pregnancy has been associated with learning disorders, hyperactivity and ADHD in the offspring as well as increased premature delivery, growth retardation and miscarriage.

We see men regularly enough who smoke cannabis. It really is a no-no. If either partner uses cannabis they need to stop and we would hope to see an improvement in sperm and ovulation after about six months.

Cocaine: There is less information about the effects of cocaine on fertility, but there are some studies showing that it may affect sperm counts and motility. Most studies have been done on animals such as rats and these certainly show an impact on fertility. It is also associated with foetal abnormalities.

Other drugs: Studies of men using opiates or narcotics, such as heroin, show reductions in testosterone and other hormones and subsequent deterioration in libido, erectile function and sperm quality. Heroin use in women is associated with irregular and failed ovulation. There are very few studies of methamphetamines or ecstasy on fertility but results in animals show a detrimental effect on sperm production and testosterone levels.

Anabolic steroids/testosterone: An ever-increasing problem that we are seeing in our clinics is the impact of certain male supplements on reproductive function. In recent years there has been a huge increase in body building, body sculpting and weight training by men. This activity takes a lot of commitment and hard work. In some cases, men are turning to medication or supplements which will speed up the rate of 'bulking up'. These agents are also used to enhance physical performance in sports. Men may be taking testosterone supplements or steroids. Many men are also taking supplements available online which they think are innocuous. However, many of these supplements contain lots of additives, including testosterone.

Testosterone supplements can be taken as tablets or in injection form and are widely available over the internet. They also have addictive properties and it can be difficult for men to stop using them. Lower doses of testosterone can be prescribed in a gel for erectile or impotence problems, but a side-effect is a lowering of sperm counts and infertility.

The interesting thing is that, while these drugs may ostensibly increase the man's appearance of masculinity, they have completely the opposite effect on his testosterone levels and hence fertility and testicular function. Sperm production is dependent on normal testosterone levels in the testis, but if the man is flooded with excess testosterone, his natural testosterone production is switched off, with drastic effects on reproduction. This can lead to complete absence of sperm (azoospermia) or very reduced sperm counts and also a reduction in the size and health of the testis.

We see a couple of men every year who have no or very low sperm counts because of anabolic steroid abuse. The good news is that four to six months after discontinuing these drugs, sperm counts and quality generally return to normal levels.

Testosterone and anabolic steroids are not often used by women but, not surprisingly, if they are they will certainly disrupt ovulation and the woman's hormones, leading to facial and body hair growth and infertility. If taken in pregnancy they will cause foetal abnormalities and altered hormone effects.

Men's underwear and heat

Men's testes (testicles) are contained in the scrotum, which lies on the outside of the body, keeping the testes two to three degrees cooler than his internal organs. There are many studies showing that increased temperature around the testes reduces sperm counts and quality. This is seen in men whose testes never descend into the scrotum but stay in the abdomen and in men with very large varicose veins around their testes. There is also evidence that the temperature around the testes increases in men who are sitting for long periods, e.g. truck drivers, men who use saunas and jacuzzis and men who wear tight-fitting underwear. However, it has not been proven that this leads to reduced sperm health and fertility problems. More recent studies have failed to show this effect and the evidence is at best conflicting (1.1).

I suppose if a man has a mild sperm problem there is no harm in trying looser underwear and avoiding heat, but for the vast majority of men, it does not really seem to make any difference and most fertility experts feel that the earlier studies overestimated the importance.

Occupation

Numerous studies over the years have looked at the effect of environmental chemicals such as metals and pesticides on pregnancy rates and foetal abnormalities. Undoubtedly chemicals have been associated with foetal abnormalities and increased rates of miscarriage, but the studies are small and it is very hard to draw conclusions. People who are exposed to a lot of X-rays, radiation, pesticides and strong chemicals in their workplace should discuss this with their doctor and also with their human resources and occupational health personnel at work.

Emotional wellbeing

It is being increasingly recognised at all levels in our society that emotional wellbeing contributes to overall health. A useful definition of emotional wellbeing is 'a positive sense of wellbeing' that enables an individual to be able to function in society and meet the demands of everyday life. Reduced emotional wellbeing can lead to stress, depression and anxiety; enhanced emotional wellbeing seems to contribute to increased coping ability, better self-esteem, better performance and productivity at work, and it even helps one to live longer.

There is absolutely no doubt but difficulty in conceiving can be one of the most distressing events in anyone's life. However, the relationship between stress and fertility is extremely complex and certainly not black and white. There are two big questions:

1) Does infertility cause stress?
2) Does stress cause infertility?

The role of stress related to fertility *treatment* is also extremely important.

I will address both these questions below and I am delighted to have the help of our counsellor at Merrion Fertility Clinic, Kay Duff, who has written an excellent piece on her experience of supporting people with all kinds of fertility-related issues.

Most of the studies on emotional wellbeing and fertility centre on heterosexual couples, but the general concepts apply to all. In a later section I discuss issues particular to same-sex couples and single men and women pursuing parenthood.

Does infertility cause stress?

Many people spend years using contraception and actively trying not to conceive. Then they may decide it is time to start a family. Even if they try not to think about it, it is only natural that thoughts will come into their minds of what they will and won't do when they have a baby, how they will cope with work, is their house suitable, will they still be able to continue doing sports, will they have time to meet friends, won't their parents be delighted, etc. Couples start out on this new venture together and it's fun!

But just imagine how it feels when a few months go by and nothing is happening. Then a few more months. They try to remain positive and not panic, try to think positively. They try another month, and another month, and another month and another ... Maybe they change their diet, reduce their alcohol intake, start taking vitamins, try to be more healthy. They start wondering if there's something 'wrong' with one or both of them. Will they need treatment? Will they be able to cope?

Meanwhile their family and friends may be asking them about their family plans or even making jokes. They may be surrounded by friends who are pregnant and having babies. And those babies look so cute and so vulnerable and so adorable.

'From the hope, expectation and excitement to the first open day we attended a couple of years ago, to all the pre-tests and exploratory procedures, we began our journey with optimism and apprehension.'

'For the first few months I was trying to play it cool and just say to myself it's going to happen next month and you try get on with life as best you can. As the months turned into a year that's when I began to worry. You become an amazing actress every time one of your friends tells you they are expecting. You shriek in delight for that person and perfect your "that's amazing" face but inside you are a blubbering mess shouting why can't it be me! The feelings of jealousy, the emptiness, the sadness can be difficult to conceal. I ask all the usual questions, how far along are you? Do you know the sex? All with a smile on my face and go home and silently sob into my pillow. I am genuinely happy for these friends who shared this news and I feel so guilty for feeling like I do. You think – how can good news like this hurt so much?'

—⟨∞⟩—

'As hard as you try not to have feelings of jealousy it's impossible as your desire for a baby is so strong. You feel you are a bad person for even having these feelings in the first place but I guess we are only human.'

—⟨∞⟩—

'Other people didn't get it. It's interesting with infertility you end up in this no man's land. We both have reasonable jobs but we had to get a credit union loan through my mother to get started which we are paying off in monthly instalments. Gone are the days of buying shoes, or weekends away. On this new health kick there is no room for partying or nights out. So it's almost like you end up with the lifestyle of a couple with kids without the joy of the kids. And yet on the outside as a colleague remarked you are DINKY – Double Income No Kids Yet – carefree. I hung on to the Yet at the end of the sentence.'

Who would not be stressed in these situations? Yet many couples have to just battle on, continue working and socialising as if everything's hunky dory. In addition, they have all the other stresses that anyone else has – work, money, relationships, family, etc.

'I don't think people realise how long it's going to take, it's definitely one of the toughest times you will face in your life.'

—⟨∞⟩—

'... the psychological impact of infertility. I don't think this can be overestimated.'

—⟨∞⟩—

'I can only speak from my experience so this might not be everyone's but it can feel like you are living month to month. Every time your period arrives it feels like grief. I feel like I am mourning the possibility and potential of what might be. I don't think this is something people understand as there is nothing concrete to actually grieve but nevertheless. Then you have to pick yourself back up and get back into the process. There is no time to process the grief as you simply cannot take this time every month.'

―∞―

'More tears, more heartache, more questions, more being on my knees in the sitting room sobbing uncontrollably with grief and despair.'

―∞―

'Wanting answers that can't be found and trying to cope with the negative tests month after month. Sarah and I focused on the bigger picture and tried to keep a positive mind-set.'

―∞―

'During this journey I find that it's very lonely. I feel like there is something wrong with me and that there is a flashing neon light over me all the time. I also feel very stupid despite having two degrees and a master's.'

―∞―

'My husband's tests are all fine so I guess I'm the one who is "broken"! Whilst my husband is extremely supportive it's very hard not to be tough on myself for not being able to get pregnant. It's upsetting that people keep asking where's baby number 2!'

―∞―

'For a woman you start to blame yourself as you are basically the one making and carrying the baby. I started questioning if it was for me. Was my body telling me what I felt all of those years ago – "I am not meant to be a mother"? I was a very healthy person I trained in the gym 4–5 times per week; I ate very healthy, no sugar, no salt, very little alcohol, so why was my body failing me when I needed it the most?'

Multitudes of studies have been done on stress levels and the emotional wellbeing of couples with fertility problems. However, the results can be conflicting. This is not surprising given that emotional wellbeing in itself is a variable thing and varies from person to person. Different people have different coping mechanisms. Despite differences between the studies, however, the overall conclusion is that infertility and fertility treatment are extremely stressful.

In one study, the psychological symptoms of anxiety and depression associated with infertility were found to be similar to those associated with other serious medical conditions such as heart disease, cancer, high blood pressure and infection with HIV (2.33). However, more recent studies show that, prior to IVF treatment, people with infertility are not any more likely to suffer depression or psychiatric problems than the general population, but they may be more stressed and anxious. And we do know that they may experience negative emotions such as low self-esteem, anger, guilt, frustration and powerlessness (2.34, 2.35). Fertility treatment, and in particular IVF, causes stress and failed IVF treatment can be followed by strong negative emotional reactions (mainly depression) that may last for up to six months, and sometimes longer (2.35). 'Treatment burden' is a term often used in studies of IVF treatments and other medical interventions. In line with this, only about half of those with infertility ever seek fertility treatment, and, of those who do, a fifth discontinue IVF treatment before completing a recommended course (2.35).

'We are going through this journey 15 months, while it may not seem like a long period of time, it's 15 times that I felt like a failure, felt inadequate.'

'Each month feels like a rollercoaster of emotion, the tears for the baby that never was, the sadness because you have to make the walk from the bathroom after your periods arrive to the sitting room where your partner sits unknowingly watching the TV. You now have to shatter his dream in three words. "I got them", our dream is over for another month.'

'In many respects we were lucky. Some people can't bear to be around babies or children. I was fine. My niece was born the day after we received our diagnosis. A friend had said nieces and nephews were different from friends' kids and she was right. I was so delighted for them – becoming a father has been the making of my brother. The timing was hard. I cried from the day we left that office I would say for at least two weeks solid.

The only time I didn't cry was in work. My manager was fantastic but actually work helped me cope. Months later, I remember ringing the clinic secretary and her surprise that it was me joking – I think she described me as bubbly. I must have been absolutely traumatised when I was with her as she didn't actually recognise me when I was my usual self.'

Fertility treatments are stressful. For example, IVF involves daily injections, frequent appointments at the clinic, blood samples, invasive investigations such as trans-vaginal scans, egg collection and always the possibility of pregnancy failure. The two weeks between embryo transfer and waiting for an outcome are particularly stressful (2.35). Some women and men may need to undergo surgery. Even in those who achieve a pregnancy, there may be increased anxiety about the health of their baby.

'I was frustrated, devastated, mortified. I felt like I was in a dark cave with no exits and It was going deeper and deeper, but at the same time I was satisfied with what we did. When we look back in the future, we would not have any regrets and if we have to give up trying to have a baby, we will be able to accept it.'

'If you had told me five years ago this would consume me I would have laughed. I was more than a bit feminist. I love my work and studying, I love going out and the craic, I have travelled the world and yet I know we would both give it up in a heartbeat. And I suppose it is the hope (which although fleeting at times) keeps you going.'

'The two-week wait is the worst part of the treatment, you try your best to stay positive and it is constantly on your mind. It's exhausting, for both the parties!'

'But fertility isn't the only concern we have. The nine months between conception and birth is like a lifetime to worried people like us. So much can happen in that time. So much can go wrong.'

Some of the things that make fertility treatment particularly distressing are the lack of control that people feel when they are going through treatment and the uncertainty of the treatment. Generally if somebody is having major medical treatment such as an operation there is some expectation of an immediate result, whereas with fertility treatments there is absolutely no guarantee of success and multiple attempts are often required.

> *'The uncertainty and how out of your control the process of fertility is, people don't realise. I think people need to talk about it more, it's only when something happens to you do you hear it has also happened to a lot of other people.'*

> *'It's very hard when it's all out of our control and we just have to wait and wait and wait.'*

> *'I think this is the hardest part about IVF or trying to conceive in general, you realise it is not in your control. I responded by trying to control everything. I turned into someone barely recognisable to myself. In our relationship we had been each to their own. I would never have dreamed of lecturing my husband on his drinking or diet. Well I went into control mode budgeting for several cycles, monitoring every morsel that went into his mouth.'*

Unexplained infertility (where no obvious cause is found for the difficulty) can be particularly distressing because there is no tangible 'reason' to focus on – I find that couples with unexplained infertility really question everything they do (and don't do) and the feelings of frustration and powerlessness are particularly strong for them. While problems such as having a low sperm count or blocked tubes pose their own particular concerns, at least people with these problems have some idea of what they're dealing with and there is some logic to undergoing specific treatments. This is not the case with unexplained infertility.

'I thought If there was some specific problem or reason it would be much easier and happier than nothing. Being unknown makes me mad and I do not know what to do or what I should. Just time is flying with no luck.'

———

'We have been through a horrendous four years and hopefully our happy ending is within our grasp! After diagnosis we actually hoped that they had found something wrong with one of us so that at least doctors could try to fix it.'

Men and women: While women may seem more vulnerable than men to developing emotional problems as a result of infertility and IVF, research shows that men also experience significant distress. A recent study that summarised 12 studies involving over 2,500 men showed that, one year following their first fertility appointment, many men demonstrated evidence of psychological distress (2.36). This was less likely to happen if men were able to access information about fertility and were able to communicate openly with their partner or others about their problems.

While there are fewer studies on men's emotional wellbeing and fertility than women's, men report higher social isolation than women during an IVF treatment cycle, probably because, in general, men discuss their emotions less with friends and colleagues than women do. We can forget that men find some of the procedures associated with reproduction embarrassing or painful (the pressure to ejaculate through masturbation on demand and pain following testicular biopsy). We also know that many men feel a bit excluded from the whole fertility process as many of the interventions and treatments are focused on the female side of things. This can, on the one hand, lead men to feel that they are 'just sperm providers' and, on the other, leave them worrying about and feeling guilty over the fact that their partner needs to undergo invasive treatments. This is particularly the case for men who have sperm issues – the treatment is ICSI, which necessitates their partner taking injections, having an egg collection, etc. Interestingly, though, one study showed that women whose partner had male factor infertility experienced higher anxiety than women with female factor.

I see this type of thing often and it shows the heartbreak of infertility – each person in the relationship is not only distressed for themselves but they have the additional burden of worry about their partner's wellbeing. For those with secondary infertility who may have a child already, there is the additional burden of worrying about their child and wanting a sibling for that child.

Here are some men's experiences:

'I was angry at the world, the government, luck, Superman and God. Now, that anger has subsided, replaced by an array of emotions I didn't know I could even feel, until now.'

During "our" pregnancy – though it was regularly relayed to us that it made no difference – almost every midwife, nurse and doctor we saw passed comment on the fact that ours was an IVF baby. Make no mistake, these comments were neither positive nor negative. They were just comments. If anything they may have been uttered in happy surprise, but perhaps I'm reading too much into it. They've all been so nice to us – the hospital staff, the staff in the fertility clinic, everyone really. I suppose it was written on that massive chart we carried around everywhere and people were just reading aloud.'

'I believe I would like to be a father just as much as Aoife longs to be a mother. I want to raise my own little Johns and/or Aoifes and teach them to be good, honest people, the best they can be. I like to think of myself as a proud Irishman, and I would like to continue my lineage, my name, as my father has done and his father before that. Cancer and heart disease are common in my family and I have lost a number of relatives to one or other of those ailments. One of my biggest fears is that my darling parents might not be around long enough to get to know their grandchild.'

'It goes without saying that it is probably usually a lot easier for the men than the women. The tests and procedures I had to undergo were minimal and non-invasive. I also got the impression that Mary held guilt on her shoulders for not achieving pregnancy even though test

results didn't show anything specifically wrong with her or me. I imagine this is probably a common issue among couples. It took a lot of time but I think she has finally come around to accepting that it's not her fault or mine. It just is what it is.'

Here are some women's experiences of male infertility:

'It was Dave's results rather than mine that were raising queries. Despite this, whenever anyone heard that we were doing IVF, the assumption was that it was my fertility that was a problem – never Dave's. It is actually quite distressing to have people (mainly men) tell you that you just need to relax and destress in order to conceive – when the evidence we had suggested that the main fertility issues were on Dave's side. I do of course now know that there can be unexplained reasons for fertility, and that even if Dave's sperm was showing healthier morphology levels, that I mightn't be conceiving anyway, so I don't want to engage in any sort of "blaming" – apart from anything else it's very unfair and I don't think it helps a relationship.'

'Given the very gendered assumptions I was encountering around responsibility for fertility and conception (and not just child-rearing as I had thought!) I was really interested then to realise that these assumptions were embedded in science too – to the point that male infertility is relatively and significantly under-researched compared to female, with the effect that even when there are clear problems with male infertility, it is the woman that is treated. I have to say I felt this quite keenly undergoing ICSI, as the whole process is very taxing on the female body and indeed daily life – and as you know, ICSI is the main treatment recommended for male infertility.'

'So when we were told my husband's tests had revealed severe male infertility I was devastated. In that meeting I wasn't able to ask how he was, I literally heaved crying. I had always had this sense that having kids wouldn't be easy – no real reason for it, I just had.'

Without doubt, working on your relationship is important and it has been shown that where both partners have similar views on parenthood and its importance, there is less stress and more relationship satisfaction. This can be a particular concern for couples where one partner has children from a previous relationship and the other has no children. Also, individuals who perceive their partner to be available and responsive experience lower infertility stress than individuals who perceive their partner to be avoidant and non-responsive. I certainly notice this.

> 'My husband and I are facing different opinions on the matter. He does not want to go ahead and do it and I would not mind. Marriage is a thing of two and I have to respect his views. Years ago this was discussed and accepted – thinking I would not have any issues.'

> 'The stress on your relationship can take its toll, so my advice to other couples on this journey is to be kind to each other because at the end of the day you both want to achieve the same goal and somewhere in the middle of all the planning, timing, constant discussions on this could be our month, or the best sexual position to conceive you can forget that at one time it was just two people who fell in love and enjoyed living in the moment.'

> 'I think the entire process is so difficult and demanding and I don't know how people do it if their relationship is not solid and supportive.'
> 'Yet some time later and from somewhere the dawn comes again. My husband and I laugh and cry together and talk it through some more.'
> 'I was blessed to have an understanding husband who was always 100% behind me.'

> 'It has made us a stronger couple all round, but there have been horrible times when the smallest of things would turn into a massive argument due to constant stress and disappointment over the years. We fought particularly bad a few weeks after our negative result. My husband has a demanding job and works late, we decided that we needed to start

spending more time together in the evenings and weekends in the weeks leading up to starting treatment again. My husband made a conscious effort to come home early one or two nights a week and that we would also spend good quality time together at the weekends, this did our stress levels wonders during the second try and it is something that we will continue. Quality time is so important as people tend to get stuck in a rut.'

'Your partner. He is your rock of support. He should be your ears when you visit the clinic because you may feel too emotional to take in information. Tasks shared are halved. Where you can involve your partner, then get him involved. Encourage him to talk to people at work and to have his support team. He may put on a brave face. He may try to be the strong person in the situation for you. But he needs an outlet too. He too has expected and hoped for a family and is more than likely experiencing the loss that you are. So involve him in the process. Put him in charge of getting the injections ready. Get him to collect the prescriptions.'

Relationships and wellbeing

Does stress cause infertility?

How often are couples struggling to conceive told to 'just relax' or 'take a holiday' or 'think positively' and it will happen? Nothing upsets people more, even though they know it has been said with good intentions. And most people wish, 'if it were only that simple'.

This is an old-fashioned concept that originated in the 1930s and was based on a small number of cases and inadequate information. Certainly there are couples who have had infertility for many years, who end up adopting a child and subsequently conceive unexpectedly. At our clinic, and every other fertility clinic, we see couples who have been trying to conceive for years, who have IVF, which may fail, and then unexpectedly conceive naturally. Or they are just about to start IVF and they get pregnant naturally. But sadly, for each of these couples, there are many more who never conceive naturally – so it is simplistic to say that 'stress' is the cause.

As mentioned above, couples with fertility problems prior to attending for treatment have not been shown to have higher levels of depression or psychiatric problems than the general population. They are more stressed and anxious, but this seems to be a result rather than a cause of the infertility (2.34). We also know that people reproduce despite very harsh conditions of war, famine, rape and poverty, so stress in itself does not cause infertility.

'The other thing that couples should brace themselves for is that pregnancy will be everywhere on their journey. Friends will be happily sharing their news, television ads will all feature babies, toddlers, mothers, and fathers.'

'If I hear "relax and it will happen" one more time! I know my family are just trying to say the right things and I can't even figure out what the right thing to say is. All I know is I have such a longing, a physical ache for a baby.'

'Another stress I found was people constantly thinking that it was acceptable to ask me when I was going to have a baby, especially after we married. I found this so insensitive, they didn't know what we were going through. I have learned to smile and just change the subject, but it really hurts. I found that over the last year, I have isolated myself from friends and colleagues to avoid these questions, which is very unhealthy. I made a conscious decision however that whatever the outcome of our second round, I was going to answer people honestly and no longer bottle it all up. We have both been living in limbo and it had to stop. I am delighted that we are going to start living our lives again and thankfully with a baby, but had it been a negative outcome we planned on doing the same. Infertility takes over your life. It has been such a long journey.'

'I find here in Ireland that people have this idea that things need to happen in a sequence, you meet, you date, you get engaged, you get married and you have babies. No sooner have you met the person than you're getting asked when is the engagement, the engagement comes and they are asking for the dates for the wedding, the wedding comes and goes and already they want to know where the babies are. It's pressure on people and I think totally inappropriate. So those questions started happening not long after we got married and I brushed them off.'

'"You'll be next, don't worry", like I am somehow let down by the fact everyone is having babies around me and I am without a child. I found my responses getting more abrupt and at one stage me roaring at someone, "I DON'T WANT KIDS SO STOP ASKING ME".'

'Friends will tell you their stories of that woman that they know who had a miracle baby eventually when nothing else worked against all the odds. People will tell you of couples they know who were struggling for years but when they stopped trying so hard they got pregnant. This is not helpful.'

However, the relationship between psychological stress and fertility problems is complex. Some studies show a correlation between stress levels and subsequent fertility problems (2.37), but others don't (2.38). We do know, however, that psychological stress can affect a couple's relationship and libido, which may impact on their chance of conception if they are not having sex often enough. A higher frequency of male sexual disturbances including loss of libido and a decrease in the frequency of sexual intercourse has been observed in couples undergoing fertility investigations and treatments. Severe stress, eating disorders and depression can affect ovulation in women (see page 168), but these are extreme cases.

What most couples wish to know is the impact of mild or moderate stress on fertility. My feeling is that most of us in modern western society are stressed due to work, money, travel, social media, the internet, constant messages and emails, etc. Any stress undoubtedly affects our health. It is unlikely that fertility is any different, but the effect is going to be different in different people and getting stressed over being stressed is certainly not going to help. Recent evidence seems to indicate that stress can reduce fertility but *only if it interferes with the frequency of sex or if it stops people going for treatment when they need it.*

Even if it does not help fertility per se, minimising stress and enhancing emotional wellbeing is important if people and relationships are not to be damaged by infertility and its treatment. Reducing stress is also essential to enable people to persist with treatment and not drop out – many people need a few attempts at treatment and it would be a shame to give up too soon. But we know that this happens and that a major cause of drop-out is the distress and burden of the treatments.

Stress and treatment success

There are lots of studies in the literature looking at the effects of stress in couples with fertility problems and the results are very variable (2.37). However, a UK study in 2011 amalgamated 14 studies with 3,583 infertile women undergoing a cycle of IVF treatment and showed that pre-treatment emotional distress was *not* associated with treatment outcome (2.38). This is very reassuring for women, who often believe that their stress may reduce their success rate with IVF. As far as we know, it doesn't.

In keeping with this, a 2016 review of 39 studies involving almost 5,000 men and women undergoing treatment showed that they were unable to conclude whether methods to reduce stress actually improved psychological wellbeing and pregnancy rates (2.39). This is disappointing, but the lack of demonstrable effect is felt to be predominantly a reflection on the quality of the studies performed to date.

Coping with stress

It seems that most patients are able to cope with the multiple demands of infertility and fertility treatment. However, studies have shown that one in five, or 20%, of patients experience significant distress, which taxes their coping resources. International groups such as ESHRE (European Society for Human Reproduction and Embryology) are now recommending that doctors and clinics should try to help patients identify their level of stress and provide appropriate help to those who need it (2.40, 2.41), while other studies are looking at the long-term psychological effects of fertility treatment and failure (2.42).

As Kay Duff describes below, it is really important for anyone with fertility concerns to recognise that it is absolutely normal to experience distress. The important thing to focus on is how to manage and cope with this distress and, rather than trying to eliminate the problem (which may not be possible), to work on ensuring that it does not take over. And it is not just the fertility-related distress that needs to be tackled – don't forget to look at other things, such as work, money, family, relationships, etc. I have seen people struggling with infertility and also trying to manage work, do a part-time degree and cope with an ill parent. We are not supermen or superwomen – however much we would like to be!

Lots of different stress-reducing programmes have been studied around the world. None has been found to be 'best' and this is probably to be expected. I generally advise people to try to figure out what has worked for them in the past. For some it may be exercise, for others socialising or going to the cinema and for others mindfulness or meditation. Discussing one's emotions and the use of meaning-based coping (e.g. thinking about the fertility problem in a positive light, finding other goals in life) seem to be associated with lower fertility-specific distress, whereas the use of avoidance coping strategies (e.g. avoiding being among pregnant women) seems to increase distress. Studies have also shown that social support and meeting people is important and even work can have a positive effect. Most fertility clinics will offer support services and counselling and most GPs will also know professionals who can help.

'Looking back on it now, that marked one of the most challenging pieces. We coped completely differently. I am quite a straight-up person and am fairly open, my husband when it comes to feelings is not. I experience my feelings fully and probably work off the motto "better out than in". It took me time to learn that my husband would manage differently. We did hit a point – a little over a year in – where we hit a crisis point in our relationship and through a friend who had also experienced fertility difficulties we began couples therapy which was probably the hardest but one of the best decisions we made. It's mad to think you are with someone ten years and in a month discover things you never knew about them. We are now much more able to support each other and able to enjoy things that are not about IVF.'

'Which leads me onto another reason for not wanting kids. I will be as discreet as possible as I want to protect my mother's privacy. My mam and dad didn't get along. There were constant fights and it wasn't nice to witness as a child. We witnessed some other things too but I won't go into that. I always in the back of my mind blamed myself and my brother for their arguments. I thought it's because they have us kids that they argue so much. So in the back of my mind I was thinking if I want my marriage to stay the way it is now then let's not have kids as that will ruin it.'

'I remember saying "I can't do this anymore." The next day I booked an appointment with a counsellor as I wanted to get my head right. It was the best thing I ever did. She taught me how to put myself first, to work through childhood issues and to realise I am not my parents and myself and my husband aren't going to end up arguing all the time. I felt like a weight was lifted off my shoulders. I could start focusing on me without feeling guilty.'

Studies regarding what fertility patients want show that less distressed patients may not wish to receive counselling, and some may cope well with support from their spouses and family (2.40, 2.41). In one study, two-thirds of patients undergoing IVF treatment reported reading newspaper or magazine articles and watching television programmes about the psychological aspects of infertility, even though few participated in a support group or sought counselling before treatment. This suggests that, for some patients, information about local and national support groups and booklets on the psychological aspects of treatment, in addition to medical information, may be beneficial.

Conclusion: The relationship of stress and fertility is complex. Certainly, fertility problems and, especially, fertility treatments, cause distress. This can have a negative impact on overall health and sexual activity, which is not good for fertility. It also leads to many people dropping out of treatment. However, stress per se has not been shown to have a direct effect on fertility or on treatment. Efforts to reduce stress are important to ensure that people are not damaged by infertility or its treatment and also to help avoid relationship problems and to help couples/patients to be able to persevere with treatment.

Supporting Those with Fertility Issues
BY KAY DUFF, FERTILITY COUNSELLOR, MFC

Most people include children in their life plan. So it is not surprising that a fertility problem causes major stress. People go from 'when' we have a family to 'if' and their life ahead becomes very uncertain.

I am an experienced professional counsellor. I originally trained as a couples counsellor with RELATE UK and continued working in this area for ten years in Marriage and Relationship Counselling Services (MRCS) Dublin. I came to the area of fertility in 2003 and have been the attending counsellor at Merrion Fertility Clinic since then. I also work as a general counsellor. In this section I will share my experience of working with those who do not conceive naturally and, as a result, undergo fertility treatment. I will give an overview of the stresses involved and the emotional impact of these on an individual's/couple's decision to access social supports.

Types of patients

People come for fertility treatment at all different stages in their life. Some have been trying to have a family for at least a year and usually at this stage they are not too concerned but want to get their fertility checked. Also there are couples who met late in life and know already that their age may be a factor and come in to get their fertility checked very early in the relationship.

There are those who already have a child, possibly conceived with little effort, and want a sibling. However, if this doesn't happen they may find themselves in the 'unexplained' category. This can be very stressful for them. It can be a big struggle trying to understand 'why' and coping with the lack of sympathy from those around them as they have a child already.

Some couples or individuals may find themselves needing a donor or surrogate. This may not be their ideal or planned route but may become the only one. Others wish to consider sperm or egg freezing, either for medical reasons such as cancer or because they are not yet in a position to conceive because they haven't met their life partner.

Stress and common themes

Having worked with so many couples and individuals I find that the uncertainty that comes with having to have medical intervention can bring along some of the following feelings and experiences.

- Overwhelming feelings of loss and grief.
- Anxiety and jealousy when others announce their pregnancy.
- Sense of guilt and failure.
- Anger and resentment.
- Feeling isolated from friends.
- Stress in the relationship.
- Upset with family and friends who don't seem to understand.
- Sex has become part of the baby-making process.
- Worried about the relationship – if no children, what then?

Losses to health

- If couples don't conceive in one year and they then have a medical diagnosis, their body image changes; they are now patients. The cumulative effect of diagnosis and treatment can lead to illness and stress.

Losses in the relationship

- Loss in the security of the relationship. The unspoken fear for many – will he/she leave me? This can be difficult to express.
- Will we be enough for one another?
- The fun's gone – will my depression drive him/her away?
- No energy to give one another.
- Loss of intimacy and sexual spontaneity.
- Sex for baby/doctor, not love – difficulties responding.
- Couples are affected and cope differently; women can be concerned with feelings and their need to express emotions, whereas men can focus on the next treatment and tend to be strong as they think it's expected of them. These different ways of coping can cause further stress in the relationship.

Loss to self-esteem

- Self-worth can change, 'when' becomes 'if'. 'I can't even do that much'. Fear of failure.

- Self-esteem is damaged with the flood of strong emotion; anger and jealousy can turn to massive guilt.
- 'I should not feel that angry, I was reared well.'
- Fear of announcements.
- 'Am I not good enough to be a parent, is this why I'm not getting pregnant?'

Loss of status (in the eyes of others)
- Society places huge emphasis on family and parenthood: How many have you? When are you starting? It's time you gave up those fancy holidays – relax and it will happen.
- Worth to society can be lessened.
- Couples can suffer comments and jokes about their sex lives, leading them to withdraw and isolate.
- Men can feel their masculinity is being questioned.
- Women – having children is central to their identity.
- They can feel they don't 'fit in' anymore.
- Friends with family can feel awkward in their company; isolation starts from both sides.
- 'We are that statistic; we don't want to be that "odd couple"!'

Loss of self-confidence
- People in control of their lives can become controlled by treatment.
- Hard work generally leads to success, but no matter how hard you try you may still fail.
- Massive sacrifice (money, persistence) but can't do what others do with no effort.
- Can't plan holidays, can't take promotion – may interfere with time off.
- Loss of security about fairness.
- If this can happen, what more can happen to us?

Loss – fulfilling the fantasy
- The fear they may never experience being a parent.
- Never experience pregnancy, giving birth, choosing schools, etc.
- Never seeing their family marry and continuing the cycle of life.
- Being an adult usually means having a family.
- Longing for the child who may never be and mourn the loss of the child who never was.

- No tangible loss for others to see.
- No sense of finality, as there is with death.
- They have to continue celebrating the births of children of family and friends.

Fertility treatment and stress

In the general population, there can be a massive lack of understanding of what people go through when they discover that they can't have a baby naturally. Infertility is often over-simplified. Outsiders often have no idea what is actually going on for the person affected. Contrary to common belief, there are those who try to have their family young, only to discover that the woman's egg supply is diminishing. A common comment from other people is, 'Relax, you have plenty of time', when they may have no idea that this 28-year-old has been told that she is in early menopause. Older women are sometimes criticised as career women who have left it too late and therefore receive little sympathy. This attitude can lead to people hiding the fact that they are having difficulties or getting treatment and this in turn makes things more difficult because they may close themselves off from valuable social supports.

We saw in the last section that there are common emotional responses to treatment. Couples can at times be alarmed by the intensity of these feelings. They can start to focus so intensely on treatment that they neglect other areas of their lives, i.e. self-care. After a long, hard day at work people often unwind by running, cycling, going to the gym or relaxing with a glass of wine. This is not always an option for those in treatment. And they may now also have been diagnosed with medical problems and are struggling to come to terms with that.

The stress that can come with infertility/fertility issues is often rated alongside family bereavement, but the grief process can be very complex. Grief is a very personal phenomenon and no one conforms to a standard grief process. Worden (2.43) has outlined a working model of grief to help those who are grieving. For example, the first task is 'to accept the reality of the loss'. This is complex in the area of fertility because the loss is often intangible and against the natural order of life. The second task is 'to work through the pain of grief' – this is complicated by the fact that a couple in treatment get new hope every month that can distract from the loss and put the grief 'on hold'. Third, 'to adjust to an environment in which the deceased is missing' – but infertility involves the loss of the child who might have been and the 'missing' is part of the future as well as the present.

Time can be a massive issue for people in treatment. They don't often have the luxury of grieving the loss because they have to keep in mind that the clock is ticking, particularly for older women.

Dealing with fertility stress

There is no point saying 'Don't be stressed' or 'You're too stressed to become pregnant'. Stress is not a decision. Treatment, trying and failing that goes on and on is very distressing. This is well documented. If we look at the list of losses and stresses that couples may experience it can look insurmountable. I have found through working for many years in the field of fertility that, if I can help people see the enormous losses and stresses that they are trying to deal with, this can help them adjust their expectations of themselves.

Some couples seek support at the beginning of treatment or when they first get a diagnosis. In this situation they can be helped to adjust to what may be ahead as they go along. This is an ideal situation, but we don't live in an ideal world. Treatment is very complex and tailored to each individual and there is no way to equip patients for everything that may be ahead. But at least they can learn to anticipate problems and build in mechanisms to address them.

Sometimes couples don't come for help until something gives, like being unable to cope with work, a big family gathering or the psychological strain of the two-week waiting period in IVF treatment. After embryo transfer, individuals have no way to predict the outcome and, to compound that, there is no reason to attend the clinic for any tests or procedures. Studies show that this is a particularly distressing time.

There are tips for dealing with stress everywhere, but I find the most important thing I can do with fertility stress is to help couples recognise the level of stress they are coping with and that these intense feelings are normal for the situation. When we are stressed our energy is sapped and we are less able to cope. Treatment may be ongoing, their batteries may be completely run down and they may be heading into another treatment. It is very difficult to have a normal life with ongoing treatment and without knowing it they may have pushed beyond their own human levels of stress. We have to work with this stress, not get rid of it or bury it. We have to acknowledge it. I can't stress enough that this is a very important step. If couples can see the stress that they are trying to manage it can help them to adjust their expectations of themselves. This in turn opens the door to looking at adjustments and strategies that will help them manage the next treatment or decisions that may have to be made.

The following stories are from two very different male clients that show that stress can manifest in many different ways.

Some time ago a male client presented with feeling low and not understanding what was wrong with him. It was just before his daughter's first birthday. He said, 'We have our little miracle and she is almost a year old, everything we ever wanted. Why am I not happy?' When we explored the previous few years there was massive loss, many treatments and miscarriages. His wife struggled physically and emotionally and he did his utmost to be strong and look after her, but he just felt helpless a lot of the time. It was useful for him to understand what he had been through. There is plenty of research in the area of loss that will support the importance of being able to put words to feelings. This is often the case when one has to be strong. Hopefully this man was able to go home with this understanding of himself and move forward with his family.

The other example is of a man who was angry and stressed all the time. He and his wife had had a few years of treatment resulting in many ectopic pregnancies and early miscarriages, which he felt were killing their relationship. He found that if there were any issues between them they got blown up out of all proportion. He tried to be strong for his wife but found it difficult when she directed her anger at him. He found himself explosive at work and resentful of others with children and hated himself for feeling this way. It was useful for him to express the pressure he felt. This couple went on to have their family but needed help through the difficult times.

The benefits of counselling

First I'd like to say a little bit about counselling to try to remove some of the secrecy and taboos. It is a practice that always takes place behind closed doors and people have different opinions on its value. Some think it is about 'tea and sympathy'; others think that counsellors 'listen and nod in all the right places' and 'give tips and advice'. To support couples/individuals having difficulties and treatment the counsellor needs the standard general training, but also lots of experience in the very specialised area of fertility. They need the training to know what may be happening with an individual (which the individual may not even be aware of), but they also need to be able to wear that expertise like an invisible cloak. No individual or couple trying to have a baby wants to be psychoanalysed. It is mainly about being human and working with where the individual/couple is at.

People with fertility issues commonly say 'How can counselling help me? All I want is to have a baby', 'I don't want my family background explored', etc. It is important to stress that fertility counselling is not therapy but could cross over into it if and when the need arises. What fertility counselling can do is offer very solid support when the going gets tough or the stress and struggle presses buttons of past unresolved issues. These could be, for example, parents' divorce, bullying in the past, a termination, previous failed relationships, rape or sexual abuse – and that's just the tip of the iceberg. Or there may be none of these issues in the background and it may be about helping people to make complex decisions, managing treatment and balancing life and work. Sometimes it can be as simple as sharing what other patients have found useful or a piece of research supporting that the person's reactions are normal.

I facilitate a fertility support group (not a therapy group) and it is proving to be a valuable asset for patients. We take feedback at the end of the evening and what patients say they are finding most helpful is the opportunity to be in the room with others who 'get it'. In the support group I facilitate rather than counsel. I provide the space for patients to support and share with each other.

As we have seen, the emotional consequences of trying to have a family can be a massive struggle for people. Many clients say that they become so consumed by the treatment that every area of their lives is affected, including their relationships and even their careers. They neglect areas of their lives, such as hobbies, thinking that it's only for a certain amount of time. The stress can build over time and they may have no outlet. Couples and individuals are often shocked when they realise after years that they have let time pass and built no memories. Having worked as a couples/relationship therapist for many years I encourage couples not to forget about their relationship and to build memories as they go along. They have no control over the outcome of treatment, but they do have control over other parts of their lives. It is very important that they attend to their own wellbeing and their relationship. They need to fill in dates on the calendar – dates that are not about conceiving. This may all seem very obvious, but sometimes it can take a couple of sessions working with individuals and couples to help them explore their lives. They can be shocked to realise the impact of treatment and how much is has taken over their lives and how they have actively avoided situations. They can become lost in getting through from one treatment/test/procedure to the next. I will always remember asking a patient many years after having her family about the emotional impact. 'We had an IVF marriage' was her answer. I think this is very telling; their lives at that time were consumed by IVF.

Most couples are optimistic when starting IVF. If treatment fails it is a painful process, but they must find the resilience to go on to have their family. Most clinics offer couples support and have counsellors available. Some couples and individuals avail of this immediately, others later in the process, and some may not want it at all. And, of course, many find the strength within that's needed to go on.

If you feel you might benefit from some support, think about seeing a fertility counsellor, either on your own or with your partner. Make sure the counsellor/psychotherapist has had a very solid training and is accredited by a reputable organisation, which will ensure the continued professional development of its members. Those seeking counselling need to shop around, as they would for any other professional, and be sure about that person's credentials, training and continued professional development.

Having a fertility problem and needing treatment is one of the most stressful situations you can find yourself in. Try to talk about it and don't underestimate the strain.

Donor treatments and counselling

When people meet their life partner they generally take it for granted that their children will be part of who they are genetically. When that proves not to be possible they can be devastated and go through a period of grieving. The idea of having a child at all can be questioned. Having to use another person's genes can seem appalling to some at first – the baby won't have 'my eyes', 'my Irish looks', it won't be 'a little me'.

After some time and healing they can begin to think again about having a child who will not be connected to them genetically and be open to looking at other options for becoming parents. In my opinion this is a very important time to have counselling. The counselling is vastly different for couples and individuals having a child with another person's genes. It is now implications counselling. The welfare of the possible child has to be a priority.

If the treatment involves an open or non-anonymous donor (e.g. in the UK and soon to be in Ireland), a donor-conceived child will be able to access information to identify the donor when they are 18 years of age. When people decide to have donor treatment where the donor will be anonymous (e.g. Spain, Czech Republic) there are many implications that need to be explored with a trained counsellor. It is of huge importance to be comfortable with decisions and feelings before starting treatment.

Donor Conception Network is a UK parent-run organisation that is over 20 years old, and which runs preparation weekends in the UK. This is a lovely way to meet others in a relaxed but structured way. As a counsellor working in this area I try to cover the following implications in a similarly relaxed but structured format.

- Their relationship – how they see it may or may not be affected; are they on the same page?
- How each person in a relationship might feel about the use of a third person's eggs or sperm or embryo.
- Thoughts about bonding with the child.
- Exploring feelings around the child being really theirs.
- What they intend to tell the child and the implications of that decision

- Do both partners agree?
- How/when they intend to tell the child – and others.
- What about left-over embryos?

I once worked with a woman who didn't allow herself to even think that donor treatment was different. This became a massive problem when she was about to have her embryo transfer. Travelling back to Ireland she began to have panic attacks and was filled with massive feelings of guilt. She came for help immediately and I was able to work with her to process what was happening. She needed to grieve the family she could not have in order to be able to go on to have a possible family through donor. I strongly believe that couples planning to have donor treatment need the best possible preparation so that they can be confident with their decisions.

Olivia Montuschi from Donor Conception Network reinforced this when speaking to the UK's fertility doctors: 'Donor conception is different to IVF treatments where there will be no genetic disconnect in the resulting family. Both clinicians and parents have a duty to keep in mind the needs of the future child and clinics have an important role to take in this. The seeds of good outcomes for adults are shown in the decisions taken before (and after) a child is conceived' (2.44).

Living and working arrangements

It might seem obvious, but in the sometimes crazy, hectic world we live in today, people's living and working arrangements can be a major contributor to infertility and difficulty conceiving.

Some people work very long hours and are exhausted all the time. It can be difficult to find time for exercise, relaxation or sex – or even to eat properly. I have seen couples where one partner is working away from home five days a week or they are both working different shifts or commuting for two hours at the beginning and end of every day. I have even seen couples trying to conceive when they are living in different countries. They try to meet up at weekends or during holiday time – but that may not coincide with when the woman is ovulating. Others are living with their parents or in a crowded house where there is little privacy. Couples with secondary infertility may have a disruptive child who has them exhausted. We have seen that, even for couples in more conducive circumstances, needing to have sex at particular times of the month or needing to attend doctors and clinics for tests and treatments can be extremely stressful. Add to that the challenges of these stressful living and working arrangements and it is not surprising that intimacy and general wellbeing go out of the window.

Sometimes people are so caught up in this crazy whirl that they don't actually see how their work or living arrangements are making things more difficult. Talking to a professional counsellor, or even discussing it together, can help highlight some of these issues. While you may not be able to change your job or change your house, the first step is to notice the problems and between you, you may be able to find ways to prioritise the things that are truly going to help you conceive.

Non-traditional relationships

Creating a baby requires a sperm from a man and an egg from a woman. Traditionally, this has meant that parenthood has been confined to couples in heterosexual relationships (even if that just lasted for the duration of one episode of sex). But not everyone is in a traditional heterosexual relationship. One of the great benefits of assisted reproduction is that it enables single people and couples in same-sex relationships to have children. However there are extremely complex social, emotional, legal and cost implications.

Not all single people or same-sex couples seek parenthood, and some others who do are raising children from previous heterosexual relationships or through adoption. However, a growing number now seek parenthood through reproductive technology. This coincides with the newfound openness and increased public acceptance of same-sex relationships and the legalisation of same-sex marriage in countries across the world. It is wonderful that Ireland is at the forefront of this liberalisation – though, sadly, reproductive services in Ireland currently lag behind other Westernised countries (see Section 5).

Same-sex or single-parent reproduction, by definition, requires a third party from the opposite sex to provide eggs or sperm and, in the case of single men or gay male couples, a surrogate is required to carry the pregnancy.

Single or lesbian women

For single women and women in lesbian relationships, the same medical issues with regard to female fertility 'fitness' apply as to all other women, i.e. the importance of female age, lifestyle issues, hormones and medical or gynaecological problems. However, the main difference is that these women need donor sperm. (Sperm donation is described in detail in Section 4.)

For a younger woman who does not have a male partner but who wishes to conceive, most clinics would initially do some investigations to ensure that the woman has no fertility-related issues herself. If she is ovulating regularly and has a normal pelvis and Fallopian tubes, IUI (intrauterine insemination, or artificial insemination) with donor sperm is usually the first line of treatment. For older women or women who have gynaecological or fertility-related issues, IVF is preferable and this is the same as for women in a heterosexual relationship, except that donor sperm is used rather than partner sperm. Some lesbian couples who require IVF may choose an option called 'reciprocal IVF', where one partner provides the eggs and the other partner carries the pregnancy.

Single or same-sex men

Men in a same-sex relationship or single men who wish to have a child will need to engage in a surrogacy arrangement in order to become a parent. This can be done via IUI or IVF. (Surrogacy is described in Section 4.)

This may be done by IUI, where the surrogate provides her own egg/s, or donor eggs may be used in addition to the male's/couple's sperm. If donor eggs are used, the surrogate has no genetic link to the child/children and IVF must be performed. In some cases male couples choose to have sperm from both partners fertilise the donated eggs before the embryo transfer to the surrogate. This allows them both to have their own genetic child. Some clinics overseas facilitate twin pregnancies in this way so that the twins born will be half siblings. It is debatable whether it is ethical to do this, given the increased risks of twin pregnancy for both the babies and the surrogate and I certainly would not support it.

Transgender people

Another group who are recently beginning to access fertility treatment and fertility preservation options are people who have gender dysphoria and are transitioning or have transitioned from male to female or female to male (i.e. transgender people). Reproductive options are diverse – although most transgender people will form heterosexual relationships after transition, many will not. Options for fertility include the following: when transgender males (female-to-male transgender) have a female partner, she may be inseminated with donor sperm. When transgender women (male-to-female transgender) have a male partner, they would need surrogacy and egg donation to have a child. Fertility preservation may be a method to help transgender people to have genetically related children in the future. Transgender males can, at least in theory, freeze eggs or ovarian tissue. For transgender women, sperm freezing is an option.

Psychosocial issues

The research that has been done on attitudes and emotional wellbeing in men, women and children involved in non-traditional family arrangements is very positive (see Section 5 for more details).

Studies show that gay males want to be fathers for the same reasons as heterosexual males (2.45). They have the desire to nurture children, want to achieve the sense of family that children provide, and to continue their family by having children. One study of motivation for parenthood compared 100 lesbian couples to 100 heterosexual couples and reported that lesbian mothers spent more time thinking about having children and that their desire for having children was stronger than the heterosexual mothers. Although adoption is a choice for parenthood for many gay men and women, research shows that lesbians who choose assisted reproduction over adoption often do so because one or both partners would like to carry a pregnancy and give birth. Gay men often choose assisted reproduction over adoption because one or both partners want to have a biological connection to the child.

Many people worry about the wellbeing of children born into same-sex or single-parent families. There is now a wealth of literature showing no significant differences between the children of gay and heterosexual parents. For example, a study of children of two-mother households found that they showed similar psychological adjustment to children of two-parent heterosexual households (2.46). A recent study of parent–child relationships in adoptive families compared 41 two-parent gay families, 40 two-parent lesbian families, and 49 two-parent heterosexual families. No differences were found between the gay and lesbian families, but compared with heterosexual families, gay fathers showed more positive functioning and less depression and stress associated with parenting (2.47).

There are presently hardly any follow-up studies regarding the psychological wellbeing of children born to transgender people. Although many transgender people already have children, the large majority were born before their parent's transition. Preliminary findings suggest that children adapt well, particularly if their parents have adapted well and if the child was younger at the time of transition. Children conceived by transgender people after their gender identity shift do not have to adapt to a new parental identity, which may well make things easier. Initial but very small studies suggest that the children are normal and happy (2.48).

The psychological effects of fertility preservation for transgender persons themselves are presently unknown. Some feel that freezing sperm for transgender females and freezing of oocytes or ovarian tissue for transgender males reinforces their former sex and does not fit with their new gender identity. Research is very much needed in this area.

The difficulties

Undoubtedly, embarking on treatment that involves donor eggs, donor sperm or surrogacy involves difficult decision-making, legal considerations, psychosocial demands, and considerable expense. Single and gay men and women face difficult decisions as they embark on reproductive treatments. Lesbians need to consider who will carry the pregnancy and whether they want a known or anonymous sperm donor. Gay men must make decisions about who will provide the sperm, whether they want a known or anonymous egg donor and how to find a gestational carrier. These issues are discussed in detail in Section 4 under third-party reproduction. Single parents need to ensure that they have the financial and social supports to rear a child or children on their own. Transgender situations are extremely complex.

Treatment is not easily accessible in Ireland, and surrogacy is particularly difficult. Donor treatments and surrogacy are banned in many countries (see Section 5). This can lead people to pursue unsafe and risky arrangements such as buying sperm over the internet or engaging in ad hoc personal arrangements where there is no medical supervision or legal certainty. I really don't think this is wise. Having and rearing a child is too important to take these risks. For this reason, most international bodies and fertility clinics highly recommend professional counselling for all those embarking on fertility treatments involving donor sperm, donor eggs or surrogacy, and I would certainly support that.

There is one aspect of reproduction for single people or same-sex couples where they seem to be at an advantage compared to heterosexual couples. Because people in these relationships can only reproduce using donor eggs or donor sperm or surrogacy, there is, of necessity, more openness in their relationships with friends, colleagues, family, etc. They are also likely to know others in a similar situation so they are more likely to feel supported than heterosexual couples. They are also less likely to suffer the feelings of inadequacy or self-doubt that those with medically related infertility experience. Talking to their children about their biological origins can also be easier as there is no way of hiding it and, also, their children are likely to be meeting lots of other (friends') children in similar situations.

Section 2 References

2.1   Menken, J., Trussell, J. and Larsen, U. (1986), 'Age and infertility'. *Science* 233(4771): 1389–94.

2.2   Baird, D. T., Collins, J., Egozcue, J. et al.; ESHRE Capri Workshop Group (2005) 'Fertility and ageing'. *Human Reproduction Update* 11(3): 261–76.

2.3   Central Statistics Office (2014) *Vital Statistics Annual Report.* Available at: http://www.cso.ie/en/releasesandpublications/ep/p-vsar/vsar2014/births2014/

2.4   Leridon, H. (2004) 'Can assisted reproduction technology compensate for the natural decline in fertility with age? A model assessment'. *Human Reproduction* 19(7): 1548–53.

2.5   van Noord-Zaadstra, B. M., Looman, C. W. N., Alsbach, H., Habbema, J. D. F., te Velde, E. R. and Karbaat, J. (1991) 'Delaying childbearing; effect of age on fecundity and outcome of pregnancy'. *British Medical Journal* 302: 1361–5.

2.6   Nybo Andersen, A., Wohlfahrt, J., Christens, P., Olsen, J. and Melbye, M. (2000) 'Maternal age and fetal loss: population based register linkage study'. *British Medical Journal* 320: 1708–12.

2.7   Franasiak, J. M., Forman, E. J., Hong, K. H. et al. (2014) 'The nature of aneuploidy with increasing age of the female partner: a review of 15,169 consecutive trophectoderm biopsies evaluated with comprehensive chromosomal screening'. *Fertility and Sterility* 101: 656–63.

2.8   Sharma, R., Agarwal, A., Rohra, V. K. et al. (2015) 'Effects of increased paternal age on sperm quality, reproductive outcome and associated epigenetic risks to offspring'. *Reproductive Biology and Endocrinology* 13: 35.

2.9   de La Rochebrochard, E., de Mouzon, J., Thepot, F. and Thonneau, P. (2006) 'Fathers over 40 and increased failure to conceive: the lessons of in vitro fertilization in France'. *Fertility and Sterility* 85: 1420–4.

2.10. Hassan, M. A. and Killick, S. R. (2003) 'Effect of male age on fertility: evidence for the decline in male fertility with increasing age'. *Fertility and Sterility* 79: 1520–7.

2.11   ASRM Practice Committee (2015) 'Obesity and reproduction: a committee opinion'. *Fertility and Sterility* 104: 1116–26.

2.12   Sim, K. A., Partridge, S. R. and Sainsbury, A. (2014) 'Does weight loss in overweight or obese women improve fertility treatment outcomes? A systematic review'. *Obesity Reviews* 15(10): 839–50.

2.13   Leese, H. J. (2014) 'Effective nutrition from conception to adulthood'. *Human Fertility* 17(4): 252–6.

2.14   Davidson, L. M., Millar, K., Jones, C., Fatum, M. and Coward, K. (2015) 'Deleterious effects of obesity upon the hormonal and molecular mechanisms controlling spermatogenesis and male fertility'. *Human Fertility* 18(3): 184–93.

2.15   Clark, A. M., Thornley, B., Tomlinson, L. et al. (1998) 'Weight loss in obese infertile women results in improvement in reproductive outcome for all forms of fertility treatment'. *Human Reproduction* 13(6): 1502–5.

2.16   Showell, M. G., Mackenzie-Proctor, R., Brown, J., Yazdani, A., Stankiewicz, M. T. and Hart, R. J. (2014) 'Anti-oxidants for male subfertility'. *Cochrane Database of Systematic Reviews*, December.

2.17   Showell, M. G., Brown, J., Clarke, J. and Hart, R. J. (2013) 'Anti-oxidants for female subfertility'. *Cochrane Database of Systematic Reviews*, August.

2.18   Orio, F., Muscogiuri, G., Ascione, A. et al. (2013) 'Effects of physical exercise on the female reproductive system'. *Minerva Endocrinologica* 38(3): 305–19.

2.19   Ferreira, L., Silveira, G. and Latronico, A. C. (2013) 'Approach to the patient with hypogonadotropic hypogonadism'. *Journal of Clinical Endocrinology and Metabolism* 98(5): 1781–8.

2.20   Augood, C., Duckitt, K. and Templeton, A. A. (1998) 'Smoking and female infertility: a systematic review and meta-analysis'. *Human Reproduction* 13(6): 1532–9.

2.21   Waylen, A. L., Metwally, M., Jones, G. L., Wilkinson, A. J. and Ledger, W. L. (2009) 'Effects of cigarette smoking upon clinical outcomes of assisted reproduction: a meta-analysis'. *Human Reproduction Update* 15(1): 31–44.

2.22   Pineles, B. L., Park, E. and Samet, J. M. (2014) 'Systematic review and meta-analysis of miscarriage and maternal exposure to tobacco smoke during pregnancy'. *American Journal of Epidemiology* 179(7): 807–23.

2.23   Sharma, R., Harlev, A., Agarwal, A. and Esteves, S. C. (2016) 'Cigarette smoking and semen quality: a new meta-analysis examining the effect of the 2010 World Health Organization laboratory methods for the examination of human semen'. *European Urology* 70(4): 635–45.

2.24   Hart, R. J., Doherty, D. A., Keelan, J. A. et al. (2016) 'Early life events predict adult testicular function; data derived from the Western Australian (Raine) birth cohort'. *Journal of Clinical Endocrinology and Metabolism* 101(9): 3333–44.

2.25   de Ziegler, D., Santulli, P., Seroka, A., Decanter, C., Meldrum, D. R. and Chapron, C. (2013) 'In women, the reproductive harm of toxins such as tobacco smoke is reversible in 6 months: basis for the "olive tree" hypothesis'. *Fertility and Sterility* 100(4): 927–8.

2.26   Coleman, T., Chamberlain, C., Davey, M. A., Cooper, S. E. and Leonardi-Bee, J. (2015) 'Pharmacological interventions for promoting smoking cessation during pregnancy'. *Cochrane Database of Systematic Reviews*, December.

2.27   Klonoff-Cohen, H., Lam-Kruglick, P. and Gonzalez, C. (2003) 'Effects of maternal and paternal alcohol consumption on the success rates of in vitro fertilization and gamete intrafallopian transfer'. *Fertility and Sterility* 79(2): 330–9.

2.28   Mikkelsen, E. M., Riis, A. H., Wise, L. A., Hatch, E. E., Rothman, K. J., Cueto, H. T. and Sørensen, H. T. (2016) 'Alcohol consumption and fecundability: prospective Danish cohort study'. *British Medical Journal* 354: i4262.

2.29   Jensen, T. K., Gottschau, M., Madsen, J. O., Andersson, A. M., Lassen, T. H., Skakkebæk, N. E., Swan, S. H., Priskorn, L., Juul, A. and Jørgensen, N. (2014) 'Habitual alcohol consumption associated with reduced semen quality and changes in reproductive hormones: a cross-sectional study among 1221 young Danish men'. *British Medical Journal Open* 4(9): e005462.

2.30   Nicolau, P., Miralpeix, E., Solà, I., Carreras, R. and Checa, M. A. (2014) 'Alcohol consumption and in vitro fertilization: a review of the literature'. *Gynecological Endocrinology* 30(11): 759–63.

2.31   Buck Louis, G. M., Sapra, K. J., Schisterman, E. F., Lynch, C. D., Maisog, J. M., Grantz, K. L. and Sundaram, R. (2016) 'Lifestyle and pregnancy loss in a contemporary cohort of women recruited before conception: the LIFE Study'. *Fertility and Sterility* 106(1): 180–8.

2.32   Klonoff-Cohen, H. (2005) 'Female and male lifestyle habits and IVF: what is known and unknown'. *Human Reproduction Update* 11(2): 179–203.

2.33   Domar, A. D., Zuttermeister, P. C. and Friedman, R. (1993) 'The psychological impact of infertility: a comparison with patients with other medical conditions'. *Journal of Psychosomatic Obstetrics and Gynaecology* 14 Suppl: 45–52.

2.34   Verhaak, C. M., Smeenk, J. M. J., van Minnen, A., Kremer, J. A. M. and Kraaimaat, F. W. (2005) 'A longitudinal, prospective study on emotional adjustment before, during and after consecutive fertility treatment cycles'. *Human Reproduction* 20(8): 2253–60.

2.35   Boivin, J. and Gameiro, S. (2015) 'Evolution of psychology and counseling in infertility'. *Fertility and Sterility* 104(2): 251–9.

2.36   Veloso Martins, M., Basto-Pereira, M., Pedro, J., Peterson, B., Almeida, V., Schmidt, L. and Costa, M. E. (2016) 'Male psychological adaptation to unsuccessful medically assisted reproduction treatments: a systematic review'. *Human Reproduction Update* 22(4): 466–78.

2.37   Rooney, K. L. and Domar, A. D. (2016) 'The impact of stress on fertility treatment'. *Current Opinion in Obstetrics and Gynecology* 28(3): 198–201.

2.38   Boivin, J., Griffiths, E. and Venetis, C. A. (2011) 'Emotional distress in infertile women and failure of assisted reproductive technologies: meta-analysis of prospective psychosocial studies'. *British Medical Journal* 23, 342: d223.

2.39   Verkuijlen, J., Verhaak, C., Nelen, W. L., Wilkinson, J. and Farquhar, C. (2016) 'Psychological and educational interventions for subfertile men and women'. *Cochrane Database of Systematic Reviews*, March.

2.40   Gameiro, S., Boivin, J. and Domar, A. (2013) 'Optimal in vitro fertilization in 2020 should reduce treatment burden and enhance care delivery for patients and staff'. *Fertility and Sterility* 100: 302–9.

2.41   Gameiro, S., Boivin, J., Dancet, E., de Klerk, C., Emery, M., Lewis-Jones, C., Thorn, P., Van den Broeck, U., Venetis, C., Verhaak, C. M., Wischmann, T. and Vermeulen, N. (2015) 'ESHRE guideline: Routine psychosocial care in infertility and medically assisted reproduction – a guide for fertility staff'. *Human Reproduction* 30(11): 2476–85.

2.42   Boden, J. (2007) 'When IVF treatment fails'. *Human Fertility* 10(2): 93–8.

2.43   Worden, J. (2009) Grief Counselling and Grief Therapy, London: Routledge.

2.44   Montuschi, O. (2016) 'Olivia Montushchi from DCN speaks at British Fertility Society conference' *DC Network Journal* 14: 4.

2.45   Greenfeld, D. A. and Seli, E. (2016) 'Same-sex reproduction: medical treatment options and psychosocial considerations'. *Current Opinion in Obstetrics and Gynecology* 28(3): 202–5.

2.46   Basker F. (2005). Lesbian mothers, gay fathers, and their children: a review. *Journal of Developmental and Behavioral Pediatrics* 26: 224–240.

2.47   Golombok, S., Mellish, S., Jennings, S., et al. (2014). Adoptive gay father families: parent & child relations and children's psychological adjustment. *Child Development* 85: 456–468.

2.48   Ethics Committee of the American Society for Reproductive Medicine. (2015) Access to fertility services by transgender persons: an Ethics Committee Opinion. *Fertil Steril*, 104: 1111–5

Fertility Problems

I nfertility is defined by the WHO (World Health Organisation) as 'a *disease* of the reproductive system defined by the failure to achieve a clinical pregnancy after 12 months or more of regular unprotected sexual intercourse'.

Traditionally it has been taught that people should try to conceive for at least a year before worrying that they might have a problem. And, in line with this, many studies in the past have shown that 80% of couples will conceive within one year of trying and 90% after two years. However, like most biological facts, life is not always that simple. As time goes on and more studies are done it is clear that the WHO definition does not fit everyone. Many organisations, e.g. the American Society for Reproductive Medicine (ASRM) also suggest that, if the woman is over 35, six months may be a more appropriate cut-off time than 12 months. That would be my opinion too as, all too often, time can march by and, before she knows it a woman is into her late thirties and early forties and time starts running out. Also some men and women will know that they have particular fertility-related issues before they even start trying to conceive e.g. women who have no periods, men who know they have a very low sperm count, women who have lost their Fallopian tubes due to ectopic pregnancies. These people don't need to wait a year to realise that they have a problem. Same-sex couples and single people also know that they don't need to wait a year before seeking help.

Other definitions

Subfertility: This term is used interchangeably with the term 'infertility'. Some people feel that subfertility is a more positive term because it suggests that a fertility problem is not absolute and can be treated. 'Infertility', on the other hand, can suggest that a person will never be capable of conceiving. I prefer the term 'subfertility' but, as infertility is more commonly used (e.g. in the WHO definitions) I have decided to use 'infertility' in this book.

Primary infertility: In medical or clinical terminology, this refers to a woman who has never been pregnant at all or a man who has never fathered a child (or had a partner who became pregnant).

Secondary infertility: In medical or clinical terminology, this refers to a woman who has been pregnant before – even if that pregnancy has not continued, i.e. has ended in miscarriage, biochemical pregnancy, ectopic pregnancy, termination. For a man it means that he has fathered children or had a partner who lost a pregnancy through miscarriage, etc.

'We have a two and half-year-old little girl who was conceived the first month after coming off the pill. Amazing! She was delivered by a planned C section as I had placenta praevia. We waited 12 months as advised after a section to try for baby number two. We conceived after four months of only half trying. This pregnancy ended after a torturous 12 weeks of bleeding and scans to determine that the baby had definitely died. After a D&C and a repeat D&C two months later as there was remaining product we braved trying again. 12 months later and we are still heartbroken. The uncertainty of not knowing why is very hard. To conceive so easily two times and to now face secondary infertility is heart-breaking.'

'As a mum of one, who had no issues getting pregnant first time, secondary infertility is very hard to get your head around and as clichéd as it sounds, I never expected it to happen to us.'

Infertility as a couple: if they have never had a pregnancy *together* we say they have primary infertility 'as a couple' even if one of them has had a pregnancy in a previous relationship.

Seeking help

As described above, the best time to seek help will depend on your individual situation. It is important that couples who are likely to have a problem are identified and seek treatment sooner rather than later but it is equally important that couples who have no problems are not dragged into the stress and expense of fertility investigations unnecessarily. I feel that the key is in identifying risk. Patients themselves, if armed with the correct information, are often the best people to determine this. Remember also that the man's history is just as important as the woman's. And, as always in medicine, getting the right balance is key.

When to seek help

The following are the main risk factors which might indicate an increased risk of fertility issues and should prompt early investigation.

RISK FACTORS

Female:

- Female age (over 35)
- Very infrequent periods (occurring every six weeks or even less often)
- Very irregular periods (with more than a week's variation from one to the next)
- Known endometriosis
- Known polycystic ovaries
- History of a sexually transmitted infection (such as chlamydia)
- History of pelvic surgery for ovarian cysts, fibroids, etc.
- History of having had an ovary removed
- History of ruptured appendix
- History of surgery for other conditions such as ulcerative colitis or Crohn's disease
- Obesity
- Family history of early menopause
- Cancer treatment
- Serious general medical problems

Men:

- Male age (over 45)
- History of testicular surgery as a child
- History of severe testicular injuries, e.g. sports injuries requiring medical care
- History of sexually transmitted infections (such as chlamydia)
- Cancer treatment
- Serious general medical problems
- History of testicular infections, e.g. mumps

If you are taking medications which need to be stopped prior to your pregnancy, consider talking to your doctor before you stop these medications as sometimes it will make more sense to have investigations done before you stop the treatment so that if there is a problem it can be diagnosed, investigated and addressed before you stop your medication.

Ask yourself three questions:

1) Is the female partner over 35 years or the male over 45?
2) Do I have any of the risk factors listed above?
3) Am I worried about anything?

If the answer to any of these questions is yes, it is better to go and have a chat with your doctor. You lose nothing by exploring your situation a little further.

Here are some patients' comments. You will see how quickly time passes!

'My advice to any couple that thinks they might have any fertility problems is to always speak to a professional, as there is always someone out there that can help them. I believe you need to be proactive with your reproductive health and get the answers sooner rather than later.'

'I have just turned 35, my husband is 32. We have been trying to conceive for a little over four years now. After the first year of trying I fell pregnant naturally but unfortunately miscarried after 7½ weeks.

We continued to try for another 6–8 months with no success and decided to visit a GP in a family planning clinic. He took basic blood tests to check my hormones and to see if I was ovulating, and referred my husband for semen analysis. Results for both myself and my husband came back normal. The GP said that he wasn't concerned and told us to keep on trying and in the meantime he would refer us to a fertility hospital, which could take up to 9–12 months to get an appointment as we opted to go public, but he was confident that we would conceive naturally in this time.

After about 9–10 months we received word of an appointment at the hospital and took it as unfortunately I was still not pregnant. More bloods were taken, I had an HSG [hysterosalpingogram] *(which I did privately due to waiting lists) and also underwent a hysteroscopy; all tests were done over a period of 6–7 months. We met with the doctor once all results had been gathered and we were diagnosed with unexplained infertility and the doctor advised that our best approach was IVF.*

We were referred to the MFC in February 2016, in April 2016 I started IVF treatment.'

'My husband and I had been trying for a baby for about three years. We took a really casual attitude to it as we expected it to be so easy. My life so far had been quite ordinary, I got a good job straight out of college, we were lucky to get a house in the area we always wanted to live in and we had a wonderful wedding. I just expected making a baby would just come easy to me and happen naturally. It was always in the back of my mind though … "It's not working – it should have worked by now". But I didn't say it out loud. I guess I didn't want it to be true. My cycles were always so irregular and I was eventually diagnosed with PCOS.'

'Before you arrive in the doctor's office you probably have gone up and down on the rollercoaster of not being pregnant each month for some time. I honestly thought, and we both did, that we would get pregnant on the first try. We were going to call our baby Boston as that's where we first tried to conceive ha ha. We started referring to the baby as Boston throughout the whole holiday. We tried plenty more times just to be sure. So when we got home and a few weeks passed my period came. I was disappointed but thought maybe the early starts and late nights and few extra drinks we were having didn't help. So we started trying again and again my period came. We felt a little deflated but said we would keep trying. Again my period came so we said that maybe we would just go see if everything was ok.'

'I still remember that day in Dr W.'s office where we were told we would need ICSI treatment. I literally couldn't believe it. I wrote notes but when I went to read them later all I had written was MFC in a circle like

a stamp over and over. It sounds like such a cliché but I just hadn't seen it coming. Things had never been better. That May we had been trying for a baby since August of the previous year but I wasn't too bothered, I was 31 when we started and thought it'll happen when it happens. In general up until this I had been fairly relaxed in my attitude to life.'

Table 3.1 When to Seek Help

	Situation	How long to wait
Female partner		
Under 35	None of above risk factors	1 year
35 – 37	None of above risk factors	6–12 months
38 and over	None of above risk factors	6 months
Any age	No periods or periods more than 2 months apart	Don't wait
Any age	One or more of above risk factors	3–6 months
Either partner		
Any age	On drugs that need to be stopped before pregnancy	See a doctor before you stop the drugs
Any age	Sexual problems	Don't wait
Male partner		
Any age	One or more of above risk factors	3–6 months

Where to seek help

The internet: Nowadays we probably all reach first for our phone or laptop and the internet to get a feel for an issue or problem. Fertility is no different. The internet is a fantastic tool – how did we manage without it? However, it has its drawbacks too. Sadly, in the area of infertility there is a huge amount written on the internet – some of it excellent but some of it irresponsible, not based on fact and completely misleading.

Sites that I would recommend are listed at the end of this book. Hopefully, this book will also help.

'I find it hard to understand all the blood results, scans, lining thickness and why we aren't pregnant! You learn all the new language, hysteroscopy,

HCG, luteal phase, TSI, IUI versus IVF! I try to avoid the internet but it seems to be the only way to interpret the results and to try and process all this new information.'

'If you don't get the answer you need or you have a clash of personality with someone, try someone else. Avoid the internet as your source of information. Each person is different, each experience is different, each medication that you are prescribed will be based on your case. Referring to parenting sites and comparing yourself to other women is not going to help you. We all do it but try to keep things in perspective. Ask your medical team for their advice. Ultimately it should be the best.'

GP/family doctor: For most people in Ireland the first port of call would be their general practitioner. If you have a GP you have been attending for a while, that is ideal as they will know your history and any medical issues that may be pertinent to you or your partner. GPs can have a very good overview of your entire situation and would be able to advise as to whether you should be concerned. Also, your family doctor is usually best placed to give advice on services in your local area. Not only do they know your history, but they will have other patients with similar problems and will have experience of helping them and of local services. GPs can also order preliminary tests such as hormone tests, smear tests and chlamydia tests. Generally there is no charge for these tests if they are organised by your GP. Ultrasound scans and semen analysis can also be arranged by the GP, but it is important that these are done by a centre that specialises in fertility. At Merrion Fertility Clinic we prefer to do our own ultrasound scans and our own semen analysis as these are tests that rely on the assessment of the individual doing the test, so different operators in different services will get slightly different results. This is not the case with blood tests, where there is one result and one result only.

Family planning clinics: If you do not feel comfortable discussing fertility with your family doctor, consider other places, such as your local hospital, a fertility clinic or a family planning clinic. However, attending a hospital or fertility clinic can be stressful and it is not always necessary, so I would recommend seeing your family doctor initially. A GP referral is also usually required for a hospital clinic or consultant. Some women will have attended a family planning clinic rather than their GP over the years, as, for many young women, their main medical requirement is for things such as contraception and smear tests. Family planning clinics often offer 'well women' services and will be able to arrange the same kind of investigations as GPs.

Hospitals and consultants: Once you have been seen by your GP or family planning clinic, it would be usual for the doctors there to do some preliminary tests and offer advice, and then, if there is no obvious solution, to refer you to what we call second-level care. This would be at a hospital, a gynaecologist's practice or a fertility clinic. Fertility services in hospitals are generally provided by obstetrician gynaecologists. All our large hospitals in Ireland provide a gynaecology service and most of the smaller hospitals do too. Your local GP is best placed to advise you of local services. However, some hospitals have more specialised services than others and if there is a hospital close to you which has a dedicated fertility clinic this is probably the best choice.

Hospitals provide public services and this is where you need to go if you want to access public care. Irish hospitals that currently provide dedicated fertility services include: the National Maternity Hospital in Holles Street; the Coombe University Women's Hospital; the Rotunda Hospital; Galway University Hospital; and Cork University Hospital. Some endocrinologists will also provide investigations and treatments. Other hospitals will have gynaecology services which can organise laparoscopies, scans and semen analysis. Private fertility care generally happens with private gynaecologists or fertility clinics. As with public gynaecological clinics, some gynaecologists specialise in infertility and its management and others have different interests. Most gynaecologists will perform laparoscopies and can help assess your situation. They generally, however, end up referring you on to a fertility clinic or fertility specialist if you need treatment such as ovulation induction or assisted reproduction such as IUI and IVF. Some gynaecologists (e.g. in Holles Street and Merrion Fertility Clinic) work in fertility clinics both publicly and privately.

If you are really worried, and especially if you have a complicated medical history, by all means go straight to a gynaecologist (for women), urologist (for men) or a fertility clinic. Also, if you have been attending your

GP or gynaecologist/urologist unsuccessfully for longer than six months it is probably wise to get an opinion from a fertility specialist.

Dedicated fertility clinics: There are several fertility clinics around the country which offer fertility treatments including assisted reproduction. These include:

- Merrion Fertility Clinic, a not-for-profit fertility clinic attached to the National Maternity Hospital, Holles Street.
- Cork Fertility Centre, which has clinics in Cork, Limerick and Waterford. Some of its doctors also work at Cork University Hospital.
- Galway Fertility Clinic, some of whose doctors also work at Galway University Hospital.
- Rotunda IVF, which operates independently of the Rotunda Hospital and has links with Sims IVF.
- Sims IVF, a large private fertility clinic in Dublin and Cork.
- Beacon Care Fertility, a subsidiary of Beacon Care UK, which operates at the Beacon Clinic in Sandyford.
- ReproMed, which has clinics in Dublin, Kilkenny, Limerick and Cork.
- Institute Marques in Clane, part of a Spanish group.
- Femplus in Dublin, which offers a smaller range of services.

All these clinics offer slightly different services but all of them have websites detailing their services. My own clinic, Merrion Fertility Clinic, is attached to a public teaching hospital and is not for profit.

> *'What I found most beneficial during the treatment is the access we have to the fertility specialists at the clinic. During the three years of trying I felt very alone during the whole process. I am very bad at communicating my feelings and I am trying to get better at this. Knowing that we have help now is such a weight off my shoulders and it helps me to stay positive. In an ideal world we would all prefer to not need fertility assistance, but when it is actually needed, having this help is a godsend. Fingers crossed this works for us.'*

Initial investigations

The first thing that needs to be done is for a doctor to take a full medical history and look at your individual situation. That will prompt appropriate tests and plans for treatment.

When I see a couple for the first time, a few simple key points go through my head and this helps me focus:

1) Is the woman ovulating?
2) Does the man have healthy sperm?
3) Are they having sex around ovulation time?
4) Is there anything in the woman's pelvis to stop the sperm and egg meeting and fertilising?

Those are the simple basics needed to conceive. Then I go into the finer detail of things that will affect those basic requirements:

1) The woman's age.
2) The woman's ovarian reserve.
3) How long they have been trying to conceive.
4) The woman's overall health, e.g. weight, smoking, exercise, medical history.
5) The man's overall health, e.g. weight, smoking, exercise, medical history.
6) The couple's views on fertility investigation and treatment.
7) The cost of the investigations and treatment and the couple's ability to pay.

Once I have this information I can plan what tests will help and what general approach to take for that particular couple. Sometimes it is easy – there is an obvious problem and I and the couple agree on a course of action. Other times the couple may have attended somewhere else and have had lots of treatments already without success. Or there may be no obvious simple problem and consequently no simple solution. This can be extremely frustrating for me – but most of all for the couple.

In order to save time for patients, our practice at Merrion Fertility Clinic is to offer some baseline tests prior to the patient's first visit so that these can be discussed at the first consultation.

Female tests

Blood tests

I have summarised the main blood tests that we do in Table 3.2. Most of these are hormone tests that can be organised by your GP. The table gives the details of when and why we do these blood tests. Further details about the actual testing process are given below. Some must be done on certain days of your menstrual cycle; for other hormones the day of the cycle doesn't matter – see the table. It is useful to look at the graph of the hormone changes in the menstrual cycle (page 10) as this helps to explain why we test certain hormones at certain times. If you have no periods, hormone tests can be done on any day of the cycle. Because the oral contraceptive pill (or indeed any hormonal treatment) interferes with ovulation, tests done while on these medications will not give a true reflection of the woman's hormone profile and so the woman needs to be off the pill or other hormones for about three months before having hormone tests done. (The only exception to this is when we are checking progesterone levels in women who are taking drugs such as Clomid to stimulate ovulation.)

In other situations blood tests may be required to look for signs of infection (rubella, chicken pox, cytomegalovirus (CMV)) or genetic problems (chromosomes) or immune system problems. These are discussed in the sections dealing with these conditions but are mentioned in the table. Not all these tests are available from your GP and some must, by law, be done by a fertility clinic.

Progesterone

As we saw in Section 1, this is a key component of fertility. If the woman is ovulating regularly it is highly likely that all her reproductive hormones are normal and there is no real need to do lots of hormone tests at this stage. Tests to check for ovulation include hormone tests and scans to look at the woman's ovaries.

Table 3.2 Blood Tests for Women

Test	Why it's done	Day of cycle
Progesterone	Is the woman ovulating?	7 days before next period
Prolactin	Why is the woman not ovulating? Irregular cycle and headaches or visual problems	Any day
Test	Why it's done	Day of cycle
FSH	Why is the woman not ovulating? Check ovarian reserve Possible PCOS Possible hypo hypo	Day 3 (2–4) if woman has a cycle
LH	Why is the woman not ovulating? Possible PCOS Possible hypo hypo	Day 3 (2–4) if woman has a cycle
AMH	Why is the woman not ovulating? Check ovarian reserve	Any day
Testosterone	Possible PCOS	Day 3 (2–4) if woman has a cycle
Androstenedione	Possible PCOS	Any day
TSH, T4, TPO antibodies	Why is the woman not ovulating? Routine screen for healthy pregnancy	Any day
Oestrogen	Why is the woman not ovulating? Sometimes helpful in early menopause or hypo hypo	Day 3 (2–4) if woman has a cycle
Rubella	Routine screen for healthy pregnancy	Any day
Hepatitis and HIV	Mandatory screen for ART treatments	Any day, but within 3 months of treatment Must be done by fertility clinic
Auto-immune tests	Recurrent miscarriage Some cases of IVF failure	Any day – must be 6 weeks after pregnancy or miscarriage
Genetic tests	Recurrent miscarriage No periods Premature ovarian insufficiency	Any day

Some women know if they are ovulating from urinary LH kits and if these show definite ovulation around mid-cycle, that is sufficient. However, the most reliable test is a blood test for the hormone progesterone. As described under ovulation, progesterone rises after ovulation and reaches its peak about a week after ovulation. A blood test at this time should show a high progesterone level. Different laboratories vary but generally a level over 20 pmol per litre is regarded as evidence of ovulation. Some clinics insist on a much higher progesterone level but I am not aware of any robust scientific evidence to state that a high level is necessary for normal conception.

It is critical that the test for progesterone is correctly timed, and this can be difficult, leading to erroneous results. If it is not done seven days following ovulation the result can be inconclusive. A level over 20 always indicates ovulation so at this level we don't need to be concerned about whether the timing was right, but a low result is only of value if it has been timed correctly. If you don't know when you are ovulating, you won't be able to calculate seven days after ovulation, but this is also seven days before your next period, so that is what we go by. That is fine if your period is regular:

- For a 26-day cycle, do blood test on Day 19
- For a 28-day cycle, do blood test on Day 21
- For a 32-day cycle, do blood test on Day 25
- For a 35-day cycle, do blood test on Day 28

If your cycle varies e.g. from 26 to 35 days, it may be best to check on two days, e.g. Day 20 and Day 27.

Usually a day or two either side doesn't make a big difference, so if the chosen day (e.g. Day 21) falls on a Saturday we generally advise having the test done on the Friday before; and if it falls on a Sunday, have the test the following Monday. However, being out by three or more days will give an erroneous result.

Another piece of advice – while the cut-off for ovulation on the test report may be 20, most women who are *not* ovulating have very low levels of progesterone, i.e. less than 10. If you get a result 'around' 20 (e.g. 17), you should repeat the test on your next cycle because it is very likely that you are ovulating and the test was just done a day or two outside the ideal time.

If the woman is not ovulating: If the progesterone has been done at the right time of your cycle and it does not show ovulation, then other hormone tests and scans may need to be done to see why. The most common reason is polycystic ovaries (PCOS), but we are also checking for hypo hypo, early menopause and other less common hormone problems which can interfere with ovulation. These conditions are all described later.

Prolactin

Prolactin can be tested on any day of the woman's menstrual cycle as it doesn't vary throughout the cycle. High stress levels, however, can cause it to be raised, so it is one of those tests that should be repeated if the first level comes back high. Often the first test is done just after the woman has been discussing her fertility concerns and this can be enough to increase the prolactin level. If it is repeated a few weeks later on a less stressed day it may be normal. Some labs report both prolactin and macroprolactin levels in their results . Macroprolactin is inactive prolactin hormone so, if this is high, it is not a problem.

FSH

It is absolutely critical that FSH (follicle-stimulating hormone) blood tests are done at the correct time of the cycle. This is ideally on the third day of the woman's period. If this is a Saturday or Sunday, day two or four is okay. If the woman has no periods a random FSH level can be taken. FSH goes up as women approach menopause, so we are hoping for a low level between 2.6 and 8 IU/L. However, we also know that FSH naturally goes up just prior to ovulation so it should not be measured at this time. Also, you can see from the diagram on page 10 that FSH is low after ovulation so, again, this is not the correct time to measure it – never have it done on Day 21.

LH

LH (luteinising hormone) varies a lot throughout the woman's cycle so its timing is important too. We usually look at FSH and LH levels together, and even the ratio of one to the other, so LH should be tested at the same time as FSH.

AMH

AMH does not vary significantly throughout the woman's menstrual cycle, so the timing of the test is not so critical. However, it can be influenced by the oral contraceptive pill and other hormones so it should really be done when the woman is not taking any other hormones. AMH is discussed in more detail later.

Testosterone, androstenedione

These hormones are mainly relevant to women with PCOS or women with hirsutism (excess facial hair). They are best tested at the same time as FSH and LH (Day 2–4 of cycle), but this is less critical than for FSH and LH.

TSH and TPO antibodies

TSH (thyroid-stimulating hormone) and T4 (thyroid hormone) reflect thyroid function and some women with thyroid disease can have elevated thyroid antibodies (TPO abs). Thyroid hormones do not vary significantly throughout the woman's menstrual cycle and so can be tested any day.

Oestrogen

Oestrogen levels vary considerably throughout the menstrual cycle and tests are not particularly useful unless a woman is not ovulating. Their main role is during fertility treatments to monitor the response of the ovaries, but during a natural cycle this is not of much benefit. If oestrogen levels are being tested, timing is critical, depending on why the level is being checked.

Rubella and other infections

Because rubella (German measles) in pregnancy can cause foetal abnormalities, it is recommended that teenagers are vaccinated and that all women trying to conceive ensure that they are immune to (protected against) infection in pregnancy. All hospitals check this in all pregnant women, so you may have had the test done already. Similar tests can be done for less common infections such as chicken pox, CMV and parvovirus.

Hepatitis and HIV

Under EU law it is compulsory for anyone having treatment involving their eggs, sperm or embryos being used for fertility treatment (IUI, IVF, egg freezing, sperm freezing) to be screened for current or past hepatitis or HIV (AIDS) infection. This is important to protect all tissues in the laboratory, and patients and staff, from cross-contamination or infection. Current rules are that the tests must be done within three months of giving the sample of sperm or eggs and that they must be done by the clinic performing the treatment.

Autoimmune tests

These tests are very controversial and are discussed in detail in the section on immune system disorders. If they are being done to investigate recurrent miscarriages (the most common reason), they must not be done for at least six weeks after the pregnancy or miscarriage or the results will not be valid. It can also take a few weeks to get a result, and these are expensive tests.

Genetic tests

These may be recommended for women with absent periods, early ovarian insufficiency or recurrent miscarriage. They may also be done if you have a family history of genetic disorders or, in some cases, of cancer, particularly breast cancer. See later sections on these conditions. These tests are expensive and specialised and may be difficult to arrange via your GP.

Ultrasound scans

I sometimes ask doctors in training, if they could do one test for a woman who comes to a fertility clinic, what would it be? My answer is an ultrasound.

A well-done pelvic ultrasound is probably the most useful test that we can do for any woman. It tells us about her ovaries, her ovarian reserve, her uterus, her Fallopian tubes and can even give clues to pelvic pain and problems with sex.

It is preferable that the ultrasound is performed vaginally. An abdominal ultrasound involves placing a probe on the woman's abdomen and looking at her pelvic organs through her abdominal wall. However, a trans-vaginal scan gets closer to the woman's uterus and the ovaries and so gives more detail. Trans-vaginal scanning may feel a little bit strange or uncomfortable but it should not be painful. The probe is generally the size of a tampon and can be inserted easily into most women's vaginas. To put it in context, it is generally more comfortable than a smear test. Studies in the past have shown that women find trans-vaginal scans very comfortable. An abdominal scan requires a full bladder and most women find that this makes abdominal scanning more uncomfortable than vaginal scanning.

Things you see on the vaginal scan include the woman's ovaries, her uterus and possibly her Fallopian tubes. I will mention the main things we look for here but, for more detail, look at the sections on the individual topics such as endometriosis or PCOS.

Ovaries

On the ovaries we are able to see **ovarian cysts** clearly and also get an indication as to whether these cysts are simple or more complex. More complex cysts would include endometriosis or dermoid cysts. Typically these tend to appear grey and grainy on a scan whereas simple cysts related to ovulation appear black (because they contain clear fluid, which shows up black on an ultrasound scan).

We can also estimate a woman's **ovarian reserve** by counting the number of antral follicles (which contain eggs) in her ovaries. We like to see six or seven of these small follicles on each ovary and a normal **antral**

follicle count (AFC) would be regarded as approximately 14. The count takes in the number of follicles in each ovary, so if there are six on one ovary and seven on the other, the antral follicle count is 13.

Ultrasound is an excellent way to detect **polycystic ovaries**, where we see more than 12 follicles and they tend to be arranged around the edge of the ovary like a 'string of pearls'.

Normal ovary and polycystic ovary

Sometimes women may become concerned if their ovaries are not seen on scan. This can happen on occasion if there is a lot of gas in your bowel and, in women who are not concerned about their fertility, it really is nothing to worry about. If there is a cyst there, we will see it. In a woman who is trying to conceive, however, we need to be sure that her ovarian reserve is normal, as a small ovary that is difficult to see may be one that has lost or is losing all its eggs. Other tests for ovarian reserve should be done and the ultrasound should be repeated.

Scans to check ovulation: By performing serial scans during a woman's cycle we can see if and when she ovulates. This is called a **tracking cycle**. Usually at least three scans are required, in some cases six or seven. This makes a tracking cycle costly, not just financially but also in terms of your time. We therefore only recommend this in cases where it really is hard to know from the woman's cycle and from her hormone test results whether she is ovulating and when. See also the sections on ovulation induction, IVF and monitoring the woman's response to fertility drugs.

Uterus (womb)

Ultrasound is an excellent way to look at a woman's uterus. We can measure the size of the uterus and look at its texture. We see fibroids and with good quality scanning we should be able to assess their size and location, though MRI scanning (see page 153) gives more information and is better for complicated cases. In some cases we may get a suspicion of adenomyosis or congenital abnormalities of the shape of the uterus but, again, MRI is better for this.

The lining of the uterus (endometrium): This is very important for fertility as the embryo (whether with natural conception or IVF) needs to be able to implant there and grow. The lining changes during the menstrual cycle. In the first few days, around the time of menstruation, it tends to be thin (2–5 mm) and we may see some blood in the uterus. Then, as we get closer to ovulation the lining of the womb gets thicker (6–12 mm) and develops what we call a triple line on ultrasound. This is a sign that the woman is about to ovulate and that her endometrium or lining of the womb is responding appropriately to her hormones. After ovulation the triple line disappears and the woman's lining becomes thicker in anticipation of a pregnancy.

If the lining of the uterus is irregular it may suggest that there is a fibroid, a polyp or some scarring in the uterus. A saline scan, HyCoSy (see page 151) or hysteroscopy is generally required to further elucidate this. Sometimes after a previous Caesarean section, the scar in the uterus where the incision was made to take the baby out may be visible. Unless the uterus appears very thin at this site, this is nothing to worry about.

Fallopian tubes

Fallopian tubes are fine structures and are generally not visible on ultrasound scans. If they are visible it is a sign that they may be diseased – see hydrosalpinx on page 212.

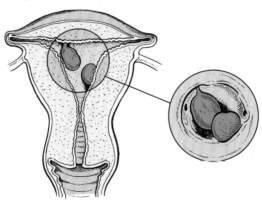

Endometrial polyps

Movement in the pelvis

Generally the ovaries, tubes and uterus should be quite mobile in a woman's pelvis and her bowel lies around these structures and can be seen contracting or moving during an ultrasound scan. However, in cases where the woman has endometriosis or severe pelvic adhesions (scarring), the pelvic organs may not slide normally over each other and the bowel and may appear 'fixed' or stuck. To see this requires a highly skilled ultrasonographer and is termed 'absence of a sliding sign'.

Pain

As stated above, a trans-vaginal ultrasound scan should not be painful. If the woman notices pain in any particular region or a particularly tender spot, it may be a sign of endometriosis, an ovarian cyst or adhesions. Women with vaginismus may find insertion of the probe painful or impossible. Sometimes if insertion is painful, it may be easier for the woman to insert it herself rather than the ultrasonographer.

Saline scan

Even though we commonly talk about the uterus or womb having a 'cavity' where the embryo implants, in fact, in its normal state, the walls of the womb lie up against each other and there is no space or cavity as such. This causes a bit of compression and can make it difficult to see abnormalities in the lining, e.g. polyps. By injecting a small amount of fluid (saline) into the womb, the walls are separated and any irregularity becomes much more obvious. This can be very useful for assessing polyps, fibroids or scarring. A speculum is used, as for a smear test, and a very fine catheter is inserted into or through the cervix (neck of the womb) and the fluid is injected using a syringe (no needle). It can be a bit uncomfortable and we generally recommend that the woman takes paracetamol or a mild painkiller about two hours before the procedure, but it is generally very well tolerated and the woman can go back to work, driving, etc. very soon afterwards.

As the saline is injected into the uterus, some of it passes out through the woman's Fallopian tubes. It may be possible to see this and to determine if the tubes are blocked or open, but it is difficult, and HyCoSy (contrast sonography) or HSG are better for assessing the tubes.

Tests for tubal patency

In order to check that there is no blockage in the woman's Fallopian tubes, dye must be inserted via the cervix and uterus into the tubes and it must be demonstrated to come out the end of the tubes. This may be done by laparoscopy (see page 153), HyCoSy (contrast sonography) or HSG.

HyCoSy or contrast sonography

This is similar to a saline scan but involves injecting a specially formulated dye rather than saline into the uterus. Its full name is **hy**sterosalpingo **con**trast **son**ography. The dye shows up clearly on the ultrasound scan. If the Fallopian tubes are healthy and open, the dye will be seen flowing freely out of the ends, whereas if they are blocked there will be no spillage. If the tubes are swollen and dilated (hydrosalpinx) they will fill with dye and be obviously abnormal.

Hysterosalpingogram (HSG)

A hysterosalpingogram is a test performed predominately to check that the woman's Fallopian tubes are not blocked or swollen and dilated. An examination similar to a smear test is performed. A speculum is inserted into the woman's vagina and a very fine catheter is inserted into or through her cervix. Some dye is injected through this and then X-rays are taken to show the dye going into her uterus and tubes and outlining the Fallopian tubes. If the test is normal the dye will be seen to pass into the Fallopian tubes and over approximately half an hour or so it will be seen to pass out through the Fallopian tubes and disappear. If the tubes are blocked the dye will not pass through, and if the tubes are swollen and dilated (i.e. a hydrosalpinx) this will show up as distended on the X-ray.

HyCoSy or HSG

Lots of studies have been done to ascertain whether HSG or HyCoSy (or contrast sonography) is better. Both use dye but one uses ultrasound to see the effect and the other uses X-ray. Like many issues, the results are inconclusive. My assessment of these studies is that both seem to be equivalent in terms of efficacy but that different practitioners and institutions will tend to have more experience with one or other test and therefore be better at their preferred method. HyCoSy or contrast sonography has the advantage of not requiring X-ray and of doing an ultrasound scan of the ovaries, etc. at the same time, but HSG produces images which are less dependent on the skill of the operator.

Risks are minimal with any of these procedures. Some information leaflets will mention perforation of the uterus with the catheter, but I have never seen this happen and even doubt that it is possible because the catheters are so small and soft. There is a very small risk of introducing infection into the uterine cavity or the Fallopian tubes. This is highly unlikely if the operator uses appropriate measures to ensure sterility (handwashing, clean instruments, etc.). However, there is a chance that bacteria or organisms present in the woman's vagina could be flushed or pushed into her uterus or tubes. This is particularly a risk if the woman has chlamydia organisms in her cervix. For this reason, some hospitals and clinics (such as ours) recommend one precautionary dose of an antibiotic prior to the test.

Need to avoid pregnancy

Because some of these tests (saline scan/HyCoSy/HSG) involve injecting fluid into the woman's uterus, it is essential that there is no chance of her being pregnant when the procedure is done. If there were an early pregnancy in the uterus, injecting fluid could disrupt or damage this. In addition, with HSG, the early pregnancy would be exposed to damaging X-rays.

In order to avoid this, most hospitals and clinics will only perform these tests in the first eight to ten days of the woman's cycle as she will not be pregnant at this time. Alternatively, the woman needs to confirm absolutely that she has avoided pregnancy by abstaining from sex or using adequate protection (e.g. condoms) since the start of her last menstrual period. In a woman with no menstrual cycle or periods, she needs to avoid pregnancy (by abstaining from sex or using adequate protection) for at least two weeks prior to the test and then perform a pregnancy test prior to the test. A pregnancy test of itself on the day of the procedure is not sufficient if pregnancy has not been avoided for the previous two weeks as it will only be reliably positive two weeks after ovulation.

MRI scans

Magnetic resonance imaging (MRI) is a type of scan that uses strong magnetic fields and radio waves to produce detailed images of the inside of the body. In gynaecology patients, it can be very useful for the following reasons:

- To delineate the exact size and location of fibroids in the uterus
- To differentiate different types of ovarian cysts (e.g. endometriosis and dermoid cysts)
- To look at small pathologies that may not be seen on ultrasound (e.g. small deposits of endometriosis)
- To look at abnormalities of the shape of the uterus

MRI scans are expensive and should only be used where an ultrasound does not give sufficient detail. Some patients find them difficult because they involve lying in a tunnel-like enclosure, which can cause feelings of claustrophobia.

Laparoscopy

Laparoscopy is probably the best way to evaluate a woman's pelvis, but because it involves surgery and a general anaesthetic it is not suitable for all women. It involves placing a telescope (laparoscope) through the umbilicus (belly button) to view inside the abdomen and pelvis. The laparoscope is attached to a camera and the image is transmitted to a screen.

A laparoscopy is usually done under general anaesthetic. Some surgeons and gynaecologists insert the telescope directly through a 5–10 mm incision (cut) in the umbilicus or belly button, while others first place a small needle into the abdomen. The abdomen is then distended with gas (carbon dioxide) and then the telescope is inserted. Once the telescope has been inserted, gas is maintained in the abdomen throughout the procedure to lift up the abdominal wall so that the structures underneath can be evaluated. It also reduces the risk of injury to the internal organs.

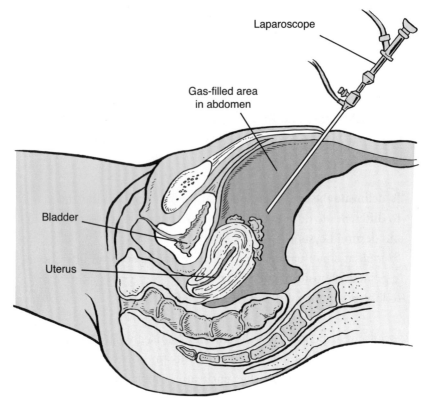

Laparoscopy and uterus

Instruments that may be used during surgery are put in through other small cuts made above the pubic hairline or on either side or in the lower half of the abdomen. These small cuts (usually 5mm wide) are usually closed with stitches. An instrument is passed through the cervix (neck of the womb) to allow the uterus to be manipulated to aid inspection of the entire pelvis. A dye may be passed through this to test the patency of the Fallopian tubes. Hysteroscopy (see page 156) may be done at the same time. Laparoscopy is usually performed as a day case but most women will require a week off work (and sometimes two) following the procedure.

Laparoscopy allows the gynaecologist to check for endometriosis, pelvic infection, pelvic scarring, etc. and to perform surgery. This is the only way to diagnose mild endometriosis and is also excellent in evaluating Fallopian tubes as the entire tube can be seen. With HyCoSy or HSG only the inner outline of the tube which has been filled with dye is seen. Subtle abnormalities such as small adhesions or damage to the lining of the tube will not be seen without laparoscopy.

When a laparoscopy is being performed it should be done with a view to treating any disease at the time of the surgery. In the past it was used purely for diagnosis, but this is not considered appropriate practice any more. Current international guidelines suggest that laparoscopy should only be performed if a significant pelvic problem is suspected either from the woman's history or her tests such as ultrasound or HSG/HyCoSy. See later sections on pelvic pathologies and treatments that can be performed at laparoscopy.

Like any operation or surgery involving a general anaesthetic, there are risks associated with laparoscopy. Insertion of the telescope or needle can inadvertently damage the underlying bowel or blood vessels. Surgery around the bladder and ureters can also damage these structures. Putting an instrument through the cervix into the uterus can rarely cause a perforation (puncture) of the uterus or a laceration (tear) of the cervix. There may also be a risk of infection and risks of chest and lung problems related to the anaesthetic. Risks are greater in women who have previously had surgery, women who are very thin, women who are overweight or smoke and those with medical problems. Complications from laparoscopy very rarely result in major surgery such as bowel surgery, hysterectomy, blood transfusion (approx. 1 in 700) or death (approx. 1 in 10,000).

As with other invasive procedures, it is essential that the woman is not already pregnant when having a laparoscopy. This might seem ridiculous to fertility patients who have been trying for a long time to conceive and who 'can't', but it happens. I have seen several occasions where women have been inadvertently pregnant when having a procedure. Here is one woman's experience of laparoscopy:

'She explained what it was and, as brave a face as I put on, I was scared of it. I'd never had surgery before so didn't know if I'd be able. I went in that morning to have my operation and wasn't nervous, I just wanted it done. All of the staff and everyone were so nice and I woke up after

the operation and felt only mild pain which was taken care of straight away. I honestly made it out in my head to be worse that it was. I was a tiny bit sore but was up walking around when I got home. Within a few days I was out walking to the shops and a week later I was feeling healed up. Within two weeks I felt back to myself and we were heading off on holidays to Portugal.'

Hysteroscopy

A hysteroscopy is a minor surgical procedure which involves gently passing a small telescope (hysteroscope) through the vagina and cervix into the womb to visualise the inside of the uterine cavity. The hysteroscope is attached to a camera and the image is transmitted to a screen. The uterus is usually filled with fluid to distend it, allowing the operator to see more clearly.

Diagnostic hysteroscopy is often done in conjunction with laparoscopy to determine if the shape of the cavity is normal and that the lining looks normal. It may be done to investigate unusual vaginal bleeding, miscarriage or suspected fibroids, polyps or scarring. Surgery can be performed in these situations.

Because of new technologies and very small hysteroscopes, it is now possible to do most diagnostic and several operative procedures as an outpatient, without general anaesthesia. Outpatient hysteroscopy is not usually painful but can be a little uncomfortable (causing period-type cramping). The advantage of outpatient hysteroscopy is avoiding a general anaesthetic, thereby avoiding a hospital stay and the inherent risks of an anaesthetic. If significant surgery is planned or if the procedure is expected to be difficult or painful, anaesthesia will generally be required.

Hysteroscopy is safe and complications are very rare, especially in the outpatient setting. Those that have been reported include injury to the cervix or uterus, infection and bleeding.

Infection screening

Infections relevant to fertility are described later in this section. Bacterial infections such as candida (thrush), trichomonas and bacterial vaginosis are detected with vaginal swabs. Chlamydia and gonorrhoea require a cervical swab, a specific urine test or in some cases, a vaginal swab. Blood tests are required to diagnose syphilis, hepatitis and HIV.

In the last two years Zika virus has been found to cause significant birth defects in pregnant women who are exposed to the virus in pregnancy. Guidelines regarding testing for the disease are evolving, but current recommended practice is for women to avoid pregnancy while in an affected area and for two months following return. Men need to avoid conception while in the affected area and for six months after they return.

Viral screening prior to ART procedures is described above under blood tests.

Post-coital test

A post-coital test involves asking a couple to have sexual intercourse at the time of or just prior to ovulation and then for the woman to attend to have a sample of her cervical mucus taken (as in a smear test). This is then examined under a microscope to see if there are actively motile sperm swimming in it. The value of this test is controversial and is a subject of continuing debate. Large studies have failed to show a great benefit. It is a difficult test to do as it has to be accurately timed to ovulation and, in my experience, and that of others, women really do not like it. Also, given that, even if it is normal, we are likely to be recommending treatments such as IUI and IVF that bypass the cervix, it is now rarely done in Ireland, Europe or the USA.

Male tests

Semen analysis

The standard and usually first test to look at a man's fertility is a semen analysis (3.1 and Table 3.3). The relevance of sperm tests is a bit controversial. We all see men who have a few abnormal results and who subsequently have a successful natural conception. This is particularly true for lesser abnormalities like abnormal morphology, mild reductions in count and/or motility and antisperm antibodies. However, with severe abnormalities, spontaneous conception is very rare and it is impossible with azoospermia (no sperm in the ejaculate). So for now, the basic semen analysis is the best test we have. But for men who have a normal test and are still not achieving pregnancy, there are almost certainly other factors in their sperm which may not be right but which can't be detected on a routine semen analysis.

Producing the sample

The man ejaculates into a container, either at the fertility clinic or at home, and the sample is analysed under a microscope by a laboratory technician called an andrologist or embryologist. It is essential that the correct container (supplied by the clinic) is used and that, if producing at home, the sample is kept at body temperature (e.g. in an inside pocket) and brought to the clinic within an hour. (If the sperm get cold they will become inactive and eventually die). Other instructions that are vital are that the man should have ejaculated 2–5 days before the test. If the man has not ejaculated for a long time, his sample may contain high numbers of dead sperm, and if he has ejaculated very recently, the volume of the sample may be low.

For men who have difficulty ejaculating by masturbation, fertility clinics can supply special non-contraceptive condoms to produce a sample via sexual intercourse. Most clinics also supply magazine and video material to help with production. However, we know that many men will have difficulty 'producing on demand'. If this is the case, please discuss it with your doctor or laboratory and they will be able to help. And don't worry – it is not unusual.

Analysing the sample

Any semen sample will contain various types of sperm. Some will be nicely active and swimming in relatively straight lines (forward progression), while others may not be moving at all or may be just twitching or even swimming around in circles. Some will have what is regarded as a normal shape and structure; others will be abnormal in shape with, for example, large heads, missing tails, etc.

The most important sperm parameters are the number of sperm or concentration, the percentage that are motile and the percentage that are a normal shape. It is also common to test the sample for anti-sperm antibodies (see page 270) and white cells, which can be a sign of infection. Some labs will also prepare the sperm as is done prior to fertility treatment to ensure that enough motile sperm come through this 'sperm prep' procedure to enable the treatment.

Most laboratories use guidelines produced by the WHO (3.2) to determine whether or not a sperm sample is normal. WHO criteria for assessing semen quality are based on populations of fertile men (see Table 3.3). Some clinics may still be using the old values (1999), so I have included those.

Table 3.3 WHO Normal Semen Parameters

	WHO 1999	**WHO 2010**
Volume	2 ml	1.5 ml
Concentration	20 million/ml	15 million/ml
Progressive motility	25%	32%
Vitality	75%	58%
Morphology	14%	4%

These criteria will accurately classify normal samples, so if the test is normal, no further testing is required. However, the criteria tend to 'over-call' an abnormality in up to 10% of cases, so it is advised that if there are any abnormal results the test should be repeated. One study showed that a single-sample analysis will falsely identify about 10% of men as abnormal, but repeating the test reduces this to 2%. Because the cycle of sperm formation takes about three months to complete, the optimal time for the second sample is at least three months after the initial sample. However, this is a long time for men and couples to have to wait so we generally schedule the repeat test after about six weeks.

DNA fragmentation tests

DNA (deoxyribonucleic acid) is a molecule that is present in all cells and that contains our genetic information. It is present in sperm. Various factors including environmental pollutants can damage DNA and it is normal for some, but not all, sperm to be damaged. The proportion of a man's sperm that is damaged has been linked with infertility and miscarriage. The amount of DNA fragmentation in sperm can be measured by several tests, including the SpermComet, SCSA and Halo. Studies with the SpermComet (which is the one we use at MFC) have shown that up to 25% damage is normal; men with rates between 25% and 49% do well with IVF and men with levels over 50% do better with ICSI.

However, the exact place of DNA fragmentation tests is somewhat controversial and not all international experts and bodies support its use. I tend not to recommend it very often.

CASA

Computer-assisted semen analysis (CASA) involves using a computer rather than a technician to read the semen parameters. It has not generally been found to be superior and is mostly used for research projects.

Sperm function tests

Some researchers have tried to assess the ability of sperm to swim through mucus or to penetrate hamster eggs. Again, these tests are not practical to do on a wide scale and are mainly reserved for research.

Anti-sperm antibodies (ASAs)

Just as we make antibodies to fight off viruses and infections, humans can also make antibodies to their own cells, e.g. patients with auto-immune diseases. Men can make antibodies to their sperm and this can affect fertility. Anti-sperm antibodies can be measured in sperm and this is usually part of a routine good-quality semen analysis. ASAs are discussed in the section on male infertility.

Testicular ultrasound

This is sometimes performed to look for swellings on a man's testicle, e.g. varicoceles, or for signs of obstruction of the ducts which carry sperm from the testes to the penis. It is usually ordered by urologists, who specialise in male genital tract issues.

Blood tests

Hormone tests may be required in cases of suspected hormonal (endocrine) problems and also in men who have azoospermia (no sperm in ejaculate) or severe oligospermia (very few sperm) – see the section on male factor infertility. Genetic tests may also be required in these instances and in couples with recurrent miscarriages.

Viral screening tests for hepatitis and HIV are required prior to ART procedures. See also under blood tests for women.

Men who have been to a Zika-infected area are advised not to try to conceive for six months after their return. If it is not possible to wait, sperm, urine and blood can be tested for the virus but the reliability of these tests has yet to be confirmed so, at present, the best advice is to avoid Zika-affected countries.

Ovarian reserve

We saw in the section on female age that a woman is born with all her eggs in her ovaries (contained in sacs called follicles) and that the number diminishes over time until by the time of menopause all her eggs have become atretic and no longer function. This process happens faster in some women than others. Some women are lucky and continue to have lots of follicles and lots of eggs in their ovaries until their mid-forties; other women will see a significant decline in their late twenties and early thirties.

Ovarian reserve is a term used to denote the number of eggs a woman may have left in her ovaries. For women with fertility problems it is important to know this as it gives us an idea as to how much time that woman has left in which she will be fertile. Measuring ovarian reserve can't tell us exactly how long a woman has, but it gives us an indication. However, it is important to remember that the number of eggs is just one parameter – the quality of the eggs is possibly more important than the number and quality is principally related to the woman's age; it starts to decline around 30 and declines quickly after 37 or so.

We can estimate a woman's **ovarian reserve** by counting the number of follicles in her ovaries or by measuring the level of hormone AMH in her blood.

Antral follicle count

The eggs in a woman's ovaries are microscopic and cannot be seen. However, they are stored in small fluid-filled sacs called follicles and these follicles are visible on an ultrasound scan. These follicles can vary in size and we saw in Section 1 that if a woman is ovulating, one follicle grows during her menstrual cycle and, at ovulation, bursts and releases an egg. However, the follicles that we are interested in when we are looking at ovarian reserve are the tiny follicles that have not yet started to grow. These are called antral or pre-antral follicles and they are small, measuring less than 9 mm (a follicle that is about to ovulate generally measures 17–22 mm).

We like to see six or seven of these small follicles on each ovary and a normal **antral follicle count (AFC)** would be regarded as approximately 14. The count takes in the number of follicles in each ovary, so if we have six on one ovary and seven on the other, that antral follicle count is 13. An AFC of less than eight is worrying as it suggests that the woman may be running out of eggs. In contrast, women with polycystic ovaries have large numbers of follicles and eggs in their ovaries and these women would have a very high antral follicle count (often over 40).

AMH

AMH (anti-Mullerian hormone) is a hormone produced by cells surrounding the egg in the antral follicles. In keeping with the decline in follicles, AMH declines with age. It is at its peak when a woman is in her mid-twenties and reaches zero by the time of menopause. In recent years, AMH has become one of the most important blood tests we do. It helps estimate whether a woman needs to hurry up with treatment or whether she can relax a bit and, in IVF and ovulation induction treatments, it helps us decide the most appropriate dose of drugs for the woman. It is also of benefit if a woman is considering freezing her eggs.

As with AFCs, a low AMH level can indicate a risk of ovarian insufficiency or early menopause, while women with polycystic ovaries typically have a high AMH level.

SHOULD ALL WOMEN CHECK THEIR OVARIAN RESERVE?

This is a controversial question and one which needs to be addressed in the next few years. The advantages of knowing one's ovarian reserve are that it might help a woman plan her reproductive life. One would hope that women with a low reserve would prioritise child bearing, or at least think about freezing their eggs. However there is a risk that women with a good ovarian reserve might be falsely reassured and think they are fine, even though because of their increasing age alone their fertility is diminishing, despite having lots of eggs – there is no value in having lots of eggs if they are poor quality.

There is also a growing concern among healthcare professionals that having an AMH test (or other test of ovarian reserve) may be very stressful for some women, particularly young women who have not yet found a partner. We at MFC have done some preliminary research in this area that shows that finding out that one has a low reserve can be devastating for women, particularly if they are not yet in a position to conceive. We also know that some women with a low reserve will have no difficulty conceiving (they may have few eggs but they may be excellent quality) so there is a risk that we could worry these women unnecessarily. However, our research also showed that, on balance, women would prefer to have this information

So my advice would be to think before having the test. If you are having fertility investigations it must be done in order to plan the best approach for you, and now is the time. But if you have not already been trying for a while, only have it done if you think you might do something positive with the result, such as starting to conceive or freezing eggs. But everyone should give some thought to their future fertility.

Problems with ovulation

We saw in Section 1 how ovulation (release of an egg from the woman's ovary) is critical for fertility and I described the signs of ovulation and how a woman will know whether or not she is ovulating. I also discussed earlier in this section progesterone hormone testing and ultrasound scans to detect ovulation. The treatments for ovulation problems (i.e. ovulation induction and IVF) are described in detail in Section 4.

Problems with ovulation can be the cause of subfertility in around 20% of couples. There are several causes and generally if failure to conceive is due to failed ovulation, it is often one of the easiest problems to diagnose and treat.

Typically women who are not ovulating do not get periods or, if they do, they are very irregular. It is therefore obvious, so women seek help early and the diagnosis is clear. Defining the exact cause and finding the right treatment can be more difficult. In many cases, conception happens very quickly with treatment but, in others, particularly women with polycystic ovaries, treatment can take time and require a great deal of patience.

Don't forget the man! Even if a woman is obviously not ovulating we usually insist on a sperm sample before starting treatment to induce ovulation. This is not because we are being difficult or trying to make money, but because sometimes there can be a sperm issue as well and we don't want to spend six months or a year treating the woman and getting her ovulating nicely only to find that she can't get pregnant anyway because of a sperm issue.

Similarly, we also perform an ultrasound scan, a chlamydia test and sometimes an HSG, HyCoSY or laparoscopy if we suspect that there may be pelvic problems in addition to ovulation problems.

Normal control of ovulation

Ovulation is a complex process. It happens in the ovaries, but only with help from hormones produced in two glands in the brain – the hypothalamus and the pituitary. The interactions between all these hormones are fascinating and, when they act together, fine-tuned ovulation takes place each month.

The hypothalamic gland in the brain produces the hormone GnRH – gonadotropin-releasing hormone. This hormone passes through specific blood vessels in the brain to another gland close by, the pituitary. GnRH stimulates the pituitary to produce the two gonadotropin hormones, FSH (follicle-stimulating hormone) and LH (luteinising hormone). These hormones circulate in the woman's blood and can be measured in simple blood tests.

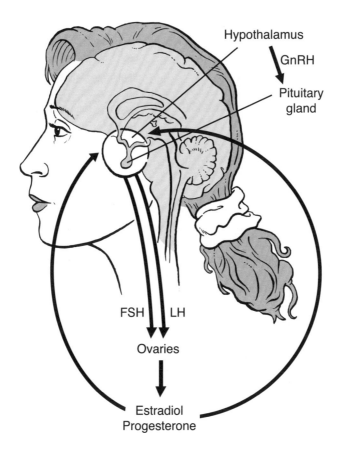

Hormonal control of the ovaries

FSH, as its name suggests (*follicle-stimulating* hormone), acts on the ovary to cause follicles to grow and develop. This happens at the beginning of a woman's menstrual cycle. The follicles start to produce oestrogen hormone and when this reaches a critical level, it sends a 'positive feedback' message to the pituitary gland, asking it to produce a 'surge' of the hormone LH. This is the surge that is picked up by ovulation detection kits. LH stimulates release of the egg from the ovary, i.e. the final stage of ovulation. The ovary continues to produce oestrogen and also begins to produce progesterone, both of which act on the lining of the uterus (womb) to prepare it for pregnancy.

Disorders at any of these levels of control can cause ovulation problems (3.3). The main causes are listed in Table 3.4.

Table 3.4 Causes of Ovulation Problems

Level of problem	Condition	Mechanism
Ovary	Polycystic ovaries	Inherited/familial
	Developmental problems	Genetic (Turner's, Down Syndrome, 46XY)
	Ovarian failure/insufficiency	Surgery
		Chemotherapy/radiotherapy
		Unexplained/familial
Pituitary	High prolactin (hyperprolactinaemia)	Tumours, microadenoma
	Enzyme disorders	Galactosaemia
	Sheehan's syndrome	Loss of blood supply
Hypothalamus	Hypothalamic disorders	Functional – exercise, weight loss, stress Chronic disease Unexplained Tumours and infection
	Kallmann's syndrome	Genetic
Other glands	Thyroid, ovary, adrenal gland	Tumours

The main causes are:

- Polycystic ovaries
- Hypothalamic due to exercise and low weight
- High prolactin
- Premature ovarian insufficiency
- Unexplained

Treatments are varied and depend on the cause.

Polycystic ovaries

Polycystic ovaries are the commonest cause of ovulation problems, accounting for about 85% of cases. This condition and its treatment are described in detail later.

Up to 20% of all women are found to have polycystic ovaries when they have an ultrasound scan, but not all of these women have disordered ovulation. Once women with polycystic ovaries (PCO) on scan have irregular or no ovulation they are deemed to have PCO *syndrome* (PCOS).

Put simply, polycystic ovaries can be associated with hormone imbalances which interfere with ovulation. Typically women have high levels of AMH, normal levels of FSH, normal or high levels of LH and oestrogen and high levels of testosterone. There are many different approaches that can be used to induce ovulation in women with PCOS, including:

1) Weight loss, if the woman is overweight. This is very effective and more than 50% of women will begin ovulating and will conceive if they can lose approximately 10% of their body weight.
2) Metformin: a diabetic drug (described in detail later).
3) Ovulation induction fertility drugs such as clomiphene citrate, tamoxifen, letrozole and FSH injections.
4) Laparoscopy and surgical diathermy to the ovaries.
5) IVF.

These topics are discussed in the relevant sections.

Hypothalamic dysfunction (hypo hypo)

In this condition the hypothalamic gland in the brain malfunctions, producing insufficient GnRH to stimulate the pituitary. In turn, the pituitary doesn't produce FSH and LH and, in turn, the ovary is not stimulated, so ovulation is blocked and the woman has very low oestrogen levels.

A short name for this condition is hypo hypo (hypothalamic hypogonadism). It can be caused by rare genetic disorders such as Kallmann's Syndrome (where affected individuals also have no sense of smell), but the most common causes are low body weight, due especially to eating disorders and also excessive exercise – see sections on weight and exercise in Section 2. Another serious consequence of the low hormone levels (especially oestrogen) is that bone formation and strength is reduced and there is a risk of osteoporosis.

The condition is diagnosed based on history, assessing BMI (body mass index) and finding low levels of the hormones FSH, LH and oestrogen. On scan, multiple follicles are seen in the ovaries and they may appear what we call 'multicystic'. AMH levels vary.

Treatment is primarily to address the woman's weight and exercise levels. If her cycle does not subsequently return naturally, the next step is to try to induce ovulation with injections of FSH and LH or a pump that delivers GnRH hormone. Only about 10% of women with ovulation disorders fall into this category. Ovulation induction is discussed in Section 4.

High prolactin

Prolactin is a hormone that is produced when women are breastfeeding and it inhibits ovulation. This is why women who are breastfeeding tend not to have periods. Prolactin can be high at other times and this can stop ovulation.

High prolactin levels are often unexplained, but a common cause is a small benign tumour called a microadenoma in the woman's pituitary gland (in the brain). This is rarely serious and can be treated with medication such as bromocriptine or cabergoline tablets to bring it down. Very rarely women with a very high prolactin level need surgery for this benign pituitary tumour and they would be referred to an endocrinologist and surgeon for this. Indeed, most women with high prolactin tend to be treated by endocrinologists, so we don't commonly see them.

Other signs of high prolactin levels include galactorrhoea (discharge of milk-type substance from the breasts) and, if there is a small pituitary tumour, headaches and/or visual problems (the pituitary gland is located near the optic nerve, which is involved with vision).

Premature ovarian insufficiency (POI)

One of the saddest things I see is young women with premature ovarian insufficiency or early menopause. Not only do they have to deal with the loss of their fertility, they also have to cope with a situation they would not have expected until they were much older.

The ovary is critical to ovulation. The follicles in it contain the woman's eggs and must grow and ovulate. As a woman nears menopause, her follicles and eggs will become atretic, or degenerate, and they become reabsorbed or disappear. Eventually there will be none left. Tragically, this happens prematurely in some women, leaving them truly unable to conceive.

Premature ovarian insufficiency (POI) is a clinical syndrome defined by loss of ovarian activity before the age of 40 years (3.4). It is characterised by menstrual disturbance (amenorrhea, i.e. no periods, or oligomenorrhea, i.e. very infrequent periods) with raised gonadotropins (FSH and LH hormones) and low estradiol (oestrogen). POI is estimated to occur in 1% of women.

The majority of cases of POI are unexplained, though it often runs in families. For that reason, if your mother or sister had an early menopause, you should be on the alert for this yourself. Some cases are due to genetic conditions, though these are rare. In the 1990s a condition called Fragile X was discovered. This causes mental retardation in affected males. Women do not get the condition, but they may be carriers, and some of these women can develop premature ovarian insufficiency. Turner's syndrome is another genetic condition that can lead to ovarian insufficiency, as is Down syndrome. Other non-genetic causes of ovarian insufficiency are surgery to the ovaries, for example for ovarian cysts or endometriosis, cancer chemotherapy or radiotherapy.

Primary ovarian insufficiency means that a woman has never had any ovarian function or periods. This is rare and is often due to a genetic reason. Secondary ovarian insufficiency occurs in women who previously ovulated and now have ovarian problems.

In women whose ovaries are not functioning adequately, the FSH levels begin to rise because the pituitary gland goes into overdrive and produces more FSH in an attempt to kick-start the ovary. Unfortunately, once an ovary has decided it's not going to work, nothing will make it do so because the problem is that the follicles and eggs are gone or atretic (degenerated). A high FSH blood level is therefore a sign of ovarian insufficiency. This happens as women enter menopause because at that stage their ovary has stopped responding to hormones. Oestrogen levels and AMH levels will be low because the ovary is no longer able to produce these hormones. On ultrasound we may see just one or two or, indeed, no follicles on the woman's ovaries.

Sadly, fertility drugs cannot stimulate the ovaries in this situation. The only viable treatment option is IVF using donor eggs. Doctors and researchers around the world have tried to use growth hormone, Clomid, FSH injections and DHEA (a testosterone-based hormone) to improve failing ovarian function, but none of these measures has been found to be effective. It is also, tragically, too late for egg freezing because there are effectively no eggs left to freeze.

Having said that, in young women with POI it is well recognised that they can have sporadic ovulation and unexpected pregnancies can occur in around 2% of cases. This is most likely in the year or two following diagnosis and I have certainly seen it on a few occasions.

Exciting work is being done in animals at a laboratory level to try to stimulate or rejuvenate atretic ovarian follicles. This research is still in its infancy but may offer hope in the future – though probably not in time for anyone currently reading this book.

Other problems with POI: Women with premature ovarian failure may develop 'menopause symptoms' due to the raised FSH levels. These symptoms include hot flushes or flashes, night sweats, vaginal dryness, reduced breast size, insomnia and difficulty concentrating. Thankfully, these can be treated with artificial oestrogen in the form of HRT (hormone replacement therapy) or the pill. There is also an increased risk of long-term problems such as osteoporosis and heart disease due to the low oestrogen levels. Again, these risks can be reduced by hormone therapy. In women with POI, we recommend regular bone scans to keep an eye on your bones, and your GP can usually organise this.

While there have been scares in recent years regarding the safety of HRT and the pill, all the risks associated with HRT (such as breast cancer) have been found in women who take HRT over the age of 50. For younger women, HRT seems to be very, very safe. HRT is slightly better for women's bones than the pill, but younger women may feel better taking the pill, and that is fine. Because, as I said above, there is a small chance of sporadic ovulation and pregnancy, the pill is better if young women wish to avoid pregnancy and HRT is better if women are hoping to conceive – it doesn't stop ovulation if it were to occur, whereas the pill does.

The psychological effects of having POI can be enormous and it is important to look for support and counselling to get through this difficult situation. My colleague Kay mentions it in her article, and there are some support groups in other countries, e.g. the Daisy Network in the UK (www.daisynetwork.org.uk), but unfortunately none in Ireland.

VERY LOW OVARIAN RESERVE

Generally a woman's ovaries don't just stop functioning overnight (except with surgery or cancer treatment). There is usually a lead-in time when the number of eggs and follicles is declining. Unfortunately, unless she has hormone tests or detailed ovarian ultrasound scans done, the woman will be unaware of this. This is where ovarian reserve and ovarian reserve testing come in. There is a debate now in medical circles as to whether all women should be offered screening for ovarian reserve in their late twenties so that they may be alerted to a low level and have time to do something about it. Options would include trying to conceive now rather than waiting, considering IVF if in a position to do this, or freezing any eggs that she may have left.

Unexplained ovulation problems

In some women, the cause of irregular or absent ovulation can be unclear. This can be very frustrating for them and indeed for the doctors and nurses treating them. While it seems good to classify cases into PCOS or hypo hypo, etc., we have to remember we are dealing with biology and humans don't always fit neatly into 'boxes'. As time goes on, it is becoming more apparent that there is overlap between many conditions and that other outside factors may tip the scales one way or another with our hormones.

We recently had a case at our clinic where a woman had normal hormone levels going into treatment. Her ultrasound suggested polycystic ovaries, as did her AMH level. However, she was borderline low BMI and then lost some more weight – just 2 kg, but that was enough to tip her hormones into the hypo hypo range. So it is likely that most women who have 'unexplained' ovulation problems are somewhere on the spectrum of PCOS or hypo hypo but it is not currently obvious.

Polycystic ovaries (PCO)

Polycystic ovaries (PCO) are a type of ovary that some women are born with. They are surprisingly common and probably occur in up to one in five women. While some women have symptoms and hormone imbalances due to these ovaries, other women have no problems, do not even know they have them and may get through life without every knowing that they have polycystic ovaries.

The term 'polycystic ovaries' is misleading as it suggests that women have cysts in their ovaries that might need to be removed. But this is not the case. The condition was first described in the 1800s when women who had irregular periods were found to have 'cysts' in their ovaries. 'Cyst', however, just means a collection of fluid or a sac filled with fluid. Some other types of cyst are big and may need to be removed, but we now know that the 'cysts' of PCO are indeed follicles, which are a normal part of a woman's ovary. Follicles are fluid-filled sacs in the ovary and are where the woman's eggs are stored.

All women have follicles in their ovaries, including women with PCO. They tend to be arranged differently, however. In women who do not have PCO, when we do a scan we expect to see about seven follicles in each ovary and these are scattered randomly throughout the ovary. In women with PCO, the ovaries are typically slightly bigger and each one contains at least 12 visible small antral follicles. These follicles are typically arranged along the outside of the ovary and have been described as looking like a 'string of pearls' – see diagram on page 148.

Polycystic ovaries are a type of ovary that a woman is born with – she has always had them and she will always have them. They can be associated with hormone imbalances which can affect fertility. However, they can be managed and fertility is usually very possible. References used in this section are 3.5, 3.6, 3.7 and 3.8.

PCO vs PCOS

PCO refers simply to the finding of polycystic ovaries on the scan. As I said above, this type of ovary can be seen on scan in 20–25% of women but many of these women behave completely normally and do not have any medical issues. In contrast, polycystic ovarian syndrome (PCOS) means that a woman with polycystic ovaries has symptoms or medical problems related to her ovaries. PCOS occurs in 5–10% of all women. Women who have PCO and no symptoms of the syndrome can develop the syndrome, particularly if they put on a significant amount of weight.

Causes of PCOS

It is not known what exactly causes PCOS and PCO. There are some genetic links and the condition tends to run in families, but a definite gene has not been identified. It is a complex condition with abnormalities occurring not just in the ovary and ovarian hormones but in the wider area of metabolism and insulin resistance. There are other important factors, which include hyperinsulinaemia (high levels of insulin), abnormal body fats and increased susceptibility to diabetes.

Many abnormalities are seen in the ovaries. They are bigger, contain more follicles and the follicles do not develop and ovulate in as predictable and orderly a fashion as those on other ovaries. Study of PCO ovaries shows overproduction of testosterone-type hormones, which in turn causes increased oestrogen levels. AMH (anti-Mullerian hormone) production is increased in the ovary, partly due to the increased number of follicles, but also due to increased secretion of AMH by these follicles. The ovaries are extremely sensitive to insulin (a hormone produced by the pancreas, which is low in people with diabetes), but tissues outside the ovary such as muscle and the liver are resistant to it (insulin resistance).

Levels of insulin, AMH, oestrogen, testosterone and LH are increased in the blood of women with PCO. All these factors interact and it is impossible to know which comes first. A typical 'chicken and egg' scenario.

The situation is further complicated if obesity is present because this in itself alters insulin sensitivity and oestrogen and testosterone levels and causes generalised inflammation and immune system changes.

Signs of PCOS

PCOS affects women in different ways. There are typical symptoms associated with the condition and these are listed in the box below. The symptoms are related to ovulation problems, high testosterone levels and metabolic problems. Some women may have only mild symptoms, while others may have all the symptoms; and the severity of the symptoms also varies from woman to woman. However, unlike other medical conditions, PCOS is not generally graded as mild, moderate or severe. Symptoms usually start in adolescence, although some women do not develop them until their early to mid-twenties.

MOST COMMON SIGNS OF PCOS

- Irregular periods (oligomenorrhoea, less often than every 35 days) or no periods at all (amenorrhoea)
- Very frequent periods (polymenorrhoea, more than once a month) or prolonged bleeding in a young woman
- Irregular ovulation, or no ovulation at all
- Reduced fertility
- Excess facial or body hair (hirsutism)
- Oily skin, acne
- Thinning hair or hair loss from the scalp (alopecia)
- Weight problems – being overweight, rapid weight gain, difficulty losing weight

---

The exact diagnosis of PCOS is controversial and several international bodies have developed different guidelines for diagnosing it. The most widely accepted guidelines are called the Rotterdam criteria and these suggest that if women meet two of the following criteria they have PCOS.

- Polycystic ovaries seen on scan.
- Menstrual irregularities (i.e. a very irregular or no cycle).
- Evidence of high testosterone levels, either on blood tests or on symptoms (excess hair, acne, hair loss).

Period problems

PCOS is the most common cause of irregular periods (cycles less than 21 or greater than 35 days apart). In fact, it's a good bet that if a woman has irregular (as opposed to absent) periods, she has PCOS. If she has some periods and they're irregular, the chance of her having PCOS is about 90%.

Many women do not realise they have PCOS until they stop taking the oral contraceptive pill in order to conceive. The pill doesn't cause PCOS, but it can mask the symptoms. We know that when a woman discontinues the pill, it can take up to a year for her periods to return naturally. This is called post-pill amenorrhoea (no periods) and it is particularly common in women with PCOS. Many such women will remember that their periods were irregular or infrequent in their teenage years and many may have even been started on the pill for this very reason. Therefore, they would have always had polycystic ovaries.

While the most common sign of PCOS is infrequent periods, some women with PCOS will actually have the opposite problem – very frequent periods and very heavy bleeding.

Irregular ovulation and reduced fertility

Fertility problems are common among PCOS patients. Up to one-third of women who present to fertility clinics have PCO or PCOS.

The irregular periods in PCOS are really a reflection of irregular ovulation. Some women ovulate from time to time and others not at all. Women with PCOS are very sensitive to changes in weight, travelling and exercise and will notice that as they lose weight they may begin to ovulate. Because ovulation happens before a period, some women can ovulate and conceive without knowing it – they miss their period but this is normal for them so they may not realise they are pregnant until they start feeling nauseated or even notice a pregnancy 'bump'.

If you are having infrequent or no periods, you are not ovulating regularly, so you will find it difficult to conceive. This can be treated. However, it is also important to make sure there are no additional reasons why you may be having difficulty conceiving, e.g. pelvic problems or sperm problems.

Excess testosterone

Because women with PCOS have higher testosterone levels than other women, they can have problems with this. Hirsutism (excessive facial or body hair) is one of the defining characteristics of PCOS. About half of women who have hirsutism have PCOS. This tends to be more obvious in women with darker colouring and it can sometimes be hard to know if it is normal for their family/genetic background or if it is excessive. However, if it interferes with life, it is likely to be excessive. Some women need to shave or wax daily or have frequent electrolysis. Other women are comfortable with greater amounts of hair.

Elevated testosterone levels can also cause or aggravate acne and can lead to thinning of the hair or alopecia.

Weight gain

A classical feature of PCOS is weight gain or difficulty maintaining or losing weight. This is important in terms of general health (see metabolic syndrome below). All the other symptoms of PCOS (infertility, hirsutism, frequency of periods) are closely linked to body weight and will get worse if the woman gains weight and improve if she can lose weight.

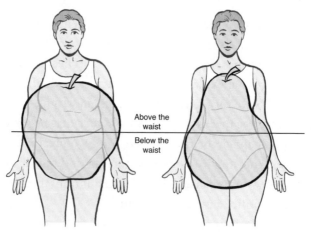

'Apple' vs. 'Pear'

Because body fat distribution is associated with hormone levels, men and women tend to gain weight differently. Many women tend to carry weight below the waist (around the bum and thighs) and tend to be 'pear-shaped'. Men typically have a more apple-shaped pattern of obesity, in which fat accumulates in the abdomen. Overweight women with PCOS also have this male-pattern obesity, all related to their PCOS and higher testerone (male hormone) levels.

Two ways of checking whether your weight is normal are BMI and waist circumference – these are discussed in detail in Section 2. In simple terms, a normal BMI is between 18.5 and 25 and a healthy waist circumference for women is less than 80 cm or 32 inches.

Emotional/psychological upset

The symptoms of PCOS are known to cause significant emotional and psychological upset for *some* women with the condition. Depression, lower quality of life scores, both on physical and mental health scales, with lower sense of self-worth, and poorer sexual satisfaction have all been described. These symptoms have been associated with the symptoms of PCOS, i.e. hirsutism, obesity, acne and irregular periods.

> *'The uncomfortable things about the whole experience was the embarrassment about having PCOS. My baby is 18 months old now and I still haven't told many people I have PCOS. I am not sure why it is so difficult to tell people and I assume people would think no different of me.'*

When should I suspect PCOS?

- If you have always had irregular periods (varying by more than a week and occurring less often than once a month).
- If your periods have stopped – particularly after stopping the pill.
- If you have troublesome facial or body hair.
- If you have bad acne that does not respond to simple measures.
- If you have difficulty conceiving and have any of the above symptoms.
- If your mother or a sister has PCO or PCOS.
- If you are overweight or gaining weight uncontrollably and have any of the above symptoms.

Diagnosing PCOS

The first factor to note is the woman's history and, as described above, a combination of irregular or no periods, a difficulty with maintaining normal weight and the presence of excess body or facial hair (hirsutism) would be absolutely typical signs of polycystic ovaries. However, not all women have these symptoms. Hirsutism, in particular, can be difficult to measure and the objective assessment of a doctor may help in deciding what is normal and what is not.

It can be difficult to diagnose the condition in adolescents and teenagers because acne and irregular periods are common in this age group anyway. Also, depending on their symptoms, patients may be referred to endocrinologists or dermatologists or obesity specialists and while these are all experts in their fields, they are not gynaecologists or fertility specialists, so multi-disciplinary care with several doctors may be needed at times.

'Unfortunately throughout my life I have faced irregular periods from a young age. Visiting my GP as a teenager I was reassured that it was a slight hormonal imbalance that would settle with time. Well, it didn't and I would go months without a period. Eventually I had an ultrasound scan at age 17 and it was negative for any abnormalities. Going into my twenties my periods started to come more regularly but I would often have very light periods or very painful heavy periods. If it was a very heavy period I would really dread those months and pain relief was a must to be able to function properly. Once I got married, I had an ultrasound scan of the pelvis and an MRI. The scan was negative for abnormalities but the MRI showed small follicular cysts throughout both ovaries that had not developed but were in excess of the normal numbers they would have expected. At last I had an explanation and looking at my blood work it confirmed a slight hormonal imbalance where my free testosterone levels were elevated with low levels of progesterone. I was diagnosed with polycystic ovarian syndrome.'

Ultrasound scan

A good quality ultrasound scan can detect polycystic ovaries. As we saw before, these are typically slightly bigger than other ovaries and contain more than 12 visible small antral follicles. These follicles are usually arranged along the outside of the ovary in a 'string of pearls' pattern. As the quality of ultrasound machines improves, polycystic ovaries are more obvious and we are seeing more and more follicles. Some international experts now feel that a diagnosis of polycystic ovaries should only be made if there are more than 20 follicles seen on each ovary.

Polycystic ovaries are easiest seen with a trans-vaginal scan and, particularly in overweight women, may be difficult to pick up during transabdominal scanning. Therefore women with PCOS do not necessarily have to have polycystic ovaries seen on scan. This is something I come across a lot as the ovaries will sometimes appear typically polycystic on a scan, but then at another stage, particularly if this scan is done abdominally rather than vaginally, or if the woman is taking the oral contraceptive pill, the polycystic appearance may not be obvious.

Blood tests

AMH is produced by the follicles in the woman's ovaries and so is high in women with polycystic ovaries. This test is rapidly becoming the most sensitive one for diagnosing polycystic ovaries and typically the level would be high (over 60 pmol/l). In the past FSH and LH hormone levels were used to look for polycystic ovarian syndrome. Typically the levels of both of these hormones should be relatively equal, but in PCOS patients we would expect the LH to be three times the FSH level (increased LH to FSH ratio). The importance of these tests is declining and they are now being replaced by AMH measurements.

Testosterone levels can also be measured to see if they are elevated. This can be helpful in monitoring hirsutism levels, but it is not a critical test to have done. Other hormone tests that have been done in the past, but which are not always necessary, include SHBG (sex hormone binding globulin), which is lower than normal; and androstenedione, another testosterone-type hormone, which tends to be elevated. In women with very high testosterone and such hormones, rarer conditions such as

Cushing's disease or adrenal disease or even an ovarian tumour need to be excluded.

Prolactin levels and TSH (thyroid-stimulating hormone) levels can also be elevated in women with polycystic ovaries and in women with irregular periods it is important to do these tests to rule out disorders due to abnormal prolactin or thyroid hormones.

Treatment of PCOS

The treatments available for polycystic ovaries depend on whether or not the woman is trying to conceive. Across all treatments the advice about maintaining normal body weight is absolutely critical and is always the first line of treatment. Typically a low-calorie, low-glycaemic index diet is probably best, combined with exercise, and there is evidence that both are critical. See under Nutrition, Diet and Body Weight in Section 2.

Women who are not trying to conceive

Young women with polycystic ovarian syndrome may have very frequent periods and in that case hormone treatment such as a contraceptive pill can be very helpful. However, it is important to try to make the diagnosis before starting on the pill.

If a woman has very infrequent periods she may be very happy with this and as long as she is having three or four periods per year that is fine. However, some women whose periods are very unpredictable prefer to take the pill because then at least they know when their period is due and it can help them to plan their life accordingly. If a woman's periods are very irregular and she is having fewer than three or four periods per year, there is a small chance of the lining of the uterus becoming over-active (described on page 186). For that reason we generally tend to recommend some medication to induce a bleed every couple of months.

For young women the pill may be most useful as it will also give them contraception, but an alternative is to use a progesterone hormone such as Provera (10 mg) or Primolut (5 mg) daily for seven days every second month. This ensures that the woman will get to bleed when she stops the medication and will prevent the lining of the uterus from getting thicker. However, it does not in any way help her to conceive and it is not a contraceptive.

Hirsutism due to PCO

Hirsutism (excess body and facial hair) due to polycystic ovaries can be difficult to treat. There are now some creams on the market (e.g. Vaniqua) which are very effective for facial hair. Alternatively, women may find electrolysis, plucking or shaving preferable. A consultation with a dermatologist may be very useful in this regard.

The contraceptive pill also reduces hirsutism and acne. Some contraceptive pills have an extra anti-testosterone hormone called cyproterone acetate and these are more effective (e.g. Dianette). However, they are slightly stronger pills with a slightly worse effect on lipids, so it is recommended that they are used for six months to a year, after which the woman switches over to an ordinary contraceptive pill. *Please note that it takes at least three months for the pill to have an effect on acne and at least six months to have an effect on hirsutism.*

The pill works by suppressing LH hormone levels and testosterone levels. Spironolactone is a blood pressure medication that may sometimes be helpful for treating hirsutism due to PCOS, but generally the oral contraceptive pill is more effective.

There have been several studies on metformin (see page 182) for the management of symptoms due to PCOS. While this can be helpful with fertility-related issues, its effects on hirsutism are marginal. Some women find it easier to lose weight when they are taking metformin, though international studies have shown no significant effect on losing weight per se. However, it is a safe drug with minimal side-effects, so it is certainly worth considering.

Fertility treatments

Weight loss: This is also discussed in detail in Section 2, where there is a great letter written by a patient with PCOS for whom weight loss resulted in pregnancy. For overweight women with PCOS the first line of treatment is weight loss. Several studies in Australia, the UK and USA have shown, without a doubt, that if women lose approximately 10% of their weight, more than 50% will conceive naturally without ever needing to do anything else. I often see women who have polycystic ovaries who conceived without much problem but now are having secondary infertility and can't conceive again. It is interesting that when I question them, they were often much lighter when they conceived on their first pregnancy. However, due to the weight gain in pregnancy, their weight went up and, given that they have polycystic ovaries, they have found it hard to lose that weight. Many of these women will conceive naturally if they can manage to get their weight back to the weight they were prior to their first pregnancy.

Countless women will find that as they start to lose weight the first thing they notice is that they will start getting more periods and then up to 50% of them will be able to conceive.

Unfortunately, losing weight is very difficult and I am not for a minute suggesting that it's easy. Hopefully you will find the excellent article on diet and nutrition by my colleague, Sinead Curran, of benefit. Please try to persevere as I have seen on many occasions healthy spontaneous (natural) pregnancies when women have managed to lose weight. These women also get a great sense of satisfaction and wellbeing from their efforts.

The next line of management in women who are not ovulating is to aim to induce ovulation with fertility drugs.

Metformin: Metformin is an anti-diabetes tablet which increases insulin sensitivity, helping the body to process and manage glucose. It has also been shown to help the symptoms of PCOS. It is a drug that has gained popularity and then gone out of popularity over the years. In the 1980s it was felt that it was a major breakthrough for the treatment of polycystic ovaries but, unfortunately, it has not always lived up to first expectations. We tend to reserve it for women who are trying to lose weight prior to considering other fertility drugs to induce ovulation. It can also be used during IVF treatment to reduce the risk of OHSS (ovarian hyperstimulation syndrome), a complication of IVF to which women with polycystic ovaries are susceptible.

Metformin is usually taken in a dose of 500 mg three times a day or 850 mg twice a day. The main side-effects are tummy upsets and diarrhoea, but these symptoms usually stop after two to three weeks. We usually start the treatment at one 500 mg tablet daily for the first week, increasing to two tablets daily for the second week and three tablets daily for the third week. It is best to take metformin at mealtimes as this reduces the number of side-effects. Scanning is not required with metformin.

Metformin alone is not associated with weight loss; however, when metformin is combined with a low-calorie diet, weight loss has been demonstrated and, in my experience, women often report that it helps them to lose weight, though this has not been proven scientifically.

Clomiphene citrate or Clomid: Clomid is a fertility drug which has been around for 30 to 40 years. It is a tablet that is taken for five days at the beginning of a woman's cycle. It acts by stimulating the pituitary gland to produce more FSH, which will hopefully act on the follicles in the woman's ovaries and cause them to start growing and ovulate. Clomid can be very effective for women who are not ovulating, particularly women with polycystic ovaries. It is described in detail in Section 4.

Letrozole: This is another tablet that may induce ovulation. It is called an aromatase inhibitor and it works on the ovary to promote ovulation. It is described in detail under ovulation induction in Section 4.

Tamoxifen: A drug similar to clomiphene, it acts in a similar way but tends to have fewer negative effects on the lining of the uterus.

FSH injections: If the woman does not respond to clomiphene, letrozole or tamoxifen ovulation induction, the next step up in terms of drugs is FSH injections. These are injections of the hormone FSH and they act directly on the woman's ovaries. Ovulation is induced and the response is monitored, as described in the section on ovulation induction. Less commonly injections of FSH and LH are used.

IVF: If ovulation induction fails to lead to pregnancy, or if it proves difficult to achieve ovulation, IVF may be the next step, particularly if there are other fertility factors such as mild endometriosis or tubal disease, sperm problems or advancing maternal age. IVF is described in detail in Section 4.

Women with PCO and PCOS undergoing IVF are more at risk of OHSS (ovarian hyperstimulation syndrome) than other women and this dictates certain approaches to IVF protocols.

Laparoscopy and ovarian diathermy: It was discovered in the 1930s that women with polycystic ovaries often started to ovulate if part of their ovary was removed. This was called a wedge resection of the ovary and involved major surgery. However, in the 1980s and 1990s, laparoscopy (keyhole surgery) was developed and this led the way to being able to perform simpler operations on polycystic ovaries. It is not understood why, but if a small amount of trauma is applied to polycystic ovaries it often induces them to start ovulating. This can now be done via a laparoscopy. It may be performed with a laser or, more commonly, with an electric current called diathermy. It is often called 'drilling' the ovary, though I prefer the term laparoscopic ovarian diathermy (LOD) – 'drilling' sounds a bit crude for something as intricate and wonderful as an ovary! The procedure involves puncturing the ovary with the laser or diathermy and causing some damage which can 'kick-start' the ovary. The other advantage of doing the procedure is that we get to see inside the woman's pelvis to make sure there are no other problems such as endometriosis or tubal disease.

Long-term effects of PCOS

PCOS is not just a reproductive problem. As mentioned above, it alters women's metabolism (processing) of insulin and glucose and alters hormone levels. This can lead to other, long-term, non-reproductive problems.

Metabolic syndrome/insulin resistance syndrome

PCOS is linked to increased risks for metabolic conditions such as obesity and type 2 diabetes. Women with PCOS are more likely to develop metabolic syndrome or insulin resistance syndrome, a group of risk factors which increase one's chance of developing heart disease, diabetes and stroke.

Insulin is a hormone made in the pancreas, an organ located behind the stomach. Insulin plays a major role in metabolism – the way the body uses food for energy. Our digestive system breaks down carbohydrates into glucose, a form of sugar that enters the bloodstream after a meal. Insulin enables cells throughout the body to absorb this glucose and use it for energy. In people who have insulin resistance, the body produces insulin but is unable to use it effectively. Glucose builds up in the blood instead of being absorbed by the cells. It is then turned into fat. The pancreas in turn produces higher levels of insulin to help overcome the insulin resistance. As long as the pancreas is able to produce enough insulin, blood glucose levels stay in the healthy range. However, over time, the pancreas is unable to keep up and diabetes develops.

'I was diagnosed with polycystic ovarian syndrome. I also had elevated blood sugar levels which confirmed type 2 diabetes. At this stage it was a lot to take in. I started treatment on metformin and worked my way up to 1,500 mg a day. In addition I embarked and am still trying to bring down my weight to a more reasonable BMI of 30 in order to start fertility treatments. I'm a few months away from this target. My husband and I are still trying in the meantime but I hope to start ovulation induction soon once my weight is more controlled.'

Another feature of metabolic syndrome is abnormal fat or lipid levels. Women with PCOS and metabolic syndrome have higher levels of bad fats such as cholesterol, LDL (low-density lipoprotein) and triglycerides, and lower levels of good fats such as HDL (high-density lipoprotein) than women without the condition.

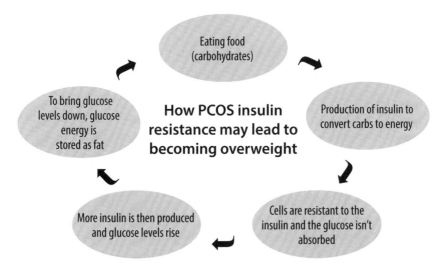

Although the exact causes of insulin resistance are not completely understood, scientists think the major contributors to insulin resistance are excess weight and physical inactivity. It has been reported that in the USA almost 50% of women with PCOS also have metabolic syndrome, whereas in Italy, where women with PCOS have a lower mean body weight and better fat profiles, metabolic syndrome is less common but still four times more frequent in PCOS patients than in the general female population of similar age. So some genetic factors related to PCOS are also at play. Women most at risk of metabolic syndrome are those who are overweight and have irregular periods, high testosterone levels and PCO on scan, i.e. all the criteria. Those with only either ovulation problems or high testosterone levels and PCO on scan are less at risk, as are those with normal weight patterns.

Insulin also acts on the ovary to increase testosterone production and this in turn causes the symptoms of PCOS that are related to high testosterone levels.

In women who are deemed to be at risk of metabolic syndrome, i.e. women who are overweight or have a family history of high blood pressure, diabetes or stroke, it is recommended that some screening tests should be performed to look at their lipids and also the risk factors for diabetes. These tests are best done by their GP or endocrinologist.

Endometrial cancer

As they get older, women with PCOS have a higher risk of endometrial cancer (cancer of the lining of the womb or uterine cancer). This is thought to be related to both excess oestrogen levels in women with PCOS and the infrequency of their periods. We know that some oestrogen hormones are made in fat tissue, so obese women have higher levels of oestrogen. If women are not ovulating, they do not produce progesterone hormone and this is known to normally keep the effects of oestrogen in balance. Also, if the woman has very irregular or no periods, the lining of the womb is not shed every month, so it can gradually thicken and start to develop abnormally. The first step in the process is often a condition called endometrial hyperplasia (overgrowth of the uterine lining). If this is not noticed or treated, it can ultimately develop into cancer. The good news is that weight loss and maintaining a normal BMI significantly reduce the risk of cancer, as does hormonal treatment. And even if a woman does develop cancer, endometrial cancer is one of the cancers which responds very well to treatment.

Quality of life

Given the host of complications and related conditions linked to PCOS, it is not surprising that some PCOS patients may have a lower quality of life than other women. Weight problems, obesity and fertility problems contribute to this. But depression is also much more common in women with PCOS than in the general population, even after adjusting for factors such as infertility. Depression can worsen problems with insulin resistance, diabetes and obesity because depression reduces the ability to undertake lifestyle interventions, such as exercise, that might help reduce the impact of those issues. Counselling can be a great help in this regard.

Pregnancy and PCOS

When they do get pregnant, women with PCOS are more likely than other women to develop pregnancy complications. The most common is gestational diabetes or pregnancy-related diabetes. This is detected by screening around six months into the pregnancy and, if diagnosed, the woman will require dietary advice and possibly insulin treatment for the duration of the pregnancy. Blood pressure problems and pre-eclampsia are also higher in women with PCOS. Again, this is monitored in pregnancy. Miscarriage is also slightly more common in women with PCOS but, having said that, most women will be able to carry healthy pregnancies to term. As described in Section 2, female age is the biggest predictor of miscarriage and this outweighs the effect of the PCOS.

As with all aspects of PCOS, trying to control weight and keeping it in the normal range helps with all these complications.

Ovarian cysts

There are many types of ovarian cyst. Some are normal or physiological and come and go without causing any problems and others indicate an underlying disorder. The following are the most common types of ovarian cyst.

Functional or physiological cysts: I explained in Section 1 how the ovary changes throughout the woman's menstrual cycle. A follicle develops on her ovary early in the cycle and grows to about 18 mm, when it ruptures and releases its egg at the time of ovulation. Then the remainder of the follicle persists as a corpus luteum producing progesterone to get the lining of the uterus ready for implantation if the woman conceives. Sometimes this activity can become a little bit disordered and can lead to what we call functional cysts. The follicle containing the egg may not rupture or, more commonly, the corpus luteum part of the cyst after ovulation can persist for two or three cycles. At the time of ovulation there can be some bleeding and the blood can track into the corpus luteum, forming a haemorrhagic, or blood-filled, cyst. On ultrasound scan, this appears similar to an endometriosis cyst (see page 192) and it can be difficult to differentiate them.

However, if it is suspected that it is a physiological cyst, which should disappear by itself within two to three months, a scan is done two to three months later, which will hopefully show that the cyst has disappeared. Functional cysts are usually harmless, rarely cause pain and usually disappear or regress spontaneously. Occasionally they can cause bleeding and pain and require surgery. They tend to be more common in women who are taking fertility drugs, in women taking certain contraceptives such as progesterone-only pills and in women coming up to menopause.

Because the oral contraceptive pill suppresses ovulation, it helps prevent physiological cysts in women who are prone to them.

Endometriomas: Endometriomas are cysts due to endometriosis in the ovary and are described in detail in the next section.

Polycystic ovaries: Women with polycystic ovaries may feel that they have cysts because of the unfortunate term poly*cystic* ovaries. However, as described earlier, the cysts seen in polycystic ovaries are actually healthy follicles and they do not need to be removed.

Dermoid cysts: These are unusual cysts. It is not known why they grow in the ovary but they develop from totipotent cells that are laid down in the ovary when the woman is an embryo. Totipotent cells are cells that occur in the early embryo and have the potential to develop into many different types of tissue, as they do when the embryo is forming. They can lead to the formation of skin, hair and teeth in the early embryo. The cells are deposited in the ovary, where they lie dormant. For no obvious reason they can begin to proliferate and grow, leading to the formation of a cyst.

Dermoid cysts are therefore complex cysts that contain, not clear fluid or blood, but hair, bone, teeth and oily secretions.

Dermoid cysts tend to be most common in women around the age of 30 and up to 15% of affected women will have them on both ovaries. They can range in size from less than a centimetre to 20 to 30 centimetres. Smaller cysts are undetectable and may be picked up incidentally by a scan, but larger cysts can cause the ovary to twist and cause pain and can occasionally rupture. Very large cysts will cause noticeable abdominal swelling. Small dermoid cysts probably do not affect fertility but larger cysts may interfere with ovulation and certainly need to be treated prior to considering fertility treatment. Treatment involves removing the cyst by laparoscopic or open surgery.

Cystadenomas: Cystadenomas are large benign cysts of the ovaries which may be filled with watery liquid or a mucus material. Again, it is not known why these cysts develop. Very rarely the cysts can become malignant, but this usually happens in older women rather than the reproductive-age population. However, from time to time we see cysts in younger women which show borderline cancerous changes. These cysts need to be removed and the women need to be followed up regularly. When they have completed their family it is usually recommended that the entire ovary is removed. However, I must stress that cancer of the ovary is exceedingly rare in young women who are trying to conceive.

Fimbrial cysts: These are benign cysts in the Fallopian tubes. They are often seen at laparoscopy and sometimes can be seen on ultrasound scan. They tend to be small and filled with fluid and are noted on scan not to be part of the ovary but to lie adjacent to it. The majority of fimbrial cysts do not cause any problems and do not need any treatment. However, they can sometimes cause confusion when interpreting ultrasound scans.

Ovarian cancer: Ovarian cancer can present as a cyst in the woman's pelvis. Thankfully, it is extremely rare in women of childbearing age. We use measurements of a blood factor, CA125 (cancer-associated antigen) to exclude the risk of cancer in women with cysts. A normal CA125 level should be under 35 kU/L, but it can be elevated in women with endometriosis or pelvic infection. The levels in these cases (usually under 400) are lower than in women with cancer (usually over 1,000).

Signs of ovarian cysts

The symptoms or signs of ovarian cysts vary depending on the type of cyst. The symptoms of endometriosis and polycystic ovaries are addressed in the sections on these conditions. An ovarian cyst in the ovary can cause the ovary to twist. This is called ovarian torsion and it can cause waves of severe crampy abdominal pain. In bad cases of ovarian torsion the blood supply to the ovary can be cut off and the ovary can die. It is therefore important to pick this up and treat it quickly. However, it is usually evident as the woman will typically end up going to hospital because of the severity of her abdominal pain.

Dermoid cysts tend to be asymptomatic unless they become very large, when the woman may notice a swelling in her abdomen; occasionally they can twist, causing abdominal pain. Most commonly, however, they are picked up on an ultrasound that is being done for other reasons. The same applies to cystadenomas. Very large cysts may be palpable abdominally and picked up by your doctor, or you may even notice yourself that your abdomen has become swollen. However, they are more often imperceptible.

Simple ovarian cysts can rupture and leak their fluid into the pelvis. This can cause abdominal pain but does not cause any lasting damage. It is very rare for endometriosis or dermoid cysts to rupture. If they do, the contents of the cysts are more toxic and surgery is required. Rarely a woman may develop an abscess on her ovary and this needs to be treated with antibiotics and sometimes surgery and drainage. This is described further under pelvic disease and damage.

Most commonly ovarian cysts are detected by ultrasound scan. Occasionally MRI scanning can also be helpful. To make a definitive diagnosis of the actual type of cyst it is often necessary to do a laparoscopy to actually look at the cyst and even biopsy it. The advantage of this is that surgery can be done at the same time.

Treatment of ovarian cysts

As described above, functional or physiological cysts disappear by themselves. Because they are caused by disorders of ovulation, the oral contraceptive pill, which stops the woman ovulating, can be helpful in preventing these types of ovarian cyst. In young women who have had one or two episodes of troublesome ovarian cysts we would generally recommend the pill to keep her ovaries quiet and prevent further cysts. This can certainly help women avoid surgery which will ultimately damage their ovaries. The treatment of endometriosis or polycystic ovaries is described in the relevant sections.

Dermoid cysts and cystadenomas need to be excised if they measure more than 2–3 cm. This is usually done by a laparoscopy, when the cyst is removed from the ovary. Various techniques can be used, including scissors, diathermy or laser. The cyst is usually put into a bag and removed through a small keyhole incision. If the cyst is very large, open surgery or laparotomy may be required. This is particularly so for dermoid cysts as the contents of the cysts can be quite toxic if they spill in the abdomen.

Any surgery to the ovary will cause a scar in the ovary and in the last ten years or so it has become evident that ovarian cyst surgery may reduce the number of follicles in a woman's ovary and so reduce her ovarian reserve. For this reason surgeons and gynaecologists have become much more conservative in recent times regarding ovarian cyst surgery. If a woman is trying to conceive and she has a small ovarian cyst, we will often now prefer to proceed with fertility treatment such as IVF rather than remove the cyst as we want to maintain the woman's ovarian reserve in order to get as many eggs as possible from the IVF cycle.

With very large ovarian cysts there may be very little normal ovarian tissue present. In older women a preferable option may be an oophorectomy – removal of the entire ovary. However, it is very important that this is not performed unnecessarily in younger women because when they comes to conceive every follicle and egg will be important. Also, in older women, if the ovaries are being removed, the Fallopian tube is usually also removed because it lies very close to the ovary and there is less chance of bleeding if both are removed. It has also been recently discovered that many ovarian cancers actually start off in the Fallopian tube, so in women over 45 it is generally recommended that both ovaries and tubes be removed. However, in younger women we would always recommend a conservative approach and, even if the ovary is being removed, the Fallopian tube should be left in place.

Pregnancy and ovarian cysts

Sometimes ovarian cysts are not detected until during pregnancy. If they are large (greater than 3 cm) and if the precise type of cyst is not known, surgery may be required. Similarly, if the woman develops symptoms of pain she may actually require surgery. Surgery is usually performed at around 12 to 14 weeks of pregnancy because at this stage the embryo has been fully formed and the uterus is not yet too big to block access to the ovaries.

Endometriosis

Endometriosis is a gynaecological condition which occurs in up to 1 in 10 women and which typically causes painful periods, pelvic pain and infertility.

The medical definition of endometriosis is the presence of 'endometrium' outside the uterus or womb. The endometrium is the lining of the uterus. During the woman's menstrual cycle this lining gets thicker in anticipation of pregnancy. If the woman is not pregnant, the lining is shed as the woman's menstrual period. If we look with a microscope at the blood released during a period, we see that this blood actually contains tiny fragments of tissue, which are part of the endometrial lining. Most of the menstrual blood and tissue is discarded vaginally as the period, but some of this blood also travels from the woman's uterus back through her Fallopian tubes into her pelvic cavity. Most women are able to process this blood in the pelvic cavity and get rid of it. However, in some women, the fragments of tissue in the menstrual blood seem to be able to implant in the pelvis and continue to grow there. Each month when the woman menstruates these fragments of endometrium in the pelvis also menstruate. This is endometriosis.

If we look inside the pelvis of a woman who has endometriosis, we can see what the disease looks like. In some women the disease is minimal or mild and in these cases we see small spots or lesions peppered around the pelvis, a bit like freckles. These can be black (old endometriosis) or pink or white (new endometriosis) or inflamed (red endometriosis). Endometriosis lesions can occur anywhere in the pelvis but the most common sites are behind the uterus in an area called the pouch of

Douglas, under the ovaries, on the ovaries themselves and in front of the uterus. Very rarely the lesions can be found far away from the pelvis in places such as the lungs or the brain.

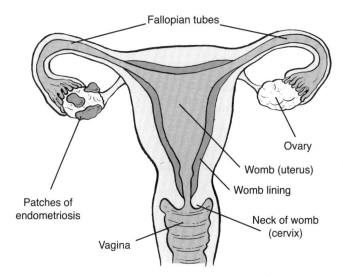

Endometriosis

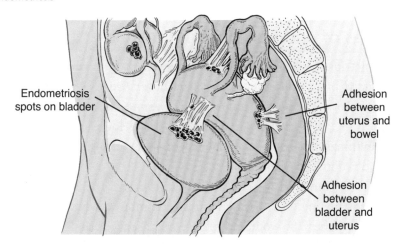

The internal bleeding within the endometriosis lesions during a period can cause pain and inflammatory and toxic factors are also released into the pelvis. In time, the bleeding and inflammation can, in some women, lead to scarring and the formation of what we call adhesions. The areas surrounding the endometriosis lesions can become sticky and can cause, for example, the uterus to adhere to the bowel or the ovaries to adhere to the walls of the pelvis. This in time can cause increasingly painful periods and even pain at other times of the cycle. If the pelvis is distorted, and particularly if the tubes and ovaries are involved, fertility problems can arise. Endometriosis in the ovary often forms into a cyst. The endometriosis bleeds into this cyst, causing a blood-filled cyst. Over time, the blood becomes thicker and darker, eventually resembling melted chocolate – these endometriosis cysts on the ovary are called endometriomas or 'chocolate cysts'.

Depending on the amount of endometriosis seen at laparoscopy and the location and type of disease, it is graded as minimal, mild, moderate or severe, also called respectively Stages I, II, III and IV.

In more severe forms of endometriosis the pelvis can be very distorted and sometimes we say that the area behind the womb (the pouch of Douglas) is 'obliterated'. All the organs in that area, including the uterus, Fallopian tubes, ovaries and bowel, become matted together by dense adhesions caused by the endometriosis. In some cases it may be impossible to even see the ovaries. A good medical reference for Endometriosis is the 2014 ESHRE Guideline on Endometriosis (3.9).

Causes of endometriosis

Endometriosis was first described in the 1800s and, since that time, thousands of scientists and researchers have tried to elucidate why it occurs in some women and not in others. Despite a wealth of information on the topic, this question remains unanswered. However, we do know of certain things that can increase the risk of endometriosis and which may be involved in its development.

It is very unusual for endometriosis to occur in a woman who is not menstruating. The disease is more common in women who bleed more than others. So women who have long, heavy periods which occur quite frequently, e.g. every 26 days, are much more likely to develop endometriosis than women who have light periods that occur at longer intervals of 35 days or so. All of this supports the theory of what we call **retrograde menstruation** – that endometriosis is caused in some way by blood going back through the Fallopian tubes and into the pelvis during menstruation. The more blood that goes back, the more likely the woman is to develop endometriosis. Because the oral contraceptive pill reduces the amount of bleeding and makes periods lighter, it tends to reduce the incidence of the disease but unfortunately does not prevent it. Other methods of contraception that reduce the amount of bleeding, such as Depo-Provera or the Mirena coil, also help. Fertility itself helps prevent endometriosis because, while a woman is pregnant, she will not be menstruating and so there is less blood to stimulate the endometriosis. Similarly, if a woman breastfeeds, this usually keeps her periods away and this in turn will help prevent endometriosis.

While we know that bleeding into the pelvis is involved in the causation of endometriosis, it is not clear whether it is the actual fragments of tissue in the menstrual blood which implant in the pelvis and lead to the development of lesions or whether there are certain factors in the menstrual blood that stimulate the lining of the pelvis to develop into endometriosis. No major differences have been found in the actual menstrual blood of women with endometriosis and those who do not have it but several studies (including some in our clinic) have shown differences in the actual uterine lining. Several differences have also been found in the fluid in the pelvis of women with endometriosis, but it is unclear whether these changes occur because of the endometriosis lesions or whether they actually predispose to the endometriosis. These changes include changes in immunological factors and other growth factors. While many women with endometriosis may have other auto-immune diseases, it has not yet been classified as an actual auto-immune disease.

It is known that some women are genetically susceptible to endometriosis. This is true particularly for the more severe forms of the disease. If you have a first-degree relative (mother or sister) with endometriosis you are six times more likely to develop the disease yourself. Unfortunately, there is not yet a genetic test for endometriosis susceptibility, but check out your mother's history.

Signs of endometriosis

The most common symptom of endometriosis is **pain**. Because endometriosis is caused by fragments of endometrium bleeding in the pelvis, most symptoms occur around the time of a woman's period or menstruation. While symptoms can occur at other times, they are typically worse during menstruation. *It is highly unlikely that a woman has endometriosis if she gets no period pain.*

So the most common symptom is painful periods or dysmenorrhea. Typically the pain starts a day or two before the period and most women who have bad endometriosis absolutely know when their period is coming. Women who don't have endometriosis often get surprised by their period and don't know it's coming until they see the first signs of blood. Because all women get some degree of cramping with their periods, it can be hard for a woman to know whether the amount of pain she has is normal or excessive. Generally I (and the medical profession generally) would grade pain as excessive if the woman misses work or school or college because of the pain or if it stops her going out and living a normal life.

Other symptoms related to endometriosis depend on where the actual endometriosis lesions occur. If there are lesions on the ovaries, the woman may complain of pain around ovulation time. A common place for endometriosis is behind the uterus. This is also the area where the bowel is located and so endometriosis in this area can cause painful bowel motions and even constipation or diarrhoea. This again occurs typically when the woman is menstruating because the bleeding endometriosis lesions aggravate the symptoms. This endometriosis behind her womb can also cause pain during sex (dyspareunia) because the affected area lies at the top of the vagina. Some women describe pain during intercourse and also a dull ache afterwards. Endometriosis in front of the womb, in the bladder area, can cause pain with urination, again typically during menstruation time.

There are other symptoms that can be associated with endometriosis but which are not typically related to lesions in the particular area. These include **fatigue**. A lot of women feel exhausted or just completely drained 'during menstruation'. Backache is another common symptom. Certainly any woman who is prone to backache will notice that it tends to be worse during menstruation. This is not always due to endometriosis but it can be more severe if the woman has the disease. The symptoms, particularly chronic pain, can also lead to depression, emotional problems and lower quality of life. Relationships can be affected, not to mention work.

The frustrating thing is that some women with endometriosis will not have any typical symptoms of pain. This even includes women who have severe endometriosis. Many international studies have shown a poor correlation between the degree of endometriosis seen and the actual symptoms caused. It is unclear why this is, but we do know that the location of the lesions (i.e. whether or not they lie close to nerve endings) can be a factor. There is also current research looking at nerve pathways and nerve endings of women who have chronic pain and there is evidence to suggest that some women do feel more pain than others because of their neurological systems.

One classic sign of endometriosis that is often ignored is what we call **premenstrual spotting**. This occurs a day or two before menstruation and women complain of a brown discharge or very light bleeding – before the period actually starts. This symptom should raise suspicions of endometriosis.

In very rare circumstances endometriosis can occur in unusual places such as the lungs or the brain. In these locations it also typically causes symptoms during menstruation times. Some women have been diagnosed because they develop a cough or even cough up blood during a period. Other women may have signs similar to epilepsy which occur only around menstruation time. However these types of distant endometriosis are very, very rare.

When should I suspect endometriosis?

If your periods are so painful that you are missing school, college or work, you could have endometriosis. Similarly, if pain during intercourse is stopping you having sex or if bowel symptoms around period time are significantly impacting your life, you should think about endometriosis. If you are trying to conceive and it's not happening and you have painful periods, endometriosis should be considered.

Endometriosis can run in families and if you have a sister or mother with the disease, you are more likely to have it than somebody who does not have any immediate relatives with the disease (aunts and cousins are not so relevant).

Diagnosing endometriosis

It is really important to consider a woman's symptoms and have a heightened suspicion of endometriosis if the symptoms are typical of the disease. Unfortunately, over the years there have been many studies showing that it can take up to seven or eight years for a woman to convince her doctors that she might have endometriosis. This is most likely because period pain is variable and not something we regularly talk about, so it can be hard for the woman herself to know if her pain is excessive. Thankfully, there is greater awareness now among doctors and other health professionals about the symptoms of endometriosis, so it is being diagnosed more frequently.

The other factor that contributes to a delay in diagnosis is the fact that, even to this day, the only sure test for endometriosis is a surgical procedure called a laparoscopy. This is, in effect, an operation, which requires a general anaesthetic and then insertion of a telescope into the abdomen to view the pelvis. Many researchers have been looking for years for a blood test that might identify endometriosis but unfortunately this has proved difficult to find.

Severe forms of endometriosis, in particular ovarian cysts due to endometriosis, can be picked up by ultrasound examination. Cysts will also be seen on an MRI scan, as will endometriosis lesions close to the bowel. However, many women can have normal examinations, normal ultrasounds and even a normal MRI and still have endometriosis. This is why laparoscopy is usually necessary to diagnose the condition.

In some women with endometriosis, thorough examination by their doctor may reveal signs of endometriosis. These include large ovarian cysts which can be palpated by a doctor, either by feeling the woman's abdomen or by doing a vaginal or internal examination. With this latter examination some women may be found to have scarring or thickening at the top of their vagina and this is indicative of deep or bowel endometriosis. Typically these women have severe pain and may have pain during intercourse. In less common situations endometriosis may be seen on the cervix when the women is having a smear test.

Treatment of endometriosis

Endometriosis can be extremely difficult to treat. However, there are several treatment approaches available and most women will find one or other option to suit them. The treatments available may be broadly divided into medical or drug treatments, surgical treatments and complementary medicine or lifestyle treatments. The treatment that works best for any particular woman will depend on several factors including her age, whether or not she wishes to conceive, the type of endometriosis she has, her symptoms, her tolerance for hormonal treatments and her suitability for surgery. Over the years I have found that women may have to try several different approaches before they find something that suits them. For this reason, a good relationship with one doctor who can work through the different options is preferable to seeing lots of different doctors and possibly getting lots of different opinions.

Medical or drug treatments for endometriosis pain typically involve medications which abolish the woman's menstruation or at least make her menstruation much lighter. The simplest drug is the oral contraceptive pill. This either makes the periods very light or abolishes them altogether and can alleviate symptoms in women who have painful periods and other symptoms related to menstruation. It can be taken in the usual fashion with a bleed every month or can be taken continuously for three or four or even more months at a time – we call this taking it 'back to back' – you start the second packet of pills when you come to the end of the first packet. The pill can be useful as a woman can stop and start it so that she has her period at a time that suits, e.g. she can avoid having a period when she is on holidays or on her wedding day! If she is using the pill for contraception, she needs to take it for at least three weeks in a row, but she can continue it for longer to 'schedule' her period when she wants it. Some women can stay on the pill continuously for months without having a bleed and this is perfectly safe. Other women, however, get irregular or what we call 'breakthrough' bleeding and if that happens they need to stop the pill for a week, have a bleed and then start again.

In a similar way, progesterone hormone given in tablet or injection form or as an implant can stop periods and therefore abolish menstrual symptoms. Contraceptive coils or IUDs (intrauterine devices) such as

Mirena or Jaydess, which contain progesterone, also tend to make women's periods very light or stop them and again can be very effective in treating endometriosis. Other drugs, GnRH analogues (described in the section on IVF) induce a temporary menopause state which again stops the woman's periods and menstruation-related symptoms. Unfortunately, these treatments are all contraceptive in action so they are unsuitable for women who are trying to conceive.

Table 3.5 Drugs to Treat Endometriosis

Drug	Route	Possible side-effects
Combined oral contraceptive pill	Tablet (cyclical or continuous)	Breakthrough bleeding, weight gain, mood swings, headaches
Progestogens Progesterone-only pill (Cerazette, Noriday)	Tablet	Weight gain, mood changes, acne, fluid retention, bloating, breakthrough bleeding
Provera, Duphaston, Primolut	Tablet	
Depo-Provera	Injection	
Mirena, Jaydess	Intrauterine device (coil)	
Visanne (not available in Ireland)	Tablet	
GnRH Analogues Decapeptyl, Prostap, Zoladex	Monthly injection	Hot flushes, headaches, dry vagina, mood swings, insomnia, decrease in breast size, irregular light bleeding during 1st and possibly 2nd month of treatment
Decapeptyl, Prostap, Zoladex	Three-monthly injection	
Suprefact, Synarel	Nasal spray	

Source: Ipsen Pharmaceuticals Limited

Surgery involves removing or destroying endometriosis lesions. This is preferably done at laparoscopy when the lesions are either excised with a scissors or destroyed using laser beams or an electronic current called diathermy. In more severe cases surgery may involve removing ovarian cysts and adhesions or, in very severe cases, removing an ovary. For women who have finished their family and who have failed with other treatments a hysterectomy (removal of the uterus) may be required but, thankfully, most women can avoid this.

Complementary medicine can be very effective for women with pain due to endometriosis. Chinese herbal medicine or acupuncture and reflexology can help significantly.

Diet may also help. Books have been written on diets for endometriosis. In my experience, no one diet works for everyone and I would not get caught up in difficult and very restrictive diets. However, some women find that reducing red meat helps; others feel better if they cut out wheat or dairy. I generally recommend 'playing around' with your diet and trying to figure out what works for you. It is important to avoid constipation and the general recommendations in Sinead's article on healthy eating (Section 2) will also help.

Fertility and endometriosis

Endometriosis is one of the main causes of reduced fertility in women. Having said that, we know that up to two-thirds of women who have endometriosis don't have any fertility problems. This is one of the enigmatic aspects of the disease.

It is easy to understand how severe endometriosis could affect fertility. If a woman's ovaries and Fallopian tubes are buried in the pelvis and distorted by adhesions due to endometriosis, it is not surprising that it will be difficult for the ovulated egg and the sperm to meet each other in the Fallopian tube, fertilise and lead to a pregnancy. While the tubes are not typically blocked, they may be stuck in a position that is too far away from the ovary for the egg to be able to bridge the gap. Similarly, ovarian cysts or endometriomas (chocolate cysts) can interfere with the ability of the ovary to produce good eggs and ovulate.

In milder forms of endometriosis, where the pelvis is not significantly distorted and where there are just small lesions on the walls of the pelvis or on the surface of the ovary, it is not so clear why there would be fertility problems. Several studies have shown that the fluid in the pelvis of women with endometriosis contains more toxins and factors that are negative for pregnancy than the pelvic fluid of women who don't have endometriosis. Some studies have also shown very minor alterations in ovulation in women with endometriosis and again these may impact on the development and quality of the eggs. More recent studies are showing very subtle differences in the lining of the womb of women with the disease and even small changes in the immune system. However, no clear cause or mechanism of subfertility has yet been internationally agreed. In some women, pain during intercourse can be enough to stop them having intercourse and this will obviously reduce their fertility.

Remember, up to two-thirds of women who have endometriosis will have no difficulty conceiving, but some do, and endometriosis is common in patients with infertility. Unfortunately it is hard to predict in advance the women who will have problems and those who won't. For that reason I always advise women with endometriosis to try to conceive as soon as is reasonable for them. The importance of not delaying pregnancy is discussed in detail in Section 2 and this is particularly important for women who have medical issues known to possibly impact fertility such as endometriosis.

It is generally recommended that all young women try to conceive for at least a year before seeking help. However, in the case of women with endometriosis I recommend referral to a doctor after six months of trying. These women may have had good control of their endometriosis because they were on the pill or other medication and they need to stop this in order to conceive. If they stay off medication too long, the endometriosis may recur or worsen. If the woman is young and all other factors related to fertility, such as AMH levels, sperm test and ultrasound scan, are all normal, it is reasonable to keep trying naturally for longer, but if there is another problem (e.g. a sperm issue) it is important to know about that too. All too often women (and their doctors) focus on one aspect of fertility and forget that there may be other issues involved too. A blood test to confirm ovulation should also be performed.

If women known to have had endometriosis have been trying to conceive for over a year it is very likely that they will require help to conceive. The two main options are surgery or assisted reproduction, most commonly IVF. (The drugs used to treat endometriosis are contraceptive and therefore not suitable for women who are trying to conceive.)

In women known to have mild endometriosis there is evidence that treating it surgically at laparoscopy may improve fertility. This is true also for more severe forms of the disease. If the woman's pelvis can be brought to a near normal state, it has been shown that somewhere between 30% and 50% will conceive in the year following surgery. Therefore, particularly in young women, a laparoscopy is usually the first option. But, as mentioned above, it is vital to first ensure that the partner's sperm is normal and that there are no other significant factors involved in the couple's fertility. There is no point doing surgery if the sperm quality is such that the couple would never be able to conceive naturally anyway. It is also important that the gynaecologist performing the laparoscopy will be able to treat the disease if it is seen.

In older women (over 35) you will need to discuss with your doctor the benefits of laparoscopy as opposed to proceeding to IVF without laparoscopy. Either approach is reasonable.

In some cases laparoscopy may not be recommended. This includes women who have had several laparoscopies in the past and who have failed to conceive after them. The presence of endometriotic cysts or endometriomas deserves particular attention. Treating ovarian endometriosis involves surgery or laser or diathermy to the ovary. Even if the surgeon is highly skilled, all these techniques can cause scarring in the ovary and reduce the number of eggs or follicles in the woman's ovaries and consequently her ovarian reserve. Therefore the pros and cons of surgery need to be carefully balanced. In particular, if a woman is known to already have a low ovarian reserve (low AMH and low antral follicle count), surgery should be undertaken only after very careful consideration as it is important not to reduce the ovarian reserve further. In a woman who has a good ovarian reserve and has not had previous ovarian surgery or in a woman who has extreme pain, surgery should be considered. As mentioned above, if there are other factors for infertility such as a significant sperm problem, surgery may not be of benefit as IVF will treat both fertility problems.

Assisted reproduction involves either IUI or IVF. These procedures are described in detail in Section 4. A few comments are worth noting with regard to endometriosis. Some studies have shown that the results of IUI and IVF are poorer in women with endometriosis compared to those who don't have the disease. Other studies have shown no difference. The poorer results may be due to some poorly understood effect of endometriosis on the woman's eggs or on her uterine lining which could interfere with implantation. Having said that, IVF is a very effective treatment for the majority of women with endometriosis.

IUI is an option only for women with mild disease (Stage I and II), but not for those with significant scarring or inflammation. The advantage of IVF is that the eggs and sperm are fertilised in the laboratory – away from the endometriosis and any inflammation associated with it. This does not happen with IUI. While IUI may be worth trying in younger women, in older women I would generally recommend proceeding to IVF. The drugs used for stimulation in IUI such as Clomid or FSH injections can lead to the development of endometriotic cysts and worsening of the endometriosis. While this can also occur during IVF treatment, it is less likely because fewer courses of treatment are generally required.

In deciding on a particular drug regime for IVF in women with endometriosis there is some evidence that protocols involving some ovarian suppression may be preferable, i.e. downregulation or pre-treatment with the oral contraceptive pill. This is because these approaches suppress the endometriosis before the woman starts the ovarian stimulation drugs. Different clinics will have different approaches and you should discuss this with your doctor. In the past when women presented for IVF and were found to have endometriosis cysts, the usual treatment would have been to remove the cysts before proceeding with IVF. In more recent years, however, it is deemed preferable to leave the ovaries alone and to proceed with IVF in order to preserve the woman's ovarian reserve. The complexities of this should be discussed with your doctor.

In women with severe pain due to endometriosis it may be necessary to perform surgery for the pain prior to proceeding with IVF treatment. Having said that, the majority of women having IVF will not develop major symptoms due to their endometriosis during their actual treatment, though there are some women who develop severe pain and will find the scanning, the ovarian stimulation, the after-effects of the egg collection and even embryo transfer more painful than other women. These women are, however, a minority. Again, if you are concerned, you should discuss this with your doctor.

Here is one endometriosis story.

'I was having an ovarian cyst removed off my left ovary through laparoscopy. While this procedure was being done the doctors discovered I had endometriosis, so therefore I was transferred to an endometriosis specialist. I had one son who is five years old but when he was two I had also a miscarriage, so I really did not understand what endometriosis was or if it would affect me having any more children. I then developed another cyst on my left ovary and had to have it removed and during this they also removed any endometriosis that they could.

We hoped this would improve my fertility and I would go on to have another child, but unfortunately that was not the case. My endometriosis was quite bad and was affecting my fertility. My only other option was IVF.

I noted during the sessions with the consultant that I had very bad period pains and at times it was so bad I couldn't get out of bed. She mentioned my options to investigate it and one was a laparoscopy and dye.

My period pain got to an all-time high. I remember being on my way to college and having to stop outside a pub and cower down against the wall in tears, the pain was that bad.'

Young women with severe endometriosis are one of the groups where freezing eggs, or oocyte vitrification, should be considered. I have come across young women who have required removal of an ovary or major surgery for endometriosis on their ovaries and this undoubtedly reduces their ovarian reserve.

There is very little research regarding oocyte vitrification in women with endometriosis, but it is certainly something that should be considered and discussed with women who have severe disease and who are not currently in a position to conceive. Oocyte vitrification is described in more detail in Section 4.

Pregnancy and endometriosis

The majority of women with endometriosis will be able to conceive, particularly if they are able to access IVF treatment and if they don't wait too long. Pregnancy itself does not generally cause problems for women with endometriosis. Indeed the symptoms of endometriosis tend to disappear during pregnancy. Because pregnancy and breastfeeding stop the woman menstruating, they have a beneficial effect on endometriosis and women who do conceive should seriously consider breastfeeding, not just because of the general benefits of breastfeeding for mother and baby but also because of the unique benefits in endometriosis.

Following the pregnancy, if you are considering contraception, it is worth considering options such as the oral contraceptive pill or a progesterone intrauterine device which will reduce the amount of menstruation and thereby help prevent endometriosis recurring or advancing.

Endometriosis and cancer

Many studies have been done to ascertain if there is an association between endometriosis and certain types of ovarian cancer. There seems to be some association but, thankfully, the risk is very low. However, more research is required. From what we know, the greatest risk is in women who are diagnosed after the age of 45 (not generally infertility patients), and who have very large cysts and no children. The link is not regarded as being enough to warrant screening for ovarian cancer in women with endometriosis. Other cancers have not been shown to be associated with endometriosis.

In my practice, I tend to monitor women with endometriomas (cysts due to endometriosis) with six-monthly or annual ultrasounds. For women over 40, if they develop increasing symptoms of pain or if the size of their cysts is increasing, I recommend surgery and continued surveillance. I have only seen one endometriosis patient who developed cancer during follow-up and she was someone who refused surgery and whose mother also had ovarian cancer.

Adenomyosis

Adenomyosis is a condition similar to endometriosis. We saw above that endometriosis involves endometrium (the tissue normally lining the uterus) being found outside the uterus. With adenomyosis that tissue is found in the muscle layer or the wall of the uterus. It is not common in women who are trying to conceive and is more common in women in their forties or fifties and in women who have had many children. In those women it tends to cause very heavy, painful periods.

With increased use of MRI scanning, we are beginning to diagnose adenomyosis more now than in the past. It presents in some women with infertility and very heavy and painful periods. The treatment is generally to proceed with fertility treatments such as IVF. In these cases the downregulation protocol with IVF may be preferable to an antagonist regime as the downregulation can be used to suppress the adenomyosis. It can sometimes be difficult to distinguish between large areas of adenomyosis and fibroids and an MRI scan can be useful. Generally surgery is not recommended for adenomyosis and ultimately some women will require a hysterectomy when they have finished having their family. In very severe cases, surrogacy may need to be considered.

Pelvic disease and damage

We saw in Section 1 how the woman's pelvis and, in particular, her Fallopian tubes are critical for natural conception. The egg is released from the ovary during ovulation and needs to be picked up by the Fallopian tube. It then must meet a sperm in the Fallopian tube and hopefully be fertilised. Then, as it forms an embryo and the cells start dividing, the embryo must move down along the Fallopian tube into the uterus. This is all a very delicate process and somewhat of a miracle. It entails some amazing signalling between the egg, sperm and Fallopian tube and also a healthy environment around the ovary and tube, i.e. in the woman's pelvis.

Any disease process in the pelvis can affect the Fallopian tubes and ovaries and their environment and can cause significant problems for natural pregnancy. Infection, surgery and endometriosis are the most common causes. The pelvis can become distorted by adhesions and scarring. The various different organs (uterus, ovaries, tubes and bowel) can be covered in scar tissue, somewhat similar to a layer of clingfilm, or can be stuck to each other. The Fallopian tubes may be blocked. If fluid collects in the Fallopian tubes it may cause a hydrosalpinx (see page 212).

Causes of pelvic damage

Unfortunately the woman's pelvis is at risk of infection as bacteria can travel up through the vagina and cervix into the uterus, along the Fallopian tubes and into the pelvis. This is how sexually transmitted infections (STIs) get into the pelvis. Alternatively, infection can occur in the appendix and if appendicitis is very bad or if the appendix ruptures, infection can travel from there to the Fallopian tubes.

The other major cause of pelvic damage is surgery. Any type of surgery in the region of the pelvic organs can cause scarring, particularly if there is any infection involved.

Endometriosis is the third major cause of pelvic disease and scarring. See Table 3.6 for more details.

Table 3.6 Causes of Pelvic Damage

Cause of problem	Situation
Infection	STIs (sexually transmitted infections)
	Pelvic inflammatory disease (PID)
	After surgery to abdomen or pelvis
	After D&C (dilation and curettage), miscarriage, termination of pregnancy
	Caesarean section
Surgery	Endometriosis
	Ovarian cyst
	Ectopic pregnancy
	Fibroids
	Tubal ligation (female sterilisation)
	Severe appendicitis/ruptured appendix
	Crohn's disease
	Ulcerative colitis
	Caesarean section
Other pathology	Endometriosis

Sexually transmitted infections (STIs) are infections that can be passed from one person to another by intimate sexual contact. They commonly affect the genitals, anus or mouth. They usually do not cause symptoms, but they may cause discharge from the vagina or penis, sores, growths or rashes. The most common STIs are chlamydia, gonorrhoea, herpes, syphilis, genital warts, hepatitis B or C and HIV. Candida or thrush is very common in the vagina. It is not generally regarded as an STI, but it can be passed from women to men and cause a rash or itching. Bacterial vaginosis is a condition where the balance of normal bacteria in the vagina becomes altered, leading to a vaginal discharge and odour. It is not sexually transmitted but it is associated with sexual activity and is often worse after sex. It can lead to problems in pregnancy.

Pelvic inflammatory disease (PID) is a term used to describe an upward-travelling infection in the female body that results from vaginal intercourse with an infected partner. The infection travels up to the uterus and Fallopian tubes and can cause pelvic damage. The most common organisms which cause PID are STIs such as chlamydia and gonorrhoea.

It has been shown that if a woman gets one chlamydia infection she will have up to a 25% chance of developing pelvic damage which can affect her fertility. If she has subsequent and repeated infections the chance of these problems increases dramatically. The amount of damage is probably related to the length of time the woman has the infection.

Signs of pelvic damage

The alarming thing about pelvic scarring and damage is that it is usually asymptomatic, i.e. the woman has no symptoms and may be totally unaware that there is a problem. It is therefore very important to know the risk factors that would raise suspicion – see Table 3.6.

Women who have a severe bout of pelvic infection will complain of pelvic pain and tenderness and may have a temperature and vaginal discharge. This is called acute pelvic inflammatory disease (PID). Occasionally such women may become very ill and require admission to hospital, but thankfully this is rare. In even rarer cases, a pelvic abscess may form and may need to be drained. Such severe disease can cause major fertility problems later on, due to scarring and damage to the Fallopian tubes.

Some women may develop chronic (long-standing) pelvic pain due to pelvic damage or adhesions (scar tissue) caused by infection, surgery or endometriosis. Symptoms of chronic pelvic damage include pain during menstruation, pain during intercourse, a dull aching feeling in the pelvis after intercourse, and infertility.

When should I suspect pelvic damage?

- If you have ever had an STI (see below), this may have caused pelvic or tubal damage, particularly if the infection was not treated quickly.
- If you have had a serious episode of illness due to any of the conditions in Table 3.6, you should be aware that there may be some residual damage or scarring in your pelvis, even if you have recovered from the original problem. The most common situations I see where surgery has led to fertility problems are surgery for Crohn's disease, ulcerative colitis, ruptured appendix, ovarian cysts, fibroids and endometriosis. You should also consider surgery that was performed when you were a child or baby.
- If you have had a temperature and signs of an infection following a D&C for a miscarriage, following a termination of pregnancy or following a Caesarean section.
- If you are trying to conceive and you know that you are ovulating well and that your partner has normal sperm, the next thing to investigate is the health of your pelvis.
- If you have had many sexual partners in the past and have not always used condoms, or if you have had abnormal smear tests, you may have had an asymptomatic infection which could have caused damage.

Diagnosing pelvic damage

The best way of assessing a woman's pelvis is to perform a laparoscopy (described earlier). This allows complete visualisation of the pelvis and accurate assessment of any damage. However, a laparoscopy requires a general anaesthetic and carries the general risks of surgery. But treatment can also be carried out at the time of laparoscopy – keyhole surgery.

Simpler tests to evaluate the Fallopian tubes include an HSG or a HyCoSy: a dye is inserted into the uterus via the vagina and an X-ray (HSG) or ultrasound (HyCoSy) is done to see if this dye passes out of the

Fallopian tubes. While these tests show the inside of the Fallopian tube and confirm whether or not it is blocked, the outside of the tube and any adhesions or scarring that might be there cannot be seen.

Ultrasound scans do not generally show up pelvic adhesions or Fallopian tubes but they will show severely damaged Fallopian tubes if they contain a hydrosalpinx (see page 212).

Treatment of pelvic damage

The treatment of tubal and pelvic disease involves surgery, followed by IVF if surgery fails.

Adhesions: Adhesions (scar tissue) may be fine and filmy or dense. It is usually easy to remove fine adhesions at laparoscopy, generally using a scissors. If adhesions are very dense and sticking internal organs together, e.g. an ovary to the bowel, there can be a risk of doing damage (e.g. to the bowel) and it may be safer to abandon surgery and proceed to IVF instead. In some women, any type of surgery may be deemed too risky and IVF may be a safer option.

Tubal surgery: This can be effective if the tubes are not too badly damaged. These would be tubes that have a thin wall and where the ends of the tubes, called the fimbrial ends, are relatively healthy. Surgery aims at opening the tubes and sometimes suturing or stitching them to keep them open. Tubal surgery can be complex and sometimes involves open surgery, preferably using a microscope. As the success rate of IVF is improving, tubal surgery is being performed less often but it can now be done by laparoscopy (keyhole surgery), so surgery would certainly be the first approach, as long as the woman is young and ovulating normally and her partner's sperm is normal. If there is another factor, such as a sperm problem, or if the woman is older or not ovulating, IVF may be the preferred treatment.

In long-standing infection the walls of the tube tend to thicken and, if this happens, no surgery whatever will allow them to be brought back to normal. Even if the tube is unblocked, the lining will be damaged and the tube will not function normally to pick up the egg, allow fertilisation and move the embryo along to the uterus. Pelvic infection with chlamydia or gonorrhoea causes the lining of the tubes to become flattened and stops them performing properly; again, this is not amenable to surgery. In these cases we definitely recommend IVF. IVF is very effective as it bypasses the

Fallopian tubes and fertilisation occurs in the laboratory rather than in the woman's Fallopian tube. Indeed, IVF was originally developed to treat blocked and damaged Fallopian tubes.

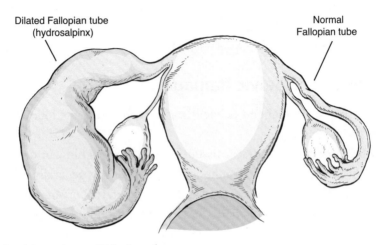

Dilated Fallopian tube
(hydrosalpinx)

Normal
Fallopian tube

Hydrosalpinx and normal Fallopian tube

Hydrosalpinx: The Fallopian tubes naturally produce small amounts of fluid (secretions) all the time and this fluid generally disappears out of the tubes and into the pelvis, where it is absorbed and disappears. If a Fallopian tube becomes blocked by infection or scarring, this fluid cannot escape and it collects in the tube, causing it to swell. A distended tube containing fluid is called a hydrosalpinx and this can be seen with an ultrasound scan.

While a hydrosalpinx itself is not harmful, it interferes with fertility and women with hydrosalpinx either require tubal surgery or IVF. We know from studies of IVF that, if a woman has a hydrosalpinx, her chance of success with IVF is reduced by up to 50%. For this reason, if we find a significant hydrosalpinx in a woman who needs IVF, we generally recommend removing it or blocking it off. It is thought that the reason it reduces success rates is that factors in the hydrosalpinx fluid travel down into the uterus and either wash the embryo out or interfere with its implantation in the uterus. By removing the tube or by clipping it at its junction with the uterus, we can prevent this fluid entering the uterus and hopefully improve IVF success rates. In some women who have had severe pelvic or abdominal infections in the past it may not be possible or safe to do a laparoscopy. In such women with a hydrosalpinx it may be possible to block the connection with the uterus by inserting an occluding device into the Fallopian tube via the uterus and hysteroscopy.

It is always very upsetting for women to need to have their tubes removed or clipped because it means that they will never be able to have a natural pregnancy with that tube. Therefore the only time we really recommend this is if (1) we are sure that the tube is highly unlikely to ever be able to lead to a natural pregnancy, and (2) the woman is contemplating IVF and we want to improve her chances of success with that.

Ectopic pregnancy: Women who have had ectopic pregnancies may also have damage to their Fallopian tubes. This can be assessed by HSG or HyCoSy and, if an abnormality is seen or suspected, a laparoscopy may be helpful. At laparoscopy the tube may be amenable to surgery to bring it back to a more normal state or, if there is a hydrosalpinx, it may need to be clipped or removed and IVF considered. Many women with an ectopic pregnancy require the affected tube to be removed. If both tubes have been removed because of ectopic pregnancies, the woman has no option but to proceed with IVF.

Uterine problems

The uterus or womb is where implantation takes place and where the foetus will hopefully live for the nine months of pregnancy. It is therefore critical for fertility and for a healthy pregnancy. Any structural abnormality or damage to the uterus will obviously impact on the pregnancy, but thankfully these conditions are rare. The whole issue of implantation and the immune system with regard to uterine implantation is very controversial and is described later.

Causes of uterine problems

When the uterus is developing in the early embryo, it forms from two halves, one from the right and one from the left – these are called the Mullerian ducts. These right and left ducts join together and fuse to form the uterus. The central area breaks down to leave a hollow organ, the uterus. In 2–3% of women this sequence of events does not happen perfectly and various types of 'uterine anomalies' may develop (3.10).

These are classified in various different ways and are probably best understood by looking at the diagram below. As time goes on we are realising that many different combinations of anomaly are possible, but the main ones are described below.

Because the ovaries and Fallopian tubes develop separately from the uterus in the embryo, they are not usually affected by uterine anomalies. However, the kidneys develop from the same groups of cells as the uterus, so women who are found to have a uterine anomaly should also have an ultrasound done to check that their kidneys are normal. Sometimes one kidney may be missing.

In some cases, one half of the uterus develops and the woman has what we call a **unicornuate uterus**. Such a uterus is smaller than usual and so these women may have a higher risk of premature labour (i.e. going into labour early). However, most women will be able to have a healthy pregnancy.

If the right and left sides fail to fuse, a woman can have a **double uterus** or **uterus didelphys**. These women may also have two cervices; some may also have a division in their vagina (a **vaginal septum**) and may also have a right and left vagina. Many women who have a vaginal septum may never realise it, while other women may have difficulty with sexual intercourse. In more rare cases the division in the vagina may totally block the cervix and when the woman

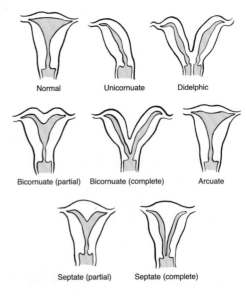

Uterine problems

begins to menstruate the menstrual blood is unable to pass out through her vagina. She can develop abdominal pain and a swelling as the uterus fills with blood. However, if the blockage is released the symptoms settle quickly.

A **bicornuate uterus** develops when the right and left uterus has attempted to fuse and has partially done so. The woman therefore has a double uterus but usually a single cervix. There is an indentation at the top of the uterus and this is critical in making the diagnosis.

All of these types of uterus do not require surgery. Indeed, it would be impossible to perform surgery without significantly damaging the uterus. In these cases the woman is at risk of premature labour but not usually infertility. There is also a slightly higher chance of late miscarriage, but this is rare. It is generally recommended that women with these abnormalities are monitored carefully in pregnancy and sometimes they may need a stitch placed in their cervix during pregnancy to try to reduce the risk of premature labour. Having said that, the majority of women with these uterine anomalies will have a healthy pregnancy.

Another type of uterine anomaly related to development is a **septate uterus**. In this case the right and left sides of the uterus have fused but the area in the middle, which is made of muscular or fibrous tissue, has been left behind, dividing the uterus. This forms a septate uterus or a **uterine septum**. Because the tissue in the uterine septum is more fibrous than in the normal uterine lining, a septate uterus can cause recurrent miscarriage and generally should be treated in miscarriage patients by removing the septum with hysteroscopic surgery. It is often also operated on in women with infertility but not always.

An **arcaute uterus** has a tiny indentation at the top of the uterus and is not significant.

Another less common uterine anomaly is a **rudimentary horn** where, at laparoscopy, it is seen that there is one fully developed side of the uterus but the second side has not developed and remains as a tiny piece of muscular tissue.

Diagnosing uterine problems

Most women with uterine anomalies do not know they exist until such time as they start having ultrasound scans. A septum or other uterine structural anomaly may be visible on ultrasound scan but MRI scans or 3D ultrasound are preferable for these cases. Hysteroscopy can also be useful.

Treatment of uterine problems

As discussed above, many uterine anomalies do not require treatment, but a septum should be treated in women who have had miscarriages. This involves surgery via hysteroscopy whereby the septum is resected or removed. Sometimes two procedures are required and the woman may be treated with hormones or a contraceptive coil for a month or two following the surgery. It is usual to perform a diagnostic outpatient hysteroscopy one to two months following the surgery to ensure that there is no scarring or adhesion formation following the surgery.

Fibroids

Fibroids are benign swellings or growths/tumours in the muscle layer of the uterus or womb. They are surprisingly common and by the age of 50 almost 70% of white women and more than 80% of black women will be found to have at least one fibroid. Fibroids may be single or multiple and can range in size from a few millimetres to 30 centimetres or more in diameter. Occasionally fibroids can grow so big that the women may appear pregnant due to the large swelling in her uterus. On the other hand, many women never know they have fibroids until they have an ultrasound scan performed. Fibroids are easily seen on ultrasound and therefore many women presenting with infertility will have a scan and will be found to have fibroids. Fibroids can also be called myomas or leiomyomas.

Fibroids can grow in any part of the uterus and their size and location are probably the biggest factors in deciding whether or not they need to be treated (3.11). Probably the most common fibroids are **intramural**, which means *in the wall*, and these fibroids are contained within the muscle wall of the uterus. They may be totally within the muscle wall (intramural) or may project onto the outside of the uterus or project into the cavity of the uterus (see diagram). Fibroids are called **subserosal**, where they project onto the outside of the uterus, or they may be **submucosal**, where they are projecting into the cavity of the uterus or womb. Fibroids may also be **pedunculated**, which means they are connected to the uterus on a fine stalk rather than being actually embedded in the wall of the uterus. Typically these fibroids are easier to remove than embedded fibroids.

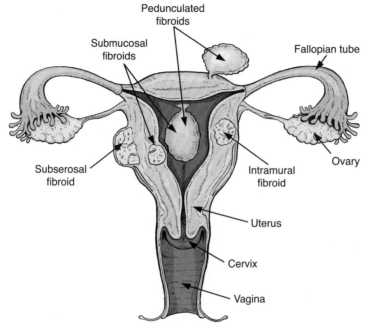

Pedunculated
fibroids

Submucosal
fibroids

Fallopian tube

Subserosal
fibroid

Intramural
fibroid

Ovary

Uterus

Cervix

Vagina

Fibroids in a uterus

Causes of fibroids

It is not known why women develop fibroids, but certain factors are important (3.12). There is definitely a genetic element, and Afro-Caribbean women are more likely to develop fibroids then Caucasians, while fibroids are uncommon in Asian women.

We know that each fibroid probably develops from just one cell in the muscle of the uterus which begins to divide abnormally, i.e. it is thought that each fibroid comes from a mutation in a single smooth muscle cell. However, this abnormal growth of cells is generally benign and highly unlikely to develop into cancer. We know that fibroids are very dependent on hormones, particularly oestrogen and progesterone. They therefore tend to be found in women of reproductive age but tend to shrink after the menopause. They also grow dramatically during pregnancy because of the increased hormone levels in pregnancy. There is also some evidence that fibroids can run in families.

Fibroids are more common as women get older and typically diagnosed in women in their forties and fifties. However, in my experience, when fibroids are diagnosed at an earlier age (i.e. at 20 or 30) they tend to be larger, grow faster and are more likely to need treatment than those found in older women.

Obese women tend to have higher oestrogen levels, so there is a link with obesity. The presence of a central distribution of body fat and metabolic syndrome are particularly associated with fibroids. There is also a possible link with a high intake of red meat. Fruits and vegetables may be protective. It is unclear whether hormonal treatments such as the pill or Depo-Provera or Implanon affect the growth of fibroids, but all these contraceptives reduce uterine bleeding and may help with heavy periods.

Signs of fibroids

Thankfully, for most women, fibroids are small and insignificant and do not cause symptoms, but are just seen on ultrasound scan. However, women with larger fibroids can have quite dramatic symptoms.

If the fibroid is submucosal, i.e. in the cavity of the womb, it is likely to cause heavy periods and also fertility issues. Once diagnosed these fibroids need to be removed. In older women with heavy periods and small submucosal fibroids medical treatments such as the Mirena coil may be effective.

The other typical symptom of large fibroids is pelvic pressure. If the fibroid is in front of the uterus it can press on the woman's bladder, causing frequent urination and difficulty emptying her bladder. If the fibroid is on the back wall of the uterus it can cause constipation and can press on the rectum, causing a pressure sensation, backache or leg pains.

Some pedunculated fibroids (which are on a stalk) can twist on the stalk from time to time and this can also cause intermittent abdominal pain. However, painful periods are not a particular symptom of fibroids and these are more likely to be due to endometriosis or adenomyosis. Women who have very heavy periods can develop anaemia (their iron levels become very low). For any young woman with anaemia, consideration should be given to her periods and, if these are heavy, fibroids could be a cause. Rarely, fibroids can block the Fallopian tubes if they are very close to the opening of the tube into the uterus.

When should I suspect fibroids?

If you are having difficulty conceiving and your periods are particularly heavy or if you feel that there might be something pressing on your bowel or bladder, then it is possible that you might have a fibroid or fibroids. However, most women with fibroids do not have any symptoms. Very occasionally when women have very large fibroids they may feel these as a swelling in their pelvis but in my experience this is not common as most women feel they are 'just putting on weight'. Fibroids are much more common in African women than in women of other races.

Diagnosing fibroids

Very large fibroids may be palpable as a swelling in the woman's abdomen or may be felt by a doctor during an abdominal or vaginal examination, but the majority of fibroids are discovered with ultrasound scans. MRI scanning is particularly useful in delineating fibroids and helping determine their exact location, something which is crucial when considering surgery. Saline scanning can be very useful for picking up submucosal fibroids as these project into the uterus and can be seen clearly. If a submucosal fibroid is suspected on an ultrasound scan, an outpatient hysteroscopy may also be helpful. HSG is not a particularly good test for diagnosing fibroids but occasionally they can be seen in the uterine cavity with this dye test.

Treatment of fibroids

Treatments for fibroids may be divided into medical, radiological or surgical. For women who are trying to conceive, surgical treatment is preferable. However, many women with fibroids do not need to have them treated so the first critical decision is whether or not treatment is indicated.

Which fibroids need treatment?

From a fertility point of view it has been clearly established that submucosal fibroids (in the uterine cavity) can interfere with fertility and these should be treated. I have seen women where the whole uterine cavity has been taken up by a fibroid. It is easy to see in such cases that it would be very difficult for an embryo to implant and grow there.

Most studies show that, unless they are very large, subserosal fibroids (on the outside of the uterus) are unlikely to influence pregnancy as they are located well away from the uterine cavity where the embryo is implanting. In general these fibroids are only removed if they are on a stalk and causing pain due to twisting or if they are particularly large (greater than 5cm).

Whether or not fibroids in the wall of the uterus should be removed is controversial and most studies have shown that if the fibroids are less than 5cms in diameter it is unlikely that they will significantly affect fertility. In order to remove these fibroids an incision needs to be made in the wall of the uterus and this itself can cause damage and scarring so a balance has to be made between the pros and cons of removing such fibroids. Certainly if fibroids are 1–2 cms in diameter it is unlikely that they will cause problems and most doctors would not recommend removing them. Consideration should also be given to the location of these intramural fibroids. The closer they are to the uterine lining the more likely they are to interfere with pregnancy and, again, this will influence the decision on whether or not to remove them.

Making a decision on whether or not to remove fibroids can be extremely difficult and it is often one of those situations 'where there is no one right answer'. It is, therefore, very important to discuss the pros and cons with your doctor who will also take into account all other aspects of your history (and your partners).

Surgical treatments

The most common treatment for fibroids for women who are trying to conceive is surgery. Submucosal fibroids are best treated hystersocopically and intramural or subserosal fibroids are treated by laparoscopy or laparotomy (open surgery). Pre-treatment is often given with drugs such as GnRH analogues or Esmya® to shrink the fibroid prior to surgery.

Myomectomy refers to the removal of fibroids (myomas) while leaving the uterus in place. Submucosal fibroids (in the uterine cavity) are removed by a hysteroscopic approach, i.e. a telescope inserted through the woman's vagina and cervix into her uterus. Removal can be achieved using a resection device whereby the fibroid is slowly chopped into small pieces which are then removed or more recently morcellation instruments have been developed. These again chop the fibroid into tiny pieces which are removed under suction control. The advantage of morcellation is that an electric current is not used and therefore any damage to the uterus itself is minimised. These techniques are, however, expensive and not all hospitals in Ireland will agree to fund them. Depending on the exact location of the fibroid they may be easy or difficult to remove. Pedunculated fibroids are relatively easy and usually can be removed in one procedure. However fibroids which are partially embedded in the muscle wall of the uterus can be more difficult to excise and two attempts at surgery may be required. A 'second look' hysteroscopy is often done about two months after surgery to ensure there is no scarring in the cavity.

Intramural or subserosal fibroids are removed with surgery performed either by laparoscopy or laparotomy (open surgery). This surgery can be difficult and can result in significant bleeding, requiring blood transfusion. If a fibroid is large, and particularly if it is extending right through the wall of the uterus into the uterine cavity, it is usually recommended that the woman have a Caesarean section in the future as the surgery leaves quite a scar in the uterus. Surgery can also distort the uterus and this is why we have to be careful when contemplating surgery. Repeated surgery can be particularly difficult because there will be scar tissue from previous surgeries. This is more common in women of African origin, who are more likely to need multiple surgeries, and I have certainly come across one case where the uterine wall was completely destroyed by repeated surgery for fibroids. With any surgery to the uterus, there is a tiny chance of getting uncontrollable bleeding, which necessitates doing a hysterectomy. This is extremely rare and, thankfully, I have never seen it happen, but we would usually warn any woman having fibroid surgery that there is a tiny chance of requiring a hysterectomy if she develops uncontrollable bleeding.

For women who have completed their family and who have very large fibroids, hysterectomy may be preferable to myomectomy. This however is not a consideration for women who are trying to conceive.

Medical treatment

In women who have very heavy periods due to fibroids, hormone treatments that reduce the amount of bleeding, such as the oral contraceptive pill, Mirena coil or Depo-Provera reduce the amount of bleeding and this may be sufficient to control the woman's symptoms. They are, however, no help to women who are trying to conceive.

New drugs have recently come on the market for managing symptoms due to fibroids. These are called selective progesterone-receptor modulators (SPRMs) and one available in Ireland is Esmya (ulipristal acetate). These drugs are not licensed for long-term treatment but are useful as pre-treatment prior to surgery or uterine artery embolisation (see below). GnRH analogues are also used to shrink fibroids but these drugs are only licensed for treatment for six months, or a year at most, and are not a long-term option for fibroid management.

Drugs are of no benefit to women with fibroids and infertility, except prior to surgery or IVF.

Uterine artery embolisation

Uterine artery embolisation is a technique, usually performed by radiologists, whereby small particles are injected into the arteries supplying the uterus in order to cut off the blood supply to the fibroids. This eventually causes them to shrink and die. If the fibroids are submucosal they can break down and be discharged through the vagina.

The role of uterine artery embolisation for fertility patients is very controversial. Because the treatment targets the blood vessels supplying the uterus there is a chance that some of the blood vessels supplying the ovary can also be affected and there have been reports of early menopause following this treatment. In addition, other parts of the uterus apart from the fibroid may be affected.

This treatment is highly effective for women who have completed their family and where surgery would be difficult, but most fertility specialists would advise surgery rather than uterine artery embolisation for women who are contemplating pregnancy. Having said that, there are certain cases where surgery might not be advisable and certainly uterine artery embolisation may be considered in these cases.

A new technique of MRI – guided ultrasound-focused treatment of fibroids – is being developed but I am not aware of any centre in Ireland currently providing this treatment. There is also very little evidence of its use in women wishing to conceive.

Fertility treatments

Most fertility patients with small fibroids do not require any treatment for these fibroids. They are therefore managed as for other fertility patients. In women undergoing IVF, it may be preferable to use downregulation rather than antagonist protocols if there are significant fibroids, as the GnRH analogues used in downregulation are known to shrink fibroids. While this has not been studied in any specific clinical trials, I have personal experience of some young women with multiple fibroids who did particularly well using the downregulation approach prior to IVF. If fibroids are submucosal and distorting the uterine cavity they should certainly be removed prior to fertility treatment. Indeed, if they are significantly large they may well be the cause of the woman's fertility problems or miscarriage and, in such cases, couples should continue trying to conceive naturally for six months to a year following such surgery.

Pregnancy and fibroids

Fibroids tend to grow during pregnancy but, thankfully, in the vast majority of cases this does not have an adverse effect. Again, whether or not they cause problems depends on the location of the fibroids. Fibroids which distort the uterine cavity can impact the way the baby lies in the uterus and there is a slightly higher chance of breech presentation. In women who have surgery for fibroids there is a higher requirement for Caesarean section during pregnancy, but this is only if the fibroids that were removed were large and were impacting the uterine cavity. There is a rare complication of pregnancy called red degeneration of a fibroid where the fibroid grows rapidly during the pregnancy and outgrows its blood supply, causing pain in the fibroid. Generally the woman is managed conservatively with painkillers and symptoms usually settle.

Fibroids and cancer

Rarely fibroids can become malignant and become what we call **sarcomas**. These are serious tumours. Luckily, they are rare in young women, occurring in less than one in 500 young women with fibroids. However, in women in their seventies malignant change can occur in up to 1% of fibroids. This risk has raised concerns regarding morcellation (breaking up) of fibroids during surgery. There have been some rare incidents where a fibroid was removed by keyhole surgery. Because of the size of the fibroid and the fact that the incisions in keyhole surgery are very small, the fibroid needs to be morcellated or broken up in order to remove it through the small keyhole incisions. An instrument such as a morcellator is used for this. There have been some sad cases where it was not known that a fibroid was malignant and then malignant cells were spread around the pelvis during morcellation. For that reason morcellation is banned in the United States. In Europe morcellation is felt to be safe as the risk of malignant change is minimal in young women, but as a precaution, when we are morcellating fibroids at laparoscopy, we now do this within an endoscopic bag which will contain all the pieces and prevent spread around the abdomen. Having said that, it is important that these risks are discussed with patients prior to surgery. Morcellation at laparoscopy should not be confused with morcellation at hysteroscopy. With hysteroscopy the procedure is contained within the uterine cavity and the uterine cavity is flushed out, so even if a fibroid has some malignant cells (which is extremely rare in these cases), the chance of spreading those cells is minimal.

Endometrial scarring (Asherman's syndrome)

Any type of surgery can leave a scar – however good the surgeon. Uterine surgery is no exception. Thousands of women have procedures performed for miscarriage or termination of pregnancy whereby a D&C is performed or suction is used to empty the contents of the uterus. In the vast majority of these cases the procedure is very straightforward with no long-term complications.

Unfortunately, in some women this surgery can lead to uterine adhesions or scarring within the cavity of the uterus. When a woman subsequently tries to conceive she may have difficulty. Scarring may also occur following the removal of fibroids or (less commonly) polyps from the uterine cavity. Such scarring is generally referred to as 'Asherman's syndrome'. Mild cases of Asherman's syndrome are easy to treat and cause few problems, but severe cases can involve quite a degree of uterine damage.

Diagnosis of Asherman's syndrome

The first sign of uterine scarring is usually very light or no periods following the D&C or other procedure. Asherman's syndrome can sometimes be suspected on ultrasound scan when an irregular uterine cavity is seen. At other times the uterine lining can appear very thin if there is a lot of scarring or, in less severe cases, pockets of fluid can be seen within the uterus. These irregularities can also show up on a HSG or HyCoSy. A definitive diagnosis is made by performing a hysteroscopy, preferably as an outpatient procedure. A telescope is inserted into the uterus to assess the degree of damage. In very severe cases, it may not be possible to pass the telescope into the uterine cavity and general anaesthesia may be required.

Treatment of Asherman's syndrome

Treatment is performed by uterine surgery via a hysteroscope. Scissors or diathermy are used for this. Mild cases of Asherman's syndrome are easily treated with very good effect but, in severe cases, it can be difficult and two or more attempts may be required. Rarely treatment may be impossible and, sadly, surrogacy may be the only option.

Following surgery, it is usual to leave a balloon device or a contraceptive coil in the uterus for a while and also to prescribe high-dose oestrogen therapy to aid healing. Some exciting trials are currently looking at stem cells to try to stimulate the lining of the uterus to heal and regenerate after damage, but these studies are at an experimental stage of development.

Cervical problems

The cervix or neck of the womb is another body part that is essential for fertility. The cervix connects the vagina to the uterus (womb) and is really a part of the uterus. It allows sperm to swim into the uterus and from there up into the Fallopian tubes to meet the egg. During the woman's menstrual cycle the cervix produces special cervical mucus. The mucus is maximal just before ovulation and this greatly helps the sperm swim in. At other times of the cycle the mucus is scanty and cloudy and does not facilitate sperm transport. The importance of cervical mucus and sex around this time is described in Section 1.

Not all women notice cervical mucus and this is not a problem. Depending on the size and nature of a woman's individual cervix she may produce more or less mucus. However, we are sometimes concerned about women who have had a lot of surgery to their cervix as this can certainly reduce the amount of mucus and affect fertility.

Cervical surgery

The most common reason for surgery to the cervix is the treatment of abnormal smear tests. Smear tests are performed to pick up pre-cancerous changes and, if these changes are found, the abnormal cells need to be removed to prevent cancer developing. The most common treatment for this is called a LLETZ procedure, where a small piece of cervix, containing the abnormal cells, is removed. (LLETZ stands for large loop excision of the transformation zone.) This procedure has been a major medical advance in terms of preventing cervical cancer in women. However, since its introduction, doctors and researchers have realised that such surgery to the cervix can, in rare cases, cause infertility and difficulties in pregnancy. If the area of abnormal cells is large or if it keeps recurring, a second LLETZ procedure may be required, or other procedures, such as a cone biopsy, which involve removing a greater part of the cervix. This is more likely to cause subsequent fertility and pregnancy problems. Many young women with early cervical cancer are now surviving the cancer, but they often need to have the entire cervix removed (**trachelectomy**).

It is now well known that if a woman has a large piece of tissue removed or if she requires several LLETZ procedures, she is at increased risk of late miscarriage or premature delivery, because the cervix is weakened and unable to carry the pregnancy to full term. Surprisingly little research has been done on the effect of a LLETZ procedure on fertility itself (i.e. the possibility of actually getting pregnant). One of my colleagues, Dr Fiona

Martyn, performed a large survey in 2012 looking at women who have had a LLETZ procedure and their subsequent fertility (3.13). This was the first large-scale study to be done in this area. Thankfully it showed that, for the vast majority of women having a LLETZ procedure, there was no impact on fertility. We can therefore reassure women having a single LLETZ procedure that it is very unlikely to affect their fertility.

However, while there is very limited data on the effects of more extensive surgery to the cervix on fertility, I have certainly seen women who have had infertility due to repeated or extensive cervical surgery. In these women the cervix can be severely damaged and this can be seen by performing a speculum examination (the examination we do to perform a smear test). The more surgery required, the greater the risk of scarring at the cervix, with subsequent reduced fertility and increased risk of late miscarriage and premature labour. However, we have to remember that this surgery is required to prevent cancer.

Treatment of cervical problems

If on examination the cervix looks scarred and the woman does not get normal cervical mucus during her cycle, IUI may be a useful treatment. This is described in detail in Section 4 – basically, sperm are inserted into the uterus around the time of ovulation. If a couple's infertility is due to cervical factors, IUI should be successful. However, there may be other factors and some couples with unexplained infertility may fall into this category.

If the woman is older or there are other problems, IVF may be preferable to IUI and this is also discussed in Section 4. With both of these techniques cervical mucus is no longer necessary as with IUI the sperm are being placed into the uterus and, in the case of IVF, the embryos are being placed into the uterus.

Sometimes the cervical scarring may make the transfer of sperm (with IUI) or embryos (with IVF) to the uterus difficult. It may be possible to dilate the cervix prior to the procedure or, occasionally, the embryos may need to be put into the uterus through the wall of the uterus rather than through the cervix.

Prevention of pregnancy problems

For any woman who has had several LLETZ procedures or who has had more invasive surgery to her cervix, such as a cone biopsy, it is important that her cervix is assessed prior to embarking on pregnancy, because of the risk of cervical incompetence and early delivery. This applies to women having fertility treatment but also to women undergoing natural pregnancy. It is common now for doctors performing cervical surgery to discuss the pregnancy implications with their patients, and this is good practice.

In any woman we suspect might have cervical problems, we would recommend that she attends a high-risk pregnancy clinic where her cervix can be monitored during pregnancy, usually with ultrasound. If it is felt that her cervix is 'incompetent', i.e. shorter and likely to be unable to hold a pregnancy to full term, she may be considered for progesterone treatment during pregnancy or the insertion of a stitch in her cervix. Cervical stitches or sutures are generally inserted during pregnancy at around 12–14 weeks and a general or spinal anaesthetic is required. In women who have a very deficient cervix, where we know they need a stitch but where there is very little cervix left, it may be necessary to put a stitch in from above via a laparoscopy procedure. This is done prior to pregnancy and involves a laparoscopy and general anaesthetic.

Problems with cervical mucus

In the past, it was felt that many women might have infertility because their mucus was in some way 'hostile' to sperm and either killed it or prevented it gaining access to the uterus. This formed the basis of the **post-coital test**. This test involves asking a couple to have sexual intercourse at the time of or just prior to ovulation and then for the woman to attend to have a sample of her cervical mucus taken (as per a smear test). This is then examined under a microscope to see if there are actively motile sperm swimming in it.

The value of this test is controversial and is a subject of continuing debate. Large studies have failed to show a great benefit and it is unclear if the mucus is really hostile or if it is just that the timing of the sample is not perfect (it has to be accurately timed to ovulation). A normal test result is very reassuring, but it is hard to know the significance of an abnormal result. It is a difficult test to do and, in my experience, and that of others, women really do not like it. Also, given that, irrespective of the result, we are likely to be recommending treatments such as IUI and IVF that bypass the cervix, it is now rarely done in Ireland, Europe or the USA.

Unexplained infertility

Unexplained infertility (UI) or unexplained subfertility refers to situations where a person or couple have had full investigation of their fertility problem and no precise cause has been found. Tests have shown that the woman is ovulating, she has no disease in her pelvis and the man's sperm test is normal. Everything seems to be okay, but they are just not getting pregnant.

UI occurs in approximately one in five couples with infertility and is extremely distressing. While, in some ways, it is good news that no abnormality has been found and nothing definite that would prevent pregnancy, the fact that there is no obvious reason is very difficult to cope with. In my experience (and that of most fertility specialists), people with UI question everything in their lifestyle and 'beat themselves up' thinking that they may be too stressed, not eating the right things, drinking too much alcohol or caffeine, working too much, not having sex at the right time or in the right way, and so on and so on. In fact, they are usually doing everything perfectly. My heart goes out to them.

There is also a huge sense of frustration – not just with themselves and their partner, but even more so with their doctors, healthcare professionals and the medical and scientific community generally: 'In this day and age how can it be "unexplained"? Surely the doctor/clinic must be missing something, just does not know enough or is not trying hard enough!'

> 'Sometimes having an issue helps. Wanting answers that can't be found and trying to cope with the negative tests month after month. Jenny and I focused on the bigger picture and tried to keep a positive mind-set. The hardest part is there are no definite answers – no real definite answers.'

As a doctor, I (and my colleagues) find UI equally frustrating. We rack our brains to think what else we can do and, unfortunately, there are no easy answers. However, the good news is that, if couples can persist and not give up hope, the majority will be successful.

Diagnosis of unexplained infertility

UI is usually diagnosed if a couple fails to conceive after one year of regular unprotected sexual intercourse even though investigations for ovulation, pelvic, cervical or uterine problems and sperm tests are all normal.

Some clinics and doctors claim that a cause can always be found if one looks hard enough. However, the difficulty here is that there are many tests and treatments related to infertility that have not been found by large, well-designed international studies to be worthwhile or effective. In addition, these tests often show up minor abnormalities that are actually what we call 'not clinically significant' and patients can spend a lot of time, energy and money on these unimportant results. Nevertheless, some clinics still offer these tests and patients can spend vast amounts of money and time without any proven benefit. I tend to follow the guidance of reputable international bodies such as ESHRE, ASRM, NICE and the British Fertility Society (BFS) and also good-quality articles in medical publications as to which tests and treatments are worthwhile and which are not. Having said that, I always tailor the tests and treatment to each individual couple's unique situation because, like all areas of medicine, one size doesn't fit all.

The assessment and investigations which must be done before one can say that any couple has UI are listed below.

Table 3.7 Assessment of Unexplained Infertility

History	No significant male or female medical problems, including infection, now or in past
	Woman has normal menstrual cycle
	Woman has no symptoms of endometriosis
	No lifestyle issues (age, weight, smoking, etc.)
	No sexual issues and having sex appropriately
Female tests	Proof of ovulation – progesterone blood test or positive LH in urine kits
	Normal trans-vaginal ultrasound scan
	Patent tubes on laparoscopy or HSG or HyCoSy
	Normal speculum exam if previous cervical surgery
Male tests	Good-quality semen analysis

Potential contributing factors

Human fertility is complex and absolutely fascinating. In order to achieve a healthy pregnancy, so many little things have to fall into place at the right time. It may be that, with unexplained infertility, lots of small factors come into play and, while none of them is enough on its own to stop fertility, a few factors combined together may just be too much!

Some of the issues that may underlie UI include the following.

Age of the woman: The problems associated with female age and egg quality are described in detail in Section 2. Studies have shown that, while UI affects women of all ages, it is more common in older women. A study of over 7,000 women in Scotland in 2008 showed that women over 35 years were almost twice as likely to be diagnosed with UI as those under 35. This is felt to be most likely due to the deterioration in egg quality with age but could also be related to an increased chance of obesity and reduced frequency of sex in older couples (3.14).

Lifestyle factors: These are discussed in Section 2. Smoking affects fertility in both men and women, as does obesity and the use of recreational drugs such as cannabis. Even if all the couple's tests are normal, these lifestyle factors can have an effect that cannot be measured by our current tests – e.g. we know that, even if a male smoker's semen assessment is normal, his smoking will still reduce his fertility.

Tubal function: The Fallopian tube is a very fine complex structure – at a microscopic level there can be damage to the lining which is invisible to the human eye and will not be picked up by HSG, HyCoSy or even laparoscopy. So, even though the tubes are not blocked, they may not be functioning perfectly. If that is the case, IVF should help because it bypasses the Fallopian tubes.

Endometriosis: A laparoscopy is not necessary to make a diagnosis of UI, so it may be that some women classified as having UI may actually have minimal or mild endometriosis. This is a difficult situation because minimal and mild endometriosis can only be diagnosed by laparoscopy, which is an invasive procedure – an operation under general anaesthetic, which has significant risks.

In the past, laparoscopy was performed for all women presenting with infertility. And I have seen many women who had this procedure done and nothing was found. International guidelines now recommend that laparoscopy is only done if the doctor (or patient) has reason to think that she might have endometriosis or other pelvic problems. We therefore do it if the woman has very painful periods or an abnormal scan or a history of issues that could have damaged her pelvis. But we don't generally recommend it for women for whom everything seems normal. One of the reasons for not always recommending laparoscopy, is that, if we find minimal or mild endometriosis we treat it and that *may* help fertility. But the woman (and her partner) need to be happy to try naturally after the laparoscopy for at least six months, and ideally a year, to give it a chance to work. Many women, particularly if they are older or have a low ovarian reserve, will be better to just get on with assisted reproduction treatment rather than having a laparoscopy. There is no evidence that treating minimal or mild endometriosis prior to IUI or IVF improves success, so if a couple with UI are happy to proceed to IUI or IVF, I do not recommend laparoscopy just to look for minimal or mild endometriosis.

Undetectable ovulation issues: Some detailed studies of women with UI, where they had their hormones measured every day over a complete menstrual cycle, show very minor hormonal abnormalities that may be relevant. But it is not practical to do daily blood tests on women and the results of these studies are not very convincing. However, it is possible that some women's eggs and ovulation are not perfect. Research is being done in this area and may give some clues in the future.

Sperm problems: In many ways, our standard semen analysis is a rather crude test and there may be small abnormalities in sperm that we are currently unable to detect in couples thought to have UI. However, IVF, and particularly ICSI, are very effective in treating sperm problems and are likely to work for most men with UI.

Fertilisation problems: Couples with UI often wonder if maybe their eggs and sperm are 'not compatible with each other', i.e. they don't fertilise. Unfortunately, the only way to currently study fertilisation is to do IVF and see what happens when the sperm and eggs are placed together in the lab. Some couples with UI can have unexpectedly poor rates of fertilisation and this suggests that there is some underlying problem, either with the eggs or the sperm, or maybe with how they interact together. Medical science has not yet found a reliable way of testing fertilisation and if a couple have very low fertilisation rates, we recommend ICSI, a specialised type of IVF.

Implantation problems: Many women with UI, not surprisingly, wonder if they are actually ovulating, achieving fertilisation and forming an embryo but then have some defect in the lining of their womb such that the embryo can't attach and implant. (Implantation is discussed later.) It is an area of fertility research that is becoming more and more important now that fertilisation can be achieved with IVF and ICSI. However, implantation is extremely complex and, unfortunately, there are currently no reliable tests to check on a woman's ability to let an embryo implant – except by doing IVF.

Immune problems: The relationship between infertility and the immune system in women is one of the most controversial and 'hottest' topics in fertility at present. This is described in detail later. I am inclined to think that there may well be immune problems in some couples with UI but, sadly, I am convinced that there is as yet no reliable and appropriate way of testing for or of treating this. And most couples with UI will conceive with IVF without any of the proposed treatments for 'immune problems'.

Treatment of unexplained infertility

Because by its very nature we don't have a defined cause for UI, our treatments are not focused on a particular abnormality or disease. This is, as I have already said, very frustrating for couples.

Expectant management: Studies in many countries have shown that a quarter of couples diagnosed with UI will conceive naturally in the year following investigation and diagnosis and up to 70% in the two years following diagnosis (3.15). This is something we also see at our clinic. However, it is very difficult to expect a couple who have already been trying for two years (or even a year) to just continue trying naturally. If they are, however, young (the woman is under 32 or 33) this is probably the best thing to do. There are no medical risks and no cost.

IUI: The role of IUI in UI is controversial and some doctors internationally recommend it, while others don't. I think a lot depends on the woman's age, her ovarian reserve and the couple's overall wishes and stress levels, and, of course, in Ireland, their ability to pay for treatment. All of these factors need to be discussed and assessed for an individual couple. For couples with UI where the woman is under 35, two to four cycles of IUI are a good option and we would expect around 20% of couples to conceive after four cycles.

IVF: For couples where the woman is over 35 or has a low ovarian reserve or for couples who have been trying naturally for more than three years, I would generally recommend going straight for IVF. The success rates here are the best one will get from any fertility treatment, though IVF, as discussed in Section 2, is invasive, stressful and expensive. IVF certainly seems to be the best option for UI if the woman is 38 or older.

Clomid: Clomid is a good drug for helping women with ovulation problems to ovulate. However, I see a lot of women who are ovulating and who want to try it – and indeed are prescribed it by their doctor. However, all the recent good-quality studies internationally show that Clomid is not effective for UI. Indeed, a multi-centre Scottish study showed that it might even reduce success rates compared to just trying naturally (3.16). It is also associated with multiple pregnancy. I therefore almost never prescribe it for UI. If it is used, women should be scanned for at least one treatment cycle to ensure they are not over-responding and at risk of a triplet or even quadruplet pregnancy.

UI is distressing and extremely frustrating for all involved. However, it is good that the man and woman involved are healthy and there is a high chance of spontaneous pregnancy – even after two to three years of failure. Failing that, IUI offers modest success and IVF is very effective, especially if the woman is under 40.

Sexual problems

The challenges of sex for couples with infertility are described in the next section by Meg Fitzgerald and male sexual problems are discussed in the section on male infertility. Apart from the very real stresses caused by difficulty conceiving and the impact that has on one's sex life, there are certain specific female problems which can cause sexual difficulties.

Table 3.8 Female Sexual Problems

Vaginal problems	Discomfort due to infection, particularly thrush (candida) or herpes
	Discomfort due to vaginal dryness
	Trauma to the vagina
	Vaginal developmental abnormality, e.g. septum
	Pain in an episiotomy scar (after childbirth)
	Pain following other vaginal surgery
	Radiotherapy for cancer
	Vaginismus
Deep (pelvic) problems	Endometriosis
	Pelvic infection/PID
	Adhesions after surgery
	Ovarian cyst
	Fibroid

Pain with sex (dyspareunia)

Sex should be comfortable and enjoyable but may be more so at some times than others. If it is always uncomfortable, there may be something wrong. Doctors and health professionals talk about the pain being superficial or deep. Superficial means that the pain occurs around the vaginal area, usually when attempts at penetration are being made. Deep pain happens after penetration and is due to the man's penis (or other object) hitting off the cervix and upper vagina. Not surprisingly, superficial pain is likely to be due to issues with the vagina while deep pain is more likely to be related to issues in the pelvis. However, there can often be a combination. If a woman with deep pain is expecting to feel pain, her vaginal muscles may subconsciously tighten up and this will cause superficial pain and discomfort also. The main conditions causing dyspareunia are shown in Table 3.8.

If any of them are severe, the woman may be unable to have sex at all and this is called apareunia.

Vaginismus

Vaginismus is when the muscles around the vagina tighten involuntarily whenever there is an attempt to penetrate it with something. This could be your partner's penis, your finger or a tampon. It is not always understood why the condition happens and this can be extremely frustrating for women. For some women, it may be caused by a traumatic past sexual experience but, in my experience, this is less common than you would think. It is also more common in women who have grown up in an environment where sex is not talked about freely or where there are strong taboos around sex. Most of the women I see can't pinpoint an obvious cause.

Vaginismus is very treatable and treatment is usually done in conjunction with a psychosexual counsellor or sex therapist. If you are in a relationship, your partner will need to be involved at some stage. Vaginismus often gets worse as time goes on and infertility can certainly aggravate it, so try to seek help sooner rather than later. If women are unable to tolerate any form of penetration during sexual intercourse, they may be able to do artificial insemination at home, i.e. insert their partner's sperm into their vagina using a quill or syringe. I have seen many couples conceive in this way.

The HSE has an excellent website regarding vaginismus which can be accessed from www.hse.ie.

Let's Talk about Sex

BY MEG FITZGERALD MSW, DipPST

Sex and sexuality may mean different things to different people. For some, sexuality may define how you see yourself as a man or a woman. How you dress, talk, laugh, wear your hair or present yourself to other people. Sex or sexual functioning may be seen as what we do to express ourselves sexually and as with every other aspect of our lives, sexual functioning will change and vary as we go through different stages of our life.

Sex may serve different purposes at different times of one's life cycle. It may be seen as a way to experience pleasure, a means of stress relief, a way of exercising and keeping fit, a means of communication, a way to feel good about oneself, a way to play and have fun. For many, it is a way to become pregnant and to start a family.

Sexual difficulties

The hope is that most individuals will develop and learn about what they enjoy sexually on their own or with a partner. This may include various ways of touching sensually or erotically. However, it's not always plain sailing. During the course of a couple's sexual relationship, it is not unusual for the individual or couple to experience sexual difficulties or problems. Some may be temporary, such as lack of arousal, painful intercourse due to infection or lack of lubrication, loss of erection due to stress or tiredness or alcohol consumption, or delayed ejaculation resulting from stress or anxiety. Sometimes these problems may develop into longer-term difficulties or dysfunctions.

If the difficulties are long term and existed prior to the couple deciding to start a family, then they may be the primary cause of, or a contributory factor to a couple's infertility. In other cases fertility problems themselves, and fertility treatments, may exacerbate the situation or even be the cause of sexual difficulties.

Perceptions and communication

We all get different messages about sex and grow up with different ideas, so it's not always the easiest thing to discuss or agree on. Different perceptions can make communication difficult.

Sometimes, due to a lack of information, there may be a perception that sex is just about penetration and that any form of touching leads to this end goal. If this is the only form of sexual contact a couple has, they may run into difficulties at some stage during their sexual relationship. They may become bored from doing the same thing every time; there may be a loss of arousal for women if attention is not given to sensual touch; or there may be pressure put on men to have an erection if the focus is on penetration every time.

Because of common perceptions that men are always ready and willing to have sex, when a sexual difficulty occurs there is a danger that it is personalised, with the man feeling a failure or perhaps the woman feeling that her partner does not find her attractive.

Since in our society sex is often not talked about in a normal healthy way, sexual difficulties tend not to be discussed at all. If a couple or individual has a sexual problem, they may feel abnormal or inadequate and too embarrassed to raise it with their partner or with a healthcare professional.

Sometimes it is the healthcare professional who is uncomfortable with talking about sex, and as a result they avoid asking the questions that may help the individual or couple to talk about their difficulties. This means that they may not be referred for professional advice such as psychosexual counselling to help them overcome the difficulty. Fortunately, many others do disclose to their doctor and are referred for help.

For others, it may not be until they are going through initial investigations for fertility treatment that they disclose their sexual difficulties and are then referred for counselling.

Some may experience uncertainty regarding their sexual orientation or sexual identity; others may have a history of sexual abuse that is difficult to share and discuss, even with a loved one.

Some couples may fear that staff in the fertility clinic will judge them and deem them not suitable for treatment if they disclose their sexual problems. It is very important to know that this is not the case.

Common problems

Vaginismus: The most common difficulty for women is called vaginismus. This is when the muscles at the entrance to the vagina tense or go into spasm and, as a result, do not allow the vagina to open up and allow penetration. Some women have primary vaginismus and may have never experienced any form of penetration; for others, it may be secondary – they were once able to have penetrative sex, but for some reason it is no longer possible.

A woman who has vaginismus may experience pain on attempts at penetration; women often describe their vagina as feeling like a 'brick wall' or being blocked. As the woman experiences pain, she may anticipate it for the next attempt and tense in advance. Over a period of several attempts, frustration and anxiety often set in for both partners and sex becomes something to avoid. This is especially the case for couples for whom penetration is their primary way of being sexual. Couples who can enjoy other ways of pleasuring may remain very sexual in their relationship but do not attempt penetrative sex.

Dyspareunia or painful intercourse: Some women may experience pain with intercourse, which may present for many reasons. Common medical causes are vaginal infection (particularly due to candida or thrush), endometriosis and pelvic inflammatory disease.

However, even if there are no medical or physical problems, women can experience discomfort. Sometimes if couples get into a habit of rushing foreplay, having sex late at night when both are tired, not dating or planning to spend fun time together, women may not be aroused enough when having intercourse. This may result in the woman's body not allowing the physical changes to take place which prepare her for intercourse – such as lubrication or lengthening of the vagina. If this happens, the woman may experience some pain upon penetration or further in around the cervix. If this happens regularly, tensing, as described above, may occur and sex may become something to avoid. Some women experience a 'lack of desire', which may not mean that they don't want to be sexually intimate with their partner but that they want to avoid being hurt or being frustrated by not being able to have full intercourse.

Erectile dysfunction: Men may experience difficulties such as loss of erection (erectile dysfunction). This may be defined as the male not being able to get or sustain an erection sufficient to allow penetrative intercourse. For some men this may be caused by physical reasons, such as illness or medication; for others it is because of psychological reasons. With repeated 'failures', men may begin to anticipate that they will not be aroused and instead of being relaxed and enjoying the pleasurable sensations that may lead to an erection, they start to obsess about their erection and this prevents the arousal happening. Like vaginismus in women, it may become a vicious cycle that the couple feel helpless to prevent, and sex becomes something to avoid as a way of avoiding frustration or failure.

Delayed ejaculation: This is another common difficulty for men. The man may be able to ejaculate on his own through masturbation but is not able to ejaculate in his partner's presence or in her vagina.

Premature ejaculation: This is when a man ejaculates too quickly, either before penetration or quickly upon insertion. For some couples, depending on how they receive sexual pleasure, this may not be a problem, but if it is interfering with conception or causing frustration, it is something to seek help about.

If you can identify with any of the above difficulties or have any sexual concern that is preventing you from engaging in a satisfactory sexual relationship, you can seek professional help either through your doctor (GP or gynaecologist) or by linking directly with a psychosexual therapist (see page 243). Please be reassured that you are not alone and that your query will be treated with respect and complete confidentiality.

(See also Professor Wingfield's discussion of possible medical and surgical causes of sexual problems.)

Fertility and sex problems

Some couples do not have a predisposing sexual difficulty, but the very process of trying to conceive may put a strain on their sexual relationship and difficulties may arise. It is often assumed that once the couple decide to start a family, they will readily achieve their goal of pregnancy in a 'natural' loving way. Initially the decision to not use contraception can allow sex to be fun and exciting as they enjoy the 'risk' of becoming pregnant. However, if multiple attempts fail, anxiety and tension may set in. They may continue lovemaking but may begin to seek medical advice or advice from the internet and start charting fertile times. Lovemaking may become timetabled so that whether or not the couple feels like being sexual, intercourse must take place at a particular time. This can lead to loss of arousal for both partners as time is not given to relaxation or pleasure. Sex becomes only about penetration and procreation and eventually equates to possible failure. In an effort to 'get it over with', there may be a loss of other forms of intimacy and a rise in arguments between the couple. Sometimes there may be doubts about a partner's commitment to the pregnancy. Pregnancy becomes all-consuming and there may be an avoidance of social situations that might include friends or family with babies. Sexual concerns may arise, with some women experiencing discomfort, and for some men there may be loss of erection. For both partners, there may be loss of desire, accompanied by lowered self-esteem.

If the above applies to you, try to focus on your relationship as a couple. Remember the things that attracted you to each other in the first place. Devote time to activities that you both enjoy doing together, so that you don't just talk about pregnancy all the time, and try to have fun together.

Talk about sex and any concerns you may have so that these can be addressed early, before they develop into bigger problems. Talking also prevents guessing what the other person is thinking or doing.

Try to make time for lovemaking – not just baby-making – by setting aside time to be intimate during non-fertile times. Play and have fun together, whatever that may be.

Know that it is normal to experience sexual challenges during this time and seek help as needed.

Fertility investigation and treatment

If a couple are referred to a fertility clinic, they may face other challenges to their sexual relationship. It may be difficult to have to talk to 'strangers' about every minute detail of their sexual activity, which used to be seen as 'private'. This is especially challenging for individuals who have not grown up with the language and confidence to talk about sex and sexuality. They may find it especially difficult to talk about it with professionals for fear that they lack the appropriate vocabulary.

The couple are also trying to come to terms with the possible 'loss' of a natural pregnancy and are thrown into a world of tests for hormones, sperm quality, pelvic or testicular problems and timing and charts. They may be asked to refrain from having sex during treatment and as a result avoid all forms of intimacy. Some women talk about what they experience as the medicalisation of their sexual organs and genitalia. Men may develop 'performance anxiety' about having to produce a sperm sample in the clinic at a particular time. And men may also have concerns about what their partner's body is going through and may feel guilty about this.

Both partners may have feelings about their bodies being 'defective' and feel they are a failure at being either a man or a woman. The stress of the process may be compounded by the possibility that friends and family members may not be aware of what they are going through. Along with the hope of a successful outcome there may be the overriding fear of failure.

If you have started the process of fertility investigation or treatment with a clinic, try to make time to talk to each other about your fears, hopes and feelings. This can be done over a meal, on a walk or by setting time aside at home.

As a couple, avail of counselling offered through the clinic. No one will judge you and it may be helpful to talk to someone who has experience in this area about your fears or concerns.

Even if you are asked to refrain from sexual intercourse, make time to be sexual. There are so many things you can do to be intimate and close that don't involve penetration. Having a shower together, giving a sensual massage, mutual masturbation, lying naked together, kissing and cuddling are just a few things you can enjoy. Maybe plan special and romantic nights out or weekends away. Take care of yourself. Eat healthily and remain active.

Reassure yourself that negative sexual experiences are normal. Just because you currently have problems doesn't mean that they will develop into a long-term issue. Try to develop a way of dealing with problems when they do occur, such as being able to talk to each other and switching to doing other things.

Post-treatment

It is worth bearing in mind that whether or not a couple succeed in achieving their desire for a child/children, sex may always be a reminder of infertility. This means that sexual difficulties may continue following pregnancy, adoption or childlessness and it is therefore advisable for couples to avail of professional help such as counselling or psychosexual therapy to invest in their future together.

Health professionals and sex

The fertility doctor or nurse will ascertain if there is any medical or physical cause for your difficulties. If nothing is found that warrants medication or surgery and it looks like you could achieve a successful pregnancy without other medical intervention, you may be referred for psychosexual counselling, in the hope that you will be successful and achieve a pregnancy on your own. This will also hopefully help you to develop a more enjoyable sex life.

For those that need to attend fertility treatment, some work may need to be done to help them overcome their difficulties with the necessary tests and treatments.

Often the best results are achieved when individuals or couples, the sex therapist and the medical/nursing team work together on an agreed and tailored treatment plan as part of fertility treatment.

Sex therapists

If you are referred to a psychosexual therapist (sex therapist), it is recommended that you see an accredited therapist. In Ireland and the UK, therapists are accredited by the College of Sexual and Relationship Therapists (COSRT). This will ensure that your therapist is a qualified sex therapist, follows a code of ethics and commits to regular training and supervision. (For further information see www.sextherapists.ie or www.cosrt.org.uk.)

Usually your therapist will arrange to meet with you and ideally your partner (if you are in a relationship) for an initial assessment. This will entail finding out what your sexual concerns are and explaining how the therapist feels they may be able to help you. Sometimes this meeting may be enough to give some suggestions on how to do things differently or look at your expectations and your sexual relationship in a new way.

If the difficulty has been there for some time, the therapist may recommend a programme in which you commit to meeting regularly (weekly or fortnightly), and the therapist will give you 'exercises' that are tailored specifically to your relationship and sexual concerns. These are done at home and are set according to your feedback to the therapist.

If it is not possible for your partner to attend, the therapist can see you on your own. However, most couples agree that they gain a lot more from therapy when both are involved. Many times, they may come in with a presenting problem to find that there are also other areas that may need to be worked on. Also, couples may develop skills and resources that help them to deal with other difficulties that may present in future years.

Miscarriage

Miscarriage is one of the most devastating thing that can happen to any couple trying to conceive and, when it follows fertility treatment such as IVF, it is particularly cruel. On the other hand, miscarriage is so common as to be a normal, though desperately sad, phenomenon in human reproduction and, in a perverse way, nature's way of trying to ensure that pregnancies that do continue are more likely to be healthy. While that may sound very insensitive, it at least offers hope that, even after miscarriage, most couples will go on to have a baby or babies.

> 'Tragedy struck just a few short weeks later with a miscarriage at 7.5 weeks. Total, utter and complete devastation. I will never ever forget those long anxious days and nights, the worry, the fear, but ultimately the knowing. I absolutely knew that I was pregnant and almost as quickly, I knew that I wasn't. Horrendous.'

> 'Our road has been littered with pain and emotion – in our quest to become parents. Of course, motherhood they say is about exhaustion, worry and fear. For a few short weeks, as I was carrying our little embryo inside me, I was a mother. That is a feeling that I will have with me to the end of my days and in a way I am grateful to have it.'

The term miscarriage refers to the loss of a pregnancy before the baby reaches viability, i.e. the ability to survive outside the uterus. Miscarriages are traditionally divided into first-trimester miscarriage, which occurs during the first 12 to 13 weeks of pregnancy; and mid-trimester miscarriages, which occur after that. As babies can now survive from as early as 22 or 23 weeks of pregnancy, mid-trimester miscarriage generally refers to the loss of a baby from 14 weeks up to around this time.

Causes of miscarriage

In order for a pregnancy to progress normally and to result in a healthy baby, two factors are crucial. Probably the most important thing is that the embryo or foetus must be capable of surviving and secondly the woman's uterus must be able to accept the pregnancy and support it. Typically, first-trimester miscarriage or early miscarriages are critically related to the health of the embryo, and the uterine environment is possibly more important in mid-trimester miscarriages. It is thought that at least 70% of first-trimester miscarriages happen because of genetic or chromosomal problems in the embryo. These are generally random events that happen in that particular pregnancy – we know that nature isn't perfect, creating a new human being is extremely complex and things often go wrong. When the genes or chromosomes are not right, nature may interrupt the growth of the embryo and the pregnancy will end as miscarriage.

The other possible causes are described below under recurrent miscarriage.

Miscarriages are extremely common, occurring in at least one in five pregnancies. Sadly, the incidence increases as women get older, as described in Section 2.

DETERMINING THE STAGE OF PREGNANCY

With modern ultrasound it is possible to detect a pregnancy on scan by six weeks of pregnancy. One confusing factor is that, traditionally, the weeks of pregnancy are counted from the woman's last menstrual period. This is based on a 28-day cycle – a woman has a period, ovulates around Day 14 and has a positive pregnancy test 14 days later. This is regarded as four weeks of pregnancy, i.e. four weeks since her last period, even though she has really only been actually pregnant for the second two weeks – the two weeks since she ovulated. Even though it is misleading, this terminology is used all over the world. It was developed before the advent of scans and ovulation tests, when her last period was the thing the woman could remember accurately.

Using this way of counting, a full-term pregnancy is 40 weeks, but a woman will actually have been pregnant for only 38 of these weeks. For the purposes of this book and to avoid confusion I will use this way of describing the length of a pregnancy. For a woman who doesn't have a 28-day cycle, she can work out her dates from the time she ovulated (if she knows that) and then add two weeks on to that time.

Diagnosing early pregnancy

At six weeks (from the last period) you should be able to see a pregnancy on ultrasound scan and this appears as a sac of fluid in the woman's uterus.

Ideally we also see what we call a 'foetal pole' which represents the embryo, and we may also see a heart beating at this stage. However, the foetal pole and heartbeat may not be evident until seven weeks' gestation. For that reason, many clinics and hospitals recommend waiting until around seven weeks before performing an ultrasound as it can be quite upsetting to have a non-reassuring scan at six weeks, just because it is too early. Once the pregnancy has been seen on scan, the pregnancy is regarded as a **clinical pregnancy**. A healthy clinical pregnancy will be seen in the uterus with ultrasound.

First-trimester miscarriage

Miscarriage occurring during the first trimester (i.e. the first 13 weeks of pregnancy) can be further subdivided into very early biochemical pregnancies and early miscarriages.

A pregnancy can fail at any time after conception. Some embryos do not develop beyond the first couple of days of life and, in these cases, they never implant and the woman does not conceive. If the embryo implants and then subsequently fails to continue developing the woman may have what we call a biochemical pregnancy. This means that the woman has a positive pregnancy test but she starts bleeding and loses the pregnancy in the first week or two after the positive pregnancy test. The pregnancy has not progressed to the stage where we are able to see it on ultrasound scan. This is called a **biochemical pregnancy** and, technically, is not a clinical pregnancy.

We saw above that a clinical pregnancy is diagnosed when we can see a pregnancy sac on scan. This will hopefully contain an embryo, referred to as a foetal pole when it is very small. The terminology gets a little bit confusing here because, in IVF and embryology, we talk about embryos right from the time of fertilisation of the egg and sperm. So the early embryo contains cells that will go on to form the placenta, but also those that form the baby. Once we get to the stage of seeing the pregnancy on scan, when we say embryo we are generally referring to this **part of the original embryo** which has formed the baby. We tend to call it an embryo until about eight weeks of pregnancy and after that stage it is called a foetus. But to the parents it is, of course, a baby. (Embryo development is also discussed in the section on IVF.)

With some early miscarriages, we see a sac on scan but we never see an embryo inside. This is termed an anembryonic pregnancy. In the past this was called a 'blighted ovum' but this term isn't really used any more – it's not a very nice phrase. In these pregnancies, it is likely that the baby part of the original embryo never developed from the 'inner cell mass', i.e. only the trophoblast which forms the placenta developed.

The next stage at which a miscarriage is diagnosed is when we see an embryo in the sac in the uterus but there is, sadly, no heartbeat. This means that something has gone wrong with the development of the baby at this embryo stage. Once the heartbeat has been seen in the uterus there is over a 90% chance that everything will progress normally for the rest of the pregnancy. However, sadly, in some cases the embryo even at this stage can stop developing normally, resulting in miscarriage.

At any of these miscarriage stages, the woman may start bleeding – sometimes very soon after a normal scan – and subsequently lose the pregnancy. Other women may not realise for a while that things are going wrong. The woman may have some light bleeding or may just go for a scan around nine to ten weeks of gestation expecting that everything is progressing normally. Unfortunately we may see that the embryo part of the pregnancy is still only six or seven weeks in size and the heartbeat is not present. It often takes a few weeks before the woman's body recognises that something has happened to the embryo as the placenta continues to produce pregnancy hormones and the woman may still feel pregnant. We therefore call such a miscarriage a **'missed' miscarriage**. This can be absolutely devastating for women/couples, but it is usually a sign that something has happened to the embryo or baby at an earlier stage in the pregnancy.

Sometimes a woman can have a 'threatened' miscarriage – there is some problem with implantation and she gets some bleeding but, thankfully, it settles and the pregnancy continues normally. This can be a really nerve-racking time.

'I had a small show of pink blood a day or two before my negative result, I usually get this a day or two before my period anyway, so I was very upset, but was hoping it was implantation bleeding or irritation of the

Crinone. I had a small show of pink blood six or seven days before my positive result and again I was convinced it hadn't worked, this made the two-week wait even worse the second time round. But thankfully it was a happy ending.'

Management of early miscarriage

The management of a miscarriage depends on how the woman presents. Some women may start bleeding heavily at home before they have had an ultrasound scan and when they arrive in the hospital an ultrasound will show no sign of a pregnancy in their uterus. Other women will be in the process of miscarrying or will have partially miscarried. If the woman is in the process of miscarrying she can have heavy bleeding associated with bad cramps and even nausea and she may feel weak. If she is examined, the neck of her womb (cervix) may be open and this is a sign that she will miscarry. This is termed an 'inevitable' miscarriage. If a woman has miscarried part of the pregnancy, some remaining placenta tissue may be seen in the uterus but the sac and foetal pole or heartbeat will usually be absent – this is called an 'incomplete' miscarriage. These pregnancies usually need minimal intervention and 'nature' takes care of it. Some women may need medication to help this along and, unless the woman is bleeding very heavily, she will probably not require surgery.

In the case of a missed miscarriage, where the sac and embryo can still be seen in the uterus and the woman has not yet started to miscarry, there are a few options for management. By waiting, a woman may miscarry spontaneously, or medical treatment (tablets or pessaries) may be used to aid this process. Alternatively a D&C can be performed under general anaesthetic; a suction device is used to remove the pregnancy from the woman's uterus. These options will be discussed at the miscarriage clinic or early pregnancy assessment clinic of a local hospital and the best course of treatment will be decided for the particular circumstances.

Pregnancy of unknown location (PUL)

In some cases it may not be possible to see the actual clinical pregnancy on ultrasound scan and then it may be necessary to establish whether it is an ectopic pregnancy (see page 254) or an intrauterine pregnancy/

miscarriage. In recent years these pregnancies have been termed pregnancies of unknown location or PUL.

Serial measurements of the level of pregnancy hormone in the woman's blood can be useful in managing this type of pregnancy. We know that in a healthy continuing pregnancy the pregnancy hormone level should double every 48 hours or so and, if this is happening, the likelihood is that this is a healthy pregnancy and it is recommended to just wait for a week or two and it will become visible on the ultrasound scan. If the pregnancy hormone level is falling, this means that, sadly, the pregnancy is failing and the woman will miscarry. If the pregnancy hormone is remaining static or increasing slowly it can be a sign of an ectopic pregnancy.

Second-trimester miscarriage

Second-trimester miscarriages are quite different from first-trimester miscarriages. Often the baby will have developed to 17 or 18 weeks of pregnancy and a miscarriage at this late stage is devastating. Such a late miscarriage can be triggered by a clot or bleeding within the pregnancy, which irritates the uterus, causing it to contract and expel the pregnancy.

Some women may have a weak or incompetent cervix either naturally or following surgery to their cervix (see cervical problems). The cervix may not be strong enough to hold the pregnancy and once it gets to a particular size the cervix can open and allow the pregnancy to slip through. Women who have a uterine anomaly are also more at risk of second trimester miscarriage as the uterus may be less well able to support the pregnancy. Infection is another cause of mid-trimester miscarriage. Intrauterine infection during pregnancy is rare but can occur and it can be very difficult to treat. Infection often occurs in combination with an incompetent cervix and it can be sometimes difficult to know whether the infection or the weak cervix was the original problem. Infection is often associated with premature rupture of the membranes (waters breaking). Sadly, in some cases a foetal abnormality becomes obvious during the second trimester and a baby that appeared healthy up to then may die during this stage. In some cases of second-trimester miscarriage, labour may need to be induced with medication to help the woman to deliver her baby.

Second trimester miscarriage is more common in multiple pregnancies, and it is one of the reasons we try to avoid twins with IVF treatments.

Recurrent miscarriage

Recurrent miscarriage (RM) refers to the tragedy of undergoing several consecutive miscarriages. Traditionally the definition of recurrent miscarriage has been three consecutive miscarriages in a woman with no live births in between. In recent years some doctors and studies refer to recurrent miscarriage as a woman who has had two consecutive miscarriages.

For a couple trying to conceive, even one miscarriage is devastating and having three or more miscarriages in a row is extremely hard to deal with. However, even in couples who have had three miscarriages in a row, the chance of finding any particular abnormality is very low, and their chance of a healthy baby in a subsequent pregnancy is high. For this reason, the normal practice has been to only perform investigations after three consecutive miscarriages.

My own feeling is that couples deserve some investigation and discussion if they have had two miscarriages, even though we know that, even after three consecutive miscarriages, the chance of a healthy pregnancy fourth time round is around 70%, even where absolutely nothing different has been done on the fourth occasion. My experience is that most couples find it very difficult after two miscarriages to do nothing and to just try again.

We also have to be aware of the limitations of finances and cost-effectiveness, and some of the investigations are expensive. If a woman has previously had healthy pregnancies and now has recurrent miscarriages it is less likely that there is a problem than if a woman has never had a healthy pregnancy. Having said that, if the woman has had a previous pregnancy but the baby was very small, and now has miscarriages, these may be connected. Sadly, in women aged 42 and older, the miscarriage is almost certainly due to age-related chromosomal problems in the embryo and doing other tests is probably not going to help (see also Section 2).

Some of the causes of recurrent miscarriage are listed below.

Genetic or chromosome problems: We saw in Section 1 that the chance of abnormal embryo development increases as women age. It is therefore not unusual for women in their forties to have recurrent miscarriages due to chromosome or other genetic abnormalities in the foetus. Unfortunately nothing can be done to prevent this, but IVF and preimplantation genetic screening of the embryos is something that some couples may wish to investigate (see Section 4). In younger women who have recurrent miscarriages, there is around a 2% chance that the woman or her partner may carry a genetic abnormality which predisposes them to an increased risk of miscarriage. These genetic abnormalities are rare and do not usually have an effect on the couple themselves but may increase the risk of a miscarriage. Blood tests can be performed to look for these genetic abnormalities. These tests are expensive and many laboratories and state systems will not fund them unless the couple has had three consecutive miscarriages. From a public health perspective, this is reasonable given that the chance of finding an abnormality is slim. It is also possible to test the actual miscarriage tissue (i.e. the placenta) following a miscarriage to see if there are genetic abnormalities. This will give information as to whether or not that particular pregnancy had a genetic abnormality but does not particularly help in predicting future risk as most of these genetic abnormalities are sporadic one-off events. However, it may be reassuring to a couple to know that the problem was with the embryo and that, if they have a healthy embryo in a future pregnancy, they are more likely to have a successful pregnancy.

Infection: In the past it was thought that infection could cause recurrent miscarriage but this is now thought to be very unlikely, unless the woman is very unwell at the time with a very high temperature.

Uterine abnormalities: After two or three miscarriages it would be our general practice to perform a hysteroscopy to exclude any uterine cause for miscarriages. The most common finding might be a uterine septum which interferes with implantation of a healthy embryo. But there is less than a 2% chance of finding this, even in women who have had three miscarriages. However, hysteroscopy can be performed as an outpatient procedure and is relatively painless. Alternatively ultrasound scan may show a uterine septum. Fibroids in the uterine cavity may increase the risk of miscarriage, but it is unlikely that polyps do so.

Autoimmune problems: These are discussed later under immune system disorders.

Superfertility: A new theory to explain some miscarriages has been emerging in recent years. The superfertility theory suggests that some women are 'too fertile' and that they allow chromosonally abnormal embryos to implant in their uterus whereas other women reject these embryos, don't get pregnant with them and therefore don't go on to suffer miscarriage. This group of women tend to get pregnant very easily but then miscarry, whereas other women may take longer to conceive but are more likely to continue with their pregnancy. The good news is that if these superfertile women actually have a normal embryo, they will accept that too and have a healthy pregnancy (3.17). This is one of the most innovative pieces of research on miscarriage that I have seen in recent years and it certainly deserves further study. I'm afraid it doesn't give us all the answers, but it can certainly be a reassurance to some couples.

Lifestyle: Smoking has definitely been linked to recurrent miscarriage, as have very high intakes of alcohol and recreational drugs. Obesity is also a factor and miscarriage is significantly more common in obese women than those with normal weight. Being underweight is also associated with an increased chance of miscarriage. These issues and their relationship to fertility and miscarriage are discussed in Section 2.

Most women who experience miscarriage will agonise over whether anything they have done in the previous few weeks may have caused a miscarriage. This is highly unlikely and it is important that women don't beat themselves up over a miscarriage. There is no evidence that miscarriage is caused by work, exercise or sex. Having said that, improving your lifestyle and in particular, cutting out smoking, aiming for a healthy BMI and reducing alcohol intake must be regarded as being of benefit.

Emotional impact of miscarriage

It can take a long time to recover from a miscarriage and some people never quite get over it. Studies have shown that, even though it was an early pregnancy, the grief reaction can be as strong as for the loss of a relative or close friend. This is understandable as the pregnancy represents a child with all the hopes and joys that that entails. The Miscarriage Association of Ireland puts it nicely: 'parents begin their relationship with their baby long before the birth'.

It is really important that women and couples give themselves time to get in some way back to normal emotionally after they experience miscarriage before they embark on another pregnancy. This can be particularly difficult for those with infertility. And, like infertility generally, those who haven't been through a miscarriage may not be very understanding and may even (unintentionally) make unhelpful comments. Counselling may help some people and there are some excellent websites (e.g. www.miscarriage.ie; www.miscarriageassociation. org.uk) and support groups.

> 'Whilst all this fertility testing and treatments are happening it's important to remember that some of us like myself are still grieving for the babies we have lost. Our hearts are broken. It's been the toughest and longest journey we have ever been on. There's no time for grieving when you are on an infertility journey.'

Ectopic pregnancy

An ectopic pregnancy is one that occurs outside the uterus. The most common location is in the woman's Fallopian tube, though ectopic pregnancies can also be found on the woman's ovaries or elsewhere in her abdomen. Unfortunately a pregnancy cannot survive in these locations and it can actually be very dangerous. As the pregnancy grows in the Fallopian tube, it can cause the tube to rupture and this can cause significant bleeding. A ruptured ectopic pregnancy is still a cause of maternal death even in the developed world. It is therefore very important to diagnose an ectopic pregnancy as early as possible.

Causes of ectopic pregnancy

In the vast majority of cases we don't find an actual cause for the ectopic pregnancy though we do know that it is more common in women who have damaged Fallopian tubes. Therefore any woman who has had a pelvic infection or surgery, or anything that increases the risk of tubal damage, is at greater risk of ectopic pregnancy. If a woman has previously had an ectopic pregnancy she is also at risk of another one. Certain types of hormone treatments such as the progesterone-only pill and intrauterine devices such as the Mirena coil can also increase the risk of ectopic pregnancy because they interfere with the tube's ability to move an embryo down the tube into the uterus (though pregnancies due to failures of these types of contraception are very rare). Ectopic pregnancies are also more common after IVF than after natural pregnancies. It is not clear whether this is due to the IVF technique or whether it relates to the fact that women having IVF may be more prone to tubal problems. Generally ectopic pregnancies happen once in 80 natural pregnancies but in 2–3% of IVF pregnancies.

Signs of ectopic pregnancy

Sometimes there are no symptoms and an ectopic pregnancy is suspected when a woman goes for a routine scan in early pregnancy. Symptoms of an ectopic pregnancy would usually be some light vaginal bleeding and some abdominal pain. The bleeding is much lighter than that associated with miscarriage. Typically the pain is sharp and aggravated by movement. If the ectopic pregnancy is bleeding, the blood collects in the pelvis where it can irritate the nerves that supply the woman's shoulder tips and an unusual symptom is shoulder tip pain. The woman may also have pain around the area of her back passage. Again this is due to blood in her pelvis. Women can also experience fainting or feeling weak and this is a dangerous sign and one that should prompt you to go to hospital straight away.

Diagnosis of ectopic pregnancy

Some ectopic pregnancies are readily seen on ultrasound scan. A pregnancy sac may be seen outside the uterus in the area of the Fallopian tubes and a foetal pole and heartbeat may even be seen. At other times the pregnancy is not so obvious and suspicion is raised by finding no signs of a pregnancy in the uterus of a woman who has a high pregnancy hormone level. There is more information on diagnosing problems in early pregnancy in the section on miscarriage.

Treatment of ectopic pregnancy

The main treatments for an ectopic pregnancy are:

- Expectant management
- Surgery
- Methotrexate

Expectant management: Very small ectopic pregnancies may resolve themselves – the pregnancy stops growing early and eventually the tissue gets absorbed by the woman's 'healing system'. With such very small, early ectopics it may be safe to just monitor events and let nature take its course. However, it is important that the woman remains close to the hospital and attends if she has any symptoms.

Surgery: Traditionally the main management for ectopic pregnancies has been to remove the pregnancy. This is generally done by laparoscopy or keyhole surgery, unless the pregnancy has ruptured and the woman is very unwell – in such cases emergency open surgery is required. At laparoscopy the tubes are assessed and a decision is made either to remove the tube which contains the ectopic pregnancy or to remove the ectopic itself. The woman's other tube should also be assessed at this time as this will give important information as regards her future chance of pregnancy. Studies have shown that the chance of a successful pregnancy after surgery is the same whether the tube is removed or the pregnancy itself is removed. This is something your doctor will discuss prior to the surgery and your entire history will be taken into account.

Methotrexate: Methotrexate is a cancer drug which is known to stop the growth of cells which are dividing rapidly. With ectopic pregnancies, it is given in a lower dose than for cancer treatment and this will stop the cells of the placenta growing without affecting the other cells in the woman's body. Methotrexate is increasingly being used rather than surgery. It is, however, not suitable for large ectopic pregnancies, those where a heartbeat is seen, those with very high hormone levels and those where there is evidence of internal bleeding. The woman needs to be monitored, usually by blood tests, until the pregnancy has resolved. If you have methotrexate for an ectopic pregnancy you should not try to conceive for three months afterwards as this is a relatively toxic drug.

Emotional impact of ectopic pregnancy

The emotional effect of an ectopic pregnancy is similar to that of a miscarriage and in some ways can be worse because, in addition to dealing with the cruel loss of her pregnancy, the woman and her partner need to also grapple with the fact that she may have damaged Fallopian tubes, or one has been removed because of the ectopic pregnancy, and this is likely to have an impact on their future fertility. Again, there are some excellent websites and support groups available. See, for example, www.ectopicireland.ie; www.ectopic.org.uk.

Fertility after ectopic pregnancy

The majority of women who have had an ectopic pregnancy will go on to have healthy pregnancies subsequently. Some women are very unlucky and can end up having several ectopic pregnancies. If the woman needs to have both her Fallopian tubes removed because of ectopic pregnancies, her only chance of further conception will be IVF, but this is a good option in these cases. Women who have had a long history of infertility and subsequently have an ectopic pregnancy are more likely to have future problems. However, if the woman has conceived quickly her chances of a further successful pregnancy are excellent, particularly if her remaining Fallopian tube is normal. Generally about 12% of women who conceive after an ectopic will have a second ectopic – but the majority of pregnancies will be in the uterus the next time.

Immune system disorders

The immune system is the body's natural defence system which helps fight disease, particularly infection. It is a complex system made up of antibodies, white blood cells, and a vast range of chemicals and proteins that attack and destroy bacteria and viruses which they recognise as foreign and different from the body's normal healthy tissues. Immunology is the study of the immune system.

Disorders of the immune system can result in autoimmune diseases, inflammatory diseases and cancer. Immunodeficiency occurs when the immune system is 'deficient', resulting in recurring and life-threatening infections. In humans, immunodeficiency can either be the result of a genetic disease, conditions such as HIV/AIDS or medication (immuno-suppressants). Autoimmune diseases result from a hyperactive immune system, which attacks the body's normal tissues as if they were foreign organisms. Common autoimmune diseases include Hashimoto's thyroiditis, rheumatoid arthritis, type 1 diabetes and systemic lupus erythematosus (SLE).

As a medical student I found immunology difficult and confusing – now, more than 30 years later, as a reproductive medicine specialist, I know a lot more about it but, sadly, I am more confused than ever. And it's not just me. In recent years, great attention has been devoted to studying the immune system to understand how abnormalities in some women might lead to infertility and particularly to an inability to allow embryos to implant and grow normally in the uterus – i.e. implantation failure and miscarriage. But scientists, researchers and doctors around the world vehemently disagree on whether immune tests should be performed for women with reproductive problems and, if so, what tests and on what tissue (i.e. blood or uterine tissue). Interpretation of the tests is fraught and there are no agreed levels of normal and abnormal. Finally, the use of treatments for suspected immune system disorders in infertility is one of the most controversial areas of reproductive medicine.

The immune system in pregnancy

A healthy, functioning immune system is critical for pregnancy and the body undergoes unique immunological changes during pregnancy. The human embryo comprises cells derived from the male as well as the female, so in order to prevent the woman rejecting the pregnancy as foreign, the woman's immune system must adapt considerably. Components involved include antibodies and immune cells.

Immune cells are white blood cells found in the blood and also in the uterus. The most important ones are natural killer cells, T cells or T lymphocytes, macrophages and dendritic cells. Most patients will only have heard of natural killer (NK) cells and these are the ones about which there is most controversy.

NK cells are the most prominent white blood cells in the uterus around the time of implantation, so they undoubtedly play a key role in fertility and successful pregnancy. NK cells and T cells in the blood play a crucial role in recognising foreign cells such as bacteria and release toxic factors that result in the destruction and/or removal of these foreign cells. (Hence the name, natural *killer* cells.) Studies in the past have suggested that women who had elevated numbers of these NK cells might be more likely to incorrectly identify their embryo as 'foreign' and 'kill' or destroy it or at least stop it from implanting. This is the basis of blood tests to look at possible immune causes of infertility or recurrent miscarriage.

However, we now know that the NK cells and T cells in the uterus are completely different to those in the blood and they play very different roles in pregnancy. Their numbers increase in the uterus around the time of implantation and they secrete substances which are critical for implantation and for the healthy development of the placenta and its blood vessels. Unlike blood NK and T cells, they do not produce toxic factors to 'kill' pregnancy cells. Some researchers feel that uterine NK cells should no longer be called 'killer' cells, but we are stuck with the name.

Antibodies are small proteins which circulate in the bloodstream. They are also called immunoglobulins. They are made by a type of white blood cell called a B lymphocyte. They work by attaching to proteins called antigens on the surface of bacteria and viruses and then destroying them.

Auto-antibodies occur in autoimmune diseases. In these conditions the person makes antibodies to normal cells in their body, causing damage to any organs involved.

Some auto-antibodies are known to increase the risk of miscarriage. These are anticardiolipin antibodies, also called anti-phospholipid antibodies. **Antiphospholipid syndrome** can cause small blood clots to form in a woman's blood vessels. This can interfere with implantation and later in pregnancy can affect foetal growth. It therefore increases the risk of miscarriage and stillbirth. It also increases the risk of the woman having blood clots during pregnancy. Another autoimmune disease that can increase the risk of miscarriage is systemic lupus erythematosus (SLE). Blood tests can be performed to diagnose antiphospholipid syndrome and SLE. These include anticardiolipin antibodies, lupus anticoagulant and anti-ß2-glycoprotein-I antibody. These tests should be done at least six weeks after a miscarriage or pregnancy and two positive tests 12 weeks apart are required to make the diagnosis. The tests are generally recommended after three, sometimes two, miscarriages (recurrent miscarriage).

For both antiphospholipid syndrome and SLE, treatment with heparin and aspirin during pregnancy significantly improves the outcomes. While it cannot totally prevent miscarriage it is associated with a 70% chance of healthy pregnancy in treated women compared to a 10% chance in untreated women.

Are NK cells good or bad?

If I could answer this question, I could retire. It is undoubtedly one of the most controversial topics in reproductive medicine at present. It is completely understandable that women and couples who have suffered recurrent miscarriages and/or recurrent implantation failure in IVF (two or more good-quality embryos transferred but no pregnancy) are traumatised and desperate to do anything that will help them achieve the baby they want so badly. And most doctors genuinely want to help. But this has led to the emergence of a plethora of blood tests and, less commonly, tests of the endometrial lining cells, looking for changes in NK cells and other immune factors that might adversely affect pregnancy.

Some excellent reviews have been published recently and they all conclude that NK cells *are* important for pregnancy and that there are differences in these NK cells in women with healthy pregnancies and women who have recurrent miscarriages and recurrent implantation failure. *But* we don't fully understand these changes yet, the tests used to diagnose them are extremely variable and unsatisfactory, and the changes in blood bear no relation to the changes in the uterus. The studies that have been done (and there have been hundreds) are conflicting and even scientists in the same lab get conflicting results (3.18).

Despite the poor evidence, many clinics and doctors prescribe treatments for these immune cell, NK cell and antibody findings. In the 1980s, treatments using white blood cells from the woman's partner were used – this was eventually banned by the US Food and Drug Administration in 2002. Since then a wide range of other therapies has been introduced, including tumour necrosis factor alpha (TNFa) inhibitors, intravenous immunoglobulins (IVIg), intralipid, prednisolone (dexamethasone) and granulocyte-colony stimulating factor. Some of these therapies certainly affect the maternal immune system, but not necessarily in a beneficial way (3.19), and many of them have serious side-effects. Some are also very expensive.

A recent survey of worldwide IVF clinicians revealed that 69% would recommend immunological investigations in patients with recurrent miscarriage, although only 8% would consider a NK cell assay; similarly, 56% would recommend immunological testing in cases of RIF but only 9% would suggest a NK cell assay (3.20).

One Australian group recently concluded the following:

> *Reproductive-aged women who are told they have high NK cell activity view their immune system as a curse, when in fact the literature suggests it may be a blessing in other respects.* (3.18)

A British scientist called her paper 'First do no harm' and concluded:

> *The functions of these uterine NK (uNK) cells are essentially unknown but available data point to a role in regulating placentation in concert with other elements of the decidua and invading trophoblast cells. Despite the lack of scientific rationale and advice from clinical governing bodies, such as the Human Fertilisation and Embryology Authority, an increasing range of tests and therapies are still offered to women undergoing IVF or attending recurrent miscarriage clinics based on the myth that uterine NK cells need suppressing to prevent damage to the embryo. New treatments can be introduced at whim with subsequent demands for expensive trials to prove/disprove their efficacy. The evidence that targeting uNK or peripheral blood NK cells assists women with recurrent pregnancy failure is lacking. Healthcare professionals and patients should very carefully evaluate the practice of immunomodulation to enhance pregnancy outcome. A discussion on how to move towards stricter regulation of immunotherapy in non-hospital settings is now needed because it is clear that the potential risks and costs of these therapies outweigh any benefits.* (3.19)

Concern has also been expressed about using steroid therapy in women not proven to have a definite autoimmune disorder. An eminent Australian group reviewed the use of steroids to prevent miscarriage and implantation failure and called this a 'faulty premise' (3.21). They stated:

> The rationale draws on the pervasive but flawed view that immune activation is inconsistent with normal pregnancy. This ignores clear evidence that controlled inflammation and activation of the immune response is essential for embryo implantation.

In summary, I concur with the reputable scientists quoted above, as do international bodies such as the British Fertility Society (BFS) and the Royal College of Obstetricians and Gynaecologists (RCOG) in the UK that, until satisfactory evidence becomes available, testing for and treating presumed immune and NK cell dysfunction in women with reproductive problems should only be done as part of clinical studies and trials. Indeed, the RCOG published a scientific impact paper on the role of NK cell testing in fertility in December 2016 and concluded:

> In response to patients who wish to discuss or request NK cell testing, clinicians should be aware that:
>
> - uNK cells are different from PB (peripheral blood) NK cells, and that measurements of the latter are of limited value in aiding our understanding of the role of uNK cells in reproductive failure.
> - There is no indication to offer routine uNK cell testing in women presenting with infertility or seeking IVF treatment; uNK cell testing in women with RM and RIF is still a matter for debate pending further evidence and should be regarded, for the time being, as within the realm of experimental medicine.
> - The measurement of uNK cells must be standardised and the definition of 'normal' and 'high' levels based on established reference ranges derived from standardised methodology.
> - Women undergoing uNK cell testing should understand that there is, as yet, no proven effective treatment for those with what may be considered abnormal results, although preliminary data suggest a possible positive effect of prednisolone. (3.22)

At MFC, we are currently collaborating with scientists in Trinity College Dublin and University College Dublin, exploring the role of the endometrium (womb lining) and NK cells in fertility. A huge amount of research in this area is being carried out around the world. Hopefully, we will have some worthwhile answers in the next five to ten years.

Male factor infertility

Across the world, and Ireland is no exception, there is a tendency for women (and some of their doctors) to assume that most fertility problems occur in the female partner. This may be because women are generally more likely to question their health and to start seeking help. However, several international studies have shown that about 20% of men have low sperm counts (though not all of these will have fertility problems) and, in couples having infertility, sperm problems are the sole factor contributing to infertility in 20% and a contributory factor in up to 50% of such couples.

In at least half of cases of male factor infertility the cause is unknown, which is very frustrating for men and their partners. This frustration is compounded by the fact that most male factor problems require IUI, IVF or ICSI treatment – treatments which involve considerable inconvenience for their partners. Even though the treatment may be necessary because of a sperm problem, the woman undergoes injections, scans, an egg collection, etc. and this is difficult for both of them. It also means that a lot of nursing and medical attention is focused on the woman and men can feel a bit left out of the whole process. And, even though IVF and ICSI are very successful for male fertility issues, it is also frustrating that the treatment doesn't actually cure the sperm problem!

Some men will know that they are likely to have sperm problems, for example, men who have had testicular surgery for cancer or bad testicular injuries. Rare cases may be hereditary and others may have a history of genital infection such as chlamydia or an endocrine (hormone) problem. Men who have had a vasectomy may also present for fertility treatment. The vast majority of men, though, will have no idea that there is a problem until they have a semen analysis or sperm test.

People often assume that if a man has had no problem fathering a child (or getting someone pregnant) in the past, everything must be fine with him. However, just as women can conceive easily first time round and then develop problems some years later, the same is true for men. Some male fertility issues are progressive and get worse as men get older. In other cases, we suspect the man may have had a problem all along, but if his partner was younger than she is now, her eggs may have been able to cope with that sperm problem, but now that the eggs are older they need better sperm!

Sperm parameters

The standard and usually first test to look at a man's fertility is a semen analysis. How this is done and the information we get from it is described in the section on male tests. The details of sperm production and the basics of the male reproductive system are described in Section 1.

Several medical terms are used to describe the different findings in a semen analysis. Some of these are:

- Normospermia: normal number, motility and shape of sperm
- Oligospermia: low numbers of sperm
- Azoospermia: no sperm seen at all
- Asthenospermia: motility of sperm is low
- Teratospermia: reduced numbers of normally shaped sperm
- Asthenoteratospermia: motility and shape is low
- Oligoasthenoteratopermia: number, motility and shape is low

The terms **mild** and **severe male factor** are used extensively in practice but there is no formally recognised definition of what this means. The term 'mild' male factor infertility is defined in the UK NICE guidelines as meaning: two or more semen analyses that have one or more variables which fall below the 5th centile as defined by the World Health Organization (3.2), and where the effect on the chance of pregnancy occurring naturally through vaginal intercourse within a period of 24 months would be similar to people with unexplained infertility or mild endometriosis. 'Severe' male factor generally means that pregnancy is highly unlikely without at least IVF and, more usually, ICSI treatment (a type of IVF).

A lot has been written in recent years about whether men's sperm counts are falling on a global level. It is actually very difficult to study this because so many different factors are involved. The way we do sperm tests has changed over the years, as has the quality of the microscopes and equipment used, so we are not really comparing like with like when looking at tests now alongside those done 30–40 years ago. It is likely that environmental and lifestyle issues have an impact, so things may well be changing. But that's not really important for the couple actually trying to conceive right now.

Causes of male factor infertility

Up to 50% of male factor infertility may be unexplained. Known causes are developmental problems, hormonal (endocrine) disorders, infection, surgery, cancer and its treatment, genetic conditions, immunological conditions, psychological and sexual function problems and general medical conditions such as diabetes. Lifestyle is also important.

These medical problems can affect the testes (testicles) or the epididymis and vas deferens (see diagram on page 6). Sperm are produced in the testes, so it is not surprising that testicular problems will affect fertility and, if the sperm cannot be ejaculated because of a blockage or difficulty ejaculating, infertility will also ensue.

Testicular failure

Primary testicular failure – the testis fails to produce adequate numbers of sperm – is the most common cause of male infertility due to very low sperm counts (oligospermia) and is the cause of non-obstructive azoospermia (no or minimal sperm production by the testis). Testicular failure may be due to the causes listed below. However, in the majority of cases (over 50%) the cause remains unknown.

The diagnosis of testicular failure is typically based on finding a reduction in testicular size and blood tests showing high levels of the hormone FSH but some men may not have these signs. Unfortunately, there is no effective treatment to reverse primary testicular failure, but if there are any sperm at all, IVF and ICSI may work. Testicular biopsy will determine if there are any sperm in the testis itself. Unfortunately, for some men with more advanced testicular failure, no sperm will be retrieved and they may need to consider using donor sperm.

Men with testicular failure may also develop testosterone deficiency and may need to be managed in the long term by an endocrinologist.

Some causes of testicular failure are listed below.

Undescended testes/cryptorchidism: During life as a foetus, the testes develop in the male's abdomen and subsequently move down, through the groin, into the scrotum at around seven months of foetal life. This is important because the scrotum is cooler than the abdomen and this is necessary to achieve healthy sperm. In some boys (particularly if they are born prematurely) the testes do not descend and are retained in the abdomen or the groin. If this is not detected and treated (by surgery to bring them down), further development of the testes and sperm production may be adversely affected. Therefore to correct this situation surgery is generally recommended before 18 months of age. In the past, surgery was often delayed. If one testis has failed to descend, there may be some but not total reduction in sperm quality.

If adult men have testes which are still in the groin or abdomen, there is an increased risk of testicular cancer and they should be removed for that reason (they will already be irreversibly non-functioning, so there is no benefit bringing them down into the scrotum at this stage). Even testes that have been treated by surgery have an increased risk of testicular cancer and men should self-examine their testes once a month and see their doctor if they notice any swelling.

'I had an operation when I was four to lower a testicle which as you know was too late and the damage was done. After trying for a baby for a year I went and got tested. As you can imagine the news was devastating. My wife and I then went to a fertility clinic where our first treatment didn't work; it was traumatising for both of us. Six months later we met you and your staff where we found the whole experience totally different. Your staff were great; on my wife's first treatment we had a little baby boy who is now 18 months old; we also have two embryos frozen in your clinic which we hope will be successful early next year. I can't thank you and your staff enough for everything you have done for me and my wife.'

Absent testes: It is exceedingly rare for men not to have testes unless they have been removed for cancer, torsion (twisting) or trauma.

Testicular injury/trauma: In the case of torsion (twisting) or a severe injury (often in sports) the blood supply to the testis can be cut off, leading to gangrene and death of the tissue, which must then be removed. If the other testis is not affected, there should be no significant effect on sperm production or quality. Injuries can also increase the risk of anti-sperm antibodies (see page 270).

Testicular infection/orchitis: In some boys who get mumps, the infection may spread to their testes – in such cases up to 12% may be rendered infertile. The childhood MMR vaccine protects against this. Chickenpox, chlamydia, gonorrhoea, TB and leprosy may also affect the testes.

Testicular cancer: This can require the testis to be removed; or chemotherapy or radiotherapy can lead to testicular damage and infertility. Fertility preservation should be discussed with all men and adolescent boys prior to such cancer treatment and they should be offered the chance to freeze sperm prior to treatment.

Genetic disorders: Rare chromosome disorders such as Klinefelter syndrome can cause testicular failure. The normal male chromosome make-up is 46 chromosomes, one X and one Y – 46XY. (Women have two X chromosomes – 46XX.) Men with Klinefelter syndrome have an extra X chromosome – 46XXY. Other men may be born missing a Y chromosome – 46XO, others may be XYY. Some chromosome problems can also increase the risk of miscarriages.

Genetic disorders may also occur in men who have a normal 46XY chromosome arrangement but who have abnormal genes in the actual chromosomes. The most common problems are called Y chromosome micro-deletions – where small genetic pieces of the Y chromosome are missing. Often these genetic problems cause no problem for the man himself apart from severe oligospermia (very low sperm count) or azoospermia (no sperm in the ejaculate). However, if he conceives with ICSI, his male children will also have the fertility defect.

Genetic disorders are complex and generally require the involvement of a genetics specialist. In some cases testicular biopsy and ICSI are possible, but in others donor sperm is required. It is our practice at

Merrion Fertility Clinic to recommend genetic testing for all men with severe oligospermia (very low sperm count – under one million) or azoospermia.

Obstruction of the vas deferens or epididymis

The vas deferens on each side of the scrotum carries sperm from the testis to the penis to be ejaculated. If one or both vasa are obstructed or blocked, sperm counts will be very low, or zero if both are blocked (obstructive azoospermia). The diagnosis is based on normal testis size and normal serum FSH levels because the testes can produce sperm but the sperm can't get out.

Some causes of obstruction of the vas deferens or epididymis are listed below.

Genetic: 5–10% of men with obstructive azoospermia will have absence of the vas deferens – called congenital bilateral absence of the vas deferens or CBAVD. About 50% of men with CBAVD carry the cystic fibrosis gene CFTR. Some of these men will be known to have cystic fibrosis; others will not but may be carriers; some may have an atypical type of cystic fibrosis. It is important to screen their partners as well to assess the couple's chance of having a baby with cystic fibrosis. If both partners carry the gene, pre-implantation genetic screening can be considered (see Section 4). Therefore we generally recommend review by a urologist and screening for the cystic fibrosis gene in men with azoospermia. CBAVD may also be associated with kidney problems.

Infection: Infections occurring in the epididymis or vas deferens can cause inflammation and damage, leading to obstruction. The commonest organisms are chlamydia and gonorrhoea. If blockage occurs, it will remain after the infection is gone. Some blockages can be treated surgically by a urologist.

Vasectomy/surgery: Male sterilisation is performed by cutting or blocking the vas deferens, preventing the release of sperm. Some men subsequently change their minds about sterilisation, most commonly because they enter a new relationship. If the vasectomy has been done relatively recently, depending on the procedure used, it may be possible to reverse the procedure. However, if this is unsuccessful or if the vasectomy was done more than ten years ago, testicular biopsy and ICSI is preferable. Vasectomy can also lead to anti-sperm antibody formation (see page 270).

Very rarely, the vas deferens may be damaged during other scrotal surgery.

Hormonal (endocrine disorders)

In the testes, the production of sperm is controlled predominantly by the hormone FSH, produced in the pituitary gland in the brain. The production of testosterone is controlled by LH, also produced in the pituitary gland. The pituitary is in turn controlled by GnRH, produced in the hypothalamus. This is very similar to what happens in the female.

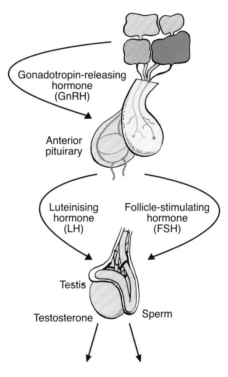

Hormone disorders affecting the hypothalamus or the pituitary gland will affect this finely tuned hormonal balance. These disorders are rare but include hypogonadotrophic hypogonadism, which accounts for less than 1% of male factor

Hormonal control of the testis

fertility problems. It results in a deficiency of LH and FSH, which is associated with failure of sperm formation and testosterone secretion.

Hypogonadotrophic hypogonadism is diagnosed with blood tests showing low levels of FSH and LH and can be very successfully treated by injections of these hormones or, if the disorder is at the level of the hypothalamus, by a pump which administers GnRH hormone. As these conditions are very rare, fertility specialists would usually work with an endocrinologist in their treatment. It is important to ensure that other hormones produced by the pituitary gland such as growth hormone, prolactin and thyroid stimulating hormone are also normal. Even if fertility is sorted or no longer an issue, maintenance hormone therapy may be required for life.

Many cases of hormone dysfunction are unexplained but some are due to failure of the hypothalamus to develop, e.g. Kallmann's syndrome (these men also have no sense of smell) or genetic disorders such as Prader-Willi syndrome. These conditions are, however, very rare. Damage to the pituitary gland can occur due to tumours (often benign) or brain injury.

Anti-sperm antibodies

Just as we make antibodies to fight off viruses and infections, humans can also make antibodies to their own cells, e.g. patients with autoimmune diseases. Men can make antibodies to their sperm and this can affect fertility. These anti-sperm antibodies (ASAs) account for about 3% of male factor infertility.

Low levels of antibodies (<50%) seem not to affect fertility, but higher levels can. For many men with antibodies, a specific cause may not be found, but typical causes are a vasectomy which has been reversed, testicular surgery, testicular trauma, testicular infection and cystic fibrosis. All of these conditions stimulate an immune response with the production in some men of ASAs. They also breach what is called the blood–testis barrier and allow blood cells such as immune cells into the testis, where they are not normally found. However, the exact cause, the effect on fertility and the percentage of antibodies which is harmful are all controversial and the subject of debate (3.23, 3.24). Most specialists would agree, however, that if ASAs are bound to more than 50% of the motile sperm, they are likely to interfere with the motility of the sperm, its ability to swim to the Fallopian tube, its ability to fertilise an egg and ultimately its ability to lead to pregnancy.

While some clinics will recommend IUI, IVF is more successful and, particularly if the levels are very high, ICSI may be preferable to IVF. As with all cases, the couple's overall situation must be taken into account, but I would generally recommend ICSI if the levels of antibodies are consistently greater than 50% and the couple have been trying naturally for a long time. In the past, steroids have been used to try to reduce the levels of ASAs but the studies have been small and the evidence not very strong. Steroids have significant side-effects, so they are rarely recommended nowadays.

Varicocele

A varicocele is an enlargement of the veins in the testis – dilated veins are also called varicose veins (e.g. in the legs). Varicoceles are found in 11.7% of men with normal semen and 25.4% of men with abnormal semen. Their relevance to fertility is highly controversial. It is thought that they may interfere with sperm quality and function because they lead to an increase in temperature in the testes.

Numerous studies have been done over the years to determine whether surgically removing or embolising (blocking) these veins might help fertility in men with reduced sperm parameters or men found to have large varicoceles. The results are, at best, inconclusive. This was the conclusion of the UK NICE guideline review of the evidence (1.1) and the authors also stated that no meaningful studies have been done comparing the results of surgery versus IVF and ICSI. And we know that IVF and ICSI are very effective for male sperm problems. The American Society for Reproductive Medicine makes the following recommendations (3.25):

- Treatment of a clinically palpable varicocele may be offered to the male partner of an infertile couple when there is evidence of abnormal semen parameters and minimal/no identified female factor, including consideration of age and ovarian reserve.
- In vitro fertilisation with or without ICSI may be considered the primary treatment option when such treatment is required to treat a female factor, regardless of the presence of varicocele and abnormal semen parameters.
- The treating physician's experience and expertise, including evaluation of both partners, together with the options available, should determine the approach to varicocele treatment.

My practice, which is the most common, is not to recommend surgery for small varicoceles or for men with a normal semen analysis. In men with poor sperm parameters and a large varicocele, we will sometimes, in conjunction with a urologist, consider surgery or embolisation. However, if a man undergoes surgery for a varicocele, we will not know for at least 3–4 months and probably longer whether it has helped his sperm – this is because of the long life cycle of sperm. Many couples may find it difficult to wait this long, particularly if the woman is over 35 or they have been trying for a long time. They are therefore more likely to wish to proceed to IVF/ICSI and this is very reasonable. Sometimes we will do IVF/ICSI and then the man can arrange the surgery after that if his varicocele is very large. If a man has had surgery, it is preferable to wait at least three months for things to recover before proceeding with IVF/ICSI.

Problems with sex or ejaculation

Despite the emphasis on sex and sexuality in the media, we saw earlier that for many people, sex and sexuality may be problematic. This is very true for many men in couples with fertility problems and infertility and fertility treatments can greatly aggravate these problems. In some cases, sexual problems may be the cause of the infertility. Luckily, these problems can usually be treated. However, they are extremely sensitive situations and, not surprisingly, very stress-inducing.

> 'We are in our late 30s and have two lovely girls already (two & four) and we had been trying for our third child for about 18 months. My wife was becoming increasingly stressed about the situation.
>
> I had read up on what I could do to increase the chances (from reputable journals and sources) and one of the things that they mentioned was my physical activity. I was always rather fit but I increased the intensity level of my activity, I found this increased my libido, something that, it feels a little strange to admit out loud, after 18 months was starting to wane. Small contribution but I found that a combination of eating better and moving more for both of us helped us.'

Erectile dysfunction (ED)/impotence

Erectile dysfunction is the persistent inability to achieve and maintain an erection sufficient to allow satisfactory sex. It is surprisingly common, especially in older men, and can have a profound effect on a person's overall quality of life. It can be associated with anxiety, depression, loss of self-esteem and self-confidence. Partners too can feel rejected, unattractive and guilty, and feel that they are to blame.

Achieving an erection is a very complex event and many processes are involved. It is initiated by sexual arousal, which causes areas in the brain to send signals via the spinal cord to the sacral area. This leads to relaxation of the muscles of the penis and an increase in blood flow into the penis, which causes the firmness necessary for sexual activity. There are many different causes of ED, including:

- Disorders of the penis itself or abnormalities in its development
- Heart disease, high blood pressure, high cholesterol
- Diabetes
- Smoking
- Neurological disorders such as multiple sclerosis, Parkinson's disease, stroke or spinal cord injury, spina bifida
- Surgical causes, particularly related to prostate surgery
- Obesity and sedentary lifestyle
- Hormonal causes
- Drugs, particularly some anti-depressants called SSRIs and some blood pressure tablets
- Recreational drugs such as alcohol, heroin, cocaine, marijuana and methadone
- Psychological causes/stress

The following patient had spina bifida and he and his wife conceived with surgical sperm retrieval and ICSI (IVF):

> *'Being someone with a congenital disability, I had gone through life with an assumption that due to physical complications, having a child was not an option. Having gotten married, I went down the route of exploring what options were available to us through fertility treatment.*
>
> *Through the support of the clinic and gaining knowledge of advances made in science, I was presented with options I did not think existed and while low percentage-based possibilities of success were flagged, I felt there was a glimmer of hope and proceeded to embark on tests and the treatment. Although the odds were stacked against us, we did conceive a child and are now the proud parents of a wonderful healthy baby boy.*

What I would say is that the skills and technology available are far greater than I ever presumed and with the support and encouragement of qualified and compassionate staff, we realised our dream. The scientific fertility knowledge and expertise available can achieve more than we sometimes realise. Through persistence in investigating our situation and analysis in assessing the potential, fertility treatment provided the key, especially for someone with a congenital physical disability such as myself.'

Psychological causes are probably the most common that we see in men with fertility problems and, as stated above, they are often exasperated by the fertility problems. The psychology of ED is complicated but the most common causes include stress, anxiety, guilt, depression, low self-esteem and indifference.

Infertility is a major cause. ED is frequently associated with performance anxiety and fear of not achieving an erection. This may become a self-fulfilling prophecy, particularly when men have to 'perform' at particular times of the month (i.e. when the woman is ovulating or at a fertility clinic). As stated earlier, having to perform month in month out without achieving pregnancy can be extremely stressful and take all the joy and excitement out of sex.

Depression is a common cause of ED and unfortunately many of the drugs used for depression can also cause it. If the female partner also has sexual problems (e.g. vaginismus or pain during intercourse) this can also contribute to the man's problems. A history of childhood sexual abuse or other sexual abuse is also a factor for some men. It has also been shown that pornography, the over-portrayal of sex in the media and 'chemsex', where people use chemicals to enhance their sexual experience, have led to an increase in the incidence of psychological erectile dysfunction. Some men may feel inadequate because they cannot match the exaggerated 'normal' sex they see on the screen.

For psychological problems of erectile dysfunction, psychosexual therapy may be very helpful and most fertility clinics would have a sex therapist or psychosexual counsellor attached. (See the article on sex by our sex therapist, Meg Fitzgerald.) It is important to look at the overall relationship because, as stated above, if there are also some issues with the female partner, these can aggravate the situation. It can be really hard to raise sexual problems with your doctor or health professional, but please try.

From a fertility point of view some men find it easier to ejaculate and masturbate to produce a sperm sample rather than achieving ejaculation during intercourse and, in these cases, the couple can be shown how to perform artificial insemination themselves at home. We have had some great success with this for couples with ejaculation problems or vaginismus.

If psychosexual therapy does not work and it is thought that there is a physical cause for erectile dysfunction, another line of treatment is drug treatment using drugs such as Viagra and Cialis. These promote the smooth muscle relaxation and increase in blood flow which is necessary for firmness in the penis. However, sexual stimulation is also necessary to achieve ejaculation. The drugs work within 30 to 60 minutes and have an effect for up to 12 hours. They have side-effects, such as headache, flushing and nausea, but are these are generally mild. They need to be avoided in men who have a history of heart disease. Other treatments include penile injections and vacuum erection devices. Rarely, penile implants are needed or penile surgery. If erectile dysfunction cannot be treated with these measures surgical sperm retrieval may be required.

Anejaculation/no ejaculation

Anejaculation is the inability to ejaculate semen despite stimulation of the penis by intercourse or masturbation. The causes can be psychological or physical. Some men are never able to ejaculate; others have what is called 'situational' anejaculation – they may have no problems when they are relaxed but it's a different matter when they are stressed. This is the most common type we see in fertility clinics because men are under pressure to 'perform' as described above. Failure to ejaculate can occur with or without orgasm.

Physical causes of anejaculation include low testosterone levels, some anti-depressant medications, hormonal treatments, multiple sclerosis, spina bifida and spinal cord injury. With the last two, the effects depend on the level of the spinal cord defect.

Men who have anejaculation but who experience orgasm may have a block in their ejaculatory ducts or damage to their ejaculatory nerves.

This can happen with diabetes and after some prostate, bladder or testicular surgery.

Treatment of anajeculation depends on the causes and includes psychosexual counselling, vibrator therapy and electro ejaculation. The vibrator acts by providing a strong stimulus to the penis for a long duration. Vibrator stimulation results in ejaculation in some men with spinal cord damage. This is a simple and quite effective way of retrieving semen in order to proceed with home artificial insemination or fertility treatments. Electro ejaculation is a procedure in which an electrical current is applied to the ejaculatory nerves through the rectum to stimulate ejaculation. Success rates in retrieving sperm vary depending on the cause of anejaculation. This treatment is not readily available and not easily repeatable as it requires a general anaesthetic. Unless it is done regularly, the sperm produced will not be of great quality and ICSI may be required. An alternative is surgical sperm retrieval.

Retrograde ejaculation

Retrograde ejaculation occurs when the semen flows back into the bladder during orgasm rather than out through the penis. It generally occurs due to weakness of or surgery to the bladder or following prostate or bowel surgery. It can also occur in men taking medications that prevent closure of the bladder neck during orgasm and in men with diabetes.

Retrograde ejaculation is rare (less than 2% of fertility patients) and is usually picked up when we see a semen sample that is low in volume and has azoospermia (no sperm in the sample). When we suspect this diagnosis, we ask the man to give us a urine sample following orgasm and ejaculation and we test that urine sample for sperm. If sperm are found, they can be used for fertility treatments. On rare occasions, medications that help to close the bladder neck (ephedrine, imipramine) may correct retrograde ejaculation.

Lifestyle

This is discussed in detail in Section 2. In summary, smoking, excessive amounts of alcohol and recreational drugs such as cannabis and cocaine have a definite detrimental effect on sperm. Excessive exercise and wearing tight underwear or anything that increases scrotal temperature is also not good.

There is some evidence that vitamins may help and there is excellent advice in Section 2 on dietary sources of vitamins.

General health problems

Any chronic illness will affect fertility, but the most common are diabetes, renal failure and thyroid disease. A bad viral infection, e.g. a bad flu (but maybe not 'man flu'!), can temporarily reduce the quality, particularly the motility, of sperm, so if we get a poor sample in a man who has recently been unwell, we would always repeat it three to six weeks after he has regained his health.

Infection in sperm sample

Sometimes we find extra white blood cells in a sperm sample and these may be a sign of infection. We therefore then test the sperm for infection. If this is found, treatment with antibiotics may help.

Male age

This is discussed in Section 2. Male fertility falls from about 45 years of age and increased male age is associated with miscarriage and health problems in their offspring, notably autism spectrum disorders.

Treatment of male factor infertility

Individual treatments for the causes of male infertility are discussed in Section 4. However, treatment really revolves around being able to get sufficient sperm of sufficient quality for natural conception, or for IUI, IVF or ICSI. Generally for natural conception, millions of healthy sperm are necessary; IUI will work with mild sperm abnormalities, but IVF and ICSI will be required for significant problems. If there is no sperm in the ejaculate and this can't be achieved, surgical sperm retrieval (testicular biopsy) may deliver sperm. If this is unsuccessful, donor sperm is an option.

Section 3 References

3.1   Practice Committee of the ASRM (2015) 'Diagnostic evaluation of the infertile male: a committee opinion'. *Fertility and Sterility* 103: 18–25.

3.2   WHO (2010) *WHO laboratory manual for the examination and processing of human semen* (5th edn). Available at: www.who.int/reproductivehealth/ publications/infertility/9789241547789/en/

3.3   Practice Committee of the ASRM (2008) 'Current evaluation of amenorrhea'. *Fertility and Sterility* 90: Suppl. 3.

3.4   ESHRE Guideline Group on POI (2016) 'ESHRE Guideline: management of women with premature ovarian insufficiency'. *Human Reproduction* 31(5): 926–37.

3.5   Norman, R. J., Wu, R. and Stankiewicz, M. T. (2004) 'Polycystic ovary syndrome'. *Medical Journal of Australia* 180: 132–7.

3.6   El Hayek, S., Bitar, L., Hamdar, L. H., Mirza, F. G. and Daoud, G. (2016) 'Polycystic ovarian syndrome: an updated overview'. *Frontiers in Physiology* 7: 124.

3.7   Carmina, E. (2006) 'Metabolic syndrome in polycystic ovary syndrome'. *Minerva Ginecologica* 58(2): 109–14.

3.8   Orio, F., Muscogiuri, G., Nese, C., Palomba, S., Savastano, S., Tafuri, D., Colarieti, G., La Sala, G., Colao, A. and Yildiz, B. O. (2016) 'Obesity, type 2 diabetes mellitus and cardiovascular disease risk: an uptodate in the management of polycystic ovary syndrome'. *European Journal of Obstetrics & Gynecology and Reproductive Biology* 207: 214–19.

3.9   Dunselman, G. A. J., Vermeulen, N., Becker, C. et al. (2014) 'ESHRE guideline: management of women with endometriosis'. *Human Reproduction* 29(3): 400–12.

3.10   Grimbizis, G. F., Gordts, S., Di Spiezio Sardo, A. et al. (2013) 'The ESHRE– ESGE consensus on the classification of female genital tract congenital anomalies'. *Gynecological Surgery* 10: 199–212.

3.11   Lumsden, M. A., Hamoodi, I., Gupta, J. and Hickey M. (2015) 'Fibroids: diagnosis and management'. *British Medical Journal* 351: h4887.

3.12   Sparic, R., Mirkovic, L., Malvasi, A. and Tinelli, A. (2016) 'Epidemiology of uterine myomas: a review'. *International Journal of Fertility and Sterility* 9(4): 424–35.

3.13   Martyn, F. M., McAuliffe, F. M., Beggan, C., Downey, P., Flannelly, G., Wingfield, M. B. (2015). 'Excisional treatments of the cervix and effect on subsequent fertility: a retrospective cohort study'. *European Journal of Obstetrics & Gynecology and Reproductive Biology* 185: 114-20

3.14 Maheshwari, A., Hamilton, M. and Bhattacharya, S. (2008) 'Effect of female age on the diagnostic categories of infertility'. *Human Reproduction* 23(3): 538–42.

3.15 Brandes, M., Hamilton, C. J., van der Steen, J. O. M. et al. (2011) 'Unexplained infertility: overall ongoing pregnancy rate and mode of conception'. *Human Reproduction* 26(2): 360–8.

3.16 Wordsworth, S., Buchanan, J., Mollison, J. et al. (2011) 'Clomifene citrate and intrauterine insemination as first-line treatments for unexplained infertility: are they cost-effective?' *Human Reproduction* 26(2): 369–75.

3.17 Quenby, S. and Brosens, J. J. (2013) 'Human implantation: a tale of mutual maternal and fetal attraction'. *Biology of Reproduction* 88(3): 81.

3.18 Templer, S. and Sacks, G. (2016) 'A blessing and a curse: is high NK cell activity good for health and bad for reproduction?' *Human Fertility* 19(3): 166–72.

3.19 Moffett, A. and Shreeve, N. (2015) 'First do no harm: uterine natural killer (NK) cells in assisted reproduction'. *Human Reproduction* 30(7): 1519–25.

3.20 Kwak-Kim, J., Han, A. R., Gilman-Sachs, A., Fishel, S., Leong, M. and Shoham, Z. (2013) 'Current trends of reproductive immunology practices in in vitro fertilization (IVF) – a first world survey using IVF-worldwide. com'. *American Journal of Reproductive Immunology* 69(1): 12–20.

3.21 Robertson, S. A., Danqing Yu, M. J., Moldenhauer, L. M., Davies, M. J., Hull, M. L. and Norman, R. J. (2016) 'Corticosteroid therapy in assisted reproduction – immune suppression is a faulty premise'. *Human Reproduction* 31(10): 2164–73.

3.22 RCOG (2016) 'The role of natural killer cells in human fertility'. *Scientific Impact Paper* 53, December.

3.23 Zini, A., Fahmy, N., Belzile, E., Ciampi, A., Al-Hathal, N. and Kotb, A. (2011) 'Antisperm antibodies are not associated with pregnancy rates after IVF and ICSI: systematic review and meta-analysis'. *Human Reproduction* 26(6): 1288–95.

3.24 Vazquez-Levin, M. H., Marín-Briggiler, C. I. and Veaute, C. (2014) 'Antisperm antibodies: invaluable tools toward the identification of sperm proteins involved in fertilization'. *American Journal of Reproductive Immunology* 72: 206–18.

3.25 Practice Committee of the ASRM and Society for Male Reproduction and Urology (2014) 'Report on varicocele and infertility: a committee opinion'. *Fertility and Sterility* 102: 1556–60.

Fertility Treatments

When it comes to fertility treatment, deciding on the best treatment approach for each case requires careful consideration. No two people will have the exact same fertility story, so it is really important that each person and couple is assessed individually and an appropriate treatment plan worked out for them. Doing the appropriate investigations and trying to find an accurate diagnosis is key, and treatment will obviously depend on this diagnosis. However, in some cases the diagnosis may be difficult – there may be several factors involved or the infertility may be 'unexplained' with no obvious factors to treat.

The social situation and wishes of the person/couple are also relevant – some people will want every possible intervention while others may prefer a more natural, low-key approach. Dialogue and trust between the patient and healthcare professional is therefore essential. I think it is really important for patients to feel comfortable asking questions and seeking clarification and it's also important for me as a doctor to feel that I explore as many options as possible with the couple. But, at the end of the day, I need to make a recommendation as to what, in my professional opinion, is the best course of action. Usually, we make the right treatment plan, but humans are not machines and there isn't always an easy formula. Sometimes one issue will initially seem the most important but as treatment progresses other factors may come to light. It can therefore be important to take things one step at a time and for patients and health professionals to do it together.

In this chapter I discuss the main treatments available and also new developments that are on the way. Other detail on treatments for specific conditions is given in the sections on those conditions. And don't forget that the tips and recommendations in the section on lifestyle can greatly enhance your chance of successful treatment.

Waiting

Strange as it may seem, sometimes the most important thing a couple can do is just wait, continue trying every month and let nature take its course. In medical terms this is called 'expectancy' and it can often be the hardest 'treatment path' for any couple to follow.

We saw in the section on unexplained infertility that a quarter of couples where no specific problem is found will conceive naturally in the year following investigation and diagnosis and up to 70% will conceive within two years, particularly if the woman is under 35. Many international experts therefore recommend no 'active' treatment for at least a year following a diagnosis of unexplained infertility. There are no medical risks and no cost but this may not always be acceptable to couples.

Following fertility surgery, it may also be important to wait. If a woman has surgery for endometriosis and if her pelvis is pretty normal at the end of that surgery, we know that she has a good chance of conceiving naturally in the following year. The same holds true for tubal surgery and the removal of ovarian cysts or adhesions. With surgery (drilling) for polycystic ovaries, we need to wait at least three months to see if there is an effect and, if the woman starts ovulating, the couple should continue trying naturally for at least six months.

For men, too, expectancy is often important. We have seen before that it takes up to three months for sperm to develop and so any intervention to improve male fertility will take a minimum of three months to have an effect. This goes for lifestyle changes, such as smoking or losing weight, but also for surgery, such as the repair of varicoceles or reversal of vasectomy. Following such surgery, couples should ideally continue trying naturally for six months to a year to give the surgery its due benefit.

A very common question for couples trying to conceive is whether they need to delay pregnancy after a miscarriage, after a Caesarean section or after an ectopic pregnancy.

In the past it was customary to advise women to wait at least three months before trying to conceive after a miscarriage or ectopic pregnancy. However, there is no evidence that this is necessary in healthy women. In the past there was poor availability of ultrasound scans and it was very difficult to determine the length of the woman's next pregnancy unless she had a few regular menstrual cycles before trying again. Also women were more likely to be undernourished and anaemic and so it was felt that they needed a few months to recover from a miscarriage. Those issues are less important now and I would generally say to couples that, following a miscarriage or ectopic pregnancy, they can start trying again as soon as they feel up to it, emotionally as well as physically. However, if the woman has received methotrexate treatment for her ectopic pregnancy, she needs to wait three months for the effects of the drug to wear off.

Following a Caesarean section it is generally recommended that women do not try to conceive again for at least a year after the birth. But it is best to discuss this with your obstetrician, particularly if your Caesarean section was complicated or if you have had more than one.

Couples having IVF often wonder how quickly they can go for a second cycle of treatment if the first cycle has not worked. There is no medical evidence that they need to wait, unless the woman's ovaries have been very hyperstimulated, in which case we need to wait for a month or two for her ovaries to settle down to normal. Otherwise there is no reason why they can't go again quickly. In my experience, however, most couples who have a failed cycle would need at least a month to get over the failure and disappointment. If they were to start treatment straight away, it would mean starting medication again on the day that the woman has had her negative pregnancy test and very few couples are ready to start again that quickly.

Surgery for women

We have seen how important it is to assess the woman's pelvis and make sure that there is no impediment to fertility there. If pelvic pathology is suspected from the woman's history (history of very painful periods, pelvic infections, e.g. chlamydia, extensive surgery) or from her ultrasound scan or other investigations, it may be necessary to perform a laparoscopy to assess her pelvis. If pathology is found, surgery may be required to remove the pathology and restore the woman's pelvis to as close to normal anatomy as possible. Pelvic surgery is generally performed by a laparoscopy, laparotomy or hysteroscopy.

Laparoscopy, which involves keyhole surgery, is described in Section 3. Laparotomy involves open surgery with a scar or incision on the woman's abdomen, usually across her lower abdomen just above her pubic hairline. For difficult surgery we occasionally need to do a midline incision, which goes from a woman's umbilicus to her pubic bone. Laparoscopic surgery is preferable to laparotomy as the recovery time is shorter and there is less likely to be scarring or adhesion formation afterwards. Laparoscopic surgery is sometimes not possible and in these cases a laparotomy may be required, for example if the woman has a very large ovarian cyst or fibroid or if she is known to have bowel and other adhesions which make laparoscopy dangerous. Generally a woman having a laparoscopy will be in hospital for a day and will need one or two weeks off work. For a laparotomy most women will be in hospital for three to five days and may require up to six weeks off work.

The surgery that is done at laparoscopy or laparotomy will depend on the pathology. Common situations where surgery is required are listed below and the specific types of surgery are discussed on the pages where those conditions are discussed.

- Endometriosis
- Ovarian cysts
- Fibroids
- Tubal disease
- Polycystic ovaries
- Ectopic pregnancy

Hysteroscopic surgery is done to remove pathology inside the woman's uterus. A telescope is inserted via the vagina into the uterus and surgery is done in a keyhole type fashion. This surgery is suitable for removing uterine polyps and fibroids and also for treating adhesions. Sometimes the surgery can be done as an outpatient procedure without anaesthetic but it is more common to require anaesthesia. However it is generally a day case procedure and two to three days off work is usually sufficient.

Surgery for men

It is rare for men to require fertility surgery. The most common situations are ligation or treatment of a varicocele and vasectomy reversal. These surgeries are discussed in the section on male infertility. Occasionally men may have problems with ejaculation and a painful foreskin and may need surgery. Male surgery is generally performed by a consultant urologist and usually requires general anaesthesia.

Testicular biopsy with a view to gaining sperm for use in assisted reproduction is best done at a fertility clinic or by an urologist linked with a fertility clinic. This is described in further detail later.

Ovulation induction

As the name suggests, ovulation induction means using treatments to induce ovulation in a woman who does not ovulate spontaneously. Weight management and ovarian drilling to induce ovulation in women with polycystic ovaries are described in Section 3. As described in the pages on ovulation problems, it is important, prior to starting ovulation induction treatment, to ensure that the male has normal sperm and that there is no pelvic reason (e.g. tubal problem or severe endometriosis) that will prevent pregnancy even if the woman ovulates.

Table 4.1 summarises the main ovulation induction drugs used. These same drugs are used to super-ovulate women for IUI and IVF/ICSI treatments. **Super-ovulation** essentially means 'boosting' ovulation in a woman who ovulates naturally with the intention of causing more than one follicle to develop and ovulate. The drugs used are described in detail below. Some drugs are not hormones (metformin, bromocriptine, cabergoline) and do not require ultrasound monitoring. These drugs are also discussed in the sections on PCOS and ovulation problems in Section 3. The hormonal stimulation drugs require monitoring to avoid the risk of multiple pregnancy.

Monitoring the response

In the case of ovulation induction, women are monitored with ultrasound scans (and sometimes blood tests) until one or two follicles are seen to be growing towards ovulation. At the beginning of a woman's menstrual cycle, her follicles measure less than 9–10 mms in diameter, but they then start growing, and one or two reach a diameter of 15–22 mm just before ovulation. Generally, when a follicle measures at least 15 mm, ovulation is deemed to be imminent and (as long as there are not more than two large follicles) the couple are advised to start having intercourse. Sometimes a trigger injection of hCG (human chorionic gonadotropin) is given at this stage to release the egg/s but this is not always necessary and in other couples we may combine ovulation induction with IUI.

One of the main risks of ovulation induction and super-ovulation is **multiple pregnancy**. All women respond differently to fertility drugs, so, while we can get an idea of what dose a woman will require from her AMH blood test and antral follicle count, weight and age, we won't know until she is actually going through the treatment how many follicles are likely to develop. The aim is to get one or two follicles developing. If three or more follicles start to grow, the risk of multiple pregnancy such as triplets or quadruplets is too high and we would cancel the cycle. This can be very upsetting for couples, but it really isn't worth taking that risk.

Very few doctors would now prescribe injections for ovulation induction without doing ultrasound monitoring as this really is imperative to avoid multiple pregnancies. However, some doctors do prescribe oral fertility drugs such as Clomid without monitoring. This is no longer regarded as good practice. All international guidelines recommend that women should be scanned for at least their first cycle of ovulation induction with oral agents, and preferably for two cycles. Contrary to popular belief, the majority of triplet, quadruplet and higher-order pregnancies come from ovulation induction and super-ovulation rather than from IVF because, in IVF, we can control how many embryos we transfer to the woman's uterus. On the other hand, with ovulation induction, if the woman releases four eggs, they may all be fertilised with intercourse or IUI and lead to multiple embryos and multiple pregnancy. I have seen some women taking half a tablet of Clomid and getting six growing follicles and other women who take three tablets daily and get no growing follicles. This is where scanning, also called follicle tracking, is essential.

Other advantages of scanning the woman are that we can time ovulation more precisely and we can see whether the lining of her uterus is sufficient for pregnancy – Clomid can cause a thin lining in some women.

Drugs used

Table 4.1 Ovulation Induction Drugs

Medical condition	Drugs used	USS monitoring required
Polycystic ovaries or unexplained anovulation	Metformin	✗
	Tablets:	
	Clomiphene (Clomid)	✔
	Letrozole (Femara)	✔
	Tamoxifen	✔
	Injections:	
	Gonal F (FSH)	✔
	Menopur (FSH/LH)	✔
	Puregon (FSH)	✔
	Elonva (FSH)	✔
	Luveris (LH)	✔
	Trigger:	
	hCG	✗
	Provera	✗
Hypo hypo	Injections:	
	Gonal F (FSH)	✔
	Menopur (FSH/LH)	✔
	Puregon (FSH)	✔
	Elonva (FSH)	✔
	Luveris (LH)	✔
	Pump: GnRH	✗
	Trigger: hCG	✗
High prolactin	Bromocriptine	✗
	Cabergoline	✗

Clomiphene citrate or Clomid: Clomid is a fertility drug which has been around for 30 to 40 years. It is a tablet that is taken for five days at the beginning of a woman's cycle and can be started on the second, third, fourth or fifth day of the cycle. It is called an anti-oestrogen and it acts by making the pituitary gland in the brain think that the woman's oestrogen levels are low. This stimulates the pituitary gland to produce more FSH (follicle-stimulating hormone) which will hopefully act on the follicles in the woman's ovaries and cause them to start growing and producing oestrogen. Clomid can be very effective for women who are not ovulating, particularly women with polycystic ovaries. It is not recommended for unexplained infertility where the woman is ovulating spontaneously.

The main risk of Clomid treatment is multiple pregnancy and up to 10% of women will conceive twins, even if monitored. Because it is an anti-oestrogen, Clomid's main side-effects are those related to low oestrogen levels. These include thinning of the lining of the womb, reduction in mucus at the cervix, mood swings, occasionally hot flushes and sometimes headaches and dry vagina. However many women will notice no side-effects and, if they do occur, they are usually mild and short-lived.

Letrozole (Femara): Letrozole is another tablet which is used to induce ovulation. It is called an aromatase inhibitor and works on the ovary to reduce oestrogen production. This in turn stimulates the pituitary gland to produce more FSH, which will hopefully act on the follicles in the woman's ovaries and cause them to start growing. Again it is recommended that women are scanned for the first one or two cycles when taking letrozole, though the risk of multiple pregnancy seems to be lower than that with Clomid. Currently letrozole is not specifically licensed for ovulation induction, but studies suggest that it is very safe and we therefore use it, particularly for women who respond poorly to Clomid. Monitoring is as for Clomid. Side-effects include fatigue, dizzy spells, hot flushes and bone, muscle or joint pains. These are usually mild and short-lived.

Tamoxifen: Tamoxifen is a drug similar to clomiphene and acts in a similar fashion but tends to have fewer negative effects on the lining of the uterus. Monitoring and side-effects are as for Clomid.

FSH ± LH injections: If the woman does not respond to clomiphene, letrozole or tamoxifen ovulation induction, the next step in terms of drugs to induce ovulation is injections of the hormone FSH, with or without LH. These hormones act directly on the woman's ovaries to induce ovulation. Generally for women with PCOS we start with just FSH (because these women usually have good levels of LH). However, women with hypo hypo anovulation have low levels of both hormones, so they need FSH and LH. Oral agents work poorly with hypo hypo.

FSH and LH injections generally have fewer side-effects than oral agents, the main ones being mood swings and bloating. The main risks are multiple pregnancy and, rarely, OHSS (see the section on risks of IVF).

GnRH pump: This is a treatment for women with anovulation due to hypo hypo (see Section 3). The problem here lies in the hypothalamus in the brain which fails to produce GnRH (which normally stimulates the pituitary gland to produce FSH and LH). GnRH must be given via an infusion pump with a needle placed intravenously or subcutaneously and this releases a 'pulse' of hormone every 90 minutes. Treatment usually lasts for 10–14 days and has similar success rates to FSH/LH injections but lower multiple pregnancy rates.

What a cycle involves

Oral tablets: Treatment generally starts on Day 2, 3, 4 or 5 of the woman's cycle (period). If she doesn't get periods or they are very infrequent (as is the case for many women with PCOS) we use Provera (progesterone tablet) for seven days to induce or 'bring on' a bleed and then we start the ovulation induction tablets. Our practice is to ask the woman to take the medication (half, one or two tablets) for five days at the beginning of her cycle and then we do a vaginal scan around Day 10 of her cycle. We aim to see one or two follicles growing. One scan may be enough or several may be needed over the next few days.

We advise the male partner to ejaculate regularly and two to five days before anticipated ovulation, to ensure healthy sperm around this time. *However, it is important that couples abstain from sex or use protection (condoms) until the scan has confirmed that there aren't excessive follicles growing.*

Once the growing follicle/s get to about 15–17 mm in size we know that the woman is about to ovulate soon and we can advise her about having intercourse around this time. If the woman does not ovulate on her first cycle, we increase the dose next time around – conversely, if she develops too many follicles, we reduce the dose in the next cycle.

FSH ± LH Injections: FSH and LH must be given as injections, either daily or weekly. Women are shown how to do these injections themselves and many companies produce patient-friendly pens to make this easier. The injections are given subcutaneously (by pinching a fold of skin in the abdomen and injecting just under the skin). The dose of hormone used is decided for each woman individually depending on her age, weight and ovarian reserve tests.

As with oral agents, treatment generally starts on Day 2, 3 or 4 of the woman's cycle (period). If she doesn't get periods or they are very infrequent (as is the case for many women with PCOS) we use Provera (progesterone tablet) for seven days to induce or 'bring on' a bleed. Women with hypo hypo may start without a bleed. Close monitoring with ultrasound is essential and generally three or four monitoring visits are required (see previous section on monitoring the response). An ovulation trigger injection of the hormone hCG (human chorionic gonadotropin) is given to cause the follicle to rupture and release its egg. Treatment with injections may take three weeks or more before a response is seen, so patience and perseverance is required!

> 'I did not have any of the symptoms typically associated with PCOS, but there you have it. We are all so different. Although when I was diagnosed, instead of being upset, I was actually relieved. We found the problem ... now we can fix it. This didn't turn out to be as easy as I thought. After one ectopic pregnancy and two failed Clomid cycles I am now going to move onto the FSH injections. I have to admit, it scares me, but I'm willing to try anything at this stage.'

> 'I have PCOS. I was lucky as my consultant immediately put me at ease and explained the condition to me; I had never heard of it before! My consultant set out a short-term and long-term plan for me. The first step was to try Clomid for four months. I went back into the Merrion for scans during ovulation to see if it was working. It worked straightaway

and I got pregnant on the fourth round of Clomid. I think the relaxed atmosphere and the set plan really helped me relax and get pregnant.'

Chance of success

As with all treatments, success is very dependent on the woman's age and to a lesser degree on her weight, duration of infertility and any other male or female factors.

Most studies show that up to 80% of women will ovulate with ovulation induction treatment, but live birth rates are closer to 40–50% with six months of treatment. In my experience, treatment either works very quickly – within the first few cycles – or it becomes protracted and really frustrating. We therefore generally recommend treatment for four to six cycles with oral agents or injections, but if these are not successful, the couple should start thinking about other alternatives such as laparoscopic ovarian diathermy for PCO, or IVF.

Artificial insemination without sperm preparation

I discussed in the pages on psychosexual problems that couples can be helped to do artificial insemination themselves at home if the woman has vaginismus or the man cannot ejaculate in the vagina. In these cases, the sperm is placed in the vagina, so there is no need for sperm preparation in the laboratory.

Some services in the past performed intravaginal or intracervical insemination of unprepared semen, predominantly for donor sperm treatments, but this is now rarely done by clinics and is not recommended.

Assisted reproductive technology (ART)

Assisted reproductive technology is a term used to describe treatments that involve the preparation or processing of eggs and sperm in the laboratory for the purpose of establishing a pregnancy. Many people would regard it as including IUI (intrauterine insemination) and donor sperm insemination, because these treatments are usually done in fertility or IVF clinics and involve processing sperm. However, some international bodies do not include these treatments under the umbrella of ART. Technically, ART refers to IVF (in vitro fertilisation); ICSI (intracytoplasmic sperm injection); embryo transfer; Fallopian tube transfer; sperm, egg and embryo freezing; egg and embryo donation; and surrogacy.

In this section on ART treatments, I have included any treatment involving the laboratory handling of eggs, sperm or embryos. All these treatments (including IUI and donor sperm) take place in fertility clinics, which must (in Ireland and the EU) hold a licence from the HPRA (Health Products Regulatory Authority) or its equivalent. There is strict technical legislation regarding the handling of eggs, sperm and embryos. One of the requirements is that men and women must be tested for infections such as hepatitis and HIV.

Intrauterine insemination (IUI)

As the name suggests, IUI involves placing the man's sperm into the woman's uterus. During natural intercourse, semen (which contains the sperm) is deposited in the woman's vagina but only the sperm actually pass through the cervix and into the uterus and Fallopian tubes. Therefore, in IUI, the man's semen sample must be prepared in the laboratory to remove the sperm from the semen. In doing this, the scientist (embryologist) also selects the most active sperm and disposes of dead and immotile sperm. The sperm are then suspended in a sample of fluid called culture media, which maintains them in an active state, and this is placed in the woman's uterus.

For IUI to be effective, it must be done at the time the woman is ovulating, so she will have been scanned to determine this. Often IUI treatment is combined with mild ovarian super-ovulation, with the ovulation induction drugs described earlier, to 'boost' her ovulation. These drugs are used in the same way as for ovulation induction and the same precautions with regard to multiple pregnancy are essential (see section on ovulation induction). Ovulation is usually triggered with an injection so that ovulation should occur 24–36 hours after this, and IUI is scheduled for this time. The couple can also have intercourse around this time – every little helps!

Having the actual IUI procedure is a bit like having a smear test. A speculum is used to locate the cervix and the opening of the womb and then a very fine catheter (tube) containing the sperm is passed into the uterus. This has a syringe attached and the sperm solution is slowly released into the uterus. This is done by a doctor or a nurse. The woman relaxes for 10–15 minutes and then she can go about her normal activities.

Success rates

Fertility specialists around the world differ in their view of the value of IUI. The NICE guidelines in the UK (1.1) don't recommend it at all except for couples unable to have intercourse. Others recommend it highly. As with ovulation induction, it is important that the sperm is normal or near normal and the same holds true for the woman's pelvis and Fallopian tubes. Female age has a large effect on success rates. Success rates reported for IUI range from 2% to 40% but in clinics with higher success rates there is often a 20–30% rate of multiple pregnancy, and that is not good. Generally, the chance of success is higher if super-ovulation with fertility drugs is used in conjunction with the IUI.

I generally quote a live birth rate of 10–15% per cycle of treatment and about 25% overall if a couple do three or four cycles. But I generally don't recommend IUI if the woman is 35 or over. My attitude to IUI has changed over the years because the success rates with IVF have increased so much and those with IUI haven't. Also, many couples, particularly younger couples, will get two children from one IVF cycle and frozen embryos.

IUI can be very helpful for couples with psychosexual problems or for women with a significant cervix problem, e.g. previous surgery to their cervix. It is also used in donor sperm treatments for single women, lesbians and heterosexual couples where partner sperm is not available and for the treatment of couples where the male is HIV positive. If couples have to travel a long distance for treatment, IVF may be preferable to IUI because, in general, one would need to do at least four (and more likely six) cycles of IUI to get the same success rate as one cycle of IVF.

IVF and ICSI

In vitro fertilisation (IVF) literally means fertilisation 'in glass'. We saw in Section 1 that during natural conception, the sperm and egg meet and fertilise in the woman's Fallopian tube. With IVF, this process actually takes place in the laboratory. Put very simply, the woman's eggs are removed from her ovary by a minor surgical procedure and placed, with the man's sperm, in the laboratory. All going well, the sperm will fertilise several of these eggs and some fertilised eggs will continue to grow further into embryos. One or two of these embryos are then placed in the woman's uterus (womb) where they will hopefully implant and lead to a pregnancy.

IVF was developed as a treatment for couples where the woman's Fallopian tubes were damaged or absent and so fertilisation could not occur naturally. IVF was a medical breakthrough for infertility due to tubal disease, enabling the bypassing of natural fertilisation in the Fallopian tube. With time it was realised that IVF is actually an excellent treatment for a number of other fertility problems and nowadays IVF is a highly effective treatment for a vast range of problems. Indeed, IVF was one of the most significant medical breakthroughs of the twentieth century.

A key part of IVF involves ovarian stimulation and, over time, this has proved to be one of the reasons why the technique is successful. Most IVF treatments involve stimulating the woman's ovaries to produce eight or more eggs during each treatment cycle. This means that, in contrast to a natural cycle, where only one or two eggs mature and develop, in one month we have the number of eggs that would generally take up to a year to produce. This can be of particular benefit for women who have a low ovarian reserve and who are running out of time because IVF enables us to harvest as many eggs as is safely possible in a short period of time.

The other situation where IVF has been a truly wonderful medical breakthrough is in the treatment of male infertility. We know that for natural conception to occur a man needs millions of healthy, swimming sperm. During IVF treatments, because we are placing the egg and sperm very close together, we do not need so many sperm, so it is an excellent treatment for men who have low sperm counts or low sperm motility. If the sperm is very compromised, a variation of IVF called **ICSI** is used. ICSI is described below under Fertilisation, which is where it differs from IVF. However, all other stages of the cycle (ovarian stimulation, egg collection, embryo transfer, etc. are the same for IVF and ICSI).

Over the years, many additions and improvements have been made to the basic process of IVF and it is now a sophisticated and complex treatment involving several stages. The stages are described below, but try not to get overwhelmed by it all. Most clinics have information leaflets and staff available to help you through the different stages – and once you actually start the treatment, it all begins to come together and make more sense. While I describe the main stages and procedures here, every clinic will have its own unique way of doing things, so if you are undergoing treatment, make sure you always follow your own clinic's instructions and advice.

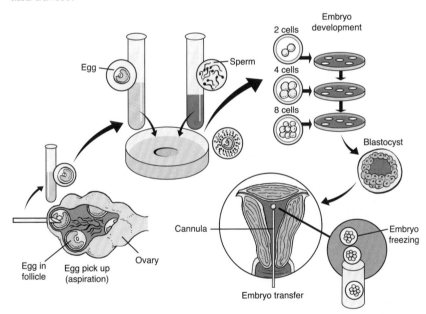

Stages of a 'typical' IVF/ICSI cycle

Ovarian stimulation and triggering ovulation

Early attempts at IVF involved natural cycles where the woman developed one or two eggs naturally and these were then removed and used for IVF. It soon became clear that a larger number of eggs would increase the chances of success and now the vast majority of IVF programmes start with stimulation of the ovaries to produce a number of eggs. We know that not all the eggs will fertilise (usually 50–70% do) and that not all of the fertilised eggs will actually go on to form healthy embryos (about 50% do). For this reason a larger number of eggs increases the chance of success. However, too many eggs are not good either (we will discuss later how overstimulation can be a problem with IVF). Most IVF programmes aim to stimulate somewhere between eight and 14 eggs during each treatment cycle. I described in Section 1 how eggs mature during a menstrual cycle and in the section on ovulation induction how the growing follicles containing the eggs can be monitored by ultrasound scan.

The ovaries are generally stimulated with FSH (follicle-stimulating hormone). LH (luteinising hormone) may also be used. FSH (and LH) must be given as injections, either daily or weekly. Women are shown how to do these injections themselves and many companies produce patient-friendly 'pens' to make this process easier. See also earlier section on ovulation induction.

The dose of hormone used is decided for each woman individually depending on her age, weight and her ovarian reserve tests. Even so, all women respond differently to the drugs, so close monitoring is required. The growth and number of the ovarian follicles (which contain the eggs) are carefully monitored using a combination of ultrasound and blood tests. Generally, three or four monitoring visits are required (see earlier section on ovulation induction and monitoring the response). When some of the follicles have reached the required size (16–22 mm in diameter), the woman is ready for the procedure to remove her eggs (egg retrieval or egg collection). In order to allow the final stages of egg development, an ovulation trigger injection of the hormone hCG (human chorionic gonadotropin) is given and egg collection is scheduled approximately 36 hours later.

In addition to the FSH/LH injections, which stimulate the ovaries, a second type of hormone is also required, this time to control the woman's own natural hormones. As the follicles grow, they cause the woman's oestrogen levels to rise and, if not controlled in some way, this will eventually trigger a surge in the hormone LH, which will result in ovulation. If this occurs, the eggs will be released from the follicles into the woman's pelvis and will be lost before egg collection. In order to prevent this occurring, additional treatment is given.

Over the years two regimes have been developed to prevent premature ovulation. The original regime is called 'downregulation'. It involves an injection or nasal spray to deliver a hormone which suppresses the action of the woman's own pituitary gland and so prevents the LH surge which can trigger early ovulation. This medication is started two to three weeks before the FSH/LH stimulation drugs and continued until just before egg collection. The other regime is called an antagonist or 'short' protocol. In this case the FSH/LH stimulation injections are started at the beginning of the woman's cycle and a second daily injection of an antagonist hormone is added on the fifth day of stimulation. Again, this is continued until just before egg collection.

The choice between downregulation and antagonist protocol will be made by your doctor. International studies show no significant difference between the two regimes in terms of success rates for the majority of women, though the antagonist protocol is shorter and more patient-friendly. The antagonist is preferable for women with PCO because of their risk of ovarian hyperstimulation, and downregulation is sometimes better for women with endometriosis or fibroids because it suppresses the condition prior to stimulation. However, different clinics may find that one or other regime works best for them, so they will advise which is recommended in your particular case. The side-effects of the drugs are described in the previous section on ovulation induction.

'The IVF cycle itself was grand. The physical aspects of the treatment were fine. When I look back on my concerns now – the time off work (I had never had a sick day in my life), would I balloon up (it wouldn't have stopped me but I remember one of my patients saying this had happened her – it didn't to me). In fact, once I remembered to drink water – and I mean a lot of water – it was fine. When I didn't I would liken it to staying up all night clubbing and then going to the beach for the day without any water. I wouldn't recommend it. I found the injections easy and it was just as well I was the one that had to take them as my husband couldn't do the needles at all – though he has become a dab hand at getting air bubbles

out. I know in this respect I am fortunate but I was on a high level of drugs and bar being a little bloated I didn't feel it at all.'

'The injections were fine, I had no side-effects from them and drank two litres of water each day as advised. My husband administered all my injections both in the evening and morning as I have fear of needles (but I can 100% say they are not painful and over within a few seconds) and also it made him feel like he was a part of the process.'

'The first injection is the hardest. Get it over with as soon as possible. I recommend that you make your dinner so that you have something to look forward to after the injection. The thought that it will get cold will motivate you to get the injection over with sooner rather than later. Then set everything up. Ideally get your partner involved in this, so as you make dinner he gets the injection ready for you. Another handy tip is to get an ice cube and put it on the area that you are going to inject. It numbs the area and takes away that initial pinch of the needle. Stick to the same time every day.'

'So we started the IVF/ICSI path. To be honest it was a very exciting time. We were warned (or more specifically 'I' was warned) that Lizzie would have mood swings, etc. in the lead-up but lucky for me she remained her usual self throughout. The injections seemed to be the hardest part for her but she soldiered through.'

Egg collection

Egg collection is a minor surgical procedure. It involves passing a fine needle through the top of the woman's vagina and into her ovaries. Gentle suction is then applied to the needle and the fluid in each follicle is drained. This procedure is done under ultrasound guidance: the needle for draining the follicles is attached to the vaginal ultrasound probe and the whole procedure is done while also scanning. This means that the doctor can see the needle, the ovaries and the follicles on a monitor and ensure that she/he is safely inserting the needle in the correct place.

The fluid that is aspirated (taken out) is passed to the embryologist and examined under a microscope. Hopefully the egg in the follicle will have been dislodged and is identified in the fluid. All follicles are drained but not all will yield an egg. Generally we would expect to get an egg from 80–90% of the larger follicles but the number retrieved can vary from woman to woman. The eggs are then prepared in the laboratory.

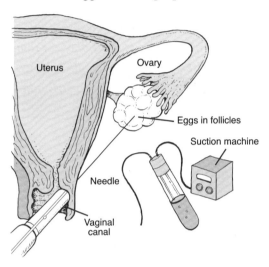

Most clinics will administer sedation or pain relief to the woman during the egg collection procedure. The type of sedation given varies from clinic to clinic but is generally given by intravenous injection or infusion. The aim is to provide good pain relief but also to avoid over-treatment – general anaesthesia is not usually necessary. Most women will experience some discomfort after the egg collection and this will vary depending on the number of follicles and the ease of the egg collection. Some follicles are easy to reach and the eggs come out easily, whereas in other women (e.g. those who have had lots of surgery in the past) the procedure can be a bit more complicated. Because of this discomfort and the sedation, it is generally advised to rest and not go to work on the day of egg collection or the day after.

'Only five eggs were collected. I was very sore upon waking up from sedation, it felt like very bad period pains and I bled quite a bit. Upon returning home that day I felt faint, hot and I vomited. The next day

I was still very sore and had severe constipation, I couldn't stand up straight for three or four days. I took a laxative the day before transfer and it seemed to help.'

'As per the previous round I had no problems or side-effects with the injections. We braced ourselves on the day of egg collection for pain, but this time I had no pain upon awaking from sedation and very little bleeding. It was the complete opposite of the previous round, I felt great. I didn't need to take any extra painkillers while at home. I had a small bit of diarrhoea that night when I came home, but nothing to complain about.'

Sperm collection

The male partner is required to provide a semen sample on the day of the egg collection, unless sperm has been frozen prior to this time. In order to optimise the quality of the sperm, the man should have ejaculated two to five days beforehand. The sperm is then examined and prepared in the laboratory and, depending on its quality on that particular day, the final decision is made as to whether IVF or ICSI is required.

We discussed earlier that having to produce a sperm sample at a particular time on a particular day can be daunting and difficult for some men. This is so true on the day of an IVF procedure. If you find ejaculation difficult at times it is important to discuss this with the team providing IVF. If there is any chance that producing sperm on the day may be difficult, we would generally recommend freezing sperm prior to the day as a 'back-up'. We will still plan to get a fresh sample on the day, but it is reassuring to know that we have some in storage. If you haven't frozen sperm and there are problems on the day, we can prescribe medication such as Viagra or Cialis, which help. In rare circumstances, if we can't get sperm, we may need to consider surgical sperm retrieval (testicular biopsy) or freezing the eggs, but neither of these scenarios is ideal.

Fertilisation

For IVF, each egg is placed in a drop of fluid with approximately 100,000 sperm and then carefully placed in an incubator. In the case of **ICSI**, the outer layer of cells around the egg is removed and a single sperm is chosen and injected into each egg. This is a highly skilled procedure performed by the embryologist

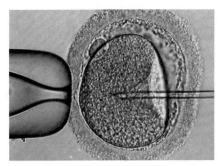

Fertilisation

using a microscope to see the tiny eggs and sperm. Great care is needed not to damage the eggs. The eggs and sperm are then placed in an incubator.

The next morning the embryologist examines the eggs to detect signs of fertilisation.

If the egg has been fertilised normally, we should see two **pronuclei** (or PNs). Each pronucleus represents half the chromosomes from each partner (23 chromosomes from the female egg and 23 chromosomes from the male sperm). These pronuclei fuse over the next couple of hours to form one whole nucleus containing the normal complement of 46 chromosomes. This is evidence of normal fertilisation. Some eggs may be abnormally fertilised and will be seen to have three pronuclei, four pronuclei or one pronucleus. Eggs which have not been fertilised will have no pronuclei evident. This assessment stage is therefore critical as unfertilised and abnormally fertilised eggs can be seen and discarded as they are genetically abnormal and will never lead to a healthy pregnancy.

Usually about 60–70% of the eggs collected fertilise, but this can range from 0% to 100%.

In some couples there will be total **failure of fertilisation** or only abnormal fertilisation and therefore no healthy embryos will develop The treatment is then over! This happens in 2–5% of cycles and is devastating. It is usually unexpected as up until then the egg development and the sperm quality will have seemed okay. Couples in this situation can feel cheated because they haven't been able to complete the cycle of treatment. Thankfully, the results are generally good if ICSI is used on the next occasion.

Development of embryos

After approximately 24 hours a normally fertilised egg should divide into two. An egg is one cell and this divides into two cells, at which stage we call it an embryo. These two cells subsequently divide into four cells, then eight, then sixteen and so on. Over the next number of days the embryologists monitor the development and appearance of these embryos. It will become evident that some will divide and grow in a normal fashion, showing two to four cells on Day 2 and six to eight cells on Day 3. Other fertilised eggs and embryos may fail to divide at all or may divide too slowly or too quickly. Other factors relating to the embryos, such as the shape of the cells and the number of fragments within the cells, are also noted.

Some incubators contain **time-lapse cameras**, which take photographs of the embryos, and this can give extra information about embryo development.

Once the embryos get to Day 4 they are called morulas. The number of cells is now too great to be counted individually and from this stage on the embryo is beginning to develop to what we call the blastocyst stage. The cells begin to rearrange themselves into a group of cells called the **inner cell mass**, which will hopefully go on to form a healthy embryo/foetus and baby, and the outer **trophectoderm cells**, which will go on to form the placenta and support for the pregnancy.

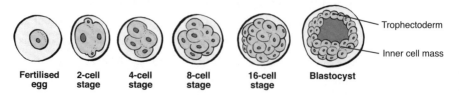

Human embryonic development

During the days when the embryos are growing and developing, the embryologists are monitoring them carefully. Depending on the number and quality of the embryos, a decision is made as to the optimal day to transfer the embryo or embryos to the woman's uterus. If a couple have many embryos, most laboratories will recommend allowing them to continue to grow in the incubator until Day 5 or blastocyst stage. This gives us the optimal amount of information about the embryos and enables the embryologist to choose the best embryo/s. If, however, a couple have a small number of embryos, it is likely that only one or two embryos will develop normally and in such a case there is no advantage in waiting any longer and the embryo/s will be transferred to the woman's uterus on Day 2 or Day 3 after egg collection.

Preparation of the woman's uterus/endometrial lining

Because of the drugs used during stimulation to suppress the woman's own hormonal responses, it is necessary for her to have extra progesterone hormone after egg collection to ensure that the endometrium or lining of her womb remains suitable to accept an embryo and allow it to implant. This progesterone is most commonly taken as a vaginal tablet or gel but may also be given as an injection. It is started on the evening of the day after egg collection and taken for at least 15 days – until the outcome of the cycle is known.

Embryo transfer

Embryo transfer is performed by placing a speculum in the woman's vagina (similar to the procedure for taking a smear test) and then gently passing a very fine tube (catheter) with the embryo or embryos in it into the uterus. The embryo/s is/are then gently expelled. Medication or sedation is not usually required for this step. An ultrasound scan is generally used so that the correct placement of the catheter in the uterus can be confirmed, though this is not essential for success.

Most clinics encourage the woman's partner to be present for embryo transfer if they wish and most couples find the procedure fascinating. It certainly seems like a miracle that this tiny embryo that we can't see, except under the microscope, could actually stay in the uterus, implant and lead to a healthy pregnancy and baby. Women often worry that the embryo will fall out after transfer, but it is truly a wonder of nature that it doesn't. The progesterone support that began after egg collection is continued until the time of a pregnancy test, and sometimes until the pregnancy scan.

The two weeks between embryo transfer and pregnancy test are often described as the most stressful time. You are waiting to see if you are pregnant, you are almost afraid to hope you are, and there is no need to go to the clinic, so it can be a lonely, anxious time.

'I 100% recommend IVF, it is not scary whatsoever – I think people
have a perception that it is. The scariest thing about it is the two-week
wait (I recommend taking a few days off work after your results, this is
so beneficial, as it gives you time to get your head together after either
outcome). IVF if anything may actually give you an answer in some
cases as to what is wrong!'

⸺

'I peed and I waited. I looked over onto the sink and sure enough it was
positive. If the stick hadn't been covered in my pee I'd have hugged it. It
was so surreal that I went straight to the chemist and did another one
to be sure.'

⸺

'I was dying to tell my husband so when my last client left I heard him
upstairs. I ran up to the bedroom, got the two tests and put them in my
pocket. I called him into the bedroom and asked him to sit down – I
needed to talk to him. His poor little face – he thought something bad
had happened. I handed him the two tests and his face said it all. We
hugged each other like crazy and lay on the bed just in absolute shock –
it had finally happened. I'll never forget that moment and how special
it was.'

⸺

Table 4.2 Summary of Timelines

Downregulation cycle	Downregulation: 2 weeks Stimulation injections: 8–14 days Egg collection (this day and next off work) Embryo transfer: 2/3/5 days after egg collection (day off work) Pregnancy test: 16 days after egg collection
Antagonist cycle	Stimulation injections: 8–14 days Antagonist injection: from day 5 to egg collection Egg collection (this day and next off work) Embryo transfer: 2/3/5 days after egg collection (day off work) Pregnancy test: 16 days after egg collection

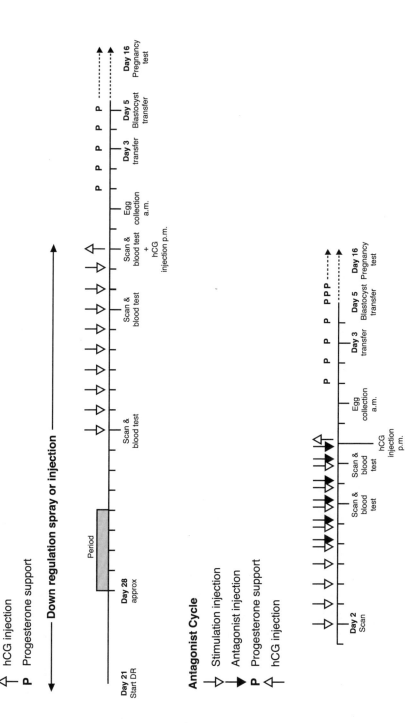

Down Regulation Cycle

▷ Stimulation injection

◁ hCG injection

P Progesterone support

— Down regulation spray or injection —

Day 21
Start DR

Day 28
approx

Period

Scan &
blood test

Scan &
blood test

Scan &
blood test
+
hCG
injection p.m.

Egg
collection
a.m.

P P P P

Day 3
transfer

Day 5
Blastocyst
transfer

Day 16
Pregnancy
test

Antagonist Cycle

▷ Stimulation injection

► Antagonist injection

P Progesterone support

◁ hCG injection

Day 2
Scan

Scan &
blood
test

Scan &
blood
test

hCG
injection
p.m.

Egg
collection
a.m.

P P P

Day 3
transfer

Day 5
Blastocyst
transfer

Day 16
Pregnancy
test

'IVF can be isolating. There isn't a lot of awareness about fertility issues in general. When you're going through it, as much as there are groups that you can join, the nature of Ireland is that it's a small country. You may not want everyone to know your business. You may not want to attend a support group in case you bump into someone that you don't want to know. I recommend building your own support team around you. At work is sometimes the easiest because you will need your close colleagues to understand why you're a bit distracted, or why you have to take more time off and also to remind you when your alarm goes off for your medication! Most people spend the majority of their day at work so it makes sense for some colleagues to understand what is going on.'

'Perspective. IVF can become a tunnel that you bury yourself into. Going relentlessly towards a life goal that you have set for yourself through expectation or desire. Both nature and life deliver the unexpected and don't always go to plan. So take a break. Go to the cinema. Enjoy a date night where you do not talk about IVF or babies or family. Talk about how you met. Talk about travel, great food, sunshine, great books, favourite friends, stupid things that make you laugh. Get away and forget about IVF. This is not easy. And you should not beat yourself up if it creeps into conversation but you should acknowledge the slip and commit to distracting yourself.'

Number of embryos to transfer

The number of embryos transferred will depend on several factors such as the woman's age, the number, quality and phase of development of the embryos, previous pregnancies, and the number of times the couple has had treatment. The ideal number to transfer is one, but in some situations we recommend two. See also elective single embryo transfer below.

Multiple pregnancy (twins and triplets) is currently the most serious complication of IVF and ICSI treatment. While many couples would love twins and many twin pregnancies proceed uneventfully, it has been shown beyond any doubt that twin pregnancies are more medically complicated than single ones, and the risks with triplets are higher again. At least half of twins and 90% of triplets are born before 37 weeks of pregnancy and with low birth weights, making them at high risk of serious health problems and death. Every single complication of pregnancy is higher in multiple pregnancy – these include miscarriage, late miscarriage, premature or early labour, diabetes, high blood pressure, haemorrhage during pregnancy and at delivery, and cerebral palsy. Premature infants often require long stays in ICU with drips, tube feeding, ventilation, etc. and have an increased risk of developmental problems, growth problems, deafness, etc. Compared to singleton births the risk of death around the time of birth is three to six times higher for twins and nine times higher for triplets.

On several occasions I have seen women with a long history of infertility deliver perfectly formed twins at about 20 weeks of pregnancy, when there is no hope of them surviving. This is absolutely heart-breaking. Multiple pregnancy also places other strains on parents, including financial difficulties, emotional distress and physical exhaustion.

The practice of **elective single embryo transfer** or **eSET** was pioneered in Scandinavia in the 1990s and is now regarded as best practice in IVF. It means that when we have two or more embryos suitable to transfer, we elect to transfer only one and we freeze the remainder for use in the future. In the past it was thought that this would reduce pregnancy success rates as the rates of pregnancy will be higher if more embryos are transferred – however, the multiple pregnancy rates will also be vastly higher and many of these multiple pregnancies will end badly. We now know that if a couple have good-quality embryos and the IVF laboratory has good IVF and freezing systems, the chance of a healthy pregnancy and a live birth are the same whether two embryos are put back together or two embryos are put back separately, one in the fresh cycle and one in a subsequent frozen embryo transfer cycle.

So I have absolutely no doubt but that for couples with a good chance of success (younger women, those with good-quality embryos, those with previous successful pregnancies and those on their first or second cycle of treatment) single embryo transfer is the way to go. For couples where the woman is older or the embryos are poorer quality, or if they have already had several unsuccessful treatments, two may be preferable.

Rarely, an embryo splits in two following transfer, resulting in identical twins. The chances of this occurring are very low – less than 1% on a Day 2/3 embryo transfer and 1–2% on a Day 5/6 transfer. However, triplet pregnancies occur if two embryos are transferred and then one of them splits.

The number of embryos to transfer is something you should discuss with your fertility team. There is a really excellent UK website called One at a Time, which deals with the issue of multiple pregnancy related to IVF and other fertility treatments. This was developed by an expert group of medical, nursing and scientific experts and co-ordinated by the UK HFEA (Human Fertilisation and Embryology Authority). See www. oneatatime.org.uk.

Freezing (vitrification) of embryos

Embryos are very precious, so if a couple have extra healthy embryos that are not being transferred in the fresh cycle, these are frozen so that they can be used in the future. If pregnancy doesn't follow the fresh transfer, or if the woman miscarries, the couple can come back to try again with their frozen embryos. A cycle of treatment using frozen embryos (often called a FET cycle, or frozen embryo transfer cycle) is much easier than a fresh cycle, because the embryos are already there. If the couple are successful with their fresh cycle, their extra embryos can be kept frozen for several years, so they can have a baby and then come back for a FET cycle. I have seen many couples get two healthy babies (and sometimes even three) from one fresh cycle of treatment and subsequent FET cycles. The logistics of a FET cycle are described later.

Embryos are usually frozen on Day 2, 3 or 5 after egg collection. Fertilised eggs can also be frozen on Day 1. Most clinics now use a process called **vitrification** to freeze eggs and embryos. Vitrification involves very rapid freezing of the embryos and is much more successful than older 'slow freezing' methods. Over 90% of vitrified embryos will survive the freezing process and be suitable for transfer when warmed (thawed). Traditionally the success rate for cycles using previously frozen embryos was lower than that for fresh embryos but this is changing and some clinics are even moving towards doing all frozen embryo cycles.

As mentioned before, every IVF clinic will have their own policies and procedures that work best for them and approaches will also be tailored for individual situations and couples.

When things don't go according to plan

Failed/inadequate stimulation: Even though the dose of stimulation drugs used is tailored to each woman, based on her ovarian reserve and age, some women respond poorly. Generally we hope for at least three good follicles to make it advisable to proceed to egg collection. In approximately 5% of cycles treatment will be cancelled prior to egg collection because of poor response, i.e. only one or two follicles develop or a low number in someone expected to produce more. If the dose of stimulation can be increased, it may be worth abandoning that cycle and trying again with a higher dose. However, if the woman is already on the maximum dose of stimulation, the couple will need to decide whether to go ahead with a very small number or to cancel and consider egg donation. This can be a very difficult decision, which you will need to discuss with your team.

Failed or abnormal fertilisation: This is discussed earlier under fertilisation.

No embryos suitable for transfer: Embryo development may be abnormal or slow and some embryos will not be suitable to transfer or to freeze. Most couples will have some such embryos but also good-quality ones. Rarely some couples are unfortunate and will have no embryos of sufficient quality to transfer.

Freeze all embryos: Apart from cases of OHSS described above, it may be advised to freeze all the embryos and postpone embryo transfer in women with vaginal bleeding around the time of intended embryo transfer or where the ultrasound scan suggests the endometrial lining may not be good (e.g. too thick or too thin or with a polyp). Occasionally women will develop a medical problem, e.g. flu or there may even be an unexpected family event and embryo transfer may have to be postponed. Rarely, embryo transfer may be unexpectedly difficult and impossible and it may be necessary to abandon it, freeze the embryo, treat the difficulty and then perform embryo transfer at a later date.

Risks of IVF and ICSI

Over-stimulation and OHSS: Some women, particularly those with polycystic ovaries, may over-respond to the chosen dose of stimulation and are at risk of a serious condition called OHSS or ovarian hyperstimulation syndrome. In this condition, the ovaries swell and very high levels of oestrogen and other chemicals are released, affecting the integrity of the woman's small blood vessels. This makes those blood vessels 'leaky'. Fluid leaks from the bloodstream into the abdomen and tissues, e.g. around the ankles. In severe cases, fluid can collect around the lungs and around the heart. Affected women feel unwell and nauseous. Ovarian swelling and fluid leaking from the blood vessels causes abdominal discomfort and pain. The kidneys may fail to work efficiently. The condition subsides as the ovaries return to normal size but it will be made worse by a trigger injection (hCG) or if pregnancy occurs. Where there is a particular concern that OHSS may develop, it is best to give a special trigger called an agonist trigger and to cancel embryo transfer. Any embryos that have developed are frozen and a frozen embryo transfer is performed at a later date when the woman has recovered fully. It may also be best to freeze all the embryos if a very large number of eggs are collected (more than 20).

Thankfully, OHSS is becoming less common now because of the use of antagonist drug regimes and the option of being able to freeze all the embryos. However, if it develops, it can still be very serious, necessitating admission to hospital and even ICU.

Side-effects of drugs: It is common to experience minor side-effects while on treatment. These may include: mild bruising at the site of injections, headaches, mood changes, menopausal symptoms and hot flushes (for those using downregulation), mild abdominal bloating and nausea. These side-effects are usually short-lived and are generally no cause for concern. If they are bothering you, don't hesitate to discuss any of these symptoms with your IVF team as they may be able to adjust your medication or offer other help.

Ovarian cysts: Approximately 5% of patients will develop simple cysts as a result of downregulation. These cysts may produce oestrogen, and may interfere with the progress of your IVF cycle. The cysts generally resolve by simply staying on the downregulation for an additional week or so. If the cyst fails to resolve, a minor procedure may be required to drain it. Some cycles may need to be cancelled and rescheduled if significant cysts are found.

Problems at egg collection: As with any surgical procedure, there are potential risks associated with egg collection. Mild pain in the first 48–72 hours is normal and usually well controlled with simple painkillers. We recommend paracetamol-based drugs rather than non-steroidal anti-inflammatory drugs such as ibuprofen. It is also better to avoid drugs containing codeine as they can cause constipation which is common after egg collection. It is common to have a small amount of vaginal bleeding after the procedure. Infection can occur but is very rare. Injury to internal organs such as the bowel, bladder or blood vessels with the needle used during the procedure is also extremely rare (about one in 1,000) but is more common in women known to have a lot of pelvic scarring and adhesions, e.g. women with a history of surgery for severe Crohn's disease or severe endometriosis. Very occasionally there will be an adverse reaction to the drugs used for sedation and pain relief during the egg collection.

Multiple pregnancy: Multiple pregnancy (twins and triplets) is currently the most serious complication of IVF and ICSI treatment. This is described in detail earlier.

Concerns about cancer: Over the years, doctors, scientists and the general public have been concerned about the possible effect of fertility drugs and IVF on the chance of ovarian, breast or uterine cancer in women and cancer generally in children born from fertility treatments. Studies in the early 1990s suggested a possible increased risk, but more recent studies have been very reassuring. The UK NICE guidelines published in 2013 (1.1) analysed 20 studies that investigated the long-term safety of ovulation induction and/or ovarian stimulation agents in women and children born after fertility treatment and concluded that fertility professionals should 'Inform women who are offered ovulation induction or ovarian stimulation that: no direct association has been found between these treatments and invasive cancer **and** no association has been found in the short- to medium-term between these treatments and adverse outcomes (including cancer) in children born from ovulation induction **and** information about long-term health outcomes in women and children is still awaited'.

However, they also advised that the use of ovulation induction or ovarian stimulation agents should be limited to the lowest effective dose and duration of use – this makes sense.

In July 2016 a very large study was published on 19,000 women who received fertility drugs for IVF and 6,000 who received them for non-IVF treatments in the Netherlands between 1980 and 1995 (4.1). Having followed these women for an average of 21 years, the authors saw no increase in the incidence of breast cancer following treatment. Large studies in 2015 and 2016 have similarly shown no increase in uterine or ovarian cancer (4.2, 4.3).

Foetal abnormalities: To date over five million babies have been born following IVF and ICSI treatment worldwide. Long-term follow up studies have been very reassuring.

IVF and ICSI are very high-tech and invasive treatments using drugs and other chemicals and manipulating eggs, sperm and embryos. They also work to allow conception in situations where nature does not. It is therefore reasonable to be concerned that these treatments might lead to an increase in foetal abnormalities in children born. Certainly this is an area that has received a lot of attention among doctors and scientists and careful research and follow-up will always be necessary as new techniques are developed.

There is no doubt that ART treatments have an effect on pregnancy and foetal development, though this has been described as a 'low-level concern'. Numerous studies have shown that babies born after IVF and related technologies are more likely to be born prematurely and to be slightly lighter than naturally conceived babies, even if they are singleton pregnancies rather than twins. However, many studies are inconclusive and even well-designed studies can show conflicting results. Some very rare disorders called imprinting disorders may be slightly higher in babies born following ICSI. However these disorders are so rare, some occurring in one out of 16,000 pregnancies, that trying to detect an increase due to ART is very difficult.

A Swedish study published in 2016 involving almost 5,000 births after IVF/ICSI showed no increased risk of foetal abnormalities (4.4). However, the authors quote other studies that did show a small increased risk. Recent studies are also showing that couples with infertility problems have a slightly increased risk of foetal abnormalities just because of their fertility history, and this may be the problem rather than the IVF and other ART techniques. This was certainly the conclusion of a large Australian study in 2012 (4.5) which involved over 300,000 ART pregnancies and which showed that couples with a history of infertility had an increase in foetal problems compared to couples with no history of infertility, irrespective of whether they conceived naturally or with ART. It is also likely that the health of children born following IVF and ICSI is followed up more closely and more completely than that of naturally conceived children, so we may be more aware of problems.

I generally explain to couples that we know that 2–3% of all babies conceived naturally will be diagnosed with a significant abnormality. This is possibly 3–4% in ART babies and may be related to undetectable genetic issues related to infertility rather than to the ART procedures themselves. We also know that lifestyle factors such as smoking, obesity, alcohol, rising age of the mother and multiple pregnancy have a much greater impact on children's health than ART treatments. And there are so many other factors in our food, drink and environment that may be having an effect on foetal wellbeing. So, like the majority of fertility specialists, I am reassured that the treatments we offer are very safe, though a small increased risk can never be completely eliminated.

Ongoing follow-up studies are essential. And unfortunately, because fertility technology is developing very rapidly, because there is a significant business and commercial involvement in ART, and because people with infertility are often desperate to have a child, some treatments are being performed on a wide scale before adequate follow-up of children and adolescents has been performed. But we can make it as safe as possible by optimising our health, doing single embryo transfer when feasible, and trying to only do treatments that have been adequately researched.

Miscarriage and ectopic pregnancy: Early miscarriage is very common in naturally conceived pregnancies – approximately one in five overall but one in two in women over 40. IVF and related treatments do not appear to either prevent or increase the risk of miscarriage. They do, however, increase the likelihood of an ectopic pregnancy. The incidence of ectopic pregnancy is 1–3% of all pregnancies resulting from embryo transfer, about twice the normal rate. Some of this is because women having IVF are more likely to have tubal disease, adhesions or endometriosis – all factors that can increase the risk of ectopic pregnancy.

Other pregnancy-related problems: Several studies, including the Swedish one mentioned above (4.4), have described an increase in pregnancy-related problems, including low birth weight and pre-term birth, in IVF pregnancies compared to spontaneous conceptions, and not just in twins, but also in singleton pregnancies; but other studies have not shown this. The Swedish study also showed an increase in placenta praevia and placental abruption, complications of pregnancy that can cause haemorrhage and foetal problems. However, it should be noted that, in this study, the authors had no information regarding the patients' past obstetric history, so there may have been other factors, unrelated to IVF, also involved.

Laboratory risks: The processing of sperm, eggs and embryos in the laboratory is a highly skilled process carried out by qualified laboratory personnel. It involves a number of complex stages involving structures that are only visible under a microscope. One couple may have 20 or more eggs and embryos in the laboratory and different patients on any one day will have sperm, eggs and embryos at various stages of development. Every patient's and every clinic's worst nightmare is a mix-up of sperm, eggs or embryos, so IVF clinics have rigorous protocols and double-checking procedures to minimise the potential for errors in the laboratory. While serious mistakes are rare, things can and do go wrong all over the world. There will be occasions when an unforeseen problem with equipment or the culture media or, indeed, human error may give rise to adverse conditions. Every effort is made to avoid this and double-checking measures are one of the reasons why IVF is an expensive process.

Success rates of IVF and ICSI

Before anyone decides to embark on treatment they need to know the likely outcome and success rate. This is important for informed consent and personal autonomy – discussed in Section 5.

The chance of an individual couple having a baby following a completed cycle of IVF/ICSI is influenced by a number of factors. The most important is female age. Other factors are previous pregnancy and births, duration of infertility, fertility diagnosis, ovarian reserve, male age and ultimately the stage and quality of embryos a couple has. Success is also affected by the clinic's treatments, practices and success rates. We saw in Section 2 that both the number and quality of women's eggs decline with age. The success rate of any fertility treatment therefore falls significantly from the age of 35 years. The older the woman, the higher the chance of cycle cancellation, the lower the chance of success and the higher the risk of miscarriage and chromosomal abnormalities in subsequent treatment cycles.

It is difficult for any person or couple to get an accurate assessment of their own individual case, and this is best given by their treating team. For a general idea, however, people need to look at published success rates based on broad categories, particularly the woman's age. However, the interpretation of different clinics' success rates is difficult as there are many different ways of presenting results and it is not always possible to be sure that one is 'comparing like with like' (see the section on interpreting success rates). Also, some clinics may be more willing than others to accept patients with low chances of success or may specialise in various ART treatments that attract particular types of patient, e.g. clinics that offer pre-implantation screening may present their results for this group of patients because they will have the highest success rates – because their embryos have been biopsied to select out only those with normal chromosomes.

The most reliable results come from large datasets such as the HFEA (Human Fertilisation and Embryology Authority) in the UK and the Society for Assisted Reproductive Technology (SART) in the USA. ESHRE (5.12) and International Committee Monitoring Assisted Reproductive Technologies (ICMART) data (5.13) also give results for large populations. The HFEA in the UK publishes standardised results for all clinics. These are available on the HFEA website and in their document 'Fertility Treatment in 2013: Trends and Figures', also available on their website. In Section 5, I discuss the lack of standardised reporting of success rates in Ireland. This makes it difficult to compare rates between different clinics and to work out your likely success rate. It is also important to look at a clinic's multiple pregnancy rate; ideally, this should be under 10%. Some clinics encourage the transfer of multiple embryos to boost their success rates – but the outcomes at the end of the day are often poor in terms of healthy babies because so many are born prematurely. This is not reflected in the success rates (even live birth rates) reported by clinics

The graphs below show results for Merrion Fertility Clinic for recent years and also the most up-to-date reported live birth rates for the HFEA (UK) and SART (USA). Please read the next section on interpreting success rates to help you understand exactly what these figures mean.

Merrion Fertility Clinic (MFC) Results

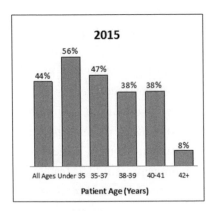

Clinical Pregnancy Rate
per embryo transfer

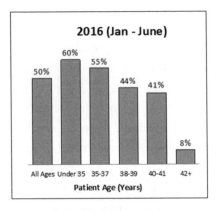

Clinical Pregnancy Rate
per embryo transfer

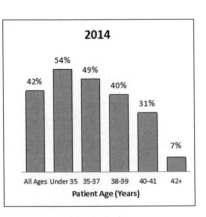

Livebirth Rate

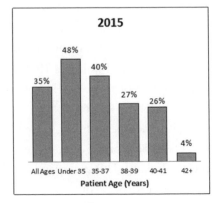

Livebirth Rate

Live birth rates per cycle started

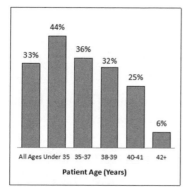

MFC 2014

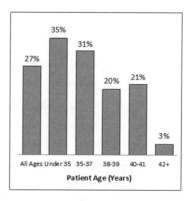

MFC 2015

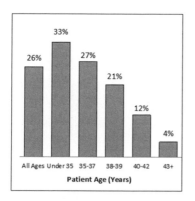

HFEA 2012

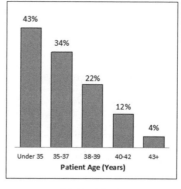

SART 2014

People often wonder whether results are better in first or subsequent cycles. Surprisingly, this question is actually quite difficult to answer. We would expect the more fertile people to conceive quickly, i.e. on their first cycle, so people having a second cycle are, by definition, people who have had an unsuccessful cycle. Having said that, if we find something in the first cycle that did not go very well and if we can address that in a subsequent cycle, that couple's chances on their second cycle may be better. Some recent studies have suggested that it is worth continuing treatment for up to six cycles, but very few people have the money or the stamina to do this. Nevertheless, overall we would expect around 70–80% of couples to be successful if they can persevere with a few treatments.

Some are lucky and can have two or three children with one fresh cycle and some subsequent frozen embryo transfer cycles.

Interpreting success rates

I cautioned in the section above on IVF/ICSI success rates that there are many ways of reporting success rates and it is really important that prospective patients have some idea how to interpret these. Ultimately you should also discuss them with your treating team.

The easy things to consider are the age of the female partner and whether the rates refer to fresh IVF and/or ICSI cycles or to frozen cycles or even a combination of both (cumulative success rates). It is also important to know the clinic's multiple pregnancy rate and this should ideally be less than 10%.

Then we need to look at what type of pregnancy we are considering. The following situations occur:

- positive pregnancy test
- biochemical pregnancy
- clinical pregnancy
- miscarriage
- ectopic pregnancy
- late miscarriage/stillbirth
- live birth.

As you know, many women will have a positive pregnancy test but then tragically miscarry early (a biochemical pregnancy). Others will get to the stage of a clinical pregnancy (visible on ultrasound scan) but subsequently miscarry. A minority will lose their baby later in the pregnancy. The success rate at all these stages is different. The best marker of success is a live birth rate, because this refers to actual babies born. Live birth rates are, however, more difficult to count and are also not available until the nine months of pregnancy have been completed. Even the live birth rate doesn't tell you whether all those babies were born healthy, at term or whether they may have been premature and had significant health problems.

> **TYPES OF OUTCOME**
>
> If someone quotes 'pregnancy rates', always ask them which rate they actually mean: positive pregnancy test rate; clinical pregnancy rate; or live birth rate.

Even before looking at the type of pregnancy outcome, there are different stages to consider:

- starting an IVF cycle
- getting to egg collection
- getting to embryo transfer.

If we report pregnancy rates 'per embryo transfer', they will be higher than those 'per treatment cycle started' because in the former group those who have done poorly and had their cycle cancelled during treatment or who did not achieve embryos suitable to transfer will have been excluded.

So we get the following scenarios:

- positive pregnancy test rate per cycle started
- positive pregnancy test rate per egg collection
- positive pregnancy test rate per embryo transfer
- clinical pregnancy rate per cycle started
- clinical pregnancy rate per egg collection
- clinical pregnancy rate per embryo transfer
- live birth rate per cycle started
- live birth rate per egg collection
- live birth rate per embryo transfer.

You will see from the MFC data on page 318 how the clinical pregnancy rates and live birth rates vary and how the rate per cycle started and per embryo transfer vary. The lowest rate will be the live birth rate per cycle started and the highest will be the positive pregnancy test rate per embryo transfer.

Most clinics report clinical pregnancy rates per embryo transfer, but try to get live birth rates if you can – but these will be less up to date than clinical pregnancy rates because they can only be compiled when all the pregnancies in a given year have been completed. The interpretation of success rates becomes even more complex when we try to do cumulative success rates for fresh and frozen embryos all from one cycle of treatment. Again, it is best to discuss this with your treating team.

Associated treatments

Time-lapse photography

Time-lapse photography is a technique whereby a camera is set to record a series of images at regular intervals. This is a well-established photographic technique that has been applied to human embryo development in recent years. Special incubators have been developed with cameras inside which photograph embryos every 15 to 20 minutes. This provides a video sequence of development and allows the embryologist to view the development of the embryos over the entire 24-hour period. Without time-lapse photography, embryologists usually assess the embryos once or twice a day – with time-lapse photography, they can play the video in the morning and see what the embryos have been doing throughout the night. This provides fascinating information which can help in selecting the best embryos to transfer. Another advantage is that there is minimal handling of the embryos during the culture period as they remain undisturbed while the computer records the image. This is in contrast to traditional assessment where the embryos must be taken out of the incubator to be viewed under the microscope.

However, even though one would expect this technology to greatly improve success rates, this has not been conclusively proven and not all clinics use the technique. It is also expensive. Time-lapse photography is of more benefit for some IVF/ICSI situations than others. The major benefit is in enabling selection of the best embryo to transfer as more information is obtained about the embryos. This can be important for a couple where there are multiple embryos to choose from, but in the case of couples who have only one or two embryos it is not going to change the embryo/s that is/are transferred. Different companies have developed time-lapse systems – at Merrion Fertility Clinic we use EmbryoScope®, but others would be Eeva®, Geri® or Esco®.

Endometrial Scratch

Endometrial scratch (ES) is a procedure which involves taking a biopsy of the endometrium (lining of the womb). It has been shown to increase pregnancy rates in some, but not all, women undergoing IVF. It is thought that by disturbing (scratching) the lining to get the biopsy, a wound healing or repair reaction is stimulated. This triggers the release of immune cells, growth factors, hormones and chemicals which may make the endometrial lining more receptive to an implanting embryo. Scientists believe that the genes which are responsible for embryo implantation are in some way 'switched on' by the procedure.

While ES has been an exciting and hopeful development in the last few years, sadly, as is the case with many interventions, it does not work for everyone. A lot more research needs to be done but at present it seems to be of value mostly in women who have what we call recurrent implantation failure (RIF – see also the section on immune system disorders in Section 3). These would be women who have never been pregnant (no live birth or miscarriage) and who have had two or three good quality embryos transferred in IVF cycles and but haven't conceived. Scratching the endometrium approximately seven days before the next fresh IVF cycle seems to increase their chance of success.

Genetic testing of embryos

We saw earlier that many embryos develop abnormally, both in natural conceptions and in IVF, and that the chance of this happening increases as women get older. As an addition to the IVF process, IVF embryos can be biopsied and tested for genetic abnormalities so that only normal embryos are transferred to the woman's uterus. This improves the success of IVF, but the technique is expensive and invasive and its long-term effects have not been fully defined. While it is becoming more commonplace in American IVF clinics, doctors and scientists in Europe are more cautious and currently only recommend it in certain situations. I think this is wise, though, like all aspects of ART, this may change as new research emerges. There are two basic types of genetic screening: PGD (pre-implantation genetic diagnosis); and PGS (pre-implantation genetic screening).

PGD: This involves screening single cells from embryos for genetic diseases and chromosomal disorders. It is used for couples/people where one partner has a risk of transmitting a known serious inheritable condition. Common diseases tested for are cystic fibrosis, Fragile X, myotonic dystrophy and thalassemia.

PGS: This refers to removing one or more cells from an embryo to test for aneuploidy (missing or extra chromosomes), which is a major cause of miscarriage and implantation failure. It is used in couples without a known genetic problem but who have had failed IVF or recurrent miscarriages. PGS screens the embryo for normal chromosome number (23 pairs of chromosomes – for a total of 46). PGS is generally only recommended for couples who have a range of embryos that have developed as far as Day 5, when the trophectoderm cells which will form the placenta can be biopsied. If embryo quality is poor, PGS offers no great advantage.

Unfortunately, Ireland does not currently have a genetics lab which can perform the required genetic analysis, so Irish clinics work with colleagues in either Europe or the UK with whom they have satellite arrangements, or biopsy the embryos and send the cells abroad for testing. Once the embryo has been biopsied, it is generally frozen until the results of the genetic testing are known and then normal embryos are transferred in frozen embryo transfer cycles.

While the techniques of PGD and PGS and the accuracy of the results are improving all the time, there is still a small error rate and it cannot be guaranteed that an embryo deemed to be normal will not still develop abnormally or that an embryo deemed to be abnormal will not correct itself. Many clinics therefore recommend prenatal genetic testing in pregnancy to confirm the result. If considering PGD or PGS, it is essential that you discuss the pros and cons in detail with the clinic performing the testing.

In vitro maturation

We saw earlier that the most common practice for IVF cycles is to hyperstimulate the woman's ovaries to produce multiple eggs and these are collected once they are deemed to be sufficiently mature. In vitro maturation (IVM) refers to collecting the eggs in an immature state and then maturing these eggs in the laboratory.

IVM has been around for some time but is less successful than standard IVF and is only performed in very specialised centres. I am not aware of anyone in Ireland performing IVM. The main indication for IVM is in women with polycystic ovaries who have proved very difficult to stimulate. These include women in whom it has been difficult to avoid ovarian hyperstimulation syndrome or women who cannot take the usual fertility drugs. IVM is also being used in ovarian tissue freezing programmes.

Most IVM cycles use only very low doses of stimulation drugs or, in some cases, no drugs at all. The implantation and pregnancy rates with IVM are generally lower than those of standard cycles and there is also not much information on the long-term safety of children born from this technique.

Adjuvant medications

These include steroids, immunoglobulins, heparin, aspirin and 'immune-modulators'. These are discussed in the section on immune system disorders in Section 2.

IMSI

IMSI – intracytoplasmic morphologically selected sperm injection – is a type of ICSI where a higher-power magnification microscope is used to examine the sperm in greater detail than with conventional ICSI. With conventional ICSI sperm are magnified 200–400 times. In the case of IMSI, sperm can be magnified 6,000 times. The extra magnification allows the assessment of subcellular structures in the sperm, for example vacuoles and neck structures. The aim in assessment of this extra information is to improve the selection of sperm and so improve clinical pregnancy and live birth rates.

Initial results from treatment cycles using IMSI did seem promising but to date there is insufficient published data to justify the additional time and expense involved (4.6). Because it takes longer to perform, there is also a delay in actually injecting the eggs. Not many centres offer IMSI and, if they do, it is generally for selected couples who have previously had failed cycles with standard ICSI.

Assisted hatching

Assisted hatching is a process whereby an artificial breach/opening is created in the outer shell (zona pellucida) of the embryo. The zona can also be thinned, rather than breached.

It is thought that the process of freezing embryos hardens the outer shell of the original egg and makes it more difficult for the embryos to expand and 'hatch out' of the egg, a process required for implantation. This is why assisted hatching is thought to be beneficial – creating an opening in the shell helps the embryo hatch from it. There are many different techniques used for assisted hatching, including mechanical, chemical and, in more recent times, laser-assisted hatching.

The process of assisted hatching is also used when embryos are being genetically screened for PGD and PGS. In this scenario, an opening is created in the zona pellucida to allow the embryologist to remove some of the cells (biopsy the embryo). These cells are then analysed.

Like many developments in ART, the role of assisted hatching is disputed and studies to date are conflicting. It may benefit a very small group of patents, but it has to be balanced with possible effects on the integrity of the embryo, i.e. a risk of damaging it in the process. It certainly has not been shown to be of value for standard IVF/ICSI (4.7).

Frozen embryo transfer

If a woman/couple wish to use their frozen embryo/s, we arrange what is called a frozen embryo transfer or FET cycle. Thankfully, this is much easier (and cheaper) than a fresh cycle because the hard work to make the embryos has already been done.

It is essential that the lining of the woman's uterus (endometrium) is at the appropriate stage of her menstrual cycle and is of appropriate thickness to allow implantation. Several protocols can be used to ensure this correct timing. The transfer can be done on a natural cycle when the time of ovulation must be calculated from ultrasound and measurement of LH levels and the embryo is transferred on the day appropriate to its stage of development, i.e. a Day 3 embryo three days after estimated ovulation and a Day 5 blastocyst five days after. It can be difficult to get the timing right, so, more commonly, we prescribe oestrogen tablets or patches (HRT) for the woman to take for two to three weeks. This inhibits ovulation, prepares the endometrium and makes scheduling easier. Several different regimes can be used, including some with downregulation, as for IVF cycles. No one regime is better than others and yours will be decided by your medical team.

The woman's lining is monitored by scan and when it reaches 7–8 mm or more, a day is scheduled for embryo transfer. The woman commences progesterone pessaries as in an IVF cycle. On the morning of embryo transfer, one or two embryos/blastocysts are warmed (thawed). Generally we would expect about 90% to survive and be suitable to transfer, but there is a chance that some may not survive. The embryo transfer is then performed as for a fresh cycle. The woman continues her oestrogen and progesterone medications until a pregnancy test, and, if this is positive, they are generally continued until her first pregnancy ultrasound.

Surgical sperm retrieval

Surgical sperm retrieval (SSR) is a method of retrieving sperm directly from the testis itself or from the epididymis. (The epididymis is a small structure in which sperm produced in the testis collect prior to passage along the urethra within the penis – see diagram on page 6.) SSR is generally performed for men who have no sperm in their ejaculated semen or where there are problems with ejaculation. It is performed with the benefit of sedation and pain relief, or general anaesthesia. It is normal to experience some discomfort for a few days following the procedure and we generally advise two days off work to recover. There may also be some testicular bruising and a small amount of swelling.

Depending on the man's individual history and the findings on examination, one or more of the following methods will be used:

- **Epididymal sperm aspiration:** A fine needle is passed through the skin of the scrotum and into the epididymal region of the testes and sperm are withdrawn using gentle suction.
- **Testicular sperm aspiration (TESA):** This technique involves inserting a fine needle into a number of areas in the testes and the removal of a small piece of testicular tissue called an aspirate.

- **Testicular sperm extraction (TESE):** This involves exposing testicular tissue through a small cut in the scrotum and removing a small piece of testicular tissue.

Tissue and needle aspirates are then processed by the embryology (laboratory) team and, if motile sperm are found, they are prepared and frozen for future use in an ICSI cycle. The number of sperm is generally small and the motility reduced, so ICSI is required to facilitate the best chance of fertilisation.

In certain circumstances (usually advised by an urologist), a sample of testicular tissue, a biopsy, may also be taken from each testicle for further tissue analysis.

Some men will get good numbers of sperm and often enough for several cycles of treatment. Unfortunately, not all men will have sperm retrieved – success rates are better with obstructive causes of azoospermia such as vasectomy or infection. Results are poorer with testicular failure but sperm may still be retrieved. If the methods above are unsuccessful, microsurgery to the testis may help. However, this is expensive and only available in specialised centres.

Sperm freezing

Sperm is very resilient and easy to freeze, and sperm freezing has been around for over 40 years. It is generally relatively easy to do and relatively inexpensive (compared to egg freezing), requiring production of a semen sample as for a semen analysis. If there are no sperm in the ejaculated semen or if ejaculation is not possible, surgical sperm retrieval is required. Prior to freezing, viral screens must be done to rule out infection – see section on blood tests.

Sperm can be frozen by a man for his own future use, either in artificial insemination or other fertility treatments, or it may be frozen to be donated. Donated sperm has to be stored for six months before it can be used in treatment, in order to screen the donor for infections.

Most clinics charge a fee for freezing the sperm and then an annual storage fee after that. There is no evidence that freezing sperm causes any foetal problems and it is safe to keep it frozen for many years.

Situations where sperm is commonly frozen include:

- Men facing medical treatment for a condition that may affect their fertility, e.g. testicular surgery, cancer treatment such as chemotherapy or radiotherapy
- Men who may have difficulty producing a sample on the day of fertility treatment
- Men with azoospermia who have surgical sperm retrieval
- men with a low sperm count, especially if the quality of the sperm is deteriorating
- Men about to have a vasectomy
- Men at risk of injury or death (e.g. soldiers)
- Men about to undergo a sex change operation.

Egg freezing

Oocyte vitrification or egg freezing is more complex than sperm freezing. The eggs must be collected from the woman's ovaries in the same way as eggs are collected for IVF or ICSI. In order to have a suitable number of eggs, fertility drugs are used to stimulate the ovaries to produce multiple eggs, as is done in IVF. The developing follicles which contain the eggs are monitored by ultrasound scan. When they are large enough, the eggs are removed from the ovary by a trans-vaginal egg collection under sedation. The eggs are then frozen by a process known as vitrification, i.e. by placing them in liquid nitrogen.

The eggs can subsequently be warmed (thawed) and used for treatment. This must be ICSI and involves fertilising the eggs with sperm, waiting for embryos to form, embryo transfer and freezing of any extra embryos.

Situations where egg freezing may be considered include:

- Women about to undergo treatment for certain types of cancer. Chemotherapy and radiotherapy can damage a woman's ovaries and eggs and therefore affect future fertility or even lead to early menopause. The eggs need to be frozen before the woman receives surgery, chemotherapy or radiotherapy.
- Women at risk of premature ovarian failure (early menopause), e.g.

when there is a strong family history of this or a young woman has very low AMH levels. N.B. This must be done *before* ovarian failure occurs.

- Women requiring ovarian surgery, e.g. for severe endometriosis or other cysts. (It is not indicated for polycystic ovaries.)
- Women who are not currently in a position to have a child due to their relationship status or other lifestyle issues – 'social' freezing.
- Ethical or religious reasons. Some people who require assisted reproduction treatments such as IVF may not wish to freeze embryos due to religious or ethical beliefs. Egg freezing may be an alternative.
- Occasional emergency situations during an IVF/ICSI cycle if the man is unable to produce a sperm sample on the day of egg collection.
- Women who are about to undergo a sex change operation.

'I have real respect for Louise McSharry*. I watched the documentary Fuck Cancer *and remember hearing how in all the time she had been diagnosed with cancer she never thought once "Why me?" but sitting there in the fertility clinic finding out her egg reserve had been decimated she thought "Why me?"'*

* Louise McSharry is a radio presenter who has spoken openly about her diagnosis of Hodgkin's lymphoma.

Success rates

As with all fertility treatments, the chance of success of ICSI using frozen eggs is affected by female age, previous pregnancy and births, medical history and female fertility factors and also male fertility factors.

We saw in Section 1 that both the number and quality of women's eggs decline with age, and loss of eggs happens earlier in some women than others. The success rate of any fertility treatment falls significantly from the age of 35 years. The older the woman, the higher the chance of cycle cancellation, the lower the chance of success and the higher the risk of miscarriage and chromosomal abnormalities in subsequent treatment cycles.

This applies also to egg freezing; what is critical is the woman's age at the time that the eggs are frozen.

The success rate of egg freezing is increasing internationally but it is still not as successful as one would hope. Unfortunately, media reports greatly inflate the chance of success and often offer women false hope. It is actually difficult to find accurate success rates for egg freezing. One of the reasons for this is that the majority of women who freeze their eggs for their own subsequent use don't plan to use them for many years so it takes time to see the results. And some women may conceive naturally in the meantime and never use their frozen eggs.

Most of the research on the success of egg freezing is based on eggs that have been collected from young women (under 35 years) who are donating their eggs to other older women. Because these egg donors are young and have no history of infertility, their eggs are usually of very high quality. It is important that older women who are considering egg freezing are aware that the success rates in older women are much lower.

In women under 35 donating eggs, it has been estimated that one egg has a 7% chance of leading to a live birth and that on average approximately 15 eggs are needed to achieve a baby. Sadly, for women aged 40 or above, more than 50 eggs would be required. As a result of the large numbers of eggs required to achieve a pregnancy, it is possible that more than one treatment cycle and egg collection will be required. In women with a very low ovarian reserve and a low AMH level, it may not be possible to retrieve sufficient eggs.

Some centres internationally report that they achieve fertilisation, implantation and pregnancy rates with frozen eggs that are similar to rates with fresh eggs. These are predominantly centres performing vitrification of donor eggs. Others report lower success rates with vitrified eggs compared to fresh eggs. A large review of the literature showed differences between the studies, but concluded that 'comparing vitrified with fresh oocytes, no statistically significant difference was observed in fertilization, cleavage and clinical pregnancy rates, but the ongoing pregnancy rate was reduced in the vitrified group' (4.8).

Egg freezing also commits the woman to an expensive, invasive procedure which seems to be safe, but which is relatively new, so we have *no* long-term data on its safety – not that many children have been born from frozen eggs, and those who have been are still very young.

So, while I would certainly recommend egg freezing for women who have no other choice, natural attempts at pregnancy, followed by IVF using fresh eggs if natural attempts fail is still far superior to egg freezing. I am sceptical about the widespread promotion of egg freezing in recent years and, sadly, much of this comes from big commercial interests. While it is a valid option certainly worth considering for some women (as listed above), it is not a panacea for the problem of falling fertility as women age and I would much prefer initiatives to facilitate women (and men) having their children earlier. I am certainly not a fan of schemes in large international companies that promote egg freezing for their staff – having a baby will affect a woman's job at any age, so what is the point in postponing it until she is older? That's when many of us are reaching the real peak in our careers! However, I think egg freezing is an important development and I see it as maybe, in the future, replacing the need for donor eggs for many women.

Recent international research is showing that most women are freezing their eggs because they don't currently have a partner. That is certainly worth considering, but *please* do it by 35 if you can. We often see women considering egg freezing when they are over 40, but by then, I'm really sorry but you have missed the boat!

Freezing ovarian tissue

Fertility preservation is becoming increasingly important for adolescents and children. Given the vast improvements in cancer treatments over the years, the majority of young cancer patients are now surviving into adulthood, so fertility becomes extremely important for them. This has led to a sub-speciality called 'fertility preservation'. We described above sperm freezing and egg freezing for adults diagnosed with cancer, but these techniques are not suitable for children prior to puberty or for very young teenagers who are not sexually active. Egg freezing, in particular, can be particularly invasive for teenage girls. Ovarian tissue freezing involves surgically removing small bits of ovarian tissue, freezing them and re-implanting them in the woman's pelvis at a later date. This allows the woman not only a chance of natural pregnancy, but also a chance to get her normal female hormonal cycle back (otherwise she would have ovarian failure and menopause). Alternatively, frozen ovarian tissue may be thawed, eggs retrieved, matured in the lab and then used for IVF/ICSI. A Danish group reported their pioneering work in 2015 (4.9). They reported on 41 women who had thawed ovarian tissue transplanted 53 times over a period of ten years. 'A total of 24 clinical pregnancies were established in the 32 women with a pregnancy-wish. The tissue remained functional for close to 10 years in some cases and lasted only a short period in others. Three relapses (of cancer) occurred but were unlikely to be due to the transplanted tissue.'

Ovarian tissue freezing is currently not available in Ireland but is becoming more common in Europe and the UK, particularly for women with breast cancer. Several women around the world have had successful pregnancies, both naturally and with IVF, following these treatments. It is also being done for teenagers and children, but this is currently still regarded by many as experimental. The first pregnancy in a woman who had ovarian tissue frozen prior to puberty (at nine years of age when she needed a bone marrow transplant) was reported in December 2016. This is an exciting development and offers great hope for children with cancer, and their parents.

Third-party reproduction

The term 'third-party reproduction' refers to the use of eggs, sperm or embryos that have been donated by a third person (donor) to enable an infertile individual or couple (recipient/s) to become parents. It also includes surrogacy.

Third-party reproduction is a complex process requiring careful consideration of social, ethical, and legal issues. Surrogacy arrangements, in particular, remain controversial. Third-party reproduction is banned in many countries.

The ethical considerations and legal situation with regard to these treatments are discussed in Section 5. In this chapter I will focus on the actual clinical procedures and what they involve. Counselling, which is critical, is also discussed below.

Sperm donation

Sperm donation is technically easy, so it has been practised worldwide for over a hundred years. The first published reports about the practice were in 1945. Prior to the 1990s, when ICSI was discovered, sperm donation was the only treatment available for severe sperm problems. It is now an important option for single women, lesbian couples and men who carry a genetic condition which they do not wish to transmit.

The donor: First, donor sperm must be sourced. This may be donated by someone known to the recipient but it is more commonly bought from a sperm bank. As mentioned in Section 2 under non-traditional relationships, I would strongly advise against setting up a personal arrangement, not linked to a fertility clinic. Buying sperm online from an international EU-approved sperm bank is safer than just using a friend or relative, but you will miss out on important medical, legal and counselling advice.

There is currently no sperm bank in Ireland, but Irish clinics source donor sperm from international banks, predominantly in Europe and the USA. These banks have strict criteria for donors. Your fertility clinic will give you a list of banks they use and will help you choose an appropriate donor.

Generally, donors must be over 18 and under 40 and have no history of genetic, hereditary or communicable (infective) disorders. A detailed personal and family medical history is taken and limited genetic screening is performed – but *it is impossible to test for all genetic conditions.* Particular attention is paid to the potential donor's personal and sexual history to exclude those men who are at high risk of communicable diseases including HIV, hepatitis and other sexually transmitted diseases. Prospective donors then undergo a physical examination with screening for visible physical abnormalities. Testing for sexually transmitted diseases, hepatitis and HIV is performed as for all those having ART treatments, with additional tests for sexually transmitted diseases. Routine blood analysis includes documentation of the donor's blood type. Since the late 1980s, because of infection risks, in Europe and the USA donor insemination has been performed exclusively with frozen and quarantined sperm. Current EU and US guidelines recommend that sperm be quarantined for at least six months before being released for use. All samples are frozen and quarantined for a minimum of 180 days. They are not released until the donor is retested for communicable diseases and the results are negative.

Prior to being accepted as a donor, the sperm donor undergoes a semen analysis, and a test sample is frozen and thawed to ensure that his sperm 'freezes well'. Donors are selected if the post-thaw semen meets a minimum standard. Depending on the quality of the post-thaw sperm, it will be classified as being suitable for artificial insemination, IUI or IVF/ICSI.

In addition to the medical information obtained from the donor, donors are asked to provide detailed information about their personal appearance, habits, education, hobbies and interests. Sperm banks may provide pictures of the donor as a child and video or audiotapes from the donor. Recipients then choose (usually online) a donor or donors of their choice. Most sperm banks will designate sufficient sperm and hold samples from that donor so that a recipient/s can use the same sperm in the future for subsequent pregnancies. Clinics place a limit on the number of donations any donor can make, but the number of children or families allowed from each donor can be high.

The sperm is kept frozen until used. It can be transported to other countries by special couriers. All sperm being imported into Ireland for use in fertility clinics must meet the EU requirements laid down in the relevant EU Directives and monitored by the Irish HPRA (Health Products Regulatory Authority) – see Section 5. Sperm bought by an individual over the internet is difficult to police, so standards cannot be guaranteed.

It is recommended that all sperm donors have a psychological evaluation and counselling by a health professional prior to acceptance for donation. The assessment aims to determine any psychological risks and evaluate for financial and emotional coercion. The donor should discuss his feelings regarding disclosure of his identity and plans for future contact. Psychological testing may be performed, if warranted.

The recipient: Before proceeding with donor insemination, the recipient woman must be fully evaluated, as for any woman undergoing fertility treatment. This involves checking her general health and suitability for pregnancy, her hormonal status, particularly that she is ovulating, and also her pelvis. In younger women with no factors that might reduce fertility, IUI will be tried initially as this is less invasive. If there is a female factor or if IUI fails, IVF will be used. The treatments proceed exactly as for heterosexual partner treatments, except that donor sperm is used rather than partner sperm.

Identity of donors, counselling and telling: See the later section on counselling in third-party reproduction.

Pregnancy rates: The pregnancy rates with donor insemination depend on similar factors to any treatment, i.e. the age of the female recipient and the presence of other female fertility factors such as endometriosis, tubal disease or ovulation problems. In general, the monthly chance of pregnancy ranges from 10% to 20% per IUI insemination and is similar to general age-related rates for IVF. The risk of birth defects as a result of conceiving with donor insemination is no different from natural conception and is in the range of 2% to 4%.

Egg donation

Egg donation is technically more difficult than sperm donation because the woman donating the eggs must undergo the equivalent of an IVF cycle (as far as egg collection) in order to obtain the eggs. These eggs are then fertilised with sperm from the recipient couple, or donor sperm in the case of single or lesbian women. One or two embryos are then transferred to the uterus of the recipient woman.

Egg donation is an option for women who have no or very few eggs themselves (premature ovarian insufficiency, premature menopause, very low ovarian reserve) and women in their forties, where we know their fertility is significantly reduced due to age, and the chance of miscarriage and foetal abnormality is rising. It is also an option for women who have had failed IVF using their own eggs, where it is thought that egg quality may be a problem. Finally, egg donation is recommended for women with certain hereditary and genetic disorders. It is also needed in surrogacy arrangements.

The donor: Eggs may be donated by someone known to the recipient (e.g. a sister or friend) or, more commonly, an unknown donor. Generally, in Ireland, unless a woman/couple has a known donor, eggs must be sourced abroad. Because egg freezing is more difficult than sperm freezing and fresh donor eggs are usually used rather than frozen, most Irish people will travel overseas for egg donation – most commonly to Spain, the Czech Republic and other EU countries. Some Irish clinics may have arrangements whereby they transport the male partner's sperm to the foreign clinic, make the embryos there and then send the embryos back to Ireland for embryo transfer. More commonly, embryo transfer is done in the overseas clinic and clinics which provide these services are highly organised as regards overseas patient services. Most Irish clinics work with overseas clinics and can provide scans and support services in Ireland, in the lead-up to and after embryo transfer. Couples end up spending a few days overseas around the time of embryo transfer.

Some clinics in the UK offer egg sharing – where a couple undergoing IVF agree to give some of their eggs to another couple who need donor eggs. The donor couple receive a reduction in the cost of treatment. This is ethically questionable because it may coerce poorer couples into donating their eggs, but some feel that it at least helps them have treatment.

Egg donors must be under 35 and are usually in their twenties. They must have no history of genetic, hereditary or communicable (infective) disorders. A detailed personal and family medical history is taken and limited genetic screening is performed – but *it is impossible to test for all genetic conditions.* Prospective donors undergo a physical examination with screening for visible physical abnormalities. Testing for sexually transmitted diseases, hepatitis and HIV is performed, as for all those having ART treatments, with additional tests for sexually transmitted diseases. Routine blood analysis includes documentation of the donor's blood type.

For known donors, e.g. a sister or friend, most clinics would recommend that the donor should be under 35 and should ideally have children herself.

The recipient: Before proceeding with treatment, the recipient woman must be fully evaluated, as for any woman undergoing fertility treatment. This involves checking her general health and suitability for pregnancy (particularly if she is in her forties), her hormonal status, and her uterus.

The treatment itself for the recipient is similar to a frozen embryo transfer cycle. The woman is prescribed medication and her cycle monitored to ensure that the lining of her uterus (endometrium) is in step with that of the donor.

Most clinics will guarantee the person/couple having an egg donation cycle a minimum number of eggs which will be fertilised. Extra embryos will be frozen for future use.

Pregnancies conceived using donor eggs: Thankfully, because of the nature of the immune system around pregnancy, which is adapted to ensure that sperm is not rejected, donor eggs are also not rejected. However, because the egg used for donor egg pregnancies is not the woman's own egg, some increased pregnancy risks have been found with donor egg pregnancies. These include an increase in high blood pressure, placental growth problems and development of blood group antibodies during pregnancy. These risks are small and the majority of donor egg pregnancies end very well.

However, due to the fact that many women having donor eggs are in their forties (and even early fifties in some cases) they run the pregnancy risks of all older women who conceive. These include increased blood pressure, including pre-eclampsia, diabetes, clotting disorders, bleeding in pregnancy and foetal growth problems.

Identity of donors, counselling and telling: See the later section on counselling in third-party reproduction.

Pregnancy rates: People can often be confused about success rates after egg donation. As regards the chance of pregnancy, miscarriage and foetal abnormalities, it is the age of the egg (or the woman donating the egg) that determines these risks, not the age of the recipient. So a 50-year-old woman having a donor egg pregnancy with eggs from a 26-year-old has the same chance of successful pregnancy, miscarriage and foetal abnormality as a 26-year-old (unless the recipient has developed other age-related issues such as fibroids). Success rates with donor egg pregnancies are therefore high, with live birth rates usually around 50% or more.

Because of these high success rates (and also the risks to the mother of being older) it is essential in donor pregnancies, more than any other, to avoid multiple pregnancy. Sadly this is not always done and the incidence of multiple pregnancy in women using donor eggs tends to be much higher than in the general IVF population. This is medically of major concern, in Ireland as well as internationally.

Embryo donation

Embryo donation means that a couple who already have embryos from IVF or ICSI decide to donate these embryos to another couple or person. These are often people who have been successful with treatment and have supernumerary embryos that they don't need themselves. Occasionally the woman may have developed a medical problem (e.g. a pregnancy complication) which makes it dangerous to carry another pregnancy. The person or couple receiving the donated embryo/s are those who have been unable to conceive themselves.

The process of embryo donation requires that the recipient couple undergo the appropriate medical and psychological screening recommended for all donor cycles. In addition, the female partner undergoes an evaluation of her uterine cavity and then her endometrium is prepared with oestrogen and progesterone in anticipation of an embryo transfer. Embryo donation is a controversial process from both an ethical as well as a legal standpoint – see below. Pregnancy following embryo donation depends on the quality of the embryos that were frozen, the age of the woman who provided the eggs, and the number of embryos transferred.

Surrogacy

Surrogacy refers to situations where a woman (the surrogate) carries and delivers a child on behalf of another person or persons. While biologically relatively simple, it is one of the most difficult treatment scenarios in terms of ethics and law as the interests of the intended parents, the surrogate and the future child must all be protected, and these interests may differ.

Medical surrogacy (also referred to as gestational carriage) requires IVF and allows a woman who is unable to carry a pregnancy herself (e.g. no uterus/womb) to have her own genetic child by performing IVF with her eggs and her partner's sperm. These are used to create an embryo, which is then transferred to the womb of another woman (the surrogate). The surrogate carries the pregnancy for the commissioning couple. Medical surrogacy is less commonly indicated where a woman has a medical condition causing serious risk to her were she to become pregnant, e.g. serious heart disease.

In other surrogacy cases the surrogate herself may provide the egg (traditional surrogacy), or either the egg or the sperm or both may be donated by a third-party donor. In recent years there has been an increase worldwide in the number of gay men having families via surrogacy arrangements. There is also an increasing trend for heterosexual couples who have failed to conceive via standard IVF to consider surrogacy using the male partner's sperm and eggs from either the surrogate or another third-party egg donor. The medical indications for this are not always clear.

The procedures for surrogacy are similar to those for general IUI (if the surrogate is using her own eggs) and IVF/ICSI where the eggs come from the commissioning woman or are donor eggs.

Counselling of all parties involved is essential, as is expert legal advice (see Section 5). Surrogacy is difficult to organise in Ireland unless one has a sister, relative or close friend who will agree to carry the pregnancy. Even in these situations most clinics are cautious in view of the lack of national legislation. Most Irish heterosexual and gay couples pursue surrogacy abroad. This is expensive, particularly in the USA, but legislation is better in the USA than in other countries.

Counselling in third-party reproduction

Donor sperm, egg and embryo treatments are different from treatments involving a couple's sperm, eggs and embryos because, with a donor, one or both parents will not have a genetic link to their child. In surrogacy, the surrogate may or may not have a genetic link with the child.

This raises questions for many people regarding their relationship with their child, and with their partner, if they have one. It also brings up the really important issue of identity and how your child will feel about the circumstances of their conception, what you will tell them and what information you can give them.

Parents' feelings

For most heterosexual couples who require donor sperm or eggs, this will not have been their first reproductive choice and coming to terms with that can be difficult. There is a sense of loss that must be acknowledged and it is easy to feel in some way 'inadequate' or 'a failure'. This may affect how you feel about your partner and your relationship. Then there may be concerns regarding how you will bond with your child and worries about the health, personality and background of the donor. Lastly, there may be concerns about how your child will feel about their conception and what you should tell them, and your family and friends. Not surprisingly, counselling by a suitably qualified counsellor with training and experience in this area can be a great comfort and help.

Children's needs and identity

A lot of research has been done in the last 20 years regarding the views, concerns and rights of donor-conceived children. Balancing the welfare and needs of offspring with those of parents and donors can be difficult and even divisive. This is an extremely controversial area and there can be significant differences in attitudes between individuals, between would-be parents, between doctors and healthcare professionals and between legislators.

The first question is *whether it is in a person's best interests to know that they were donor-conceived.* The research seems to say that this is the majority view of those who have been conceived with donor sperm and also of adoptees. (Offspring from donor egg treatments are only now getting to the age where they can give an opinion, as donor egg treatments didn't start until the late 1980s.) Others (mainly healthcare professionals and parents) argue that it may not always be in the child's best interests, particularly in closed and conservative communities or environments where there is a strong religious influence.

If parents do not tell their children, they commit themselves to withholding important information from their children for ever. This has led some donor-conceived offspring, who found out in their teenage years or later that they were donor-conceived, to express feelings of distress because they felt their relationship with their parents had been 'based on a lie'. It is also acknowledged that it is extremely difficult to keep such a secret and that 'if one person knows, it is no longer a secret'. There have been many cases where donor-conceived offspring were told by a relative or family member for the first time at their parent's funeral that their parent was not their genetic parent. This is, not surprisingly, devastating and can seriously affect an individual's trust in humanity. On the other hand, children generally are open to any possibility, have not yet developed the hang-ups that some adults have and the evidence is that they assimilate and accept information regarding their genetic origins really well.

I am in no doubt but that, except in very closed societies, it is in the child's best interest to have an open and honest relationship with his or her parents.

The second question is *whether children should, on reaching maturity, be able to access the identity of the person who donated sperm or eggs.* This is not possible in every jurisdiction and there is a widespread difference of opinion about the pros and cons. There is now a strong body of opinion that it is a person's right to know their genetic origins and that donor-conceived people should be able to access the identity of the donors. However, it is generally acknowledged that the donor should have no legal or other responsibility for any children conceived using his or her sperm or eggs.

Studies of donor-conceived adults show that the majority would like to know their genetic origins and be able to identify their genetic parent/s and also genetic siblings. However this does not seem as important to them as actually knowing that they were donor-conceived as described in the section above. There is now an active online community of donor-conceived persons and many make great efforts to meet their siblings or half siblings. Similarly, donors who have donated in the past can post their details online and allow any offspring conceived from their eggs or sperm to contact them.

The arguments in favour of disclosing information include the value of openness and honesty and the avoidance of identity confusion. In addition, the need of children to discover their genetic heritage is met. Having access to genetic origins is potentially of profound importance for people's understanding of their identity in a psychological, genetic and historical context. Apart from the psychological need to trace one's roots to establish a sense of identity, there may also be a need to discover one's genetic health for medical reasons. One may be able to preserve one's health by altering behaviour to prevent problems such as heart disease, alcoholism or breast cancer if one has knowledge of a genetic predisposition in the family.

Arguments against telling children include statements that many naturally conceived people have different genetic parents (fathers) to whoever they regard as their father. This is, however, an entirely different scenario and not really applicable to donor pregnancies, which are highly planned and deliberate. Another argument in favour of not making sperm and embryo donation open is that this might lead to a shortage of sperm or eggs to donate. Again this is extremely controversial and the medical literature contains very conflicting reports as to whether lack of anonymity actually reduces the numbers of donors available.

In certain jurisdictions all third-party donation must be open, with full traceability. This includes countries such as the UK, Sweden, Switzerland, Austria and many states in Australia. In these jurisdictions, once the donor-conceived person reaches 18 he/she can apply to the relevant reproductive medicine legislative body to enquire as to whether he/she was donor conceived. Donors can only donate on the basis that their full identity will be available to any offspring conceived with their sperm or eggs.

In other countries, such as Spain and the Czech Republic, donors are guaranteed anonymity and children born using their sperm or eggs will never be able to trace their genetic parents. The legal situation in Ireland is discussed in Section 5.

While the issues relating to donor anonymity and children's rights to know their genetic origins are currently controversial and the subject of much debate, this is likely to change entirely in years to come. Several scientists have recently commented that it is now becoming possible for people to establish their entire genetic make-up and so, in the future, it will be possible for any person to determine whether his/her genetic make-up matches that of his/her presumed parent. This is becoming an argument very much in favour of giving donor-conceived offspring as much information as possible about their conception and their genetic parents.

As society becomes more open and liberal generally, more and more donors are accepting that any offspring of their donations may wish to contact them in the future and many young donors are comfortable with this, as, surprisingly, are older donors. In Ireland there seems to be a trend towards open donation, particularly with sperm donation. However, it is extremely difficult to access open donors for egg donation and most couples currently have no choice but to go to countries such as Spain and the Czech Republic, where anonymity is guaranteed and their children will not be able to access their genetic origins. Nevertheless, the studies suggest that, if these children at least have an open and honest relationship with their parents, this will not do them harm.

Once the Children and Family Relationships Act is enacted in Ireland, any donor treatment in this country will, by law, need to be open, and donor-conceived offspring will, on reaching the age of 18, be able to access the full identity of their genetic donor parent. However, in line with other jurisdictions, this genetic parent will have no legal or other responsibility to the offspring. Similarly, offspring who wish to be contacted by any siblings or half siblings will be able to facilitate that (see Section 5).

Surrogacy and counselling

With surrogacy arrangements, if donor sperm, eggs or embryos are used, the issues described above need to be considered. However, there are additional ethical and social considerations with surrogacy.

The commissioning couple in a surrogacy arrangement have usually undergone the very considerable mental, physical and financial pain of infertility prior to entering into a surrogacy arrangement. They fund the treatment and, in medical surrogacy cases, generally provide the genetic material (sperm and egg). It may be difficult for them to hand over care of the child during pregnancy to another woman – the surrogate. What do they do, for example, if the surrogate smokes during pregnancy or refuses medical care? Even in countries (e.g. the UK) which have legislation regarding surrogacy, the arrangement may not always be enforceable if the surrogate at or after birth changes her mind and decides to keep the baby.

On the other hand, the surrogate in any arrangement is placing herself at emotional, physical and financial risk and discomfort by virtue of being pregnant. She needs control of her own body and medical care while pregnant.

This may cause conflict in certain cases. Commissioning couples may be encouraged to have multiple embryos transferred in IVF, leading to multiple pregnancy in the surrogate, with significantly increased maternal as well as foetal risks. In many developed countries, e.g. Ireland, there may be no legislation governing surrogacy, or laws may be restrictive (it is banned in many European countries). This has led to a large international phenomenon of 'reproductive tourism' whereby persons from richer countries engage women (usually with limited education) from poorer countries to become surrogates. Exploitation of these women is very real and has been well documented in the media. There is also the issue of who is responsible for the child if he/she is born with a medical or genetic problem – witness a recent Australian/Thai case.

A fourth group, often forgotten about when considering rights and ethics in surrogacy arrangements, are the existing children of surrogates. These children must witness their mother being pregnant, with the limitations that that puts on the time and energy she can devote to them, and at the end of the pregnancy, they do not have the compensation of another sibling. In many countries where exploitation has been documented, surrogates are kept in institutions for the duration of the pregnancy – to ensure adequate nutrition, etc. but leaving their own children without a mother for the duration.

The importance of counselling

Given all the complexities described above, it is not surprising that best medical practice insists on what is called implications counselling for all those embarking on any kind of treatment that involves third-party reproduction. Most international bodies and fertility clinics strongly recommend professional counselling for *all* those embarking on fertility treatments involving donor sperm, donor eggs or surrogacy. Indeed, it is mandatory in many countries, including the UK.

Counselling is strongly recommended (and often mandatory) for all parties involved in third-party donor arrangements. These include the person/couple who are hoping to have a child with donor sperm, eggs or embryos and also those who are donating sperm, eggs or embryos. In the case of known donations where a friend or sister/brother are donating sperm, eggs or embryos or embarking on surrogacy, it is essential that everyone involved and their partners, if relevant, also receive counselling. This is particularly important in the case of surrogacy arrangements. In the case of surrogacy it is often recommended that the surrogate and her partner (if she has one) receive counselling from a different counsellor from that of the commissioning person/persons so that there can be no conflict of interest between the counsellor and their clients.

I have no doubt that counselling is essential as the issues involved are extremely complex and, unless someone is working in the area, they may not foresee all these issues. Kay, in her section, mentioned a woman who got as far as having a baby before she realised the implications of what she had done. This is obviously not the ideal way to do it and good counselling will hopefully help avoid these difficult scenarios.

There are some excellent websites on third-party donation. These include the HFEA, ASRM and Donor Conception Network UK. Written and binding consent is essential for all ART procedures, but particularly for those involved in third-party donation.

Adoption

Adoption has been legalised in Ireland since the first Adoption Act in 1952 and since 2010 by the Adoption Act of that year. The Adoption Authority of Ireland, an independent body, was established in 2010 to regulate, grant or refuse adoption orders in Ireland. When adoption is granted in Ireland it is done with an adoption order, which gives an adopted person full legal standing in their adoptive family.

Adoption can occur of children born in Ireland (domestic adoption) or children born elsewhere (inter-country adoption). Domestic adoption can occur within families (by a step-parent, where the husband/partner of a parent of the child adopts the child, or by an extended family member or relative of the child). Other cases of domestic adoption are those of children who have been in foster care and a tiny number of babies who are 'given up for adoption' by their parent/s – so-called domestic infants. There are few Irish babies currently available for adoption and the majority of children are adopted from overseas.

Since 2010, inter-country adoption in Ireland can only occur of children from countries that are Hague-compliant (i.e. countries that have ratified the Hague Convention). The Hague Convention is an international agreement assigned in 1993 to safeguard inter-country adoptions. It sets out international standards and practices for inter-country adoption. At present 96 countries or states carry out adoptions under the guidelines.

Tusla, the Child and Family Agency, is the Irish state agency that provides services to adopted people and birth relatives. They also assess applicants for inter-country and domestic adoption. Tusla was established by law in 2013 and took over many functions from the HSE. There are several other accredited bodies in Ireland which can perform adoption assessments and these are listed on the website of the Adoption Authority of Ireland (www.aai.gov.ie). These include www.cunamh.com, www.helpinghands.ie and www.pact.ie.

In order to adopt a child, a person/couple must have a declaration of eligibility and suitability. This is given by the Adoption Authority of Ireland following an assessment of the prospective adoptive parent(s) carried out by Tusla or another specific accredited body. A declaration of eligibility and suitability is valid for two years and this may be extended for a year. The assessment leads to a report regarding the potential parents' family, education, employment, relationships, stability and attitudes. It also gathers information about how parents deal with stress and what their reasons are for wanting to adopt, how they feel about other cultures and how they feel about having contact with birth relatives. The assessment period, which includes waiting times, completion of a HSE course, social worker assessment, production of a report and decision from the AAI, can take up to two years.

Prospective parents must be 21 years of age, but there is no official upper age limit for adoption. However, all adoption agencies apply their own upper age limits and, if adopting from abroad, different age limits may apply in different countries.

For inter-country adoption, during the assessment process the person/couple make a decision about which country they wish to adopt from. At present, the number of approved countries is small (Bulgaria, China, India, Philippines, Romania, Thailand, UK, USA, Vietnam) and there are long waiting lists for children. The prospective parents choose a country and then work with the appropriate agency in that country. The Adoption Authority of Ireland contacts the national central authority of the country of origin of the child, if that country is satisfied with the Irish assessment report and other paperwork.

Pre-adoption counselling is considered important, not just for the wellbeing of the adopting parents but also for the needs of the child. An adopted child may need help coming to terms with any losses and perhaps the difficulty of growing up in a country that is not their country of birth. Parents are encouraged to educate their adopted children in the lifestyle and practices of their country of origin and to visit these countries with the child, if possible, as the child grows up.

The Adoption Authority of Ireland also maintains a National Adoption Contact Preference Register. This applies to domestic adoptions and enables adopted people, natural parents and any natural relative of an adopted person to sign up to facilitate contact and meetings. Contact will only be initiated if both parties agree.

Sadly, the numbers of children available to adopt is currently very small. For domestic adoption, this relates to societal changes in Ireland where very few children are placed for adoption. In the case of inter-country adoption, the Hague Convention, which rightly requires stringent safeguards and more transparent processes than previously, has made the process difficult. This is particularly so for developing countries which may not have the resources or administrative processes to support the enactment of the convention. There are also more restrictions on children who may be legally adopted abroad in order to protect against trafficking. So, in effect, this has meant that there are fewer countries and fewer children who enter into inter-country adoption – despite the fact that, sadly, there are still lots of children in institutions in some countries.

Adoption is also expensive and most couples find it costs a minimum of €20,000. The USA is particularly expensive – up to €50,000. More information is available on the following websites: www.tusla.ie; www. aai.gov.ie.

Table 4.3 Irish Adoptions 2013–2014 (4.10)

	2013	2014
Domestic		
Infant	10	6
Foster care to adoption	17	23
Intercountry		
Bulgaria	4	1
China	1	3
India	3	10
Romania	0	0
Thailand	2	0
United Kingdom	?	?
United States	5	7
Vietnam	4	0
Total	19	21

Complementary medicine

Complementary medicine refers to treatments or therapies which fall outside our concept of conventional or 'Western' medicine. It includes treatments such as acupuncture, Traditional Chinese Medicine, osteopathy, naturopathy, reflexology, etc. There is growing interest in these treatments, partly because they are seen as more holistic and natural than conventional medicine. They are often thought to have less risks and side-effects. Practitioners of complementary medicine are often also, rightly or wrongly, perceived to be more approachable, patient-friendly and sympathetic than doctors. Unfortunately, this trend towards complementary medicine is also fuelled by a growing societal distrust of and scepticism towards science, the pharmaceutical industry, governments and 'experts'.

In my experience, complementary medicine greatly helps some people and I have seen patients who have noted big improvements in their general health and wellbeing with acupuncture, Traditional Chinese Medicine (TCM), meditation, mindfulness, etc. I have worked with practitioners of acupuncture and TCM over many years and their holistic approach to lifestyle, diet and stress management is usually excellent. I have seen endometriosis patients whose cysts and CA125 levels (see Section 3) reduced with Chinese herbs and acupuncture and several IVF patients who have done really well with a combination of Chinese medicine and ART.

The precise place of these treatments in fertility is, however, controversial. The research to date is conflicting and, given the variability between treatments and practitioners, it is unlikely that we will get clear answers in the near future. I have explored and describe below the current international research on acupuncture and TCM. There is evidence that these may have a role to play and certainly they have not been associated with harm. I have not, however, seen any scientific or medical evidence to suggest that reiki, reflexology, naturopathy, etc. enhance fertility, but they may well enhance wellbeing.

There is an ever-increasing array of complementary new therapies and approaches to fertility and I think we must be cautious. Fertility is complex, as this book shows, and, much as we would like it, there is no wonder cure. I am sceptical of any simple remedy or technique that is promoted as a major breakthrough. On a more sinister note, I am dismayed at the commercialisation of infertility, not just in medical and pharmaceutical circles, but also in the fields of so-called complementary medicine and dietary and other supplements. People with fertility problems can spend a fortune on these approaches, many of which are no better than 'quackery'.

I would be the first to say that Western medicine, despite all our advanced technology, doesn't have an answer for many of the medical problems we face. But neither does complementary or alternative medicine. We all need to enhance our physical and mental health and things like meditation, mindfulness, yoga, tai chi, Qigong, proper diet and exercise all have their part to play. I would urge people to use their common sense, have a healthy degree of scepticism and find what is right for you.

Acupuncture

In its original form, acupuncture is based on the principles of Traditional Chinese Medicine and involves the insertion of fine needles into the skin along 'the meridians', providing a means of altering the flow of energy (life force or Qi, pronounced Chi) through the body. In a typical treatment, between 4 to 10 points are needled for 10 to 30 minutes. Needles can be stimulated by manual twirling or with a small electric current, as electro-acupuncture.

For many years acupuncture has been widely used in fertility treatments, and, in particular, as an add-on to ART. Opinions about the effectiveness of acupuncture vary. Some researchers regard acupuncture as effective whilst others consider it primarily a placebo treatment or even a treatment that is unscientific and futile. Initial studies suggested that acupuncture on or around embryo transfer improved IVF outcomes. The first study was by Paulus et al. in Germany (4.11) and the acupuncture technique most used in IVF today is the Paulus treatment protocol. Since then many studies and trials have been done, but, sadly, there is disagreement among doctors, researchers and Chinese medicine and acupuncture practitioners regarding the effects.

A meta-analysis of seven studies in 2008 (4.12) suggested that acupuncture increased the odds of clinical pregnancy. However, as more trials were completed, it seemed that this limited dose of only two or three acupuncture sessions does not improve pregnancy rates overall. In a review of 14 trials by the Cochrane group in 2013 (4.13), two to three acupuncture treatments administered around embryo transfer did not improve clinical pregnancy or live birth rates compared with controls. Another very large review of 16 trials, also in 2013 (4.14), confirmed these findings. However, this study did find that acupuncture improved success in populations where the overall pregnancy rate was low, suggesting that in IVF settings where the baseline pregnancy rates are already high, the relative added value of additional co-interventions, such as acupuncture, may be insignificant but there may be sub-groups of patients where it may be of value. Unfortunately these subgroups have not been clearly defined.

One of the difficulties in interpreting the studies on acupuncture is that, in clinical practice, acupuncture treatment is not standardised and, instead, treatment is very much individualised for each patient. This is one of the hallmarks of complementary medicine and a benefit of a holistic approach. But it makes research and trials difficult. A course of treatment can range from 6 to 24 treatments depending on the complexity of the case. Also, in trials of acupuncture, some studies use 'no treatment' for the control group whereas others use 'sham acupuncture' (needles are used but not in the usual sites). This further adds to the difficulty in interpreting the results.

Apart from its possible effect on IVF success rates, acupuncture has been shown to relieve stress in many women undergoing ART and may help them cope with the challenges of treatment. This has been shown in both randomised controlled trials and observational studies. This can only be beneficial. In addition, no detrimental effect has been shown with acupuncture.

Traditional Chinese Medicine (TCM)

This is even more complex than acupuncture because it is a multi-dimensional intervention that can include any combination of modalities classified under the system of Traditional Chinese Medicine. These include acupuncture, moxibustion (the burning of processed herbs on or near the body), Chinese herbal medicine, Chinese medical massage, Chinese medicine-based dietary recommendations and breathing exercises (Qi Gong) or movement exercises (Tai Chi). It places a large emphasis on the woman's menstrual cycle, aiming to improve uterine blood flow and stop period pain and clotting. It focuses on replenishing and enhancing the patient's 'reserves' and resources and uses techniques such as monitoring the pulse and the appearance of the tongue to make a diagnosis. Some of the terms used are very different to those of Western medicine, e.g. body 'heat' or 'cold'.

A recent US study (4.15) compared standard IVF, IVF with acupuncture only around egg collection and embryo transfer and a comprehensive TCM approach. They found no effect with acupuncture only, but a possible effect with the integrated approach. However, this study was retrospective and involved relatively small numbers. Treatment was not standardised, but patients needed an average of 12 TCM visits to see an effect.

Other herbs

A wide range of herbs are promoted in health food shops for hormonal and fertility problems. These include agnus castus, black cohosh and maca. Laboratory studies have shown that these agents have definite hormonal effects (4.16). In the case of agnus castus and black cohosh, their effects have been shown to be similar to those of the medicines Bromocriptine and Clomid respectively. As mentioned above, there are no good studies regarding the effect of these drugs on standard medical treatments and I do not recommend them. I have seen several women with very abnormal hormone profiles, particularly when taking agnus castus. So, while they are marketed as being harmless, we cannot be sure and it is safer not to take them. Certainly, if you are undergoing medical treatment and you are taking any supplements, make sure to inform your doctor or fertility clinic.

Safety and effectiveness

Acupuncture and TCM seem to be safe and the benefits on stress reduction are clear. For couples with a good prognosis, i.e. young women (<35) with no particular period problems starting out on their first ART treatment, no benefit has been shown in terms of pregnancy and live birth rates but I would like to see further studies tailored to women and couples with specific fertility-related conditions.

My advice generally is that acupuncture and TCM seem to be safe – as long as they are provided by suitably trained practitioners. That is key. There have been some cases of serious medical complications and even death around the world with patients taking herbs that were not properly regulated and sourced. Also, there are no studies on possible interactions between herbs of any kind and standard Western fertility drugs. For that reason, I , and most fertility specialists, would advise against the use of herbs and other 'natural' supplements during IVF treatment as we just don't know the effects. However, acupuncture seems to be safe and may help, particularly in those with a poorer prognosis or those who find treatment very difficult. Patients also need to accept that it is not a 'quick fix' treatment but something that takes generally at least three months and attention to lifestyle to have an effect.

TCM, including herbs, from appropriately qualified practitioners can be excellent for many patients with chronic pain due to endometriosis and also women with heavy, difficult periods. The best results are likely to occur when the practitioner works with the gynaecologist and this is certainly my practice. I don't recommend it for everyone but I am certainly happy to consider it and to recommend it in certain situations, tailored to the individual patient or couple.

New developments

Reproductive medicine is one of the fastest-developing and most exciting areas of modern medicine. New ideas and research are constantly coming on stream. This makes it really interesting but also exposes patients and the public to unfounded and poorly researched advice. All too often, new research is hailed as a breakthrough when it is still at the stage of animal studies and very far from being applicable to the average patient.

Exciting areas of research and development that will hopefully come to fruition over the coming years include:

Uterine transplantation: Doctors have been working on the possibility of uterine transplantation since the 1930s, but it has proved extremely difficult. It offers an alternative to surrogacy for women born without a uterus. In recent years uterine transplantation has been pioneered by a Swedish professor of obstetrics and gynaecology, Mats Brännström. The first birth from a transplanted uterus was described by his team in October 2014 (4.17). The Swedish woman, aged 36, received a uterus from a live 61-year-old donor. Prior to surgery the mother and her husband had IVF and froze embryos. The transplant procedure was then performed. The woman needed high doses of immune-suppressant drugs during pregnancy because of the risk of rejecting the transplant. Despite this, she developed pre-eclampsia (very high blood pressure in pregnancy) and the baby, a boy, was delivered prematurely at 32 weeks, by Caesarean section. The transplant is intended to be temporary – the plan is that the woman will undergo a hysterectomy after one or two successful pregnancies. This is to avoid the need for her to take immunosuppressive drugs for life with a consequent increased risk of infection.

The first uterine transplant performed in the United States took place in February 2016 at the Cleveland Clinic. The transplant failed due to a complication and the uterus was removed less than two weeks later.

Uterine transplantation is exciting but should still be regarded as experimental. It is only available in very specialised centres and is extremely expensive.

Some ethics specialists regard the risks to a live donor, as opposed to a post-mortem donor, as being too great, and some find the entire procedure ethically questionable, especially since the transplant is not a life-saving procedure. Time will tell.

Mitochondrial transfer: Mitochondria are present in almost all human cells, including eggs, and are called the 'powerhouse' of the cell as they generate the majority of a cell's energy supply. Mitochondria carry separate genes to the genes found in the nucleus of the egg. Mitochondrial genes are involved in energy production but determine no other human characteristics. However, mitochondria with gene abnormalities can cause severe medical disorders known as mitochondrial disease. Mitochondrial disorders range from mild to life-threatening conditions. Unlike nuclear genes, mitochondrial DNA is inherited only from a person's mother. Very recently the technique of mitochondrial transfer has been developed to treat mothers who carry serious mitochondrial gene defects. In this technique, nuclear DNA is moved from a patient's egg or embryo containing unhealthy mitochondria to a donor's egg or embryo, which contains healthy mitochondria, from which the donor's nuclear DNA has been removed. Therefore, this embryo has nuclear genes from the proposed mother and father but mitochondrial genes from the donor.

Mitochondrial transfer was licensed in the UK in 2015 but is highly regulated and confined to specific clinics and clinical situations. However, it is extremely controversial and many feel the creation of an embryo with 'three genetic parents' is morally wrong. A baby was born following mitochondrial transfer by a US team in 2016 but these researchers carried out the procedure in Mexico because 'there is no regulation of ART there'.

Human cloning: Human reproductive cloning is the creation of a genetically identical copy of a human. This happens naturally with identical twins, where the embryo splits, creating two or more embryos that carry almost identical DNA. Reproductive cloning has been used in animals (e.g. Dolly the sheep). Basically, researchers remove a mature non-reproductive cell, such as a skin cell, from an animal that they wish to copy. They then transfer the DNA of this cell into an egg that has had its own DNA-containing nucleus removed, i.e. an empty egg.

The egg is then allowed to develop into an embryo, which is then transferred into an adult female animal's womb. Ultimately, the adult female gives birth to an animal that has the same genetic make-up as the animal that donated the non-reproductive cell. This young animal is referred to as a clone. Reproductive cloning of humans is not allowed anywhere in the world. There have been some reports of human cloning in recent years, but these have all been found to be false.

Therapeutic cloning, on the other hand, involves the production of stem cells from embryos and using these to create tissues to replace injured or diseased tissues. This is still very experimental, but it offers hope for the treatment of conditions such as Alzheimer's disease and spinal injury.

Cloning and embryo research are also discussed in Section 5.

Section 4 References

4.1 van den Belt-Dusebout, A. W., Spaan, M., Lambalk, C. B. et al. (2016) 'Ovarian stimulation for in vitro fertilization and long-term risk of breast cancer'. *Journal of the American Medical Association* 316(3): 300–12.

4.2 Saso, S., Louis, L. S., Doctor, F. et al. (2015) 'Does fertility treatment increase the risk of uterine cancer? A meta-analysis'. *European Journal of Obstetrics & Gynecology and Reproductive Biology* 195: 52–60.

4.3 Gronwald, J., Glass, K., Rosen, B. et al.; Hereditary Breast Cancer Clinical Study Group (2016) 'Treatment of infertility does not increase the risk of ovarian cancer among women with a BRCA1 or BRCA2 mutation'. *Fertility and Sterility*, 105(3): 781–5.

4.4 Ginström Ernstad, E., Bergh, C., Khatibi, A., Källén, K. B., Westlander, G., Nilsson, S. and Wennerholm, U. B. (2016) 'Neonatal and maternal outcome after blastocyst transfer: a population-based registry study'. *American Journal of Obstetrics and Gynecology* 214(3): 378.

4.5 Davies, M. J., Moore, V. M., Willson, K. J., Van Essen, P., Priest, K., Scott, H., Haan, E. A. and Chan, A. (2012) 'Reproductive technologies and the risk of birth defects'. *New England Journal of Medicine* 366(19): 1803–13.

4.6 Teixeira, D. M., Barbosa, M. A., Ferriani, R. A., Navarro, P. A., Raine-Fenning, N., Nastri, C. O. and Martins, W. P. (2013) 'Regular (ICSI) versus ultra-high magnification (IMSI) sperm selection for assisted reproduction'. *Cochrane Database of Systematic Reviews* July 25(7) CD010167.

4.7 Carney, S. K., Das, S., Blake, D., Farquhar, C., Seif, M. M. and Nelson, L. (2012) 'Assisted hatching on assisted conception (in vitro fertilisation (IVF) and intracytoplasmic sperm injection (ICSI)'. *Cochrane Database of Systematic Reviews*, December 12 CD001894.

4.8 Potdar, N., Gelbaya, T. A. and Nardo, L. G. (2014) 'Oocyte vitrification in the 21st century and post-warming fertility outcomes: a systematic review and meta-analysis'. *Reproductive BioMedicine Online* 29: 159–176.

4.9 Jensen, A. K., Kristensen, S. G., Macklon, K. T., Jeppesen, J. V., Fedder, J., Ernst, E. and Andersen, C. Y. (2015) 'Outcomes of transplantations of cryopreserved ovarian tissue to 41 women in Denmark'. *Human Reproduction* 30(12): 2838–45.

4.10 Adoption Authority of Ireland (2016), *Statistics*. Available at: www.aai.gov.ie/statistics

4.11 Paulus, W. E., Zhang M., Strehler, E., El-Danasouri I. and Sterzik K. (2002) 'Influence of acupuncture on the pregnancy rate in patients who undergo assisted reproduction therapy.' *Fertil Steril* 77(4): 721–4.

4.12 Manheimer, E., Zhang, G., Udoff L., Haramati A., Langenberg, P., Berman, B. M., Bouter, L. M. (2008) 'Effects of acupuncture on rates of pregnancy and live birth among women undergoing in vitro fertilisation: systematic review and meta-analysis.' *British Medical Journal* 336: 545–549.

4.13 Cheong, Y. C., Dix, S., Hung Yu Ng, E., Ledger, W. L. and Farquhar, C. (2013) 'Acupuncture and assisted reproductive technology'. *Cochrane Database Syst Rev.* Jul 26(7): CD006920.

4.14 Manheimer, E, van der Windt, D., Cheng, K., Stafford, K., Liu, J., Tierney, J., Lao, L., Berman, B.M., Langenberg P. and Bouter L.M. (2013) 'The effects of acupuncture on rates of clinical pregnancy among women undergoing in vitro fertilization: a systematic review and meta-analysis'. *Hum Reprod Update* 19(6): 696–713.

4.15 Hullender Rubin, L. E., Opsahl, M. S., Wiemer, K. E., Mist, S. D. and Caughey, A. B. (2015) 'Impact of whole systems traditional Chinese medicine on in-vitro fertilization outcomes'. *Reprod Biomed Online* 30(6): 602–12.

4.16 Gonzales-Arimborgo, C., Yupanqui, I., Montero, E., Alarcón-Yaquetto, D. E., Zevallos-Concha, A., Caballero, L., Gasco, M., Zhao, J., Khan, I. and Gonzales, G. F. (2016) 'Acceptability, Safety, and Efficacy of Oral Administration of Extracts of Black or Red Maca (Lepidium meyenii) in Adult Human Subjects: A Randomized, Double-Blind, Placebo-Controlled Study'. *Pharmaceuticals (Basel)* 9(3)

4.17 Brännström, M., Bokström, H., Dahm-Kähler, P., Diaz-Garcia, C., Ekberg, J., Enskog, A., Hagberg, H., Johannesson, L., Kvarnström, N., Mölne, J., Olausson, M., Olofsson, J. I. and Rodriguez-Wallberg, K. (2016) 'One uterus bridging three generations: first live birth after mother-to-daughter uterus transplantation'. *Fertility and Sterility* 106(2): 261–6.

Ethical and Legal Issues in Fertility

The management of fertility issues and, in particular, treatments involving assisted reproductive technology (ART) evoke extremely complex and often controversial debate relating to ethical and legal considerations. The advent of ART means that families can now be created outside the traditional male and female relationship and also that human eggs, sperm and embryos can be manipulated in a laboratory. This is challenging for society from both ethical and legal perspectives.

These are issues that I, and my colleagues, working in the area of reproductive medicine are faced with daily. We are, however, becoming increasingly disillusioned and frustrated by the failure of successive Irish governments to address the legal aspects of ART in Ireland and the ethical arguments in favour of making fertility treatment with ART available in our public health system.

In this chapter I have drawn together the major ethical considerations around fertility treatment and have summarised the current legal situation in Ireland. I have deliberately focused on issues that are relevant to the majority of patients that I see every day, rather than more 'exciting' but less relevant issues such as stem cell research and cloning. In my day-to-day practice, I see people who need to consider the affordability (or not) of treatment, the decision to embark on IVF or ICSI with the associated issues related to embryo freezing and the complex considerations around donor eggs, donor sperm and surrogacy.

People who have never experienced infertility or who have not had to consider having treatment with ART can sometimes be dismissive of the very genuine and heart-breaking needs of those who need treatment. Society can even be unkind and unsympathetic. This lack of understanding and empathy can make it even harder for those with problems and it is not surprising that fertility patients are not a very vocal group. Infertility is a very personal and private issue. In this section I provide some internationally accepted information and arguments which I hope will help inform those who are unaware of the issues and which will also reassure those with infertility that their needs are genuine, ethically and morally acceptable and absolutely deserving of support.

For those who require more detail, the book *Medicine, Ethics and the Law* by Professor Deirdre Madden, University College Cork, is excellent (5.1).

Ethical issues in fertility

We all have our own personal views on ethical issues and this is the essence of personal autonomy and conscience. I don't think it would be correct for me to impose my personal ethical beliefs on patients or readers. However, what I aim to do in this section is to raise awareness of the issues involved. It is essential that prospective patients and other readers are aware of the varied and complex considerations around treatment, particularly those involving access to treatment, the handling of embryos, the implications of technological advances, donor treatments and surrogacy. It is important to be aware of and to address and understand these issues prior to embarking on treatment. Most fertility services will have counsellors and other staff available to discuss your concerns, or you may have your own spiritual/religious adviser, guide or mentor.

Medical ethics

Medical ethics can be defined as an application of moral principles to the practice of medicine. Bioethicists often refer to four basic principles of medical ethics which were first suggested in 1979 (5.2). These are autonomy, justice, beneficence and non-maleficence. All of these principles are relevant to fertility treatment, and particularly ART.

Autonomy relates to a person's right to make decisions about matters that concern him or her. In order to do this they must be appropriately informed and understand the implications of these decisions. This can be difficult with ART because of the highly technical nature of the treatments, the lack of long-term data on the effects and outcomes of many treatments and new developments, the stress and emotion associated with treatment and the increasing commercialisation of fertility medicine. The involvement of others (a partner, the hoped-for child, egg, sperm or embryo donors or a surrogate) in ART treatments adds a further complexity.

Justice concerns fairness and equality. Important here are access to treatment and the need to ensure that medical treatment is available without discrimination on the grounds of socio-economic status, age, health, gender or relationship status.

Beneficence requires that the procedure be provided with the intent of doing good for the person involved. In considering ART treatments, it is important to consider the need to do good, not just for the person or couple desiring children but also the paramount needs of any children that may be born and also those of egg, sperm or embryo donors and surrogates. The commercialisation of the fertility sector must also be considered here.

Non-maleficence refers to the need to 'first do no harm', i.e. to ensure that a procedure is safe for the patient and for society. This brings up the need to ensure that new developments in ART are monitored appropriately and that internationally agreed principles of best practice are followed. It also highlights the needs of children born from ART, both in terms of their physical health and in terms of imparting information to them about their genetic origins. Again, the needs of donors and surrogates and the influence of commercialisation in the sector must be considered.

Sometimes the principles of beneficence and non-maleficence must be weighed up and balanced. Many treatments carry some risk of harm and this must be balanced against the hoped-for positive outcome of the treatment. This emphasises the need for informed consent with regard to any treatment and the person's right to autonomy and to decide for himself or herself, also bearing in mind the needs of others and of society. While some human actions would be regarded by all rational persons as being wrong (e.g. rape or murder) others, such as ART, will have pros and cons, harm and benefit and these are the areas where there is controversy and lack of consensus. People of different religions, beliefs and cultures will have differing views and these must be respected.

In an attempt to put structure on the ethical arguments relating to ART treatments, several international reproductive medicine bodies have formed multi-disciplinary ethics committees which regularly evaluate and update ethical issues with regard to ART. Foremost among these are ESHRE (European Society for Human Reproduction and Embryology) and ASRM (American Society for Reproductive Medicine). I have referenced these in this section. These issues were also considered by the Irish Commission on Assisted Human Reproduction (5.3).

The right to reproduce and access fertility treatment

The Universal Declaration of Human Rights 1948 provides that 'Men and women of full age, without any limitation due to race, nationality or religion, have the right to marry and to found a family'. It does not, however, stipulate that those with infertility have a right to treatment (see later section on law).

People sometimes argue that infertility is not an illness and that therefore, when health resources are stretched, we cannot afford to or it is not in the common good to fund it. I hope that by reading Sections 1 to 4 of this book, it will be obvious to all that infertility is absolutely a medical disorder with major life and health consequences. In 2009 the WHO (World Health Organisation) defined infertility as a 'disease of the reproductive system' and the WHO report in 2011 showed that infertility in women is the fifth highest cause of serious disability globally. Like many other medical conditions, infertility can be caused by infection, surgery, hormone disturbances, drug treatments, cancer or birth defects. Some cases are unexplained and lifestyle can also be contributory (delaying pregnancy, obesity, smoking). There is undisputed evidence showing that the inability to conceive is a significant cause of depression and anxiety and that fertility patients have similar stress levels to those with cancer. So infertility is a 'disease' and those affected need treatment.

The ESHRE task force on Ethics and Law defines infertility as a serious handicap that prevents people from realizing an important life goal and states that fertility treatment 'allows people to express their autonomy by realizing their reproductive choices and substantially increases their well-being' (5.4). The authors state that 'in relatively affluent societies, like most European countries, it is difficult to justify that no public funding at all would be provided.' However, they also acknowledge that, 'given the righteous claims of other types of health care and other fundamental needs in society, funding cannot be expected to be unlimited.' They also state that 'practitioners have a moral obligation towards their patients and the health care system to reduce the cost of treatment as far as reasonably possible' (5.4). Similarly, the Ethics Committee of ASRM 'encourages all reproductive medicine stakeholders to pursue opportunities for establishing affordable, safe, effective infertility services and treatments for underserved populations' (5.5).

Access to treatment and cost in Ireland

The topic of access to fertility care is one that is close to my heart. As a doctor, it is unacceptable to me that medical health care should be preferentially available to those in our society who can find the money to pay for it and not available to all. In Ireland, we pride ourselves on having a comprehensive public health system. Our health system is far from perfect but most of us agree that all Irish citizens should be entitled to care.

A significant proportion of the population (approx. 40%) is entitled to a medical card, which entitles holders to free GP care, free hospital services and prescribed medications for a small prescription charge of €2.50. However, they are not entitled to fertility treatment involving assisted reproduction. The 60% of the population who don't have a medical card must pay for GP visits (but not tests organized by the GP at a public hospital) and must pay €80 per day for in-patient hospital care or day case care and €100 for attendance at A&E. They pay a certain amount (currently €144 per month) for prescription drugs. With these relatively modest charges, they are entitled to medical care for any illness. However, they are similarly not entitled to fertility treatment involving assisted reproduction.

I am not aware of any other valid medical treatment that is not provided in our public health system. Certainly, as a gynaecologist and doctor, I can provide free care for public patients for any gynaecological complaint (including fertility surgery) but I can't provide fertility treatments such as ovulation induction, IUI or IVF/ICSI. I am allowed to perform multiple expensive surgeries for a woman with severe endometriosis and infertility but I can't provide IVF which is more likely to result in a baby. A man with blocked tubes (vas deferens) similarly is funded to have surgery, but not surgical sperm retrieval and ICSI.

Pregnancy care is available to all in the public system, as is gynaecological care, whether that be for period problems, menopause, endometriosis, fibroids, polycystic ovaries, etc. For men, surgery for testicular problems, ejaculation problems or testosterone treatments are all available publicly, as is Viagra for medical card holders. Treatments for obesity, smoking, drug and alcohol use and other lifestyle-related health problems are covered by the public system, as are mental health problems. And all that is as it should be in a country where we believe in social justice and universal access to appropriate health care. Beyond doubt, assisted reproduction is currently the 'Cinderella' of our Irish health care service. It doesn't need to be like this and it shouldn't be.

In May 2014, the Irish Institute of Obstetricians and Gynaecologists, under the chairmanship of Professor Harrison, submitted an opinion piece to government, detailing the need for public funding of fertility services including ART. Representatives of the Irish Fertility Society (including myself) have met successive ministers for health to discuss these disparities, but, despite promises made prior to the last general election, no help has been forthcoming. NISIG, the National Infertility Support and Information Group, has also been proactive in calling for funding.

Just recently there is evidence of some progress. In March 2017, the Health Research Board Dublin published a 207-page evidence review of international approaches to public funding mechanisms and criteria (5.6). This review was commissioned by the Irish Department of Health as part of its current consideration of public funding for assisted reproductive technology. I am delighted to see this and I sincerely hope that some degree of funding will be provided in the near future.

Here are some patients' comments about funding. They demonstrate how it can be hard for those with infertility to vocalise their views that in public so they are not in a position to form a vocal lobby group!

'Public healthcare and even private health insurance are remiss in their lack of support for these couples. In the dark times I discovered articles from so many others in despair, seeking help in their efforts to reproduce. My luck may have changed but, sadly, theirs has not. It feels almost as though I have abandoned them, just as the politicians they voted for and the healthcare they paid for have done.'

'The opinions and outrage of the Pro-Life and the Pro-Choice groups are widely publicised. There is another group however, a silent minority. These people may never know the joy of parenthood but they hope to, one day. Sometimes all they have is their hope but for some reason, sometimes many reasons and often for unknown reasons, they may never have children. I call this group the Pro-Hopers. Being the silent minority, Pro-Hopers are unlikely, unwilling even, to fight for support. So, I ask you to lend a thought to the hopeful ones. Lobby for the silent minority who long for life.

Life is such a delicate thing. As Jane and I try and try again to bring new life to this Earth, hope is very often the only survival tool we possess. We are diligent taxpayers and loyal servants of a Republic that ceased to care about its public long ago. No one lobbies or protests in favour of Pro-Hopers, but perhaps someone should. In other countries, such as our neighbours across the Irish Sea, the NHS offers free IVF treatment. In Ireland they do not.'

'I was traumatised and I was raging. But it wasn't really about the injections, or the traffic or the nursing staff. I was raging that I lived in a country where adoption was non-existent (and you have to wait six months on a list to find this out), where there is little or no support for infertility – honestly, you can get acupuncture for a pain in your toe but not for a biological medical difficulty which in my husband's case he has had since birth. Actually, underneath the rage I was terrified.'

'Usually, if there was something going on I will talk about it – with this I felt a mixture of wanting to keep it private, but not wanting people pitying me or viewing me differently. At another level I refuse to be silenced. I wrote to every TD and representative in my local area laying it out exactly as it was – the government get away with ignoring this very real difficulty because shame keeps people silent.'

Table 5.1 ART Reimbursement in Europe (5.7)

Country	State Funding	Public Clinics
Austria	✔	8
Belgium	✔	34
Bulgaria	✔	3
Croatia	✔	7
Cyprus	✔	0
Estonia	✔	3
Finland	✔	10
France	✔	50
Georgia	✘	0
Germany	✔	30
Greece	✔	9
Hungary	✔	3
Ireland	✘	0
Italy	✔	63
Lithuania	✘	0
Macedonia	✔	1
Netherlands	✔	13
Norway	✔	6
Poland	✔	4
Portugal	✔	11
Romania	✘	2
Serbia	✔	5
Slovakia	✔	1
Slovenia	✔	3
Spain	✔	41
Sweden	✔	6
Switzerland	✘	7
Turkey	✔	25
UK	✔	78

Other developed countries

A survey published by ESHRE (European Society for Human Reproduction and Embryology) in May 2015 showed that Ireland is one of only 5 of 29 countries in Europe and one of only three in the EU where fertility treatments such as IUI or IVF are not funded by the state (5.7). (Other countries with no funding are Georgia, Lithuania, Romania and Switzerland.) I, for one, feel ashamed of this. It is a reflection of a lack of commitment by successive politicians and ministers for health in Ireland to all issues related to assisted reproduction (see also under legal issues).

Funding in other EU countries varies from country to country. These are extensively reviewd in the recently published HRB document (5.6). Belgium and France fund six and four IVF treatments per person, while Scotland funds three cycles and the UK funds one to three, depending on the patients' health region (see www.fertilityfairness.co.ok). Scandinavian countries also fund generously. Most countries, however, have restrictions in terms of whether or not a person or couple has children already, the woman's age, smoking history and female weight or BMI. For example, in Scotland, couples must have no more than one child in the home, both must be non-smokers and the woman must have a BMI <30. If the woman is under 40 she is entitled to three funded cycles, if she is 40–42 she gets one cycle and there is no funding for women over 42. Worldwide, Australia and New Zealand have good levels of funding, as does Israel, but in the US funding is poor as is South America and the Middle East. ART is not provided in many low-income countries. Globally, it has been estimated that only 30% to 50% of the world demand for assisted reproduction is being met (5.8). What is really interesting is that even in countries with high levels of state funding (e.g. Australia, Scandinavia) treatment with assisted reproduction amounts to less than 0.25% of the healthcare budget – and that includes private as well as public ART treatments (5.9). This contrasts with the cost to the individual, which varies from 15% to 50% of their annual disposable income.

Several studies have also shown that it makes economic sense for countries to fund ART, especially in these times of falling birth rates and increasing numbers of elderly people needing support. A UK study in 2004 estimated that to produce one baby from IVF costs £13,000 but that over its lifetime that child would produce £110,000 in tax, so that the government would get an eight-fold return on its investment in IVF (5.10). Similar findings have also been shown in studies in Denmark, the USA and Sweden.

Wider implications of lack of state funding

Commercialisation

Sadly, worldwide, there is a trend for fertility treatments, particularly ART, to be provided in the private sector. In the last 10–15 years this has mushroomed with many fertility services internationally now being provided by large commercial corporations which are listed on the stock exchange. Ireland is no exception and currently only three of the Irish ART clinics providing IVF/ICSI are independent and Irish-owned.

In 2014, an Australian company paid €15 million for a 70% share in one Irish clinic. In 2015, this same Australian–Irish company bought another Irish fertility clinic, previously run by one of our state hospitals. In 2016, another Irish clinic sold a 51% share to a billionaire Czech finance minister while a fourth Irish fertility clinic has been taken over by a large Spanish group. Worryingly, this last clinic has boasted in the Irish media that 'Spain has soft touch legislation in relation to egg donation' and that they 'really hope to change fertility treatment in Ireland because it is something that is really needed'. (5.11)

In showing these facts, I must stress that I am not opposed to private medicine per se. In Ireland, private medicine supports our state system which currently could not survive without the input of private hospitals and practitioners. However, the difference with ART treatment is that, contrary to all other medical and health needs, ART is not provided for at all in our public system. While all Irish citizens have a choice of private or public healthcare in all other areas, there is no choice with ART. And we know that, like the privileged in our society, less well-off people also need ART.

Commercial corporations have a duty of care to their investors and shareholders and, while they may provide excellent services, there is a concern that financial considerations may affect clinical care.

'IVF gets bad press for being a money making business but that wasn't our experience. Any consultant we had was realistic with us – we were up against it. It was a little like playing the lottery.'

Reporting of data

We saw in the earlier descriptions of the principles of medical ethics that prospective patients should be accurately informed of the chance of success with various fertility treatments. International bodies such as ESHRE (European Society for Human Reproduction and Embryology) and ICMART (International Committee for Monitoring Assisted Reproductive Technologies) produce excellent reports every year and every three years respectively, detailing the numbers of ART treatments and their success rates in Europe and around the world (5.12, 5.13). Some but, unfortunately, not all Irish clinics contribute to this data. This is partly because there is no national monitoring centre in Ireland. The Irish Fertility Society (IFS) has tried over the years to co-ordinate data collection but reporting has been incomplete because the IFS is not a statutory body, it relies on voluntary submission of data and it is not supported by all clinics. Given the increasing commercial competition between clinics, there has been a reluctance to report results on a national basis.

Looking at the most recent (2010) global data from the ICMART group, overall 72% of clinics worldwide reported their data and in 28 European countries, Australia and New Zealand 100% of clinics reported their data outcomes. Only 57% of Irish clinics reported. Internally, Irish patients must rely on success rates mentioned on individual clinic websites. These can be very misleading (see section on reporting success rates in IVF section). Unlike the UK, where the HFEA (Human Fertilisation and Embryology Authority) or the US where SART (Society for Assisted Reproductive Technology) specify the exact parameters which must be reported, e.g. clinical pregnancy and live birth rates per cycle of treatment started for specific female age groups, there is no requirement for Irish clinics to provide uniform rates and so it is impossible to compare one clinic's success rates with another. This makes it difficult for Irish patients to be truly informed about proposed treatments.

Medical practice

It may or may not come as a shock that the level of state funding of ART treatment has been shown to even affect medical practice. We saw in the chapter on IVF that the most serious adverse effect of IVF and ICSI is multiple pregnancy. Compared to singleton pregnancies, twin and triplet pregnancies are associated with markedly increased risks for babies, and to a lesser extent, their mothers. The financial cost of multiple births is also significantly increased. It has been shown that, on average, a twin pregnancy costs 3 times more than a singleton and a triplet pregnancy 10 times more – and these costs are just for the first 6 weeks of life – they do not include the cost of caring for the lifetime needs of pre-term infants (cerebral palsy, blindness, respiratory problems etc.). This presents a compelling case for reducing multiple pregnancy rates with ART.

Elective single embryo transfer (eSET) was pioneered by the Scandinavians in the late 1990s and has been shown to very effectively reduce multiple pregnancy rates following IVF and ICSI. Global monitoring of IVF outcomes by ESHRE and ICMART shows that, in countries with affordable IVF (affordable either because of state funding or low costs), eSET rates are higher and multiple pregnancy rates lower. Belgium was the first country where the benefits of eSET were incorporated into a state funding model, following very meaningful discussions between its ART doctors and government. Couples in Belgium are funded for up to six cycles of IVF/ICSI but they must follow strict guidelines regarding eSET in younger women. It was shown that, by doing this, the reduction in the cost of caring for premature infants from multiple pregnancies, was sufficient to cover the costs of IVF cycles for those who needed them. In the first year following implementation of the scheme, they managed to reduce twin deliveries from 28% to 14% and triplets from 5% to 0.5%, with a gain of €7.25 million in reducing the number of premature infants. The benefit in terms of the reduction in handicap and long-term morbidity was actually €50 to €70 million per annum (5.14).

Contrast that with Ireland, where there is no incentive for patients or clinics to advocate eSET and where our maternity services are increasingly bearing the burden of multiple pregnancies following ART treatments.

This has been highlighted by the Masters of some of our maternity hospitals. Indeed, a significant proportion of these multiple pregnancies result from treatments in private clinics, many of them overseas and it is the Irish taxpayer who bears the substantial cost of caring for these mothers and babies. Increasingly, Irish patients are travelling overseas to clinics in countries which have lower employment and other costs and, hence, lower cost IVF. But is this false economy for our government?

Another effect of the lack of state funding for ART treatments in Ireland is that doctors are sometimes left with no option but to provide suboptimal care for patients. I know that I will sometimes suggest a laparoscopy for a patient with for example endometriosis when I know that IVF would be better. But if the couple can't afford IVF, then at least a laparoscopy may be of some benefit. But this is not good medicine. Others may prescribe Clomid or a wide range of adjuvant medical treatments of unproven benefit but which will be funded under the Drugs Payment Scheme. Other problems are that patients often have to save up for a year or two to be able to afford treatment. During this time, the woman will be getting older and progressive conditions like endometriosis or fibroids will be deteriorating. Finally, the lack of integration of our fertility and ART services with the main teaching hospital system has an adverse effect on the training of doctors, nurses and other health professionals in the area of reproductive medicine.

The following male patient's case is a typical one where a couple need the funding now – they don't have years available in which to save:

> 'By the time we were finished with our final attempt at IUI we had exhausted all options within our price range. We felt satisfied that we had done all we could in our situation. It was now my turn to feel some guilt, and I did so because I felt that at my age if I had made some of my career choices earlier in life we could have afforded to try IVF. I was confident that in four or five years the price tag would not be an issue but by then it would probably be too late for Majella.'

Some clinics in Ireland offer a limited amount of funding for those who can't afford it. My clinic has a charity, Merrion Fertility Foundation, which funds treatment for such couples. All couples attending the fertility clinics at the National Maternity Hospital or Merrion Fertility Clinic are eligible to apply for funding through our grant application process. However, funds are limited and strict financial and clinical eligibility criteria apply.

> '*In our last consultation we were told of the Merrion Fertility Foundation and we were given some information on how to apply. We did so and forgot about it until the day we got a reply telling us we were granted full funding. It was an amazing feeling and we felt extremely lucky and grateful. Although we were fully aware that it was by no means a guarantee of having a child it was a free chance to try and then be able to say one way or another that we had given everything a go. We'll forever be grateful to Merrion for treating us so well and particularly for granting us funding. It's a gesture we'll never forget.*
>
> *This was very worrying for us as we were not in the position to be able to afford IVF, but with the help from the Merrion Fertility Clinic, it was possible. We were accepted for funding and I then started my IVF journey. I was very tired and emotionally drained as I was not a hundred percent sure that it was going to work, but all the doctors and nurses were very assuring and very helpful to me if I needed any question answered. My IVF journey is now finished and we received the best news any young couple could ever get. I am now pregnant with my second child, and after a long wait we could not be any more happier.*'

Access on grounds of age, health and lifestyle

Access to fertility treatment may be limited not just by financial arguments. Many caregivers and members of the public believe that fertility treatment should only be provided for those of reproductive age, i.e. between 18 and 45. However, ART using donor eggs and sperm and surrogacy has extended the boundaries, making it possible for older men and women to conceive. We have all heard media reports of pregnancies using donor eggs in women aged 50, 60 and even older. This has significant implications for the health of the mother but, just as importantly, for the wellbeing of any children born. Do children have a right to healthy, relatively young parents? Do children have a right to parents who will be able to look after them into their teenage and early adult years? Is it fair that teenagers and young adults should have to care for an elderly parent? The death of a parent is extremely stressful for a child or adolescent and more likely with an older parent. Should the same restrictions with regard to age apply to men as well as women?

These are all difficult questions which, given the increasing liberalisation of society and the high priority Western society places on reproductive choice, are becoming more difficult to answer. However, most people in the field and, I suspect, many in our society, would feel that treatment should not be offered to women over the age of 50. Having said that, the recent ASRM Ethics Committee Guidelines consider up to 55 – but only after extensive counselling and assessment regarding the mother's general health (5.15).

General health and lifestyle issues related to fertility have been discussed in Section 2. The ESHRE (European Society for Human Reproduction and Embryology) task force on Ethics and Law has written a detailed document on the ethics of fertility treatment in patients with issues related to obesity, smoking and alcohol consumption (5.16). They discuss patient autonomy and the right of patients to access treatment, even if their lifestyle means that they will have a reduced success rate, as long as these patients are aware of the implications of their lifestyle. However, they also argue that such patients also have a responsibility, not only for their own health but also for the wellbeing of their future offspring. We saw in Section 2 how smoking, alcohol and obesity affect pregnancy risk, foetal and neonatal risk and the overall growth, development and health of children. The Ethics and Law task force suggests that doctors and clinics must obey the principle of non-maleficence ('first do no harm'). While they dispute whether doctors can morally refuse treatment based on lifestyle risks, they state that these risks 'give fertility doctors a reason to insist that making lifestyle changes should at least be seriously attempted before considering the requested treatment'. The interests of society must also be considered, particularly if ART treatment is state funded.

Similar weighing and balancing of the principles of patient autonomy, the welfare of the child and the cost to society need to be considered in women with serious medical conditions who request fertility treatment. Given the advances in medicine and surgery generally, these cases are becoming more common as women with severe medical conditions which in the past would have precluded pregnancy, e.g. cystic fibrosis, can now be managed through pregnancy with reduced, albeit still significant medical risk. Such complex medical and ethical issues are prompting many clinics to appoint multi-disciplinary committees with medical experts, anaesthetists, feto-maternal specialists and ethics experts to help make these difficult decisions.

Access on grounds of gender and relationship status

Medically assisted reproduction is mostly offered to heterosexual couples (either married or in a stable relationship) – the 'nuclear' family. However, a growing number of people in 'non-standard' relationships are now requesting fertility treatment. These include single women, single men, homosexual male (gay) couples, lesbian couples and, more recently, transgender men and women. These cases raise ethical issues regarding access to medically assisted reproduction and some of these cases may be especially controversial. Again, both the ESHRE task force on Ethics and Law and the Ethics Committee of ASRM have written detailed documents on this subject (5.17, 5.18, 5.19). Objections raised by some include arguments that these practices are unnatural and that there may be harm to both the future child and society, and in some cases surrogate mothers. I discuss these issues in more detail in Section 2 under non-traditional relationships and in Section 4 under third-party reproduction. The evidence is that, all else being equal, children fare just as well in same-sex relationships. However, these treatments involve third party donation which is complex and counselling is highly recommended, and in many jurisdictions mandatory, prior to treatment. As always, it is important to safeguard the needs and interests of all involved – the children, the would-be parents, the donors and the surrogates.

Long-term follow up and consequences of ART

The perceived and known risks of ART are discussed in Section 4. While it may be seen as a moral duty of those providing these treatments, to ensure adequate and appropriate follow up of patients treated and children born, this is actually very difficult to do, particularly in countries such as Ireland where there is no state support for ART, no national register, etc. There is also an argument that patients undergoing ART and their children should not be exposed to any greater scrutiny than children who are naturally conceived.

The major source of long-term data on fertility treatments and ART is scientific and medical research. However, it is increasingly being acknowledged that medical practice and clinical studies are unable to keep up with the pace of scientific developments in the area of human reproduction. For that reason it is essential that new techniques, particularly if they are commercially lucrative, are not introduced too quickly and without due consideration of their risk profile. It is absolutely incumbent on all those working in the field to ensure that they keep up to date with developments and their effects and consequences. Continuing medical education is compulsory for doctors and is now monitored by the Medical Council.

Donor treatments and surrogacy

Treatments that involve third party donation or surrogacy result in children that are not genetically related to one or both parents. In such cases, serious consideration must be given to the ethical issues surrounding the needs of the donors or surrogate, the needs of the 'commissioning' parents and, most importantly, the needs of any children conceived. In the case of surrogacy, the needs of the surrogate's own family must also be considered.

The issues surrounding the imparting to offspring of knowledge regarding their genetic origins is particularly controversial and difficult.

I have addressed these topics in detail in Section 4. It is essential that anyone considering treatment involving donor eggs, donor sperm, donor embryos or surrogacy read this section. Indeed most service providers, and countries where there is regulation of ART, insist on counselling before embarking on such treatments. When people individually source sperm over the internet, they do not receive this counselling and that is not a good idea. Issues particular to single parents, lesbians and gay men and transgender people are discussed in Section 2.

Another topic of ethical debate is whether donors or surrogates should be paid for donating or for carrying a pregnancy. Most international bodies, including the EU Directives on ART, allow only altruistic donation, i.e. donors or surrogates may only be paid reasonable expenses for donation. There is some ambiguity and flexibility around what is a 'reasonable' expense – e.g. should it cover loss of income in addition to medical expenses. Most would agree that it is important not to exploit those in poorer socio-economic situations, particularly in the developing world.

The Ethics Committees of ASRM and ESHRE have produced detailed guidelines regarding third-party reproduction and the arguments around informing offspring of their conception by sperm, egg or embryo donation. (5.20. 5.21, 5.22, 5.23)

Posthumous reproduction

This refers to treatments where frozen sperm, embryos or eggs are used in treatment after the death of the person who produced the sperm or eggs. There are ethical issues here with regard to consent and honouring the wishes of the person who has died. Critically, the best interests of any child born must be considered. There have been high-profile cases where distraught spouses/partners or even parents have wished to use the sperm, eggs or embryos of a deceased partner or son or daughter to conceive a child with the deceased person's genetic makeup. One has to question whether the welfare of the prospective child or of the distraught partner/parents is the most important issue here. A differentiation must be made between treatments involving sperm or eggs and those involving embryos which have been formed prior to the death of the individual.

The ESHRE task force on Ethics and Law has made this distinction and is unanimous in its agreement to posthumous reproduction where the gametes or embryos were part of a prior 'parental project' and where the deceased partner had given consent to such use by the surviving partner after his or her death (5.24). Ethics committee members disagreed regarding the use of gametes or embryos outside of such a prior parental project (e.g. use by parents of the deceased), even if the deceased had consented to this. The committee stresses the importance of the welfare of the child and notes that no research is available on the follow up of children born posthumously. They do, however, note that such children benefit from being aware of their genetic origins, in contrast to children conceived from anonymous donation. The committee also notes that 'there is a certain danger for the autonomy of the child if the parent looks at the child as a "commemorative child" or as a symbolic replacement of the deceased. Extensive counselling is therefore recommended before the treatment.' It is also important that the grieving process is complete before a person embarks on posthumous conception. For this reason, ESHRE and other bodies insist on waiting for at least a year after the person's death before treatment can take place (a cooling-off period). The Ethics Committee of ASRM has similar views (5.25).

Embryos and their moral status

The introduction of human IVF in 1978 allowed, for the first time in history, the creation in a laboratory of a human embryo. This posed one of the biggest ethical dilemmas of the twentieth century. When the first IVF baby (Louise Brown) was born in 1978, the doctor and scientist who were responsible (Steptoe and Edwards) were denounced publicly and it wasn't until 32 years later (2010) that one of them, Bob Edwards, received the Nobel Prize for this work. In the intervening years there has been intense international debate regarding the ethical and legal status of the human embryo.

Ethical concerns regarding the human embryo centre on one's beliefs regarding 'when does human life begin?' While this may seem a simple question, it is one to which there is no universal agreement. Scientists disagree over this. Religions disagree over it. Ethicists have different opinions. And in my experience, the general public and patients have their own individual beliefs regarding this crucial issue.

The Ethics Committee of ASRM described this clearly in 1994 when they outlined the diversity of views on the status of the human embryo. This continuum of views has also been used by other groups including the Irish Commission on Assisted Human Reproduction (5.3). The viewpoint at one end of the spectrum asserts that human embryos are entitled to protection as human beings from the time of fertilisation (union of the sperm and egg) onwards. This is based on the fact that a new genetic entity is formed at fertilisation and that this fertilised egg and subsequent embryo has the potential to become a human being or person. A second viewpoint is that human embryos do not have any moral status until a later stage of development. Some believe this to be at the stage of implantation in the uterus because, without implantation, the embryo cannot achieve its potential and the woman is not pregnant. An embryo in a laboratory cannot become a human in the laboratory. Even after implantation, only a minority of embryos survive to become babies – the majority are lost as miscarriages at various stages of development (biochemical pregnancies, blighted ovums, miscarriages – see Section 3). In many of these early pregnancy losses, the foetal or baby part of the embryo may not have developed at all but rather the placental type cells have. We saw in Section 2 under age considerations that the majority of embryos formed are genetically and chromosomally abnormal, particularly in older women. Also, usually by the completion of implantation, the division of a single embryo into identical twin embryos will or will not have taken place. At the other end of the spectrum are those who believe that an individual does not exist until 14 days after fertilisation when the 'primitive streak' has formed – this the first sign of brain and nervous system development. As brain activity, in particular that which controls breathing and the heartbeat, is necessary for human existence, this ethical position defines basic brain activity as necessary to define human life. In ancient times, life was deemed to begin when the foetus had a soul and 'ensoulment' was thought to occur around 28 weeks of pregnancy.

Irrespective of the stage at which one believes that an embryo becomes a human life or person, the moral and legal status of that embryo must be defined and protected. Again, opinions vary. International reproductive ethics committees such as ASRM and ESHRE concur that an embryo has a distinct moral status that differentiates it from other tissues and cells, but that it does not equate with an actual human or person. ESHRE suggests that an embryo is 'human and has a specific symbolic significance'(5.26). It therefore deserves respect but can be treated differently before and after implantation. ASRM takes a similar view and states that 'our moral obligation to embryos' before implantation 'can be outweighed by other moral duties, for example, the duty to develop new and better methods of providing care to infertile couples' (5.27). The status of the pre-implantation human embryo according to the Irish Constitution (and its Eighth Amendment) is discussed in the section on Law.

In simple terms and in my experience, couples who have embryos formed by IVF but which are still in the laboratory are further along the road to having a baby but they are still, sadly, a long way from actually having that baby. Once an embryo has been transferred and has implanted (the woman is pregnant) the couple is even further down the road but still at risk of miscarriage or other pregnancy complication. Hopefully that embryo will develop into a live-born baby – but this is by no means guaranteed. These are all stages on a continuum and every person will have his or her own view as to the importance and 'moral status' of each stage. In a tolerant and secular society, we should respect all views. However, having an embryo in the lab is not equivalent to having a baby in your arms. This is, tragically, the reality for couples who have had several apparently very normal and high-quality embryos transferred but who have not conceived or couples who repeatedly miscarry. People who have been through IVF, and those who work in the area, will be more aware of the intricacies, complexities and uncertainties of 'having a baby' than those who have been fortunate enough to conceive naturally. I truly wish I could say that every embryo we produce will lead to a baby. It breaks my heart that so many fail – but that is the nature of human reproduction, both naturally and with ART.

One of the ethical dilemmas of modern IVF is that it entails the production of numerous embryos, not all of which will be used to create a pregnancy, i.e. many couples will end up with surplus embryos which they don't need. Options are then to donate these to other patients/couples, to donate them for research or to allow them to be thawed and to perish. Undoubtedly, the vast majority of patients and those who work in ART would ideally support a situation where surplus embryos and the subsequent need to freeze those embryos was not necessary. Ideally we would retrieve one egg, fertilise that and then transfer the resulting embryo. However, fertility treatment is, unfortunately, not that simple.

In general, less than 10% of human eggs will develop to a baby and this applies to natural pregnancy as well as those achieved with IVF and ICSI. This figure varies with the age of the female partner but maximum fertility for an egg even in young fertile women with a fertile partner is at best around 30%. To have a reasonable chance of success with ART treatment, a couple need several eggs and the older the woman, the more they need. Some studies suggest that the ideal number for the best chance of success is between 10 and 15 eggs. However, biology is not an exact science and some couples will do IVF and get 10 eggs which will lead to five or six very good quality blastocysts (Day 5 embryos) while a very similar couple with 10 eggs also will be lucky to get one nice blastocyst to transfer. I have seen couples who have had three healthy babies with one fresh cycle of IVF treatment, i.e. they had a successful first fresh cycle, followed by two successful frozen embryo transfer cycles. However, I have also seen couples where the woman produced more than 20 eggs but they didn't get a baby from any of those eggs. I have also seen a couple who had three years of infertility and then conceived with their first IVF treatment. They also had three embryos frozen. After that first IVF pregnancy, they went on to have three natural pregnancies and ultimately four very healthy children. It had never been their intention, but they ended up with three frozen embryos that they no longer required.

These are the vagaries of fertility treatment which demonstrate the limitations of our current treatments. Despite our best efforts, and a wealth of research occurring around the world, it is not possible to accurately predict in advance how successful any particular couple will be. For this reason, most IVF programs aim to produce around 10 eggs per cycle. Given the high cost of IVF, not just in terms of finance, but in terms of the physical, medical and emotional strain, it is hard to justify putting people through the treatment without maximising their chance of success.

'Eventually the day came; I played my part and she went under general anaesthetic to play her part. Our hope now rested in the labs of Merrion. We got updates as the days progressed. Things looked reasonable at the beginning. The day before we were due to go back in, there were two average embryos and one weak one. When we got in the next day there were just two left and neither looked promising. This was disappointing news for us because we had hoped that we could freeze one and get a second chance if the first failed. Both embryos were transferred in the hope that maybe one would survive. That morning was the first negative news we had received and we knew in our hearts that it wasn't going to work when we left the clinic.'

—∞—

Of the five eggs that were collected, four fertilised on Day 1, by Day 3 there were still four embryos, a 7-cell, two 5-cells and a 4-cell. We were advised to proceed to Day 5 transfer. On Day 5, there was only one blast left and it was of fair grade, I was also told that my follicles still looked flared. The transfer went ahead and unfortunately it was a negative result after my two week wait. My period arrived the night of the blood test, only a few hours after we had received the bad news.

—∞—

Eleven eggs were collected this time, on Day 1 eight had fertilised, on Day 3 six were still there, three were top grade (two 8-cells and one 6-cell), the other three where fair grade. We were advised again to continue to Day 5 for transfer.

On Day 5, three were left, one of which was a good grade and two that they wanted to monitor overnight to see if they were strong enough for freezing. We were disappointed that we only had one and went ahead with the transfer, this time I was told that my follicles and lining looked perfect. I waited for the call after 24 hours of monitoring and was delighted to be told that one of the blasts had come on leaps and bounds and was suitable to freeze. We were delighted, we certainly didn't expect a call with such good news.

I am delighted to confirm that this time round, we got a positive result. We are over the moon, but still very cautious after miscarrying previously, but will patiently wait till our 12-week scan.'

The recent trends in IVF, which have improved success rates and reduced risks such as ovarian hyperstimulation syndrome and multiple pregnancy, are leading to more manipulation of embryos including embryo freezing. There is evidence that some women will have higher pregnancy rates if all their embryos are frozen and then transferred to the uterus at a later stage when the high hormone levels related to ovarian stimulation have resolved. Allowing embryos to grow to blastocyst stage in the lab also aids in choosing the best embryo to transfer and the promotion of elective single embryo transfer to reduce multiple pregnancies, by definition, involves the freezing of all healthy embryos except the one being transferred. Ovarian hyperstimulation syndrome (which can be fatal) is now extremely rare due to the practice of freezing all the embryos in women who are at risk of the syndrome and transferring them at a later stage.

While freezing eggs and using them one at a time is proposed by some as a means of avoiding the formation of surplus embryos and the freezing of embryos, it is not really practical. Difficulties would almost certainly occur because not all eggs fertilise and only a minority generally go on to form healthy embryos. We would have to thaw one egg and allow up to five days to see if it developed to a healthy embryo. The transfer of that embryo to the woman's uterus has to be accurately timed so if that one egg does not develop appropriately, another could not be thawed until the woman's next menstrual cycle. Couples with a long history of infertility generally don't have the time, the financial resources or the emotional resources to keep coming back month after month for drawn out, stressful medical treatments. Most couples prefer to allow all their available eggs to be inseminated at the same time, allow them to develop to embryos and then freeze if required. However, if patients are particularly opposed to embryo freezing or other aspects of ART, treatment can be tailored to suit their beliefs. But careful consideration and counselling must be given regarding the effect of this on success rates etc.

In my experience, most patients accessing ART treatments and most of those working in the field take the pragmatic view that the benefits which treatment affords them, their families, their future children and society in general greatly outweigh any negative consequences for a limited number of early, pre-implantation embryos, many of which are not destined to lead to pregnancy.

Research and developments

As ART treatments evolve and new scientific developments come on board, more and more ethical issues come to light. Many of these centre around the moral status of the embryo and one's attitudes to this. For those who believe that human life begins at fertilisation, any treatment that involves manipulating embryos is wrong – this may include freezing embryos, biopsying them for PGD or PGS (pre-implantation genetic diagnosis or screening), newer techniques such as mitochondrial transfer and embryo research.

Embryo freezing and its pros and cons are discussed in the previous section. PGD and PGS are described in Section 4. Of their nature, these treatments involve the selecting out and disposal of embryos affected by a genetic disorder. Some view this as acceptable to prevent miscarriage and the birth of children with serious disabilities while others find it offensive and unacceptable. There is also debate as to what constitutes a 'serious' disability.

The donation of surplus embryos for research is viewed by some as a very moral, generous and good thing to do while others find it morally unacceptable. An interesting question is whether those who oppose embryo research should also refrain from using the benefits of embryo research carried out elsewhere. People also differ in whether it is acceptable to only use for research those embryos which were produced to treat infertility but are now surplus or whether it is acceptable to create embryos purely for research purposes. The ESHRE Task Force on Ethics and Law (5.26) states that it is preferable to use surplus IVF embryos than to create them specifically for research and that research should not continue after Day 14 (the formation of the primitive streak). ASRM and the HFEA in the UK have similar guidelines regarding embryo research. All guidelines prohibit the transfer of research embryos into a uterus for the purpose of achieving a pregnancy and stress the need for informed consent for all procedures.

At present, all international bodies oppose reproductive cloning, i.e. the creation of an embryo using embryo splitting or somatic cell nuclear transfer where the nucleus of a non-reproductive cell is transplanted to an egg cell and used to 'clone' the animal from which the non-reproductive cell nucleus came from. However, many believe that research should be allowed in this area. Therapeutic cloning uses the same technique of somatic cell nuclear transfer to create cell lines or organs which can be used to treat disease. This is viewed by some as being acceptable. These techniques are not currently deemed safe and much work will be needed in the coming years to establish their place from an ethical perspective. Human embryonic stem cell research involves the use of stem cells taken from the inner cell mass of the embryo to develop pluripotent stem cells which are theoretically capable of being induced to differentiate into any type of cell found in the human body. It is hoped to be able to use such cells to treat a wide range of diseases and conditions, including Parkinson's disease, Alzheimer's disease, cancer, spinal cord injury and juvenile-onset diabetes. Again, the ethical issues revolve around whether the benefits to humanity derived from such research outweigh the destruction of donated surplus IVF embryos.

Legal issues in fertility

The management of infertility and, in particular, assisted human reproduction (AHR), is extremely multi-faceted and I think by now any reader will have seen that there are very complex medical, scientific, social, ethical and legal issues involved. As society expands and evolves it becomes necessary to adapt the law – the rules and regulations that govern society. These generally reflect the values of that society and protect its citizens, supporting the common good. In Ireland, the law is found in our Constitution of 1937 (approved by the people) and in legislation, which is passed by the Houses of the Oireachtas (parliament). The provisions of the Constitution and of legislation are interpreted by the courts in case law.

Because fertility treatment involves the creation of families and because assisted reproduction opens up the way for 'non-traditional' family arrangements, complex legal issues arise with regard to:

- parentage
- rights of and responsibilities towards children
- rights of and responsibilities towards donors and recipients of eggs, sperm and embryos
- obligations on those providing services to do so in a law-abiding fashion.

Due to the complexity of these issues, specific legislation is required to cover the appropriate management of sperm, eggs and, most particularly, human embryos and embryo research.

While some may argue that fertility treatment is 'just a medical treatment' and, as such, should be left to doctors and their patients, I think most people would agree that the days of 'doctors playing God' are long gone and the complexity of ART demands that legislation protects all those involved. It is equally important, however, that ART legislation is not over-restrictive and that it is formulated in a way that facilitates change to keep up with the rapidly evolving medical and scientific developments in the area.

The law with regard to reproductive medicine is vast and, for those who would like more detail, I recommend the excellent book by Professor Deirdre Madden, *Medicine, Ethics and the Law* (5.1). In this section I will focus on the current legal situation in Ireland with regard to infertility treatment and ART, issues that need attention and a brief comparison with the international situation. As in the pages on ethics (above), I will focus on the issues that are relevant to the vast majority of patients I see.

Current legislation in Ireland

Legal right to reproduce

It seems reasonable to expect that national and international laws and declarations on human rights would determine whether an individual has a right to reproduce and have a family. Some Irish legal cases have considered this question. The first was *Murray v Ireland*, in 1991 (5.29), which considered the case of a married couple who were in prison having been convicted of capital murder. The judge acknowledged that they had rights under the Constitution to 'privacy and procreation' but that these were not absolute and that the need for prison security, in terms of the common good, trumped these rights.

In the case of *Roche v Roche*, 2009 (5.30) (see page 388), which involved a couple with frozen embryos – the woman wished to use these embryos but her husband (who had provided the sperm) did not wish to use them – it was noted by the Supreme Court that, while the woman had a right to procreate, her husband had 'an equal and opposite right not to procreate'. A critical issue in this case was consent to treatment, and mutual consent was deemed essential before any treatment could be performed. Other legal cases have used the argument of a right to privacy to justify intimate and personal relations between persons, regarding contraception – *McGee v Attorney General*, 1974 (5.31) – and regarding homosexual acts between males – *Norris v Attorney General*, 1984 (5.32).

While the rights to procreate (or not) and to privacy are not absolute in Irish law, it is likely that they would be upheld by the courts, except in very extreme cases where upholding such rights would be deemed to be contrary to the common good. However, to date, no jurisdiction (including Ireland) has advanced this right to procreate as implying a right to fertility treatment as such. These rights to privacy and to procreate are seen as so-called 'negative or non-interference rights', i.e. the state should not interfere with the right to have a child by ART, but this does not mean that this is a positive right: the state is not required to enable someone to have a child by providing fertility treatment to them.

Legal status of the embryo

The moral status of the human embryo plays a key role in ethical debates about IVF and ART. Accordingly, the legal status of the embryo must be defined before laws can be made regarding the acceptability of ART procedures such as embryo freezing, embryo biopsy for PGD and PGS, disposal of embryos, research on embryos and new developments in embryo manipulation. Thankfully, this is something that has been clarified by the Supreme Court in Ireland in recent years, although more detailed legislation implementing this judgment has not been forthcoming.

Article 40.3.3 of the Irish Constitution (also known as the Eighth Amendment, passed by referendum in 1983) states that 'The state acknowledges the right to life of the unborn and, with due regard to the equal right to life of the mother, guarantees in its laws to respect and, as far as is practicable, by its laws to defend and vindicate that right.' Since the introduction of IVF in Ireland in the mid-1980s, practitioners and lawyers have debated whether or not the term 'unborn' in this provision of the Constitution applies to human embryos prior to implantation, i.e. embryos in the laboratory.

In the landmark case of *Roche v Roche* (High Court 2006 (5.33), Supreme Court 2009 (5.30)), this question was finally answered. As described above, the case involved a married couple who had three frozen embryos but who had separated subsequent to the IVF cycle in which the embryos were produced. The woman wished to use these embryos but her husband did not. One of the arguments proposed by the woman's legal team was that these embryos had a right to life under Article 40.3.3 of the Constitution and that they should therefore be transferred to her uterus. I was involved as an expert witness for the state in this case and the lawyers consulted widely with experts from many disciplines and many countries regarding the status of the human embryo.

Justice McGovern in the High Court addressed the issue of whether the term 'unborn' was, at the time of the amendment, intended to include embryos, and he held the view that the intent was to legislate against abortion, not to make provision for pre-implantation embryos. He concluded that 'there has been no evidence adduced to establish that it was ever in the mind of the People voting on the Eighth Amendment to the Constitution that "unborn" meant anything other than a foetus or child within the womb.' He therefore held that 'the word "unborn" in Article 40.3.3 does not include embryos in vitro and therefore does not include the three frozen embryos which are at the heart of the dispute.' He noted, however, that 'because of their nature, embryos are deserving of respect' and that such issues 'should be governed by a regulatory regime established by an Act of the Oireachtas.' This case was subsequently appealed to the Supreme Court, which unanimously upheld the findings of the High Court.

The outcome of the Roche case has made a major contribution to the practice of ART in Ireland and to clarity around what we do. Prior to the judgment, because of concerns about the application of Article 40.3.3 to embryos outside the uterus, fertility clinics did not feel they could legally dispose of surplus embryos or consider treatments such as PGS. Couples were left in the unenviable position of having to maintain their embryos indefinitely in storage or abandon them. At least now, clinics can introduce policies to deal with this difficult issue. Legislation is, however, still required to ensure that this is done appropriately and that there is clarity around the content and applicability of these policies.

Children and Family Relationships Act 2015

Under Irish law, a woman who gives birth to a child is legally the mother of that child, but the legal parentage rights of fathers have historically been less clear. The Children and Family Relationships Act (CFRA) was introduced in an attempt to modernise Irish law on parentage, particularly in non-marital relationships and in families created outside the traditional male/female relationships, i.e. families created with the help of assisted reproduction. The Act also addresses the important issue of disclosure to donor-conceived persons of information about their genetic parentage.

While this legislation was enacted in April 2015, sadly and in typical Irish fashion, large sections of the Act relating to assisted reproduction and donor conception have not yet been 'commenced'. (Prior to this Act, I did not realise that such procrastination in applying an already approved law was possible.) The official position is that parts 2 and 3 of the Act (which deal with donor-assisted human reproduction and parentage in such cases) will be commenced on a date 'appointed by the Minister for Health'. Given that several requirements of the Act, e.g. a National Donor-Conceived Persons Register, have yet to be established, it is likely to be some time before these parts of the Act are actually implemented. This continues to leave patients undergoing treatment with donor sperm, eggs and embryos, and their children, in an unacceptably uncertain situation.

At present, virtually all treatments involving egg donation for Irish patients use eggs donated by women overseas. Many Irish couples travel to other countries (most commonly Spain and the Czech Republic) for donor egg treatment. Donor sperm treatment occurs in Ireland, but clinics almost exclusively use sperm that has been donated abroad to international sperm banks (most commonly in Denmark, the USA and the UK) and imported by the clinics. Embryo donation is very uncommon. The CFRA will apply only to treatments taking place in Ireland and covers all treatments in ART clinics whether or not the sperm or eggs were provided in Ireland or imported by the clinics from abroad. It will therefore not apply to the vast majority of couples undertaking egg donation treatments outside Ireland, but it will apply to sperm donation and egg or embryo donation occurring in this country.

Parentage

Prior to the CFRA, mothers and fathers who were married to each other had automatic guardianship rights over any children born into their family. However, there was significant uncertainty and ambiguity over issues of guardianship, custody and access for men who were not married to the mother of their children. The CFRA contains provision whereby a man who is not married to the mother of his biological child to acquire guardianship rights over that child. This can happen in three ways:

1) The parents complete and sign a statutory declaration for joint guardianship in the presence of a Peace Commissioner or Commissioner for Oaths. They state that they are the parents and they agree to the appointment of the father as guardian of the child.

2) If the father has been living with the mother continuously for 12 months, and at least three of these months were after the birth of the child, he will automatically be the guardian of the child.

3) The father can apply to the local district court to become a joint guardian of his child, whether or not his name is on the birth certificate. The best interests of the child will be considered by the court prior to granting guardianship in these cases.

In terms of children born via fertility treatments and, in particular, cases involving donor sperm, eggs or embryos, the Act introduces much-needed legal clarity. Prior to this Act, there was no legislation regarding parentage in cases of sperm donation. If a married woman conceived a child with donor sperm, her husband was presumed to be the father and was registered as such. However, if the couple were not married, the man could only be registered as the father with the consent of the birth mother. He would not have been able to apply to the court for guardianship in relation to the child as he would not be its biological father. In the case of a single woman having a child with donor sperm, no man would be registered as the father.

Under the CFRA the parents of a child conceived by donor sperm, eggs or embryos will be the mother (who gives birth to the child) and her spouse, civil partner or co-habitant, if such exist and as long as they have given consent. This applies to both heterosexual and same-sex relationships. Donors of sperm, eggs or embryos will not be the legal parents of any child born from their donation and will have no parental rights or duties in respect of the child. Adoption provisions have also been revised to enable cohabiting couples as well as civil partners to be eligible to apply to adopt a child jointly.

The Act clearly defines the duties and rights of sperm, egg and embryo donors, the detailed information that must be provided to them before they make a donation and the issues to which they must consent. Similarly it specifies the information that must be given to the woman or couple who will receive the donated sperm, eggs or embryos and issues of consent for them. Donors must be 18 years of age and intending parents must be 21 years of age. The Act also stipulates that donors cannot be paid for a donation but that they can be given reasonable expenses, in relation to travel costs, medical expenses and legal or counselling costs.

It must be noted, however, that the Act only applies to donor treatments that take place in a recognised and licensed donor assisted human reproduction (DAHR) facility in Ireland, i.e. an Irish fertility clinic. The law does not apply to private arrangements that people may make using a friend's sperm or sperm sourced from the internet or to donor treatments undertaken abroad.

Disclosure of information about donor conception

I have discussed the arguments for and against giving donor-conceived persons information about their genetic origins (i.e. the identity of the donor) in Section 4. The CFRA stipulates that for any donor treatments taking place in approved facilities in Ireland, any children born will, on reaching maturity at age 18, be entitled to access information about their genetic origins, including the name and contact details of any donor. The use of anonymous donation of eggs, sperm or embryos will be prohibited other than for embryos that were created prior to commencement of the Act. If a person or couple had a child conceived from anonymously donated sperm or eggs prior to commencement of the Act and if some of that sperm or eggs remain, they may use the sperm or eggs for up to three years after commencement of the Act if they wish to have a sibling using the same sperm or eggs so that the children will be full genetic siblings.

The Act makes provision for a National Donor-Conceived Persons Register on which fertility clinics will be obliged to register detailed information regarding all donor treatments and their outcomes. All those taking part in donor conceptions (donors and recipients) will have to consent to this information being registered. There are also provisions for donor-conceived siblings to access (with consent) information about each other.

A provision deemed by many to be controversial is that, where a person who has attained the age of 18 years applies for a copy of his or her birth certificate, the Register of Births will contain a note stating that the person is donor-conceived. When issuing a copy of the birth certificate, the registrar will be obliged to inform that person that further information relating to him or her is available. This will lead to disclosure of the fact that the person was donor-conceived. While the intent of the Act is to encourage all parents to disclose their origins to donor-conceived persons, this cannot be enforced and there is therefore a chance that a person who was donor-conceived will hear this for the first time when they apply for a copy of their birth certificate. Like many of the provisions of the Act, it has not yet been determined exactly how this information will be imparted, e.g. will the person giving the information be appropriately trained to deliver such complex and potentially life-changing information to the donor-conceived person? Will appropriate counselling be available? This is a concern that the Institute of Obstetricians and Gynaecologists and the Irish Fertility Society highlighted on numerous occasions prior to finalisation of the Act – one of the 'interesting' reassurances we were given was that this will not happen for 18 years after commencement of the Act so there will be plenty of time to figure out the detail!

Surrogacy

Legislative issues regarding surrogacy are extremely complex because so many people are involved and so many combinations of sperm and egg providers and carriers of the pregnancy are possible. The legal rights of the following need to be protected:

- The intended parents – these may be a heterosexual couple, a same-sex male or female couple, a single man or a single woman.
- The surrogate.
- The child or children to be born by surrogacy and also any existing children of the surrogate.

- The sperm, egg or embryo donor(s), who may or may not be one of the intended parents.
- The partner, if any, of the surrogate.

Due to the complexities of this area it is not surprising that many countries lack relevant legislation. Indeed, many countries prohibit surrogacy on moral or public policy grounds. The needs, interests and rights of the people mentioned above differ and there have been many sad and controversial cases internationally where conflict has occurred between the surrogate and the intended parents. Although studies show that it is unlikely, it is nonetheless possible that surrogates may change their mind and this is hard to legislate for. Additionally there is concern about the trend towards the use and potential exploitation of surrogates in poorer cultures and countries.

Unfortunately, surrogacy was not addressed by the CFRA, partly because a case regarding surrogacy was at the time pending in the Supreme Court. This case, *MR and DR (suing by their father and next friend OR) and CR v an t-Ard Chlaratheoir* (5.34) was decided in 2014. It involved two sisters, one of whom acted as an altruistic surrogate for the other. The embryos which were transferred to the surrogate came from the sperm and eggs of the intended parents and twins were born. Under Irish law at the time (and currently) the surrogate was deemed the legal mother of the children and the intended father was regarded as the legal father because he had provided the sperm. Although he was not married to the surrogate, she consented to his being registered as the legal father on the birth certificate. However, there was no mechanism for the genetic mother to have parentage or guardianship rights over the children. The High Court ruled that the biological or genetic mother should be the legal mother, based on her 'bloodlink' to the twins, in the same way as fathers are recognised legally as such (5.35). While this was the intended outcome of all the parties in this particular case, and undoubtedly in the best interests of those involved, especially the children, it would, if applied generally, have serious implications for the much more common instance of donor conceptions where the donor of the biological material should have no right to be the legal parent of any child born. This decision of the High Court was appealed to the Supreme Court, which overturned it and held that 'the gestational mother (the surrogate) should be regarded as the legal mother, unless and until the legislature provided otherwise' (5.34).

At the current time, the legal status of Irish citizens who have children through surrogacy is complex and all those interested should definitely seek expert legal advice prior to embarking on treatment. In simple terms, the surrogate mother (whether she is in Ireland or abroad) is the legal mother of the child. A man who has provided the sperm in a surrogacy arrangement may become a parent and guardian of his child. To do this he must firstly satisfy the Court that he is in fact a parent of the child. This is done through DNA tests. If so satisfied the Court will make an Order of Declaration of Parentage. Having been declared to be a parent of the child he can then apply to the Court for a guardianship order. The consent of the surrogate and her husband if she is married is vital. In considering this application the Court will determine whether this is in the best interests of the child. The genetic mother does not have a similar right to apply for parentage or guardianship because the law recognises only the position of the birth or surrogate mother. Therefore, she has no legal relationship to the child whom she wishes to raise along with the genetic/legal father, irrespective of whether or not she is genetically related to the child.

There is one ray of hope for a commissioning mother and that can be found in Section 49 of the CFRA. Essentially, it contains a provision whereby a person who is not a parent may apply to the court to be appointed a guardian provided certain conditions are met. Being appointed a guardian will permit the commissioning mother to make certain decisions in relation to the child.

For surrogacy arrangements where the child has been born to a surrogate abroad, the Department of Justice in Ireland has issued guidelines (5.36) to assist parents in getting the child back to Ireland. The intended father will need to provide evidence of paternity (usually DNA evidence) in support of an application for an emergency travel paper for the child. If the Department of Foreign Affairs is reasonably satisfied based on the DNA test results that the child is the child of an Irish citizen, the authorities may issue an Emergency Travel Certificate. One of the preconditions to the issue of an Emergency Travel Certificate is that the genetic father will give an undertaking that he will register the child with the Health Services within three days of the child coming into the country and will apply to the Court for a declaration of parentage and a guardianship order within 10 days unless there are exceptional circumstances, and in any case within 20 working days.

In surrogacy cases where donor sperm is used, the intended father will not have a genetic link with the child. This would occur, for example if a woman required a surrogate for medical reasons and her partner had azoospermia (no sperm). How such cases would be treated in the Irish courts remains to be seen. The case of a single woman engaging a surrogate and using donor sperm would be similarly difficult, as would the case of a person or couple (heterosexual or same-sex) using a surrogate and a donor embryo.

Posthumous conception

This refers to treatments where frozen sperm, embryos or eggs are used in treatment after the death of the person who produced the sperm or eggs. Clinics in Ireland have very different policies with regard to this. Some allow it; others don't. However, there is no national legislation and this is something that could be challenged in court. Indeed, there have been many high-profile international legal cases regarding posthumous use of sperm, eggs or embryos.

There are concerns regarding parentage in such cases and consequently issues such as inheritance rights. In Irish law (Status of Children Act 1987), where a woman gives birth to a child within a period of ten months after the death of her husband, he will be presumed to be the father of the child. In cases of posthumous conception by assisted reproduction, it is likely that birth will be significantly outside this ten-month period.

When I am signing consent forms for treatment with couples undergoing IVF with the prospect of having embryos frozen, the area of posthumous conception is something that, understandably, bothers them. I really feel this needs to be addressed as a matter of urgency by the Irish legislature. I would hate to see another Irish person (especially someone traumatised by the death of a loved one) have to battle through the High Court and Supreme Court to determine their legal position in such a case.

We urgently need legislation to clarify posthumous reproduction in Ireland, including whether it should only be allowed if the deceased consented to it prior to his or her death, and the legal status of any children born.

European Union Directives on AHR

In March 2004, the EU introduced Directive 2004/23/EC of the European Parliament and of the Council, which aims to set 'standards of quality and safety for the donation, procurement, testing, processing, preservation, storage and distribution of human tissues and cells'. This was followed by three technical directives: Commission Directive 2006/17/EC (February 2006); Commission Directive 2006/86/EC (October 2006); and Commission Directive 2012/39/EU (November 2012). These directives have been transposed into Irish law by statutory instruments SI 156 of 2006, SI 598 of 2007 and SI 209 of 2014.

The directives apply to organ donation and to tissues and cells. These include cells such as eggs and sperm and tissues such as embryos. For the purpose of this directive the term 'donation' means 'donation to a clinic for treatment' and includes donation of sperm or eggs for one's own use as well as for what we usually mean by donor conception, i.e. donation for use by a third party.

These directives lay down extensive and stringent requirements for any centre or clinic offering assisted reproduction services. Requirements include a quality management system, a designated 'person responsible' with appropriate qualifications, and strict conditions regarding the quality of the laboratory and laboratory methods, the labelling and storage of tissues and cells, traceability of tissues and cells, management of infection risks and other adverse events and the movement of tissues and cells from one laboratory to another and between countries.

In Ireland, the HPRA (Human Products Regulatory Authority), previously the IMB (Irish Medicines Board), is the competent authority that oversees compliance with the legislation. Any clinic or group providing ART services in Ireland must be licensed by the HPRA and this entails a detailed inspection every two years or so.

These directives have greatly standardised the laboratory components of ART across Europe, but this has come at significant cost in terms of finances and manpower, costs which ultimately contribute to the cost of treatment for patients.

Regulation of AHR in Ireland

EU regulation of issues related to the tissues and cells used in ART treatments is described above. While this regulation is important, it focuses on the tissues and cells, not on the more medical or clinical issues such as medical suitability for treatment, number of embryos to transfer, counselling, donor conceptions, surrogacy, adjuvant therapies, research, etc.

Medical Council

The Medical Council is the statutory body that regulates doctors under the Medical Practitioners Act 2007. It functions to protect the public by 'promoting the highest professional standards amongst doctors practising in the Republic of Ireland.' It consists of 13 non-medical members and 12 medical members. It sets the standards for medical education and training in Ireland and oversees the maintenance of doctors' professional competence.

The Medical Council also publishes a *Guide to Professional Conduct and Practice* (5.37). One section of the most recent edition of this guide (8th edn, 2016) relates to assisted reproduction and states the following four points:

1) Assisted human reproduction treatments such as In Vitro Fertilisation (IVF) should only be used after thorough investigation has shown that no other treatment is likely to be effective. You should make sure that patients have been offered appropriate counselling and have had enough time to consider the information before giving informed consent to any treatment.

2) Assisted human reproduction services should only be provided by suitably qualified professionals, in appropriately accredited facilities, and in line with international best practice. You should do regular clinical audits and follow-up of outcomes.

3) If you offer donor programmes to patients, you must have strong governance structures and keep accurate records so that the identity of the donor can be traced. Donor programmes should be altruistic and non-commercial. You should also comply with industry accreditation standards for donation programmes.
4) You must not take part in the creation of new forms of human life solely for experimental purposes. You must not engage in human reproductive cloning.

It can be seen that these guidelines are extremely short and do not cover the vast areas of complexity described above in the sections on Ethics and Law. Also, while all registered medical practitioners in Ireland must adhere to the guidelines, they do not apply to others working in the field of ART, e.g. nurses, scientists, counsellors, etc.

Institute of Obstetricians and Gynaecologists

The Institute of Obstetricians and Gynaecologists is the national professional and training body for obstetrics and gynaecology in Ireland. Established in 1968, it is one of six postgraduate specialist training bodies based in the Royal College of Physicians of Ireland. Most Irish obstetricians and gynaecologists are members of the institute and some of these have a particular interest in fertility and reproductive medicine. The institute makes representations to government and other national bodies regarding issues of concern to fertility patients in this country. It does not, however, have any regulatory role.

Nursing and Midwifery Board

This regulates nurses under the Nurses and Midwives Act 2011.

Irish Fertility Society (IFS)

The IFS, founded in 2005, represents doctors, nurses, scientists and counsellors who work in infertility and reproductive medicine in Ireland. The society holds a scientific meeting each year where international experts are invited to lecture and those involved in fertility in Ireland present research and engage in workshops and discussion groups. The society is a member of the International Federation of Fertility Societies. IFS also makes representations to relevant bodies regarding issues of concern to fertility patients in this country. The society produced comprehensive and evidence-based practice guidelines in October 2010 and these were circulated to the Department of Health and to all members of the Institute of Obstetricians and Gynaecologists. Unfortunately, not all fertility practitioners in Ireland are members of the society and the society has no statutory role.

Irish Clinical Embryologists (ICE)

Founded in 1998, the Irish Clinical Embryologists (ICE) association is a professional body for embryologists working in Ireland. Together they work to provide a better and safer service of assisted reproduction to couples in the North and South of Ireland. Members were/are involved in the Commission on Assisted Human Reproduction (CAHR), the IFS, the Association of Clinical Embryologists, and the Steering Committee set up by the Department of Health and Children to look into the introduction in Ireland of the EU directives on tissues and cells. ICE also has representation on the European Assisted Conception Consortium (EACC).

The members of ICE have acted in an exemplary fashion and, in the absence of national regulation in this regard, have introduced self-regulation for all ICE fertility clinics in Ireland with regard to the numbers of donor conceptions that should be allowed nationally from any one sperm donor.

Irish Fertility Counsellors' Association (IFCA)

IFCA was founded in 2008. Its members are professionally qualified counsellors and psychotherapists who specialise in the area of fertility. As professionals working throughout Ireland they provide support and counselling to anyone contemplating or undergoing any aspect of fertility treatment. The association has no regulatory role.

Commission on Assisted Human Reproduction (CAHR)

CAHR was a multidisciplinary body set up by the Minister for Health in 2000. Its task was 'to report on possible approaches to the regulation of all aspects of AHR and the social, ethical and legal factors to be taken into account in determining public policy, in this area'. Chaired by the excellent Professor Dervilla Donnelly, the commission included experts from a wide range of disciplines, including reproductive medicine, embryology, genetics and law, with additional input from philosophers, sociologists, a director of ecumenical studies and a Roman Catholic theologian. I was honoured to be a member of the commission and it was one of the most rewarding things I have done.

The commission made 40 recommendations, which were published in 2005 (5.3). I have read these recommendations again 12 years later and they are still excellent and applicable. They cover all the areas that are relevant today and the issues that cause concern and uncertainty for my patients. The first recommendation was that 'a regulatory body should be established by an Act of the Oireachtas to regulate AHR services in Ireland'. Recommendations were also made regarding the collection and dissemination of information; good practice; the protection of children; the freezing of eggs, sperm and embryos; the management of surplus embryos; counselling and consent; donor pregnancies; surrogacy; quality assurance; access to treatment; PGD; and research.

It is interesting to note that, following on from this report, legal decisions regarding the status of the embryo and surrogacy and the principles of the CFRA have mirrored the recommendations of the commission. It is a real shame that, 12 years on, legislation on AHR and a regulatory authority have not been introduced. The legislation and clarity contained in the CFRA is to be welcomed – but in some ways this has been putting the cart before the horse in legislating for donor conception without first establishing legislation for basic ART procedures. Consequently this legislation is effectively on hold until AHR legislation is introduced.

The need for AHR legislation in Ireland

The setting up of the CAHR by the Minister for Health in 2000 is evidence that there have for many years been calls for the introduction of legislation and regulation in the complex area of AHR. Such calls have been made by the medical profession under the auspices of the Institute of Obstetricians and Gynaecologists, the Medical Council and the IFS, as well as by individuals.

The judiciary has also in recent years become quite vociferous in this regard. In the *Roche v Roche* case in 2006 (5.33), the judge stated, 'It is a matter for the Oireachtas as to whether it implements the recommendations of the commission. In the meantime the courts are being asked to deal with a complex dispute involving social issues which should be governed by a regulatory regime established by an Act of the Oireachtas.' In the subsequent appeal to the Supreme Court (5.30), the need for legislation was repeatedly noted: 'But the fact that difficulties are raised does not absolve the legislature from the obligation to consider the degree of respect due to fertilised embryos and to act upon such consideration "by its laws". There has been a marked reluctance on the part of the legislature actually to legislate on these issues.'

In the Supreme Court decision in the surrogacy case I referred to earlier (*MR and DR and OR v an t-Ard Claratheoir*, 2014 (5.34)) all the judges commented on the need for legislation. One in particular, Judge Hardiman, was particularly strong: 'I wish to join with my colleagues in pointing out the urgency of the need for legislation on this topic. There is at present a serious disconnect between what developments in science and medicine have rendered possible on the one hand, and the state of the law on the other. It is as if road traffic law had failed to reflect the advent of the motor car.'

Since my time on the CAHR, I have listened to successive ministers for health telling us that legislation is imminent. Most recently, the Department of Health met with stakeholders in the area to discuss planned legislation – that was in August 2015. It is expected that the general scheme of a bill dealing with AHR will be published in 2017. I sincerely hope this happens.

In July 2015, the Institute of Obstetricians and Gynaecologists, under the chairmanship of Professor Robert Harrison, submitted a document to the Department of Health on the 'undoubted need for national legislation regarding all aspects of AHR to protect the patients using the services and the health professionals working therein.' This advised the opinion of those working in the field concerning policy development. Key issues were:

- A Regulatory Authority should be established to regulate ART Services in Ireland. This body should be independent and have statutory powers. It should license clinics, develop a Code of Practice to govern AHR practices. It should also act as a resource for clinics, provide standardised national consent forms and information for patients and maintain confidential registers of all AHR treatments commenced including success rates and neonatal and other safety outcomes. The authority should be at the forefront of research in AHR and should act as the arbiter for the introduction of all new therapies.
- The Code of Practice should address the following and should be supported where necessary by legislation: safety of treatments for parents and children, in particular the minimisation of multiple pregnancy, informed consent, management of surplus embryos, including cases where embryos are abandoned, counselling, particularly for treatments involving a third party.
- Legislation should be enacted to cover posthumous conception and allow non-commercial surrogacy.
- PGD and PGS should be allowed where clinically indicated and under stringent regulation.

It is important when devising legislation and regulation of ART that consideration is given to ensuring a relatively flexible system. Reproductive medicine and, particularly, assisted reproduction are areas that are advancing rapidly in medical and scientific fields. If every change had to be debated and decided by the Oireachtas or a referendum on the Constitution, we would never be able to keep up and there would be an enormous waste of resources. This is where the establishment of an appropriate Regulatory Authority with statutory powers is essential.

International legislation and regulation

Legislation and regulation regarding ART varies widely between countries. It would be impossible to cover all aspects of it in this book, but several international studies have been performed. (5.5, 5.38, 5.39).

The most recent is a review of the situation in Europe performed by ESHRE and published in 2015 (5.7). Its findings are shown in the table below. It is noteworthy that Ireland stands out as being one of the few countries that has not yet legislated in this area. In the commentary regarding Ireland it is stated, 'No legislation to ban any procedures though law in preparation to make gamete donation non-anonymous'. All countries, except Switzerland, allow embryo freezing, but in Germany this is allowed only in very limited circumstances. The majority of countries allow PGD and PGS and place a limit on the number of embryos that can be transferred. With regard to donor conception, some countries allow anonymous donation, some only non-anonymous, and some allow both. Interestingly, surrogacy is banned in most countries and only allowed in Belgium, Cyprus, Greece, Macedonia, the Netherlands, Romania and the UK.

In 2013 the IFFS (International Federation of Fertility Societies) published a 148-page document entitled 'IFFS Surveillance' (5.39). This gives a lot more detail which concurs with the ESHRE data in Europe. The table also shows the findings for Australia, New Zealand and the United States. Surrogacy is allowed in all three countries.

IFFS mentions posthumous conception, and it is allowed in only Argentina, Australia, Belgium, Brazil, Denmark, Greece, India, Kazakhstan, New Zealand, the UK, the USA and Vietnam.

It is worth noting that many international groups have cautioned against the imposition of restrictive legislation, as this can lead to unforeseen problems. Italy is a prime example. Restrictive legislation was introduced there in 2004 which prohibited, among other things, embryo freezing. Many of these restrictions have since been reversed in order to facilitate best medical practice. In both Italy and Germany, restrictive practices relating to embryo freezing led to unacceptably low pregnancy rates and unacceptably high multiple pregnancy rates in both countries. Doctors in those countries have campaigned to change the laws in order

Table 5.1 ART regulation in Europe (5.7)

Country	Legislations or Guidelines	Limit on number of embryos to transfer	PGD allowed	PGS Allowed	Embryo Freezing allowed	Gamete donation allowed and anon vs non-anon	Surrogacy allowed
Austria	L	✔		Not yet	✔	✔ non-anon	✘
Belgium	L	✔	✔	✔	✔	✔ anon & non-anon	✔
Bulgaria	L	✔	✔	✔	✔	✔ anon	✘
Croatia	L	✔	✔	✔	✔	anon	✘
Cyprus	L + G	✔	✔	✔	✔	✔ anon & non-anon	✔
Estonia	L	✔	✔	✔	✔	✔ anon	✘
Finland	L	✘	✔	✔	✔	✔ non-anon	✘
France	L + G	✔	✘	✘	✔	✔ anon	✘
Georgia	None						
Germany	L + G	✔	✔	✔	✔	non-anon sperm only	✘
Greece	L + G	✔	✔	✔	✔	✔ anon	✔
Hungary	L + G	✔	✔	✘	✔	✔ anon	✘
Ireland	G	✘	✔	*	*	*	*
Italy	L + G	✘	✔	✔	✔	✔ anon	✘
Lithuania	No ART Regulations	✔	✘	✘	✔	✘	✘
Macedonia	L	✔	✔	✔	✔	✔ anon & non-anon	✔
Netherlands	L + G	✔	✔	✔	✔	✔ non-anon	✔
Norway	L	✘	✔	✘	✔	non-anon sperm only	✘
Poland	G	✔	✔	✔	✔	✔ anon	✘
Portugal	L	✔	✔	✔	✔	✔ anon	✔
Romania	L + G	✘	✔	✔	✔	✔ anon & non-anon	✘
Serbia	L	✔	✔	✔	✔	✔ anon	✘
Slovakia	L	✘	✔	✔	✔	✔ anon	✘
Slovenia	L + G	✔	✔	✔	✔	✔ anon	✘
Spain	L + G	✔	✔	✔	✔	✔ anon	✘
Sweden	L + G	✔	✔	✘	✔	✔ non-anon	✘
Switzerland	L + G	✔	✘	✘	✘	sperm only	✘
Turkey	L + G	✔	✔	✔	✔	✘	✘
UK	L + G	✔	✔	✔	✔	✔ non-anon	✔
Australia	L + G	✔	✔	✔	✔	✔ non-anon	✔
New Zealand	L + G	✔	✔	✔	✔	✔ non-anon	✔
United States	L + G	✘	✔	✔	✔	✔ anon & non-anon	✔

* No regulation to ban any precedures, though law in preparation to make gamete donation non-anonymous.

to encourage elective single embryo transfer, which is undoubtedly safer, not only for women but, most significantly, for the babies born.

The variations in legislation and regulation in countries across the world have led to a surge in what is called 'reproductive tourism' or 'cross-border reproductive care'. I think Irish patients are very aware of this. Almost all those who need donor egg treatment must travel abroad, as do many couples who need PGD and PGS, though the latter is changing. Similarly, surrogacy is most commonly accessed abroad. Studies of cross-border reproductive care have shown that more than half of cross-border patients travelled to evade the law of their own country. While this type of travel opens up opportunities for patients not available in their own country, it is not without risk. Travel and dealing with a strange medical system, and even a different language, adds to the stress, cost and risk of fertility treatments. International bodies such as ESHRE have advocated co-operation between doctors and other healthcare professionals in different countries to ensure continuity of care for patients. This is certainly our policy at Merrion Fertility Clinic, where we endeavour to develop professional links with reputable services abroad. Sadly, some jurisdictions have at times introduced penal restrictions for doctors who helped patients to access treatment abroad that was not allowed in their own country.

Legislation and regulation in the UK

The regulatory situation in the UK deserves special mention because that country has one of the most comprehensive systems available and also one in which Irish professionals working in AHR are well versed in. Many of us have worked in the UK and, indeed, we often envy some of the provisions of the UK HFEA (Human Fertilisation and Embryology Authority) Act and the appointed regulatory authority, the HFEA. The Act was originally passed in 1990 and amended in 2008. The HFEA is responsible for applying the regulations of the Act and for licensing both IVF clinics and scientists carrying out research on human embryos.

On its website, the HFEA proposes to:

- be an effective regulator commanding stakeholder confidence by ensuring compliance with the law
- inform patient choice, securely hold personal data, and maximise public understanding (of available and developing treatments, embryology research, and the HFEA and its role)
- encourage consistently high quality standards of treatment and research in the sector by putting the patient experience first
- be an effective organisation with strong governance that adds value and reduces bureaucracy
- ensure the HFEA and the sector keep abreast of new scientific and research developments through continued collaborative working with scientific and professional bodies
- recognise and address the needs of the HFEA's many and varied audiences, and specifically to consider the patient experience in all our work.

Apart from regulating the area, the HFEA acts as a great source of information and guidance for doctors and patients. These is a wealth of patient information available on its website and it produces regular reports of national trends and figures in fertility treatments. The most recent was in 2014 and ran to almost 50 pages. The HFEA produces a Code of Practice which must be followed by all those providing fertility services. This is very comprehensive – the most recent (eighth) edition was published in July 2016 and runs to 258 pages. Changes in regulations can be added to the code without the need for changes to primary legislation and this makes for a responsive and timely regulatory framework. In addition, the HFEA provides standardised national consent forms and maintains registers of ART procedures. It also deals with issues related to the provision of information to donor-conceived persons.

Section 5 References

5.1   Madden, D. (2016), *Medicine, Ethics and the Law* (3rd edn). Bloomsbury Professional.

5.2   Beauchamp, T. M. and Childress, J. F. (1979) *Principles of Biomedical Ethics* (1st edn), Oxford University Press.

5.3   Commission on Assisted Human Reproduction (CAHR), *Report* (2005), Available at: http://health.gov.ie/wp-content/uploads/2014/03/Report-of-The-Commission-on-Assisted-Human-Reproduction.pdf

5.4   ESHRE Task Force on Ethics and Law 14 (2008) 'Equity of access to assisted reproductive technology'. *Human Reproduction* 23(4): 772–4.

5.5   ASRM Ethics Committee (2015) 'Disparities in access to effective treatment for infertility in the United States: an Ethics Committee opinion'. *Fertility and Sterility* 104: 1104–10.

5.6   Health Research Board, Dublin (2017). *Assisted reproductive technologies: International approaches to public funding mechanisms and criteria. An evidence review.* Published by Health Research Board, Dublin © Health Research Board, www.hrb.ie

5.7   ESHRE (2015) 'ART regulation and reimbursement in Europe'. *Focus on Reproduction*, May.

5.8   Chambers, G. M., Hoang, V. P., Sullivan E.A. et al. (2014) 'The impact of consumer affordability on access to assisted reproductive technologies and embryo transfer practices: an international analysis'. *Fertility and Sterility* 101(1): 191–8.

5.9   Chambers, G., Sullivan, E. A., Ishihara, O., Chapman, M. G. and Adamson, G. D. (2009) 'The economic impact of assisted reproductive technology: a review of selected developed countries'. *Fertility and Sterility* 91(6): 2281–94.

5.10   Connolly, M., Gallo, F., Hoorens, S. and Ledger, W. (2009) 'Assessing long-run economic benefits attributed to an IVF-conceived singleton based on projected lifetime net tax contributions in the UK'. *Human Reproduction* 24(3): 626–32.

5.11   'Fertility tourism sparks Spanish takeover of clinic', *Irish Independent*, 10/7/16

5.12   Kupka, M. S., Ferraretti, A. P., de Mouzon, J., Erb, K., D'Hooghe, T., Castilla, J. A., Calhaz-Jorge, C., De Geyter, C., Goossens V. and the European IVF-monitoring (EIM) Consortium for ESHRE (2014) 'Assisted reproductive technology in Europe, 2010: results generated from European registers by ESHRE'. *Human Reproduction* 29(10): 2099–113.

5.13   Dyer, S., Chambers, G. M., de Mouzon, J., Nygren, K. G., Zegers-Hochschild, F., Mansour, R., Ishihara, O., Banker, M. and Adamson, G. D. (2016) 'International Committee for Monitoring Assisted Reproductive Technologies world report: Assisted Reproductive Technology 2008, 2009 and 2010'. *Human Reproduction* 31(7): 1588–1609.

5.14   De Neubourg, D., Bogaerts, K., Wyns, C. et al. (2013) 'The history of Belgian assisted reproduction technology cycle registration and control: a case study in reducing the incidence of multiple pregnancy'. *Human Reproduction* 28(10): 2709–19.

5.15   ASRM Ethics Committee (2016) 'Oocyte or embryo donation to women of advanced reproductive age: an Ethics Committee opinion'. *Fertility and Sterility* 106(5): e3–7.

5.16   ESHRE Task Force on Ethics and Law (2010) 'Lifestyle-related factors and access to medically assisted reproduction'. *Human Reproduction* 25(3): 578–83.

5.17   ESHRE Task Force on Ethics and Law 23 (2014) 'Medically assisted reproduction in singles, lesbian and gay couples, and transsexual people'. *Human Reproduction* 29(9): 1859–65.

5.18   ASRM Ethics Committee (2015) 'Access to fertility services by transgender persons: an Ethics Committee opinion'. *Fertility and Sterility* 104: 1111–15.

5.19   ASRM Ethics Committee (2013) 'Access to fertility treatment by gays, lesbians, and unmarried persons: a committee opinion'. *Fertility and Sterility* 100: 1524–7.

5.20   ESHRE Task Force on Ethics and Law (2002) 'Gamete and embryo donation'. *Human Reproduction* 17(5): 1407–8.

5.21   ASRM Ethics Committee (2013) 'Interests, obligations, and rights in gamete donation: a committee opinion'. *Fertility and Sterility* 102: 675–81.

5.22   ASRM Ethics Committee (2013) 'Informing offspring of their conception by gamete or embryo donation: a committee opinion'. *Fertility and Sterility* 100: 45–9.

5.23   ASRM Ethics Committee (2012) 'Using family members as gamete donors or surrogates'. *Fertility and Sterility* 98: 797–8.

5.24   Pennings, G., de Wert, G., Shenfield, F., Cohen, J., Devroey, P. and Tarlatzis, B. ESHRE Task Force on Ethics and Law 11 (2006) 'Posthumous assisted reproduction'. *Human Reproduction* 21(12): 3050–3.

5.25   ASRM Ethics Committee (2013) 'Posthumous collection and use of reproductive tissue: a committee opinion'. *Fertility and Sterility* 99: 1842–5.

5.26   ESHRE Task Force on Ethics and Law (2001) 'The moral status of the pre-implantation embryo'. *Human Reproduction* 16(5):1046–8.

5.27   ASRM Ethics Committee (1994) 'Ethical considerations of assisted reproductive technologies'. *Fertility and Sterility* 62(5 Suppl 1):1S–125S.

5.28   ASRM Ethics Committee (2013) 'Donating embryos for human embryonic stem cell (hESC) research: a committee opinion'. *Fertility and Sterility* 100: 935–9.

5.29   *Murray v Ireland* (1991) ILRM 465.

5.30   *Roche v Roche* (2009) IESC 82.

5.31   *McGee v Attorney General* (1974) IR 284.

5.32   *Norris v Attorney General* (1984) IR 36.

5.33   *Roche v Roche* (2006) IEHC 359.

5.34   *MR and DR (suing by their father and next friend OR) v an t-Ard Chlaraitheoir* (2014) IESC 60.

5.35   *MR v an t-Ard Chlaraitheoir* (2013) IEHC 359

5.36   Department of Justice and Equality (2012) *Citizenship, parentage, guardianship and travel document issues in relation to children born as a result of surrogacy arrangements entered into outside the state.* Available at: www.justice.ie/en/JELR/20120221%20Guidance%20Document.pdf/Files/20120221%20Guidance%20Document.pdf

5.37   Medical Council of Ireland (2016) *Guide to Professional conduct and Ethics for Registered Medical Practitioners* (8th edn). Available at: www.medicalcouncil.ie/News-and-Publications

5.38   Busardò, F. P., Gulino, M., Napoletano, S., Zaami, S. and Frati, P. (2014) 'The evolution of legislation in the field of medically assisted reproduction and embryo stem cell research in European Union members'. *BioMed Research International* 2014: 307160.

5.39   International Federation of Fertility Societies (IFFS) (2013) *IFFS Surveillance.* Available at: www.iffs-reproduction.org/resource/resmgr/iffs_surveillance_09-19-13.pdf

Afterword

When it Doesn't Happen – A Life Without Children

Very sadly, despite their own absolute best efforts, and those of their fertility team, a minority of individuals/couples will be unsuccessful in achieving their dream of having a family. They leave our care and are often left to their own devices, faced with the prospect of life without children. This can often be where counselling and support is most needed.

Surprisingly little research has been done on this group. On the other hand, maybe it is to be expected. Once they stop treatment, patients no longer have a reason to attend a clinic, and may even want to get away from the clinic and unhappy memories of failed treatment. An ESHRE guideline published in 2015 (2.41) gives lots of information about couples before and during treatment, but it concluded that 'the evidence about the behavioural and emotional needs of patients after unsuccessful IVF treatment is too limited for supporting recommendations'. Having said that, they advised that:

- *Fertility staff should be aware that former patients who remain childless five years after unsuccessful IVF/ICSI treatment may use more sleeping pills, smoke more often and consume more alcohol than former patients that become parents via adoption or spontaneously.*
- *Former patients that remain childless five years after unsuccessful IVF/ ICSI treatment are three times more likely to separate than former patients that become parents via adoption or spontaneously.*
- *Women with a persistent desire for pregnancy three to five years after unsuccessful treatment may experience more anxiety and depression*

than women who find new life goals or women who become mothers but women who remain childless 10 years after unsuccessful IVF/ICSI treatment are not more likely to develop psychiatric disorders than women of the same age who never underwent fertility treatment.

A UK study published in 2007 also gives some idea of what people go through after unsuccessful treatment (2.42). This study was comprised of 33 interviews with people who had had unsuccessful IVF five years previously. Of these interviews, 18 were with couples and 15 were with female partners only. Some of the findings were as follows:

- For some, the effects can be traumatic and long lasting.
- Hope was an important factor. Treatment offers hope and this provides the motivation for treatment, alongside the urgent need to avoid future regrets.
- Once the support provided by hope is removed, patients can struggle to make sense of their lives.
- Some form of closure regarding the ending of treatment is required.
- Some couples are able to reinvest in life goals and re-establish their relationships
- However, a significant proportion of couples were still struggling five years after their last treatment.
- Sadly, not all couples recover from the trauma of the inability to parent at will, and some relationships break down.
- There is a lack of psychological support offered to couples going through assisted conception, and findings suggest that more support should be offered on a regular basis to couples going through this process and beyond.

In my experience, different people have different ways of coping with disappointment, heartbreak and adversity. I suppose this is true for every misfortune in life. Many couples grow stronger in their relationship throughout the fertility journey and are a great support to each other when it doesn't work. Sadly, I have also seen relationships break down where one or other partner just can't take it anymore. It is really important that those of us who work in the area try to help patients protect themselves, their relationships and their lives from the ravages of infertility and its treatments.

Generally, it tends to be women that I see after couples have been unsuccessful with treatment because they may come back for management of an ongoing gynaecological issue such as endometriosis. My impression is that they all eventually find their way. They adjust to their new life without children – some may develop their career or get involved in the arts or voluntary work and others may even move on to new relationships. No one finds it easy and it is more difficult for some than others. If a person can know deep down that they have tried their best and done all they could, they usually can come to terms with the huge loss and move on.

The person's situation and attitude right from the beginning can be important. Some, particularly younger, patients may have never contemplated a life without children or considered that they might not be able to conceive. They have often been very successful in their enterprises to date – education, work and even finding a partner. Now – wham! They have come up against a brick wall. They may spend an absolute fortune – not just in terms of money – but also time, emotions and happiness – seeking after a retreating goal and moving from clinic to clinic. They are also likely to be under immense societal pressure. They are often in the age group where all their friends are having babies and, because they are young, their friends and family may have no idea that they have a problem. Not surprisingly, their life can become consumed. This is absolutely understandable but can be a recipe for disaster – if they don't conceive, they have nothing left. Counselling and support can be invaluable here. Finding new life goals and paths can seem impossible but, with some professional help, it is usually eminently doable.

Older couples and patients are often in a different place. They may have the added pressures of time and their biological clock, but they have also had a longer life experience with more hard knocks and uncertainties. They may come to the fertility scene with less expectations and a realisation that it may not happen for them – if it does, it is a bonus. They are also more likely to find acceptance and empathy from their peers who are also older.

Often the most difficult thing for any person or couple can be deciding when to stop fertility treatment. People often talk about getting on the treadmill and not being able to stop. Fertility treatments like IVF can certainly do this. The outcome is unpredictable and there is always the chance that the next treatment just might work. Some couples may get really close to success – they may have decided to do one last cycle of treatment and then they get a positive pregnancy test but suffer an early miscarriage. It is very hard not to want to try again in this situation, even if there have been many failed attempts in the past. Others get lured or sucked in by new therapies and technologies that are being proposed all the time (not always justified or proven) – they read about someone who tried and tried for years, and then tried a certain thing which worked. The internet can be very misleading in this regard and can entice people into trying more and more unscientific and spurious treatments.

I am greatly saddened when I see people or couples who have really tried everything and have been unsuccessful. It is often hard as a doctor to know what to say. Having worked so long in the area, I know that our treatments and technologies work very well in most situations. But there are definitely some patients and couples who are really unlucky. Sadly, science does not yet have all the answers. I really do believe that we should try fertility treatment and, while most people will be successful, unfortunately some will not. All any of us (patients, doctors and other staff) can do is do our best and, then accept that sometimes in life, 'que sera, sera', and some things are beyond our control.

I'll finish up with a few insightful quotes from some of our patients.

'When we started this journey, my husband and I said that we did not want to look back in 20 years' time asking ourselves what if, if only we had tried one more time. But we also said we did not want to be one of the those couples who simply could not or would not accept what is meant to be, is meant to be.'

'For us our battle is still ongoing and there may be no happy ending, but my husband actually said to me just the other day that he would not change one minute of it – and all things considered, I don't think that

I would either. We have a picture now that we didn't have before. The picture might not be our favorite one, but it's clear and we can build a life around it and be proud of it.'

'Your journey may be successful. That success may be a family. Or that success may be accepting that you have tried your best to get what you both wanted and life has decided that you are going to follow another path. So plan for both. And enjoy life.'

Useful Websites

Adoption
www.adoptionboard.ie
www.tulsa.ie

Funding
www.fertilityfairness.co.uk

General medical information
www.mayoclinic.org

Infertility
www.infertilityireland.ie
www.oneatatime.org.uk

International monitoring and professional bodies
www.eshre.eu
www.sart.org
www.hfea.gov.uk

Miscarriage/pregnancy loss
www.miscarriage.ie
www.isands.ie
www.feileacain.ie
www.ectopicireland.ie
www.miscarriageassociation.org.uk
www.anamcara.ie
www.ectopic.org
www.ectopicpregnancy.co.uk

Nutrition
www.bodywhys.ie
www.bestinseason.ie
www.fsai.ie
www.indi.ie
www.safefood.eu

PCOS
www.pcosupport.org
www.jeanhailes.org.au

Premature ovarian insufficiency, menopause
www.daisynetwork.org.uk

Sexual problems
www.sextherapists.ie
www.cosrt.org.uk

Index